What people are saying about *Fearless* . . .

"*Fearless* will challenge you to walk in faith and to believe the most amazing things that Christ can do. Dr. Wood's devotional book will help you to face with courage the things you are facing right now in your everyday life. *Fearless* will give you step by step antidotes to fear and uncertainty. If there is anyone who knows how to live and lead with courage it is Dr. George Wood. This is a book to read again and again!"

—Choco de Jesús, senior pastor, New Life Covenant church, Chicago, Illinois; author of *Amazing Faith* and *In the Gap*

"I am so thankful for the teaching of Dr. George O. Wood. In *Fearless*, Dr. Wood reminds us that the same Jesus who changed the world 2,000 years ago is still changing lives today. His power is our power. His hope is our hope. His peace is our peace. His love is our love. Dr. Wood—once again—leads us to higher places."

—Roma Downey, producer, actress, president of LightWorkers Media

"Whenever I get to hear Dr. Wood's insights on the Scriptures I can't wait to get some great insights and deep material. Dr. Wood doesn't realize how deep and profound his thoughts are. They impact me deeply and I know they will impact you. If you're looking for a fresh look at the Word of God, I highly recommend Dr. Wood's devotional on the gospel of Mark."

—Rob Ketterling, lead pastor River Valley Church, Apple Valley, Minnesota; author of *Change Before You Have To* and *Thrill Sequence*

"*Fearless* invites you on an inspiring devotional journey through the action-packed book of Mark's gospel. Dr. George Wood is known for his keen insight into Scripture, a great love of history, and a wealth of minister mentors who invested their wisdom in him. All comes together here as the author explores Jesus through Mark's eyes and shares fresh applications for believers today. You'll return to this book again and again!"

—Dr. Beth Grant, codirector of Project Rescue, author of *Courageous Compassion*

"Dr. George Wood is my spiritual overseer and mentor. He is fearless! But he hasn't written about himself in this, his seventh book. Once again he writes about the central character in his life and mine: Jesus Christ. After reading *Fearless* you will be encouraged to run toward the outer borders of faith. I guarantee it!"

—Rich Wilkerson, co-pastor, Trinity Church, Miami, Florida; author of *Private Pain* and *Straight Answers to Tough Questions About Sex*

"In a world where words are abundant and multitudes are vying to be heard, a few voices stand out. These always make my heart perk up and take notice, not because they're *louder* than the rest, but because they are *deeper* . . . with meaning, with insight, with spiritual gravitas. Dr. George Wood is one of these voices. In *Fearless: How Jesus Changes Everything*, Dr. Wood masterfully uses his words to connect us, heart and soul, to the Word, Jesus, through a fresh compelling look at the gospel of Mark. While reading *Fearless*, I found myself constantly highlighting, making notes, and often weeping, as God's truth is superimposed over the human condition. Jesus really *does* change everything, and this book is changing me."

—Dr. Jodi Detrick, author of *The Jesus-Hearted Woman* and former *Seattle Times* columnist

"Dr. Wood's reflections from Mark's gospel will provide valuable insight into your understanding of your leadership and pastoral roles. I am so excited about this valuable insight from a great pastor and leader."

—Roger Stacy, home missions director and leadership coach for the Minnesota District of the Assemblies of God, Church Multiplication Network

"Dr. George Wood's fresh and heartfelt approach to the gospel of Mark will cause a daily invasion of the power and grace of God. It will cause a vital daily shift to enliven your life and expand the way God uses your story."

—Mike Quinn, lead pastor, Newbreak Church, San Diego, California

"*Fearless* delivers! In an age of biblical illiteracy, Dr. George Wood's amazing wisdom from the gospel of Mark is a must-read for anyone who wants to understand better the heart and the message of the Bible."

—Scott Hagan, lead pastor, Real Life Church, Sacramento, California; author of *They Walked with the Savior* and *They Felt the Spirit's Touch*

"I'm so excited about this book! It has been in the making for over six years! These thoughts from Dr. Wood will have a great impact on your life. His mind is anointed by the Holy Spirit, and his insights will inspire you!"

—Dary Northrop, lead pastor, Timberline Church, Fort Collins, Colorado; author of *Garage Door Evangelism*

"The healthy areas of our lives flow from a strong devotional life. Dr. George Wood shares tremendous insight from the gospel of Mark to help us in our walk with the Lord. *Fearless* will draw you closer to Jesus!"

—John Van Pay, lead pastor, Gateway Fellowship Church, San Antonio, Texas

"More than anything, the gospel of Mark presents a Christ who is God's servant, a Savior who came to serve and give His life as a ransom for many. Dr. Wood's devotional provides a rich tapestry of biblical and deeply personal reflections that point us to this Christ with the challenge to embrace and be transformed by His grace so that we too may serve as He did. This is a rich resource for reflecting deeply on the gospel of Mark."

—Carol A. Taylor, PhD, President, Evangel University

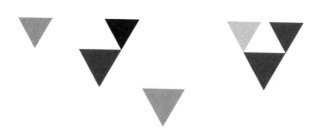

FEARLESS
HOW JESUS CHANGES EVERYTHING

GEORGE O. WOOD

FEARLESS—How Jesus Changes Everything

Copyright © 2015 by George O. Wood
ALL RIGHTS RESERVED

Published by Vital Resources
1445 N. Boonville Ave.
Springfield, Missouri 65802

www.vital-resources.com

No part of this book may be reproduced, stored in a retrieval system, or transmitted in any form or by any means—electronic, mechanical, photocopy, recording, or, otherwise—without prior written permission of the publisher, except for brief quotations used in connection with reviews in magazines or newspapers.

Cover design by Sheepish Design (www.sheepishdesign.org)
Interior design by Tom Shumaker

Produced with the assistance of Livingstone, the Publishing Services Division of Barton-Veerman Company. Project staff includes: Bruce Barton, Ashley Taylor and Tom Shumaker.

Unless otherwise specified, all Scripture quotations are taken from the Holy Bible, New International Version®, NIV®. Copyright © 1973, 1978, 1984, 2008 by Biblica, Inc.™ Used by permission of Zondervan. All rights reserved worldwide.www.zondervan.com. The "NIV" and "New International Version" are trademarks registered in the United States Patent and Trademark Office by Biblica, Inc.™

Scriptures marked KJV are from the King James Version of the Bible, which is held in public domain.

Scriptures marked NKJV are from The New King James version®. © 1982 by Thomas Nelson, Inc. Used by permission. All rights reserved.

ISBN: 978-1-68066-006-7

Printed in the United States of America

18 17 16 15 • 1 2 3 4

CONTENTS

FOREWORD 13
INTRODUCTION 14
NEVER-ENDING GOOD NEWS 17
WHAT IS YOUR MISSION? 19
REVIVAL IN THE DESERT 21
THE JORDAN RIVER PROTEST MOVEMENT 23
TRANSITIONS 25
TEMPTATION 27
THE LAUNCH 29
THE MAIN THINGS 31
ELEVEN LIFE-CHANGING WORDS 33
THE PARADOX OF CALL 35
POWER IN THE PULPIT 37
DEEP EVIL 39
AMAZED 41
OUT OF BED 43
INTO THE STREET 45
ALONE IN PRAYER 47
SOMEWHERE ELSE 49
THE YES AND NOT YET OF HEALING 51
KEEP YOUR ENTHUSIASM IN CHECK! 53
DISABLED, BUT NOT ALONE 55
THE PARALYTIC'S OWN TESTIMONY 57
SIN AND FORGIVENESS 59
THE AUTHORITY OF JESUS 61
ONE FROM THE CROWD 63
HE DREW A CIRCLE THAT TOOK ME IN! 65
OUTSIDE OUR COMFORT ZONES 67
UNHAPPY PEOPLE 69
A NEW WAY 71
LAW AND GRACE 73
SHRIVELED 75
NEVER A TIME NOT TO DO GOOD 77
CONSTRUCTIVE AND DESTRUCTIVE ANGER 79
RETREAT AND ADVANCE 81
WHAT FAMOUS MINISTERS MAY FORGET 83
TO BE WITH HIM 85
THE GIFT OF A NEW IDENTITY 87
ENERGY BOLTS 89
SPIRITUAL STEM CELLS 91

THE BETRAYER	93
PERSPECTIVE	95
NASTY RELIGIOUS PEOPLE	97
DEALING WITH CRITICISM	99
THE UNPARDONABLE SIN	101
MISUNDERSTOOD BY FAMILY	103
THE NEW FAMILY	105
THE TEACHER	107
THE FARMER	109
THE SOILS	111
THE SECRET	113
THE PATH	115
ROCKY PLACES	117
THE THORNS	119
THE GOOD SOIL	121
SECRET MESSAGE OR SECRET SINS	123
THE LEARNING PRINCIPLE	125
UNDER DEVELOPMENT	127
THE MUSTARD SEED	129
CAPACITY	131
JUST AS HE WAS	133
I'M SWAMPED, HE'S SLEEPING	135
GREAT PEACE	137
QUESTIONS	139
LIFE'S SURPRISING TWISTS	141
TORMENTED	143
LEGION	145
JESUS AND THE DEMONS	147
PIGS OR PEOPLE?	149
ZOOM OUT, ZOOM IN	151
A DESPERATE DAD	153
A DESPERATE WOMAN	155
THINKING, SAYING, DOING	157
THE TOUCH AND THE FRUSTRATION	159
THE WHOLE TRUTH	161
FAITH, NOT MAGIC	163
JUST BELIEVE	165
DEATH AS SLEEP	167
BETTER TO BE INSIDE	169
ORDERS NOT TO TELL	171
THE NAZARETH MENTALITY	173
PROPHET WITHOUT HONOR	175
MICROWAVE AND OVEN	177
AUTHORITY AND POWER	179
IS YOUR VISION SMALL ENOUGH?	181

IN WORD AND POWER	183
THE WRONG VIEW OF JESUS	185
GENERALITIES OR SPECIFICS	187
THE PERIL OF INDECISION	189
RASH PROMISES	191
THE CHILD DESERVED BETTER	193
PURE EVIL	195
DO YOU NEED TO TAKE A BREAK?	197
SLOW BOAT, FAST CROWD	199
THE INCONVENIENCE OF MINISTRY	201
WHAT'S IN YOUR HANDS?	203
THREE DON'TS FOR SUCCESS	205
SAFE	207
"IT IS I!"	209
RECOGNIZING JESUS	211
CONFLICT	213
WHAT QUESTION WOULD YOU ASK?	215
TRADITION	217
CROSS YOUR FINGERS	219
KOSHER IN THE HEART	221
THE HOME AND THE LESSON	223
THIRTEEN BAD THINGS	225
A MOTHER'S DESPERATE PLEA	227
A WINNING RESPONSE	229
HELP FROM FRIENDS AND FAMILY	231
BE OPENED	233
THE AMAZING JESUS	235
COMPASSION	237
LEST WE FORGET	239
SATISFIED	241
NO SIGN	243
YEAST	245
MISSING THE POINT	247
AMONG THE "SOME"?	249
I CAN SEE CLEARLY NOW!	251
OPINIONS OF JESUS	253
LIFE'S GREATEST QUESTION	255
A STUNNING ANNOUNCEMENT	257
CROSS AVOIDANCE	259
COME AND DIE	261
WHAT DO YOU WANT MORE THAN ANYTHING?	263
HIS COMING	265
WHEN THE KINGDOM COMES IN POWER	267
METAMORPHOSIS	269
VETERANS AND ROOKIES	271

MY SON, WHOM I LOVE	273
THE SECRET	275
ELIJAH COMES FIRST	277
FROM ARGUMENT TO WONDER	279
THEY COULD NOT	281
WHEN JESUS IS NOT PLEASED	283
HELP THE CHILDREN	285
GROWING IN FAITH	287
LIFTED UP	289
WHY?	291
REFRESHED AND CONFUSED	293
FIRST OR LAST?	295
LESSONS FROM A LITTLE BOY	297
NO FRANCHISE	299
REWARD AND PUNISHMENT	301
HAND, FOOT, EYE	303
BE AT PEACE	305
A "GOTCHA" QUESTION	307
MARRIAGE BREAKUP AND HARDNESS OF HEART	309
GOD'S DESIGN FOR MARRIAGE	311
A PRIVATE CONVERSATION WITH JESUS ABOUT DIVORCE	313
JESUS LOVES THE LITTLE CHILDREN	315
AFFECTIVE KNOWLEDGE	317
TWO GREAT QUESTIONS	319
IS BEING GOOD ENOUGH?	321
IF ONLY	323
THE CAMEL AND THE NEEDLE EYE	325
ETERNAL LIFE MADE POSSIBLE	327
FIRST AND LAST	329
IN THE LEAD	331
NECESSARY	333
WHATEVER WE ASK	335
REQUEST DENIED	337
JOSTLING FOR PROMINENCE	339
SERVANT LEADER	341
HE HAD A NAME	343
SON OF DAVID, HAVE MERCY	345
HOW MUCH DO YOU ASK?	347
WHAT DOES THE LORD NEED?	349
UNDER AUTHORITY	351
SAVE NOW!	353
HE LOOKED AROUND	355
HUNGRY	357
CLEANING HOUSE	359
THIEVES IN THE HOUSE OF GOD	361

THE GATHERING STORM	363
TEACHER AND RABBI	365
FAITH IN FAITH, OR FAITH IN GOD?	367
FORGIVENESS	369
THE QUESTION OF AUTHORITY	371
LITTLE LIES LEAD TO BIGGER ONES	373
OWNER AND TENANTS	375
AMAZING RESTRAINT	377
AMAZING LOVE	379
OUR CAPSTONE	381
THE ATTACK DOGS	383
WHAT BELONGS TO GOD	385
SEVEN BROTHERS, ONE WIFE	387
LIKE THE ANGELS	389
THE GREAT "I AM!"	391
THE MOST IMPORTANT	393
THE GREATEST COMMANDMENT	395
THE SECOND GREATEST COMMANDMENT	397
NOT FAR	399
AT THE RIGHT HAND	401
SON AND LORD	403
RELIGIOUS FAKES	405
COUNTING THE OFFERING	407
MORE THAN A TITHE	409
DASHED EXPECTATIONS	411
THE INSIDER QUESTION	413
WATCH!	415
WARS AND EARTHQUAKES	417
TROUBLE AND TRIUMPH FOR DISCIPLES	419
WARNING AND PROMISE	421
FAMILY BETRAYAL	423
THE ABOMINATION OF DESOLATION	425
WOMEN AND WINTER	427
NO QUICK FIX	429
WHEN NOT TO BELIEVE	431
CATASTROPHE AND CLIMAX	435
GATHERED BY ANGELS	435
THE FIG TREE	437
THE LAST GENERATION?	439
THE UNKNOWN DAY OR HOUR	441
WORK AND WATCH!	443
STAY AWAKE!	445
THE ROOT OF RELIGIOUS PERSECUTION	447
THE EXTRAVAGANCE OF LOVE	449
QUICK TO CRITICIZE	451

SOMETHING BEAUTIFUL FOR JESUS	453
WHAT YOU COULD	455
REMEMBERED	457
KEEP ME TRUE!	459
DIVIDED LOYALTY	461
ANONYMOUS FOR JESUS	463
PREPARING A ROOM FOR JESUS	465
SURELY NOT I?	467
SO CLOSE, BUT SO FAR	469
GRATITUDE	471
THE THIRD AND FOURTH CUP	473
THREE PROPHECIES	475
GOOD INTENTIONS	477
KNOWS US BEST, LOVES US MOST	479
THE PRAYER LIFE OF JESUS	481
JESUS: OUR MODEL FOR DEALING WITH DEPRESSION	483
YOUR WILL BE DONE	485
FALLING ASLEEP?	487
THE AGONY OF GETHSEMANE	489
TIME TO WAKE UP	491
FALL FROM GRACE	493
BETRAYED WITH A KISS	495
RETURNING GOOD FOR EVIL	497
RELIGION GONE BAD	499
THE COME-BACK DISCIPLE	501
TOO NEAR THE FLAME	503
THE RIGGED TRIAL	505
JESUS' OWN TESTIMONY	507
CRACKED UNDER PRESSURE	509
THE ARRAIGNMENTS	511
THE CROWD, THE GOVERNOR, AND THE RELIGIOUS LEADERS	513
THE VERDICT	515
THE ABUSE	517
GOLGOTHA	519
THE CROSS AT 9 A.M.	521
FAITH AND FAMILY	523
FINAL WORDS FROM THE CROSS	525
THREE POST-CRUCIFIXION MOMENTS	527
THE BURIAL OF JESUS	529
WOMEN AT THE TOMB	531
UNLIKELY RECIPIENTS OF GOOD NEWS	533
SHATTERED DREAMS MENDING	535
REFUSING TO BELIEVE	537
COMMAND AND PROMISE	539
TO BE CONTINUED...	541

FOREWORD

I remember the first time I heard George O. Wood preach. My father-in-law, Bob Schmidgall, had invited Dr. Wood to speak at Calvary Temple, the church he pastored in Naperville, Illinois. I had never heard Dr. Wood before that time, but by the end of his sermon, I remember thinking, *I want to preach like that.*

Dr. Wood combines two traits that rarely appear together: intellectual acumen and spiritual insight. He pays attention to the proper exegesis of Scripture, as well as its theological import. But he also knows how to tell a good story, capturing attention with a telling anecdote. One of the reasons I love and respect him is because his approach to preaching and teaching the Word of God simultaneously inspires me to think and to seek God more than I do currently. My prayer is that this book will inspire greater thinking and greater seeking in you, too.

Ancient Christians had a spiritual discipline called *lectio divina*. It was a way of reading the Bible that emphasized slowing down and getting small. Rather than rushing through the Bible in a fifteen-minute daily quiet time, the ancients lavished time on reading and thinking about God's Word. And in addition to looking at the big picture of Scripture—its majestic story of creation, fall, and redemption—the ancients sought God's will in the Bible's small details: this noun, that verb, a particular phrase or clause. The combination of slowness and smallness helped them see more clearly how they should live as disciples of Jesus Christ.

In *Fearless*, Dr. Wood takes this slow-small approach and works his way through the gospel of Mark one or two verses at a time. As you read the good news about Jesus through Dr. Wood's eyes, you'll find it working its way into the everyday details of your life. And as the gospel permeates more and more of your life, you'll see the truth in the words of this book's subtitle: *Jesus changes everything.*

May this book be to you what Dr. Wood's ministry has been to me—a catalyst for knowing and experiencing God in ever greater measure.

—Mark Batterson, lead pastor of National Community Church;
New York Times bestselling author of *The Circle Maker*

INTRODUCTION

I once asked the biographer of a famous twentieth-century Christian how she would deal with an unfortunate incident in the life of the person she was writing about. Her reply: "I will give it all the attention those few moments merit in considering an otherwise worthy and productive life." When the book was written, the failure was omitted. It didn't merit mention.

Not so with the man named Mark. His failure is written for us all to see; two of them in fact. Both relate to cowardice in the face of danger.

The first is the incident told in Mark 14:51–52, a young man fleeing naked in the night from Gethsemane after the arrest of Jesus. The fact that Mark's gospel alone records the incident telegraphs to us that it is an autobiographical reference. When the heat was on Jesus, Mark deserted. But, that was not the only time.

The second incident came when he abandoned Paul and Barnabas after the beginning of the first missionary journey (Acts 13:13). Paul completely lost confidence in Mark and refused to take him along on the second missionary journey (Acts 15:38).

But thanks be to God, Mark's failures did not define his life. He overcame them. In fact, he proved himself so well that during the apostle Paul's incarceration in Rome while he waited execution, he summoned Mark "because he is helpful to me in my ministry" (2 Tim. 4:11).

Like Mark, you don't have to let your failures define you. God wants to write His good news through you also!

Mark overcame his failures, and the Spirit used him to write what we call the second gospel. It is the shortest of the four Gospels. It leaves a lot out. It doesn't cover the nativity events, as does Luke. Mark doesn't focus a great deal on the teaching ministry of Jesus, as does Matthew. Mark doesn't reference extensive dialogues of Jesus with His disciples and others, as does John.

Instead, Mark's gospel focuses on the actions of Jesus. He moves quickly from incident to incident, frequently connecting accounts from Jesus' ministry with the oft-repeated word *immediately*.

Early church tradition tells us two things about the nature of Mark's gospel: First, it was written to Romans to tell them who Jesus was. So, the emphasis on the power ministry of Jesus was natural in writing to that audience. Second, behind Mark's account stands the reminiscences and preaching of Peter. If you want to know how Peter would talk to others about Jesus, then read Mark.

There is a moment when the eyewitness picture is so vivid it had to have come from Peter since Mark was not personally present. It happened in the storm at sea. Mark, alone of the gospel writers, tells us Jesus "was in the stern, *sleeping on a cushion*" (4:38, emphasis mine). Why did none of the other Gospels give us this detail? I suspect it was Peter who woke Jesus and noted what others may have missed. The detail went from Peter's lips to Mark's ears.

My prayer is that your journey with me through the gospel of Mark will increase your love for Jesus and help you realize anew that He is indeed the Messiah, the Son of God (1:1)!

NEVER-ENDING GOOD NEWS

*The beginning of the gospel about
Jesus Christ, the Son of God.*

MARK 1:1

HAVE YOU EVER NOTICED that Mark's gospel begins with an incomplete sentence? My suspicion is that Mark gave this verse as a title only when he had completed the last sentence of the last chapter.

Mark wrote about thirty years after the ascension of Jesus. The gospel, in its entirety, looks back on the three years of Jesus' public ministry. It's as though Mark got to the end of what we know as chapter 16, doubled back, and said to himself, "Well, the earthly ministry of Jesus was just beginning. Decades later, it is still ongoing. His story has no ending—He is still saving, teaching, healing, delivering—so I must make that clear. I'm going to add a sentence at the beginning that simply says, 'All you are about to read is just the commencement. When you get to the end of my gospel, please know that everything He did in the flesh was only the beginning.'"

It is the never-ending good news.

The word *gospel* in the original Greek means simply "good news."

When Jesus comes into your life, the good news begins. No matter how bad the news has been for you up to that moment, with His entrance the good news of salvation, forgiveness, abundant life, and eternal life begins!

The good news remains true even for the dark nights of the soul that you may endure as a follower of Jesus. Without Him there is no light at the end of the tunnel. He may be the only good news you have in a time of difficulty.

Jesus is the source of all good news. All other forms of good news are transitory because they are of this earth. Health, wealth, position—all will pass away. Jesus remains, and because He abides, we will inherit forever the benefits He provides.

He comes to you, in human form, as Jesus: Yeshua, Savior, Joshua. The very meaning of His name informs our human condition. We are lost and in need of a Savior. Without Jesus, we do not know God because we are ignorant of Him, unlike Him, and distanced from Him.

He comes to you as Christ: Messiah, the Anointed One. In the Old Testament, three offices carried the investiture of anointment: priest, prophet, and king. Jesus is all of these to you. He is priest because He bears your sins, carries your burdens, and intercedes for you. He is prophet because He speaks words of life to you, and He is king because He rules over you.

He comes to you as Son of God. Whereas the titles Savior and Christ describe His relationship to you, the title Son of God describes His relationship to the Father. Jesus is man, but far more. You may not understand the essence of His nature as Son of God because there is hiddenness in Him that no one but Himself knows. His being defies your ability to describe Him. We are no more able to fathom the mystery of the Trinity than a mouse is able to comprehend calculus. Jesus has revealed Himself sufficiently, however, that we may know and love Him, fall down and worship Him, and get up and serve Him.

The life of Jesus is never finished because He reigns without end. His work in you is never finished. The gospel must never be an old story for you. The One who brings you the good news has power to save you, rearrange you, deliver you from bondage and the power of the Devil, and continually reveal Himself to you so that each day in your life will witness your own new chapter of Christ's ongoing good news in you.

A Prayer

Lord Jesus, I give You thanks that Your good news has begun and continues in me. In every peak and valley of my life, You are always there with good news.

WHAT IS YOUR MISSION?

It is written in Isaiah the prophet: "I will send my messenger ahead of you, who will prepare your way"—"a voice of one calling in the desert, 'Prepare the way for the Lord, make straight paths for him.'"

MARK 1:2–3

IN HIS EARLY YEARS OF MINISTRY, the late Philip Crouch, past president of Central Bible College, served with his wife, Hazel, at the Lillian Trasher Orphanage in Assiout, Egypt, during the last years of Mama Lillian's Life.

Lillian Trasher had broken her engagement with Tom Jordan in North Carolina ten days before the wedding as an act of obedience to the missionary call upon her life. Eight months later, she welcomed the first baby into her orphanage in Egypt. Over the next fifty-one years, about 10,000 children were raised in her home; and since her death, probably another 10,000 children have called her orphanage their home.

Knowing that she had never married, I asked Philip Crouch if he had ever talked with Lillian about whether she regretted breaking her engagement to Tom.

He said, "As a matter of fact, I did. About a year before she died, I was talking with her one day and put the question to her, 'Do you ever regret not marrying Tom?' She became very quiet and finally said, 'If I had married Tom, what would have happened to all these children?'"

We sometimes blithely think, "Well, if I don't do what the Lord wants me to do, there will be someone else to take my place." But, there was no one standing in line to take Lillian Trasher's place. If she had not done what God wanted her to do, it would not have been done! And there is no one waiting in line to take your place either!

What is your mission in life?

John the Baptist stepped into the role cut out for him by the prophetic work of Isaiah. There was no one who could have taken his place either.

WHAT IS YOUR MISSION?

You may not have had a biblical prophet foretell your purpose on earth, but as God's child you just as surely have a mission. You can say with David, "You have laid your hand upon me" (Psalm 139:5).

"It is written" is not only a phrase describing John; it is meant to objectively anchor you when you are driven by the subjective impulses of life. God's written Word and the guidance of His Spirit will always lead you to effective service.

Like John, when we follow the Lord's will we prepare the way for others.

Sometimes we may not initially like where the Lord puts us. John's posting was the desert—water was scarce, varieties of food limited, and air-conditioning nonexistent. But in our difficult places we truly prepare the way of the Lord for others.

John was called to prepare the way of the Lord by making straight His paths. The imagery is of a road worker called to fill in the potholes, level the bumps, and take out the winding curves in order to make a good highway for the King to travel on. All the work on the road makes no sense if the King is not coming.

Similarly, you are working on some section of the Lord's highway in your life today. You have a purpose and a mission because the Lord is traveling on the segment of the road where you are.

A Prayer

Lord Jesus, when I stand before You on that Day, may You say to me, "Friend, well done. You did with your life what I asked of you." May I never be anywhere except in the very center of Your will.

REVIVAL IN THE DESERT

*And so John came, baptizing in the desert region and
preaching a baptism of repentance for the forgiveness of sins.
The whole Judean countryside and all the people
of Jerusalem went out to him. Confessing their sins,
they were baptized by him in the Jordan River.*

MARK 1:4–5

ISAIAH HAD PROPHESIED that before the Lord came, a messenger would be raised up in the desert.

Why the desert? Why not the city, the seacoast, or verdant plain?

On about thirty occasions, I have been in the location where John the Baptist ministered. I always marvel that he could attract people down to where he was at 1,200 feet below sea level. Jerusalem is a steep twenty-mile climb up over 3,500 feet, and the Judean countryside is highland area. It is only a thirty-minute drive, but try walking!

Perhaps you would not mind the day's walk downhill to where John preached and baptized, but you certainly would not like the walk back up! Who today would walk one day to get to church, and then another day to get back home?

When planning strategically for new church buildings, we want location, location, location. We want to make it easy for people to come, park, and walk to the front door. We are all about access.

That is all well and good, but John was not about access. You had to want to get to him.

God wanted John out in the desert—that is why Isaiah prophesied it 800 years earlier.

Throughout church history, the Holy Spirit has used unusual places to begin powerful spiritual movements: a small town in Germany called Wittenberg where Luther posted his 95 Theses; a mission in London where Wesley felt his heart strangely warmed when he heard someone read Luther's commentary on Romans;

a former stable in Los Angeles converted into the Azusa Street Mission where the Pentecostal Movement caught fire, a rented opera house in Hot Springs, Arkansas, where the Assemblies of God was born.

God is not impressed with the grandeur of a place. He is concerned about the emptiness in the heart. John addressed that emptiness by passionately proclaiming that God forgives sins.

That is why people went out to John near the place where the Jordan River empties into the Dead Sea. They came because he had an authentic message from God.

When an authentic message from God is wedded to an authentic hunger in the heart, a powerful spiritual movement gets underway.

That is the challenge before us today. Those who proclaim God's Word must do so with conviction and passion. People will not be attracted by those who mumble religious words or simply say interesting things—even if they do so in multi-million-dollar buildings.

On the other hand, the greatest preachers of God's message will see no results if people's hearts are not open to receive, repent, and be cleansed of sin.

A Prayer

Lord Jesus, I pray for an authentic work of Your Spirit in my church and community. Just like the mass of people from Judea and Jerusalem who came to John, I pray for a great movement toward You in this land.

THE JORDAN RIVER PROTEST MOVEMENT

John wore clothing made of camel's hair, with a leather belt around his waist, and he ate locusts and wild honey. And this was his message, "After me will come one more powerful that I, the thongs of whose sandals I am not worthy to stoop down and untie. I baptize you with water, but he will baptize you with the Holy Spirit."

MARK 1:6–8

JOHN THE BAPTIST'S CLOTHING certainly was not from Versace or any contemporary designer of his day. Out in the hot desert he wore a thick garment of camel's hair and ate simply.

He had retreated early in life to the shimmering, blistering desert—the lowest point on earth at 1,200 feet below sea level, just north of the Dead Sea.

His appearance probably belied his age—skin deeply burned from the desert sun; his feet, hands, and knees heavily calloused; hair and beard untamed by comb and mousse—you would have thought him more an eccentric hermit in his fifties than a prophet of the Almighty just turning thirty.

John the Baptist was the sort of person you would expect to see at the front of a demonstration. Modern news reporters might have dubbed him the leader of the Jordan River Protest Movement. But what was John protesting against?

Religion without repentance: If the religion of the time had been meeting the people's needs, they would not have walked into the desert to hear John and to be baptized.

John didn't appear in the wilderness preaching, "Improve, for God is about to raise up a new society." Instead, he proclaimed, "Repent, for the kingdom of God is at your doorstep."

Life can only be better when we begin at the right starting place—where John started, where Jesus started, where the apostles started—with the first word of the gospel, the good news: *repent!*

Liturgy without salvation: The banks of the Jordan River were lined with people who found no peace from the guilt of sin even though they had gone to the temple and offered animal sacrifice, prayed prayers of penance, and trusted in the ecclesiastical system of the day.

Public or private acts of worship afford no guarantee that sins will be pardoned or salvation will come. Any worship is empty if it calls attention to the worshiper rather than to the God who saves us.

Liturgy without salvation is an external performance that does not affect the internal.

History without fulfillment: Life in Jerusalem could go on with little sense of impending crisis. But, out in the desert, John knew that history was headed someplace. The Messiah was coming!

John did no miracles. Neither could he forgive sin or grant eternal life. John knew he was unworthy, but Jesus is worthy. John baptized people in the external and physical element of water, but Jesus baptizes people with the Spirit, a baptism that transforms from the inside out and empowers people to live for God far beyond their human potential.

A Prayer

Lord Jesus, help me never to think that religious ritual substitutes for a genuine relationship with You. You are the All Powerful One.

TRANSITIONS

At that time Jesus came from Nazareth in Galilee and was baptized by John in the Jordan. As Jesus was coming up out of the water, he saw heaven being torn open and the Spirit descending on him like a dove. And a voice came from heaven: "You are my Son, whom I love; with you I am well pleased."

MARK 1:9–11

ARE YOU FACING A MOMENT OF TRANSITION in your life? We can learn much from the example of Jesus as He transitioned from the private life of His first thirty years to His public life of His last three years. His baptism by John marks the turning point.

First, Jesus identified with John. Although Jesus had no need for a baptism of repentance for the forgiveness of sins, His example teaches us to position ourselves on the side of those whose hearts and motives are pure.

Politicians talk a great deal about change, but change can move us from good to bad or bad to worse depending on whether we identify with the wrong person or persons. In your time of transition, are you closest to those who truly know the Lord? Have you sought the counsel of those who walk near to Him or are you just charging ahead because it seems like a good idea to you?

Second, Jesus received confirmation personally from the Father—the heavens opened. Interestingly, none of the Gospels report that anyone else saw the heavens open except Jesus. He, not "they," saw the heavens open!

Your journey in life will involve experiences with God that you alone will observe and apply. You must be sensitive to what the Holy Spirit shows you in your personal times of waiting on Him. When you act in obedience, as Jesus did by going to the Jordan, God will reveal Himself to you. That revelation may not be something outward or spectacular—it may be an inner, still small voice—but get the mind of the Spirit before you set forth with transition.

Third, Jesus experienced the peacefulness and gentleness of God in the descent of the Spirit as a dove upon Him.

Transitions need to be marked by calmness. Any hyperactivity by Jesus at His baptism would have shooed away the dove of peace. If you are filled with anxiety, fear, and stress as you anticipate transition, back off until you are filled with peace.

Fourth, Jesus experienced the Father's honest and wholesome perspective—"You are my Son, whom I love; with you I am well pleased." Jesus emerged from the transition with the unmistakable assurance that the Father both loved and approved of Him.

Do you really know deep inside yourself that God dearly loves you, that you are known to Him, and that He is pleased with all who put their trust in His Son? What greater security or sense of wholeness is there than this?

Jesus knew He was not alone because He knew in His time of transition that the Father approved of Him, and the Holy Spirit descended and remained on Him. It is the same with you. You are not alone in your time of transition. God is with you!

A Prayer

Lord Jesus, may I never make decisions that exclude You.
In every transition moment, may I remain centered in
Your will, seeking Your voice and experiencing
Your favor and blessing.

TEMPTATION

*At once the Spirit sent him out into the desert,
and he was in the desert forty days, being tempted by Satan.
He was with the wild animals, and angels attended him.*

MARK 1:12–13

MARK GIVES US THE READER'S DIGEST condensed version of Jesus' temptation. It tells us all the essential elements we need to know when facing our own temptations.

First, how are we tempted in the first place? Three forces are always at work in the process of temptation: (1) our personal tendency to desire what is opposite of the Spirit, (2) the activity of the Enemy, and (3) the prodding of the Spirit that directs us into engagement with the Devil. For Jesus, it was the third one—but for us, it can be any or all of these three.

Second, the place of temptation is the wilderness, at least symbolically. The wilderness represents the barren and dry place. When you find yourself relationally, emotionally, and spiritually empty, you are far more vulnerable to temptation. When everything is going well—in your life, your family, your marriage, your finances, your health, and your walk with the Lord—you are far less likely to fall into sin. But the desert represents the places where you don't have many resources to fall back on and you are most likely to give an ear to the Devil's pitch.

Third, the time of temptation is always for a period. It isn't forever—at least, in its intensity. For Jesus, the period of time lasted forty days, and then the Devil left Him for a season (Luke 4:13). Your temptation, likewise, will not last forever. It will come at you thick and furious, but when you steadfastly resist the Devil he will flee from you (James 4:7; 1 Peter 5:9).

Fourth, the agent of temptation is your adversary, Satan. For Jesus, no intermediate agent of testing was used—just the Devil himself. For you, the temptation may come through the world or the sinful human nature. But never forget, no matter how temptation comes to you, the Devil stands behind the curtain. He is the puppeteer, pulling the strings. Your contest is with him (Ephesians 6:12).

Fifth, the atmosphere of temptation may involve frightful dimensions. Mark is the only gospel writer to note the presence of wild animals. When the Devil came to Jesus with the three temptations (as recorded in Matthew 4 and Luke 4), he seems to have donned a rather civil appearance, as he often does when he wants to beguile. But temptation may also involve a nightmarish time of danger. Jesus experienced in the wilderness things similar to what Daniel experienced in the lion's den. What "wild beasts" are present in your own time of temptation?

Sixth, God will protect you in the place of temptation as you put your trust in Him. Arrayed against the wild beasts are the angels of God. The angels didn't assist Jesus in saying no to the Devil, but they protected Him from the other ravages of the wilderness. Likewise, the Lord will protect you from whatever seeks to tear you apart. He has promised to provide a way of escape (1 Corinthians 10:13).

A Prayer

Strong Lord, help me to understand that I will never be tempted by what is unattractive or by that for which I do not have an appetite. Help me to say yes to You and no to everything that harms my relationship with You.

THE LAUNCH

After John was put in prison, Jesus went into Galilee, proclaiming the good news of God.

MARK 1:14

I GRADUATED FROM COLLEGE at the age of twenty with a call to full-time vocational ministry. One problem! Nobody wanted to hire me on a church staff or call me as pastor. So, I decided to go to seminary for three more years.

Some older believers counseled me: "Don't do that. Jesus is coming soon and you need to be out winning people to the Lord, not going for more schooling." I didn't know enough to answer them well, but the way I saw it, if Jesus could wait until He was thirty years of age to begin His public ministry, I could wait until I was twenty-four!

Just as Esther came to the kingdom "for such a time as this" (Esther 4:14), and Jesus came in "the fullness of time" (Galatians 4:4, KJV), so also you are alive for a reason at this time on planet earth (Psalm 139).

Mark tells us that Jesus launched His public ministry when four things had happened: (1) John the Baptist's preaching had created a public movement of awareness and expectancy, (2) Jesus had been baptized and (3) tested, and (4) John had been imprisoned.

Nothing ever happens randomly in life. There are wheels within wheels, purposes within purposes. God is always setting out the building blocks of our lives in a precise manner—just as happened with Jesus.

As a young person, I got frustrated several times when the Lord seemingly had not answered my prayers. I wanted some things He evidently did not want for me. Looking back, I realize that if I had gotten what I wanted when I wanted it, my life would have been far less productive for the Lord.

If I were Jesus, I might have wanted to skip some of the "hoops"—the quiet thirty years of waiting and learning the trade of a carpenter/mason, along with the temptation in the wilderness. It must have been difficult for Jesus to wait until the right time for His ministry to begin. Likewise, it's difficult for us to be patient while waiting for the perfect timing of God's will to unfold in our lives.

But, like Jesus, you must not become impatient with the data of your own life. Sure, we want everything to happen today. Many times I have wanted to do things without self-examination, repentance, and personal inside cleaning. I have wanted to avoid trial and temptation, and certainly all dangerous circumstances. As the saying goes, "I want it and I want it now!"

Had I been Jesus, would I have begun my ministry following the imprisonment of John? That doesn't seem like a good or comfortable time to me! The same forces that silenced John surely threatened to silence Jesus as well.

At the very worst of times, with John imprisoned, Jesus appeared bringing good news. Good news meant so much more when all around there was so much bad news.

God has a plan for your life! His design is to help you, shape you, guide you, and make of you what you could never become on your own. God's good news never ends for those who follow Jesus!

A Prayer

Lord Jesus, help me to remember that Your way is best.
Protect me from making stupid or sinful choices
that would bring harm into my life.

THE MAIN THINGS

"The time has come," he said. "The kingdom of God is near. Repent and believe the good news."

MARK 1:15

WHEN I WAS A YOUNG PASTOR, an older minister advised me: "George, the main things in Scripture are the plain things; and the plain things are the main things."

That is certainly the case with Jesus. He never bothered to talk about a Bible code as a means of discerning hidden things in Scripture. In fact, none of the things we really need to know are hidden at all—God's Word completely reveals them.

Jesus began His ministry in the synagogues of Galilee by focusing on the main things and the plain things. He evidently repeated the same message everywhere He went, because when Mark wrote his gospel thirty years later, he still remembered Jesus' four-points.

First, the time has come. While others were looking for the Messiah to bring a political kingdom, Jesus instead brought a kingdom that was internal rather than external. His kingdom is voluntarily received and not imposed from without. Do you know that on this very day God desires to insert a piece of the future age—an age of unbounded love, joy, and peace—into your life? Then His kingdom will be within you!

Second, the kingdom of God is near. How near?

Perhaps you are passing through a difficult season in your life. You wish you could either get it over with or go on to be with the Lord. But, Jesus is telling you that His kingdom is present with you this day. It is near, not far. It is at hand.

His rule enters this present moment. While you may long for His kingdom in the age to come, He longs for His kingdom to rule in you today. He wants you to turn your thoughts, emotions, moods, and relationships over to Him. He desires to be Lord in you!

The first two points of Jesus' sermon in the synagogues of Galilee deal with God's activity: the time has come and the kingdom is at hand. The last two points deal with our response: (1) repent and (2) believe the good news.

The word *repent* is from the Greek word that means to change your mind. How so? Our thoughts and way of life need to conform to Jesus' way of life. As His followers, we know that forgiveness of sin, salvation, and eternal life reside only in Him. There is no other way to God. Education, religion, philosophy, or material wealth will not save us. Repentance means we throw away our false ideas of relating to God and embrace the life of Jesus.

Repent has sometimes been called the first word of the gospel because it is where John the Baptist, Jesus, Peter (Acts 2:38), and Paul (Acts 26:20) all began. It is the starting point of the Christian life.

Finally, we are to believe the good news, the gospel. The good news is that God sent His Son to earth to teach us how to live and to pardon our sins through His death on the cross so that we might have eternal life. The good news is that defeat, despair, and death never have the last word because through His resurrection from the dead, Jesus is Victor!

A Prayer

Lord, there are days when there is no news or there is only bad news. Help me to see that every day You bring good news: that I am personally known to You, deeply loved, and embraced eternally.

ELEVEN LIFE-CHANGING WORDS

As Jesus walked beside the Sea of Galilee, he saw Simon and his brother Andrew casting a net into the lake, for they were fishermen. "Come, follow me," Jesus said, "and I will make you fishers of men." At once they left their nets and followed him.

MARK 1:16–18

NO ONE OUTSIDE their own small fishing village knew them. They were just two young brothers trying to make a living at commercial fishing. Then Jesus gave them an invitation that changed their lives forever. It's an invitation He also gives to you.

1. **Come!** Before Jesus can do anything in your life, you must begin to move in His direction. The whole of the Christian life involves coming to Him—culminating in that great day when you will live with Him forever.

2. **Follow!** When you start following Jesus, you do not know where you will go. But, one thing is for sure, you will go *with* Him. Better to go with Him than anyone else!

3. **Me!** Jesus does not call you to follow an ethical system, a religious ideal, or a code of restrictions. His invitation is personal. It calls for exclusivity—follow Him, and no other.

4. **And!** Jesus has more in mind for you than just being a follower. The "and" connects you to a larger meaning for your existence. Without the "and," you are only responsible to follow, but He has bigger plans for you than you have for yourself.

5. **I!** Jesus proposes to take charge of your life. All of us have family and friends who influence us—but Jesus brings deep change. We know Simon and Andrew because they were known first to Jesus. He revolutionized their lives, as He also seeks to revolutionize yours.

6. **Will!** Jesus does not say "may." There is no uncertainty in His voice. You can rely on His ability to transform you.

7. **Make!** From the Gospels, it is clear that the making didn't happen all at once. He may have to demolish some stuff in your life in order to make room for His splendid purposes, but you will love the makeover of His finished work in you.

8. **You!** That means *you* specifically! His call is not generic—it is personal. He knows your name and what you are doing with your life, just as He knew the names and occupations of His first disciples.

9. **Fishers!** Simon and Andrew, by trade, fished. That is the only natural ability ever noted of them. You probably are not a fisher, but you have some interests, some talents. Jesus will build on what you offer Him.

10. and 11. **Of Men!** Is wealth your goal? Then accumulate things. Is being smart your goal? Then gather facts. Is fame what you seek? Then find whatever brings you attention. But, Jesus offers something far better than wealth, smartness, or fame. He calls you to people.

These eleven words in the English text of Mark's gospel changed the destiny of Simon and Andrew. They dropped everything at once and followed Jesus.

What will you do? Jesus comes to you as He did to these two young brothers. They never regretted accepting His invitation, and neither will you.

A Prayer

May I truly follow You, Lord Jesus. I don't want to run ahead of You, away from You, or lag behind You. I want to stay close to You because I am only at my best when I keep You just in front of me.

THE PARADOX OF CALL

*When he had gone a little farther, he saw James son of
Zebedee and his brother John in a boat, preparing their nets.
Without delay he called them, and they left their father
Zebedee in the boat with the hired men and followed him.*

MARK 1:19–20

SEVERAL WEEKS AGO I VISITED the Vietnam Veterans Memorial in Washington, DC. Engraved into the long Memorial Wall are the 58,195 names of all American military personnel killed in that war. I looked for the one I knew, Phillip A. Nichols. I found him at section 7W, line 133. I reached down and placed my hand on his name.

Phil and I entered college at the same time. Both of us planned to be ministers of the gospel; Phil through military chaplaincy and I through pastoral ministry. We lived in the same dorm and attended the same small classes. Phil married his college sweetheart, JoAnna, at the beginning of their last year in college.

Time went by. Phil went on to seminary, as did I, only to different schools. He received his chaplaincy appointment after two years of pastoral ministry and headed off to Vietnam, leaving behind JoAnna and their three young children.

While bivouacking with his troops one night, someone hit a tripwire and all the men in the company were killed in the explosion. To this day, Phil is the only Assemblies of God chaplain ever to lose his life in the conflict of war.

When I read the above verses about James and John, I think of Phil and me. The brothers James and John, and two friends—Phil and I—were all called to follow Jesus.

But you know the gospel history. James became the first of the Twelve martyred for his faith (Acts 12:1–2), and John lived longer than all the others. We are never told why. That is the paradox of the call. Its beginning is the same; the ending is different for each one called.

The fourth gospel tells us that John had actually been a follower of John the Baptist when he and Andrew heard the Baptist say of Jesus, "Look, the Lamb of God." So, they asked Jesus where He was staying and He told them, "Come and see." Sixty years later, when writing his gospel, John still remembered the exact time of the call—about 4 o'clock in the afternoon (John 1:35-39).

That first brush with Jesus had been down by the Judean desert, just north of the Dead Sea. Evidently, John didn't stay with Jesus long at that time because in the verses above we find him up north on the Lake of Galilee plying his trade as a commercial fisherman with his brother James and the hired help.

Suppose we could interview James and John today: "James, you were killed early on, and John you lived longer than all the others, and spent your last years as an exiled prisoner on a lonely wind-swept island. Do either of you regret having obeyed Christ's call so instantly? Looking back, would you have taken more time for reflection before leaving everything to follow Him?"

"We have absolutely no regrets!" I hear them answer. "Jesus gave us the greatest privilege in life—to follow Him, all the way to eternity. And if we had it to do all over again, we would leave everything instantly to follow Him!"

Phil and I would say the same thing. His life was cut short. I have lived long. But following Jesus is the greatest thing of all!

A Prayer

May I never hesitate, Lord, to follow You—whether the journey with You in this life is long or short. Your way is best for me.

POWER IN THE PULPIT

They went to Capernaum, and when the Sabbath came, Jesus went into the synagogue and began to teach. The people were amazed at his teaching, because he taught them as one who had authority, not as the teachers of the law.

MARK 1:21–22

I WILL NEVER FORGET my first attempt to deliver a sermon in a preaching class in seminary. Twenty of my fellow students were scattered throughout the 200-seat auditorium, all holding a legal size critique sheet—waiting to pounce on every weakness in delivery and any hint of weak content.

My idea of preaching at the time was to start high, loud, and fast. The more anointed you felt, the higher, louder, and faster you shouted. I reached full pitch by the end of my twenty-minute rant, thinking I had done rather well.

My professor stood by my side while my student colleagues came together and gave their painful analysis. My roommate said, "Who was that up there? I never heard that voice before." Another of my friends said, "Who did you think you were, the Pope, speaking *ex cathedra*?" I was devastated. When they were all done, my prof saved me by saying, "You leave my Ozark hillbilly preacher alone. At least when he gets up there, he has some fire. All some of you do is read your sermon with no emotion."

I have learned a lot about preaching since then. Volume doesn't equal anointing or authority. You cannot give others what you do not have yourself. Lack of preparation always shows. Prayerlessness produces dryness. Preaching must be rooted in the Word but made applicable to life. It is inexcusable that preaching should ever bore people.

Jesus' words have a way of getting inside people. That is what we notice when Mark tells us about the Lord's first sermon in the Capernaum synagogue.

Just a few days prior, Jesus had called two sets of brothers from Capernaum to follow Him. The first Sabbath after their call found Jesus in their town synagogue. Every ear was tuned to His commanding voice. Mark doesn't tell us His scriptural text that day or the content of His message, just the reaction of the audience—amazement that Jesus taught with authority and not as the teachers of the law.

The audience was used to being bored by religious leaders who read the lesson in monotone, quoting authorities from the past and present, and doing nothing to make the Scripture come alive in the hearts of the hearers. Their sermons were like term papers—fully footnoted.

Jesus didn't rely on the authority of others but on Himself. We see a sample of that later in the Sermon on the Mount when He repeatedly said, "You have heard it said . . . but I say to you . . ."

Two questions hit us for application.

First, do you take the authority of Jesus seriously? In your moral and ethical behavior, do His words provide the direction for your life or do you feel free to disregard what Jesus says when it is inconvenient for you?

Second, are you amazed with Jesus? Oh, I realize we haven't heard Him audibly, but the Gospels give us His words in written form. His words crackle with authority, amazing us with their clarity, revelation of God, and insight into human behavior.

I wish I could have been in the Capernaum synagogue that day and heard Him in person; but every day I can read again what He said and arrange my life accordingly. How about you?

A Prayer

Lord Jesus, may I listen to You as I would to no other. May Your voice alone be supreme in my life. Bend my will and heart to Your authority.

DEEP EVIL

Just then a man in their synagogue who was possessed by an evil spirit cried out, "What do you want with us, Jesus of Nazareth? Have you come to destroy us? I know who you are –the Holy One of God!" "Be quiet!" said Jesus sternly. "Come out of him!" The evil spirit shook the man violently and came out of him with a shriek.

MARK 1:23–26

HOW DO YOU FIGHT deep evil?

When a bully comes along and taunts and hits a weaker child in the playground, you can do something about that.

When a maniac gains control of a nation, terrorizes and seeks world control, armies come together in justice to defeat him.

But who can help a person possessed by an evil spirit? Who can deliver the person trapped and dominated by an agency not his or her own?

There are evils so deep only God can deliver.

Mark gives us several accounts of that deep evil. Later, in Mark 5, Jesus frees a man bound by a legion of demons—a man so wild he lived among the tombs and was often bound with ropes and chains. This possessed man in the Capernaum synagogue had a lighter case of demonic possession. He didn't live away from people. Others would even have thought him normal; after all, he attended synagogue along with everyone else.

But in the presence of Jesus the deep evil came spilling out. The man knew two things about Jesus: His identity (the Holy One of God) and His mission (to destroy the Devil and his demons).

Perhaps you have never witnessed demonic possession. Maybe you think it is simply a misdiagnosis of schizophrenia or some other mental illness. Jesus took demonic possession as fact and gave a treatment for it—deliverance!

This passage in the gospel always sets me to wondering whether in our own church meetings there are people who come Sunday after Sunday, go through the motions of worship and hearing the Word, but the evil in them never comes out because there is no powerful presence of Christ in the service.

Is there deep evil in you? Oh, you may not be possessed by a spirit other than your own, but are you dealing with things in your life that, despite your best efforts, you cannot control or get free from? Bulimia? Anorexia? Pornography? Addiction to alcohol, nicotine, prescription or illegal drugs, to name a few? Our society is full of people who deep down cry out to be free from denigrating and life-controlling destructive behaviors.

Jesus' goal for you is totally different than the Devil's. The Devil wants to destroy you, to completely ruin your life. Jesus wants to save you, to set you free. The good news of Jesus is that He not only wants to eradicate the deep evil in you, He also has the power to do so.

Today, multiplied millions of people have been set free by Jesus. There is no bondage He cannot break, no evil strong enough to resist His power. How do you tap into that power? Go the source—Jesus—and ask Him to help you! He cares for you!

A Prayer

Strong Lord Jesus, You have power to root out from my life all that is unlike You, all that is harmful to me. I invite You to set me free so that I can live joyfully and productively.

AMAZED

The people were all so amazed that they asked each other, "What is this? A new teaching—and with authority! He even gives orders to the evil spirits and they obey him." News about him spread quickly over the whole region of Galilee.

MARK 1:27–28

A FEW YEARS AGO, over 2,000 ministers and laity gathered in Springfield, Missouri, for an annual Assemblies of God Prayer Summit. At that meeting, we experienced once again the living authority of Jesus.

In a morning session devoted exclusively to prayer, a request was made for a young pioneering pastor who had spent the previous twelve days in a coma. A virus had attacked his brain, leaving a damaged area the size of a pecan. That morning his father had emailed me saying the doctors had detected bleeding in that area. The son's situation was critical. No one knew whether he would live, and if he did live whether he would be physically or mentally impaired.

His wife was expecting their first child in a few weeks, and he had no health insurance.

We all went to prayer. After a time of intercession, a man stood and began groaning loudly. At first, it sounded inappropriate—but as he called out from his depths to God, the congregation began weeping in intercession. Then the noise of several thousand saints praying rose to a crescendo. I sensed immediately in my spirit that something had happened in the heavens. You could feel it in the room—healing had gone forth.

Within hours, the father called me and told me the bleeding had stopped. Six days later, this young church planter was sitting up in his hospital bed, using his computer. Two weeks and four days after we prayed, he attended the Easter service at his small but growing church.

Another pastor in that Prayer Summit felt his heart warmed as with a heating pad and knew he was being healed. A nuclear stress test taken a week earlier had revealed no activity in a portion of his heart. After the Prayer Summit, he was re-examined and his heart was completely well.

I reflect on these healings and the reaction of the Capernaum synagogue folk to the deliverance Jesus brought to the demoniac in their midst.

There are some things only the Lord can do. It is vital that we, His people, recognize that.

It is so easy to settle into the routine of going through a church service or even our own personal devotions. If we just trip through the motions, there will never be amazement. But when we throw our hearts wide open to the ministry of Jesus, wonderful things happen.

The reaction at Capernaum came in response not only to what Jesus did but to what He said. They were amazed at His teaching. Jesus certainly never bored people; He spoke with vitality. He never preached just to give information; He spoke to change hearts.

When words and deeds combine to communicate the love and power of God authentically, the news will always "spread quickly over the whole region." What happened in Capernaum became known throughout all Galilee. If the reality of the Lord's presence becomes known in any one place—large or small, obscure or at the crossroads—the good news will get out.

A Prayer

Lord Jesus, may I never take You for granted. May I never skim over Your words as if they were those of any ordinary person. May I always be amazed at what You say and what You do.

OUT OF BED

As soon as they left the synagogue, they went with James and John to the home of Simon and Andrew. Simon's mother-in-law was in bed with a fever, and they told Jesus about her. So he went to her, took her hand and helped her up. The fever left her and she began to wait on them.

MARK 1:29–31

MARK IS TANTALIZINGLY BRIEF in his account of the healing of Peter's mother-in-law. He doesn't even give us her name.

It is also a mystery why Jesus didn't go to the home of James and John. After all, they too lived in Capernaum. Why go to Simon and Andrew's home when the hostess is sick in bed? In fact, the third gospel tells us one additional detail—she had a *high* fever. You would expect an exact diagnosis from the medical doctor, Luke (Luke 4:38)!

Not only did Peter's mother-in-law have a raging fever, but Jesus didn't go to her home alone—He entered with a group of people about Him, simply identified by Mark as "*they* went with him."

So, what is going on here?

I suspect a correlation between what had just happened in the synagogue with the deliverance of the demoniac and an expectation on the part of Jesus' disciples. They believed that if He could exorcise an evil spirit then He might also be able to cure a sickness.

Here is an important lesson for us in our faith journey. We must connect the Lord's past deeds to our present situation. So many times when we are in an immediate crisis we forget that the Lord has helped us in the past. When we don't remember, we become filled with fear rather than faith.

I remember a time when I was "in bed"—not literally in bed with a fever like Peter's mother-in-law but proverbially with a depression that hung on for a couple of years. I wish my cure had been as quick as this healing, but I see a similar process that Jesus used both for me and for this woman.

He comes to us. That is first and foremost. He is in our "house," in our lives. He is not absent.

Then, He takes us by the hand. There is a gospel chorus that says, "He touched me." I know personally the touch of that hand. Oh, not the physical hand; but I do know that Jesus pulled me out of the depths.

When Jesus took Peter's mother-in-law's hand, He didn't just hold it. He "helped her up." Jesus will lift you, whether through the process of time or immediacy of action. The songwriter put it well, "He brought me out of the miry clay, He set my feet on the rock to stay."

Mark doesn't say the fever left her and then she got up, but the reverse. She got up and the fever left her. All during depression, I would say: "What would I do today if I weren't depressed?" And I got out of bed and fulfilled my duties. Over time, the "fever" left me!

The last time we see Peter's mother-in-law she is well and serving. That is the whole purpose of Jesus' work in our lives—that we might be about the work of caring for others.

A Prayer

Lord Jesus, take me also by the hand. Transfer Your strength and wholeness to me that I might serve You and those to whom You have called me.

INTO THE STREET

That evening after sunset the people brought to Jesus all the sick and demon possessed. The whole town gathered at the door, and Jesus healed many who had various diseases. He also drove out many demons, but he would not let the demons speak because they knew who he was.

MARK 1:32–34

ON FEBRUARY 9, 1958, a twenty-six-year-old Assemblies of God pastor in a rural Pennsylvania town watched late-night television while his wife and small children slept. "How much time am I spending in front of the TV each night?" he asked himself. "A couple of hours at least. What if I sold the TV set and spent that time praying?"

The next day he and his wife placed an ad, agreeing to sell the TV if a buyer appeared within thirty minutes of the newspaper landing on their doorstep. At twenty-nine minutes, the TV sold.

Sixteen days later, while praying late in the evening, the young pastor's eyes focused on a nearby issue of *Life Magazine*. After resisting the temptation to interrupt his prayers, he finally picked it up with this question, "Lord, is there something you want me to see?" On pages thirty and thirty-one he found the answer: a sketch drawing and story of seven young New York City gang members on trial for the brutal murder of fifteen-year-old Michael Farmer.

David Wilkerson, the young pastor, began weeping for these lost boys. Two days later he was in New York City, a place he had never been before, and his appearance in the courtroom that day opened the door for ministry to gang members. Soon, Teen Challenge was established. Over the past five decades, multiplied thousands have experienced the deliverance of Jesus Christ from addictions, life-controlling problems, and bondage.

David Wilkerson simply followed the pattern of the Lord—he went into the street. The people who met Jesus in the street at sundown had not been to the place of worship that day, the synagogue; nor had they been inside the home of Peter because it was too small for them all to fit.

Indeed, the opening paragraphs of Mark's gospel show us that Jesus is present in the house of worship, the home, and the street. That is also where His activity is today. The street is where His people must carry His presence as well.

It isn't enough just to be gathered in the church. Nor can we just keep Jesus in our homes. He is looking for the wider venue—out in the public place where people are needy and hurting.

Picture the citizens of Capernaum. They waited until the Sabbath was past and with clay lamps illuminating their faces they gathered outside the door of the home where Jesus was present. For the first time in many years, the broken in body and spirit, the broken-hearted, had hope. There is hope when Jesus is in the street!

One demoniac was healed in the synagogue and one sick mother-in-law was healed in the home (Mark 1:21-31), but *many* were healed and delivered in the street. It is the same today. Yes, there are results in our church worship services—people come to Christ. But if we want to see many come instead of the few, then, as Christ's followers, we too must be out in the street.

A Prayer

Lord Jesus, I am grateful for the comfort zone of my church and home, these safe places. Help me, Lord, to see that You also want me out in the street.

ALONE IN PRAYER

*Very early in the morning, while it was still dark,
Jesus got up, left the house and went off to
a solitary place, where he prayed.*

MARK 1:35

PICTURE THE SCENE. On Saturday, the Sabbath, Jesus ministered in the Capernaum synagogue and cast out a demon. He then healed Peter's mother-in-law in her home. Next, from sundown into the evening hours, He healed various diseases in those gathered in the street. It had been an exhausting day.

But Jesus didn't sleep in the next day! Before the crack of dawn, before anyone else in the house had arisen, He slipped off quietly to find a solitary place to pray.

I can understand His restlessness in rising early. When I am on the verge of plunging into something major, I don't feel like sleeping. Jesus knew that the years of quietness and isolation in Nazareth were forever behind Him. The events of the previous day in preaching, exorcism, and healing had launched His public mission.

From now on His days would be filled with people who had needs. He would teach, heal, and cast out demons, but He would also be questioned, accused, and misunderstood.

Whom did He have to turn to for respite from the pressing demands? The Father, of course!

Do you remember a time when you had been away from home and longed for the fellowship of family? Then imagine how Jesus felt.

He had left His home in heaven. But in the quiet of the dark and dawning morning hours He spoke the language of heaven. He continued in the fellowship of the Father and the Holy Spirit. He drew strength and assurance through prayer.

If Jesus found it necessary to spend time alone in prayer, how much more do we?

Certainly, our schedules are no more exhausting or full than His. He shows us that if we are to draw divine strength for our lives we are better off spending an hour or two in prayer than sleep. We often think the reverse—that we need sleep rather than prayer. Why not follow the example of Jesus and cut out some sleeping time for prayer?

One of my seminary professors, Harold Lindsell, said this about prayer:

> "God cannot do some things unless we work. He stores the hills with marble, but He has never built a cathedral. He fills the mountains with iron ore, but he never makes a needle or a jet airplane. He leaves that to us.
>
> "If then, God has left many things dependent on man's thinking and working, why should He not leave some things dependent upon man's praying? He has done so. 'Ask and you shall receive.' And there are some things God will not give us unless we ask.
>
> "We cannot suppose that God will do for us *without* prayer what He has promised to do for us only *through* prayer."

Jesus knew He could not function effectively unless He prayed; neither can we. Prayer must become our everyday habit. If you haven't already done so, find a time alone each day to adore and praise God. Unpack your burdens and intercede for others. You will be amazed at how near you will draw to Him and how He will respond to your prayers!

A Prayer

Lord Jesus, I cannot get through this day or any day without You. I need time alone with You. In Your presence I am strengthened and renewed. My will, character, and attitudes become aligned to You. I cherish my time alone with You.

SOMEWHERE ELSE

Simon and his companions went to look for him, and when they found him, they exclaimed: "Everyone is looking for you!" Jesus replied, "Let us go somewhere else—to the nearby villages—so I can preach there also. That is why I have come." So he traveled throughout Galilee, preaching in their synagogues and driving out demons.

MARK 1:36-39

IT WAS EARLY SUNDAY MORNING in Capernaum. The previous day (on the Sabbath), Jesus had preached in the synagogue and delivered a demoniac, raised Peter's mother-in-law from a bed of sickness, and after sundown He had stood in the street for hours while the sick and demon-possessed came to Him for healing and deliverance.

After only a few hours' sleep, Jesus got up while it was still dark and went to a solitary place to pray. The disciples had slept in. When they awakened, people were already gathering again out in the street—so many, in fact, that when Simon found Jesus he declared, "Everyone is looking for you!"

At first it appeared that Jesus had vanished. They looked for Him in the home, but He wasn't there. He certainly wasn't in the crowd that waited for Him. Normally, when a group of people look for a lost person, they split up; but these disciples hung together for the search. They found Him in a solitary place.

Three years later, Judas knew exactly where to look when he led soldiers to Jesus in Gethsemane. Here, early in Jesus' ministry in Galilee, they had not known where to look and it had taken them some time to locate Him.

In both Galilee and Gethsemane Jesus sought out solitary places to pray. If Jesus knew He couldn't be effective without spending time alone in prayer with His Father, how much more do we need to follow His example? If others went looking for us, would they ever find us praying? Or would they always find us busy?

When they found Jesus, the disciples' solution was for Him to remain in Capernaum and have a ministry that paralleled John the baptizer's. John stayed in one place and people came out to him. Jesus wanted to model the lifetime vocation He would call Simon and the others to—a vocation that required the word "Go!"

No doubt Jesus could have had a vast ministry by staying in one place. Indeed, He may have reached as many people by being stationary as He did by being itinerant. When people are desperate for healing, they will go any distance. So long as Jesus healed and exorcised, the crowds would have remained undiminished. As a side bonus, Capernaum could have developed a nice tourism industry off the business of hotel and dining accommodations, the sale of religious trinkets, and travel packages.

But Jesus held the long view. What was needed in each community was His presence. Each village did not need to be vacated in order for people to go and find Him in a fixed spot at Capernaum. No, He would go to them. He would be in their midst.

There is always a temptation in our lives to get stuck, to not venture out beyond the confines of what we know. But is the Lord nudging you to get out of your familiar or comfortable routines and go with Him to some person, some place, some ministry where you have never been before?

We follow the example of Jesus when we go.

A Prayer

Lord Jesus, somewhere today there is a person to whom You are sending me. It would be easier for me to stay in my safe place, but You ask me to go in Your name. And I will.

THE YES AND NOT YET OF HEALING

A man with leprosy came to him and begged him on his knees, "If you are willing, you can make me clean." Filled with compassion, Jesus reached out his hand and touched the man. "I am willing, he said. "Be clean!" Immediately the leprosy left him and he was cured.

MARK 1:40–42

I AM A MISSIONARY KID raised in northwest China and Tibet. One of my earliest memories is of beggars on the streets—toes, fingers, and noses eaten away by the dread disease of leprosy. I never saw any of them healed, although I have witnessed other types of healing.

This leper that came to Jesus had a double whammy: the illness itself and the isolation caused by the illness. His disease reduced him to the position of outcast and separated him from friends, family, and community. Luke, the doctor, notes this man was "full of leprosy" (Luke 5:12, KJV), a diagnosis that put him in the latter stages of the deterioration caused by leprosy.

If he had a wife, had she remarried? If he was a father, were his children calling someone else Daddy? Or, if he had a family, were they still hoping against hope for some miracle of disease arrest?

For sure, Jesus was the leper's last hope. Without healing, his disease inevitably would lead to a lonely death. He only asked Jesus to make him "clean." He didn't ask for a restorative miracle of lost body parts but for a complete end to the progression of the disease so that a priest, functioning by Old Testament law, could declare him able again to return to society.

Here is the mystery for us. Individuals we know have also come to Jesus for healing and have not yet been cured. How is it that the Lord had compassion for this leper, but others are not healed? Why doesn't the Lord say to all, "I am willing"?

The healing evangelist Kathryn Kuhlman once said that is the first question she will ask the Lord on the other side.

THE YES AND NOT YET OF HEALING

Perhaps if the Lord healed all, there would be nothing left for us to do. Would we be motivated to care for the poor, the sick, and the dying? Although Jesus is full of compassion, would our compassion be empty?

I certainly don't understand the mysteries here. Maybe our problem is that we are too quick to universalize the experience of one, to say, "Well, Lord, if You did it for one then You should do the same for all." That attitude keeps us from rejoicing for the one who has been healed.

I was once in a Kathryn Kuhlman meeting when a student of mine was healed of a broken toe while another young friend of mine with a fatal illness was not healed. I found it hard to rejoice with the one who had been healed.

While we don't understand why some are healed now and others are not, we do know as believers that in short time the hand of Jesus will touch us all with life immortal. Let us rejoice in the healing grace given to some now, and rejoice also that a complete healing lies ahead for all who put their faith in Christ.

A Prayer

Lord, help me to live with the mystery of "I am willing . . . but not yet." It is in your hands, Lord. Meantime, I will continue with an active faith that asks You for healing but trusts You no matter what.

KEEP YOUR ENTHUSIASM IN CHECK!

Jesus sent him away at once with a strong warning: "See that you don't tell this to anyone. But go, show yourself to the priest and offer the sacrifices that Moses commanded for your cleansing, as a testimony to them." Instead he went out and began to talk freely, spreading the news. As a result, Jesus could no longer enter a town openly but stayed outside in lonely places. Yet the people still came to him from everywhere.

MARK 1:43–45

A MAN FULL OF LEPROSY came to Jesus, begging for compassion. Jesus did more than speak healing to him. He touched the man and in so doing Jesus rendered Himself unclean under the Law of Moses.

The law of the leper (Leviticus 13 and 14) taught that the unclean contaminated the clean. But Jesus brought a new way. He decontaminated the contaminated by healing them.

The leper was beside himself with joy. Understandably so!

Then Jesus gives him a seemingly and totally illogical command, "Don't tell anyone!" Evidently the healing took place without a crowd milling around; had more people known, they would have quickly spread the word. No, this was a private encounter between the leper and Jesus.

How could Jesus expect the leper to retrain himself from telling such good news? Shouldn't the Lord have permitted him to express enthusiasm immediately?

Jesus knew ahead of time the result of the man's obedience or disobedience. Jesus always knows more about the future than we do, and that is why it is important for us to obey Him even when we do not feel like it, or when our emotions or thinking disagrees with Him!

Look at the consequences of the healed leper's disobedience.

One, he broke the Old Testament law that provided for a time period of cleansing and restoration to society. In so doing, he jeopardized his return to normalcy because he had not been properly certified as clean by the priest. He violated God's word through his enthusiasm.

Second, he missed the opportunity for the priesthood to validate the healing Jesus performed. The official validation of the priestly system on the healing work of Jesus would have been a genuine headache to those who later sought to destroy the Lord.

Third, Jesus was forced to change His itinerary. It took eight days to validate the cleanness of a former leper (Leviticus 14:10). Those extra eight days would have provided freedom of movement for Jesus within towns and villages. Instead, Jesus had to avoid going into population centers.

Fourth, others were inconvenienced. If the man had obeyed, there would have been no need for the multitudes to trek out to lonely places where Jesus taught and healed. Jesus would have ministered in their hometowns.

The healed leper didn't take the Lord seriously. The Lord asked him to do something counter to his feelings. His emotions took over from his volition. The disease of leprosy had not resisted the Lord's command of "Be clean!" But the man himself resisted the Lord's orders, "Do not tell."

If the Lord asks you to do something that doesn't seem to make sense, do it anyway! He always has the better idea!

A Prayer

Lord Jesus, I am full of good intentions but You have all wisdom. May I always and instantly obey what You tell me to do.

DISABLED, BUT NOT ALONE

A few days later, when Jesus again entered Capernaum, the people heard that he had come home. So many gathered that there was no room left, not even outside the door, and he preached the word to them. Some men came, bringing to him a paralytic, carried by four of them.

MARK 2:1–3

MOST OF US ARE FORTUNATE enough to use our own two legs to get us where we want to go. Others are disabled either through birth, injury, or disease and become dependent on family and friends for mobility.

I have a friend who was disabled at the age of fourteen from a car accident. For her whole adult life she has been confined to a wheel chair. Despite her handicap, she is an incredibly joyful person with a multitude of friends.

About thirty years ago, I preached a sermon on Amram and Jochebed, the parents of Moses. I mentioned that if they had been afraid of the times, they would never have borne children and we would not have had Moses, Aaron, and Miriam.

My friend and her husband listened with their hearts to that sermon. They had already decided that because of her condition they would not have children—it would just be too difficult to be a wheelchair mom. But the Lord spoke to their hearts not to be afraid of the circumstances. In time, a daughter was born and then a son. The daughter today serves with her husband and three small children as a missionary in Asia.

I think of my own friend when I read this story of the paralytic. What I note is that he had friends.

When tragedy happens to you, the wind can be knocked out of your sails. You can become bitter, withdrawn, sullen, full of blame, cynical, and almost impossible to live with. People who become that way have few friends. They've driven them away.

But this paralytic at Capernaum must have been like my own friend. He had lots of people who wanted to help him. We are told that four of them carried him, but there were actually more than that helping him because "some men came, bringing to him a paralytic, carried by four of them." In other words, there was a whole group—but only four of them were needed logistically for transportation.

The application from this story is inescapable. If you suffer, don't turn bitter. Be the kind of person who keeps friends around. You will need them to carry you—spiritually, emotionally, and physically.

Two of my favorite sayings are: "What happens *in* you is more important than what happens *to* you," and "The same wind that uproots a tree lifts a bird." The paralytic, despite his suffering, had not permitted his spirit to become bitter. That's why he still had plenty of friends. Nasty people don't get carried around voluntarily.

Evidently when Jesus was in Capernaum at sundown a few days earlier (Mark 1:32–34), the paralytic and his friends had missed out; or perhaps they had tried to get near and were unsuccessful.

But Jesus is again available, and they are now determined not to miss this new opportunity.

How about you? Whether able or disabled, do you have a sweet and joyful spirit that invites others to be your friends?

A Prayer

*Lord Jesus, life throws some pretty tough things at me. I
need Your help to remain tender, pliable, and joyful.
I want to follow the advice of the apostle Paul,
"Rejoice, and again I say, rejoice!"*

THE PARALYTIC'S OWN TESTIMONY

*Since they could not get him to Jesus because of the crowd,
they made an opening in the roof above Jesus and,
after digging through it, lowered the mat the paralyzed man
was lying on. When Jesus saw their faith, he said
to the paralytic, "Son your sins are forgiven."*

MARK 2:4–5

HERE'S WHAT HAPPENED.
"An hour earlier, a company of friends came to my home, excitedly announcing that Jesus had slipped back into town. They told me they were taking me to the house where He was—that they believed I would be healed if they could get me to Him.

"Now healing is an option I had given up on long ago. But my friends' enthusiasm couldn't be dampened. They insisted. So, they picked me up on my mat, headed out the door and down the street. By the time we got to the house where Jesus was, a huge crowd had already gathered. My friends weren't deterred. Up on the roof they went and started tearing a hole over the place where Jesus stood near the door. Then, their work completed, they tied ropes to the corners of my mat. Four of my friends each grabbed a rope and lowered me in front of Jesus.

"I had absolutely no idea how He would react: Either He would chew out the friends who tore up the roof and interrupted Him, or He would heal me. Certainly, He couldn't ignore me. But never in a million years would I have guessed His first words to me: 'Son, your sins are forgiven.'

"How do I take that? Did He agree with those who held that sickness comes as a result of others' sin or my own? Was He saying my paralysis, therefore, resulted from some sin?

"Or was He first addressing my inner need before my outer?

"I think the latter. God knows how I felt at being laid up. Sometimes I was angry with God; other times, at myself. I hate confinement and helplessness. I hate not being able to be normal like others. Oh, I had friends, and the fact that I had them meant that I wasn't a grouch. No, people didn't stay away from me. They loved me, but way down deep inside I hurt badly. I sometimes secretly blamed God for the whole unfairness of my condition.

"Jesus first exposed my thoughts before He extended my limbs. He wanted me to be healed at a layer deeper than my flesh, muscles, and bones. He wanted me whole on the inside.

"You see, a paralytic cannot commit some of the kinds of sins done by ambulatory people. Paralyzed people don't rob banks, steal old ladies' purses, or commit assault and battery. No, our sins are weighted on the side of mental. It's what we think. It's our attitudes and verbal expressions. It's the damage we do to ourselves both in body and mind.

"Jesus knew I would never be whole if the only thing He gave me was the power to walk again. Something had to change first on the inside of me. He knew I wanted forgiveness, so without my even asking, He read my mind. He forgave me and gave me a clean heart."

A Prayer

Lord Jesus, my own friends don't know about the depth of my pain. But You know. You understand where I have gone wrong, how I have sinned in thought, word, and deed. You come to me and amazingly, You forgive. Thank you, Lord!

SIN AND FORGIVENESS

Now some teachers of the law were sitting there, thinking to themselves, "Why does this fellow talk like that? He's blaspheming! Who can forgive sins but God alone?"

MARK 2:6–7

THEY WERE RIGHT. In the last analysis, only God can forgive sin!

True, there is such a commodity as human forgiveness. Jesus called us to forgive one another—even seventy times seven.

My mother taught me that when I was a boy. She told me that when other kids picked on me, I was to turn the other cheek. But one little bully became my nemesis, always hitting and insulting me and trying to pick a fight.

One day, my mother noticed me putting marks on notepaper. Responding to her inquiry, I said that every time this other kid, Billy, bothered me I was making a mark. When I reached 491, then I had permission from Jesus to hit him back.

My mother must have begun praying harder because in a few days Billy suddenly announced in class that his parents were moving. My count by then was around 250!

I had a very childish view of Jesus' words, not realizing that "seventy times seven" was Jesus' way of describing the infinity of forgiveness.

If the Lord tells us to forgive one another seventy times seven, don't you think He does the same . . . and far more?

Ultimately the forgiveness of all sin—even the sins we do against one another—belongs to God.

After his affair with Bathsheba and his murder of her husband, Uriah, David admitted in Psalm 51, "Against you, you only have I sinned" (v. 4). What? Hadn't he sinned against them too? Why this statement to God, "Against you only . . ."?

All sin ultimately is a sin against God. Sin involves: (1) falling short of God's will and ideal, (2) stepping across the line of His commandment into forbidden thought or conduct, or (3) intentionally rebelling against Him or negligently failing to do His will.

David knew he had failed in all these respects. His stain was deeper than human forgiveness could reach. Thus, he cried, "Cleanse me with hyssop, and I will be clean; wash me, and I will be whiter than snow" (Psalm 51:7).

Even when another forgives you, you still need God's forgiveness. The forgiveness of another is like erasing a chalk board—the smudge and tracer effects remain. It takes a wet sponge to wipe the slate clean, and God's forgiveness does that.

Suppose I were to visit your home and carelessly or intentionally knock to the floor a family heirloom, breaking it, then asked for your forgiveness. When you say unconditionally, "I forgive," you pick up the tab for what I owe. I am released from payment because you have discharged me of my debt. I have no further obligation.

Through sin, I have caused irreparable damage to my soul. I can try all my life to atone for what I have done wrong, but I can never do enough. I need God to say, "I forgive your sin," because He alone has the depth of riches to do for me what I can never do for myself.

Jesus knew all that. So did the teachers of the Law. Only God can forgive sin.

A Prayer

I come to You today and ask You for the full remission of all my sins. And You speak to me as You did to Isaiah, "Your guilt is taken away and your sin atoned for" (Isaiah 6:7).

THE AUTHORITY OF JESUS

Immediately Jesus knew in his spirit that this was what they were thinking in their hearts, and he said to them, "Why are you thinking these things? Which is easier: to say to the paralytic, 'Your sins are forgiven,' or to say, 'Get up, take your mat and walk'? But that you may know that the Son of Man has authority on earth to forgive sins . . ." He said to the paralytic, "I tell you, get up, and take your mat and go home." He got up, took his mat and walked out in full view of them all. This amazed everyone and they praised God, saying, "We have never seen anything like this!"

MARK 2:8–12

THE ROOF OVERHEAD had been torn up. A paralytic was dropped down through the opening by four of his friends.

Jesus didn't address his physical need first, but said to him, "Your sins are forgiven."

The theologians in the crowd thought to themselves, "He can't do that. Only God can forgive sins, and He's not God."

At this point, Jesus disclosed several things about Himself that we need to take to heart.

First, He can read our minds. Jesus immediately knew what His critics were thinking. He also perceives your thoughts from afar (Psalm 139:2). He knows what's really going on inside you.

You may fool your family, your spouse, your closest friends, the people you work or worship with—but He knows you inside and out.

Second, He has more power than His critics. His question is rhetorical, "Which is easier to say . . . ?" They can say neither. They cannot get the paralytic to walk nor can they forgive his sin. Jesus makes a connective and rational argument. If He can heal the outer man, then He can also heal him on the inside.

Third, Jesus reveals Himself as the Son of Man. "Son of Man" is Jesus' favorite term for Himself. In Mark's gospel, this is the first time He used the term of Himself. It is a code word that is often misunderstood.

Reading it today, we think Jesus may be referring to His humanity. Not so!

The term is lifted from Daniel 7 to refer to the One who appears before the Ancient of Days to claim an eternal kingdom when all this world's empires have passed away.

Jesus often used parables. To outsiders, truth was concealed; to His disciples, truth was revealed.

The term *Son of Man* is like a parable. His critics couldn't possibly link the majestic Son of Man in Daniel 7 with the humble Jesus from Nazareth in Galilee. But Jesus' disciples would come to understand Jesus' self-identifying term. He is the Lord of human history and "his dominion is an everlasting dominion that will not pass away, and his kingdom is one that will never be destroyed" (Daniel 7:14).

The Son of Man forgives sin because He is God in the flesh. If He has authority over the future, He has authority over the present. If He has authority over worlds and peoples, then He also has authority over one man, and to that one He says, "Get up and walk out of here." The man does so and all are amazed.

A Prayer

Lord, Your healing of the outer man, the mending of paralysis, is a sign of Your authority over the human spirit, that You exercise the power of God to forgive sins. Thank You for forgiving and healing me also!

ONE FROM THE CROWD

Once again Jesus went out beside the lake. A large crowd came to him, and he began to teach them. As he walked along, he saw Levi son of Alphaeus sitting at the tax collector's booth. "Follow me," Jesus told him, and Levi got up and followed him.

MARK 2:13-14

THE NARRATIVE in Mark's gospel constantly shifts from the crowd to the individual or from the person to the group.

Jesus heals one person, Peter's mother-in-law; then the whole town gathers in the street (1:29-34). Jesus cures a man with leprosy; then He is so beset with multitudes He can no longer openly enter a town (1:40-45). He slips back into Capernaum, but word gets out and the house becomes dense with people. The spotlight then shifts to one paralytic coming down through an opening torn into the roof (2:1-12).

Jesus breaks away. The crowd follows Him as He walks along the shore. He stops. No mention is made of miracles. He simply teaches. Perhaps this was the occasion when He delivered the Sermon on the Mount (Matthew 5 to 7), which Mark omits.

Mark turns our attention instead on one individual, the tax collector Levi.

Days earlier, while walking along the shore, Jesus called His first four disciples, two sets of brothers (1:16-20). None of the four had volunteered—they were drafted. The same was true of the tax collector Levi, whom we know as Matthew. We see no record of him running up to Jesus and saying, "I want to follow You. Will You let me?"

We have something in common with the four and with Levi. None of us feels worthy enough to follow Jesus. We think, *He is looking for someone more qualified, more holy, more eloquent, better prepared, and more experienced.*

Jesus comes to us nevertheless and says, "Follow Me."

Like the first disciples, you don't know where that will take you. None of the first five followers could have imagined the course of events over the next years.

James, for example, couldn't foresee that he would be a martyr early on, and his brother John had no inkling he would live the longest. Levi didn't know he would write the gospel that opens our New Testament. Levi's ability to log tax records made him an ideal person to take shorthand notes of Jesus' teaching and thereby give us an extensive record of Christ's discourses and parables.

The Lord never shows us the full picture—He just asks us to take the next step. Like Levi, though, we have to be willing to "get up." Had Levi continued to sit at his tax post and ignored or declined Jesus' invitation, he would have missed his destiny in life.

I can almost hear the murmur that went up from the two sets of brothers, "Lord, we can't stand this man, Levi. He's a collaborator with the Romans. He collects tariffs from us, pays off the Romans, and then keeps a cut for himself. Surely You wouldn't ask us to hang out with the likes of him?"

But when you start walking with Jesus, you find that you don't follow Him by yourself. You don't get to choose His friends. His friends must also become yours, even when their viewpoints and personalities totally diverge from your own.

A Prayer

Lord Jesus, I am amazed that You would invite me to follow You. I am so unworthy. Since You have asked me, then I, too, will follow You alongside those whom You have also called.

HE DREW A CIRCLE THAT TOOK ME IN!

> *While Jesus was having dinner at Levi's house, many tax collectors and "sinners" were eating with him and his disciples, for there were many who followed him. When the teachers of the law who were Pharisees saw him eating with the "sinners" and tax collectors, they asked his disciples: "Why does he eat with tax collectors and 'sinners'?"*
>
> MARK 2:15–16

IN THE EARLIER YEARS of his ministry, Billy Graham was frequently criticized for associating with members of Christian traditions different from his own. He defended himself with this poem:

> He drew a circle that shut me out;
> Rebel, heretic, a thing to flout.
> But love and I had the wit to win,
> He drew a circle that took me in.

That's exactly what Jesus does for us, and with Levi and his "sinner" friends. He took them in!

This is the third time in Mark's gospel that Jesus was in a home: first, Peter and Andrew's for the healing of Peter's mother-in-law (1:29–31); then the home where the paralytic was let down through the roof (2:1–12); and now, third, the home of the tax collector Levi.

Jesus told Levi earlier in the day, "Follow me!" And the first place Jesus took Levi was Levi's own home.

Too frequently I look at Jesus' call as a romanticist: faraway places, splendid fields of glory, euphoria in life. But, like Levi, the first place Jesus calls you and me is to our homes—where the issues of life unfold daily.

And look who comes to dinner with Jesus at Levi's house! Not your average church crowd!

I tend to hang around people I know because that's where

my comfort level is. How different is the gregarious Son of God! While He Himself is righteous and without sin, He continually opens Himself to the company of those whose standards fail to meet even the demands of the "good moral persons" within His own society: He dined with political pariahs—tax collectors who collaborated with an occupying military force and sinners—those who kept neither the ceremonial nor the moral law.

It is often true that the longer we follow Christ, the fewer non-Christian friends we have. We enjoy the company of those who share our faith and values. We need to more carefully assess how our own friendship circle aligns with what Jesus did.

Recently our family was on a cruise and, on the last night, a young lady who had been our server asked me privately if she could ask a question. Evidently, she had listened to our table conversations as she brought food and observed our time of prayer at the beginning of each meal. Her question was profound: "How can I know which way is the right way?"

How can we answer spiritual hunger like that? Of course, I gave a verbal witness and have sent follow-up material. But the best answer can be given only in the context of presence. Jesus was present at the table with sinners and tax collectors. Rather than give them a lecture or sermon, He took time to be with them.

Once people know you, they can begin to trust you and open their hearts. In turn, you will have earned the right to be heard. So let's draw a circle that takes them in!

A Prayer

Thank You, Lord, that You ate with sinners and tax collectors for I now feel welcome at Your table. I see that my own sinfulness is not a barrier to Your availability to me. You welcome me into Your presence.

OUTSIDE OUR COMFORT ZONES

On hearing this, Jesus said to them, "It is not the healthy who need a doctor, but the sick. I have not come to call the righteous, but sinners."

MARK 2:17

E.S. WILLIAMS SERVED the Assemblies of God as general superintendent from 1929 to 1949, bringing godly leadership to a church that grew rapidly and benefitted greatly from his doctrinal stability, pastoral wisdom, and personal kindness.

After retiring at the age of sixty-five, he lived well into his nineties. Not too long before he died, my wife and I visited him at his small apartment. He had been my mother's teacher in Bible school in the early 1920s, and my motive for seeing him that day included asking him for any counsel he could give me as a young pastor.

I put this question to him, "What do you see as the main problem of the church?"

Without a moment's hesitation he answered, "Socialization." Then he explained what he meant.

"When a church is younger, most of the people in it are new converts—and they are very focused on evangelism," he said. "They have a lot of family and friends who aren't followers of Christ. But as time goes along, more and more they enjoy the company of their fellow-Christian friends. They have fewer and fewer non-Christian acquaintances. The church then begins to settle down and become more of a social club than a soul-saving agency."

I have never forgotten his words. They correspond to Jesus' response when He was criticized for eating with tax collectors and sinners.

Jesus got out of the box of safe associations by fraternizing with persons not on the invite list of the religiously respectable. He explained that He was like a doctor. Physicians don't do any good when they open their offices only to the well. Doctors are for sick folk, and Jesus came for sinners.

Jesus' example forces us to ask some uncomfortable questions. Do you or I get criticized by religious types for spending social time with people who are in suspect categories? Or do we only hang out with people who only share our church associations, political beliefs, or social networks?

One of our young ministers tells the moving story of how he and a small group around him planted a church in a new community. They spent nine months making friends before they even launched a public service. One evening a week they wrote on a long sheet of butcher paper the names of the new friends they had met that week. They prayed over each name—while the list grew to over 900, most or all of whom were non-Christian.

In fact, before they held their first Sunday service, this young minister conducted a funeral for a young husband and father whom he had befriended while sitting on a park bench and ultimately led to the Lord. Is it any wonder that people were saved at the funeral? On the first Sunday they launched, 283 attended and twenty-eight people came to Christ!

What did this young minister and his friends do? Exactly what Jesus did! They built relationships with "sinners." May we go and do likewise!

A Prayer

Thank you, Lord Jesus, that You eat with sinners and tax collectors, which makes me feel welcome at Your table. I see that my own sinfulness doesn't prove a barrier to Your availability to me, and I am so grateful.

UNHAPPY PEOPLE

Now John's disciples and the Pharisees were fasting. Some people came and asked Jesus, "How is it that John's disciples are fasting, but yours are not?" Jesus answered, "How can the guests of the bridegroom fast while he is with them? They cannot, so long as they have him with them. But the time will come when the bridegroom will be taken from them, and on that day they will fast."

MARK 2:18-20

YEARS AGO, WHEN I WAS A YOUNG PASTOR, an older minister gave me this piece of advice: "George, you can spend a lot of time trying to make unhappy people happy. You may make them less unhappy for a while, but sooner or later they will go back to their original state.

"On the other hand," he continued, "you may make happy people less happy for a while, but sooner or later they also will return to their original state."

I thought that was good advice and took it to heart. There are some people you just cannot make happy no matter how hard you try.

That was the case with the Pharisees. They were unhappy that Jesus ate with sinners and tax collectors (2:15-17). Next they complained that Jesus' disciples were not fasting. It is obvious they wanted Jesus to do something about the behavior of His followers.

The disciples were only following the example of their Leader. If Jesus was feasting, then they would be too!

Jesus responded to the criticism by giving the first veiled reference to His mission: "the bridegroom will be taken from them." Of course the disciples and the critics had no idea at the time what this meant. Much later they would understand.

Jesus didn't give in to the criticism. He came to the defense of His disciples and in so doing gave us an important lesson.

From the beginning Jesus knew why He had come. The cross was ever before Him. But, He didn't let that impending event cast a shadow of sadness over Himself or those who were with Him. He didn't prematurely disclose to His disciples what was going to happen.

If I knew years in advance that I was headed for crucifixion, it would be very difficult for me to enjoy the present moment. But Jesus lived what He taught. He didn't show anxiety about tomorrow. He didn't throw a blanket of sorrow over His disciples that would have prevented them from experiencing the great joys of being with Him.

He feasted, and so did they! In the very face of impending suffering, He taught His friends to enjoy the moment.

The Pharisees didn't like that. Everything had to be done by their rules. They were not happy on the inside—and unhappy people don't enjoy seeing or being around people who are happy.

I have heard it said that every baseball team could use a player who always gets a hit, always makes a key fielding play, and never strikes out or makes an error—but there is no way to make him lay down his hot dog and come out of the grandstand!

Let's avoid a Pharisee spirit that is always looking for what is wrong rather than what is right. An attitude that is predominantly looking to nitpick and find something to condemn rather than keeping an eye out for whatever is true, noble, right, pure, lovely, admirable, excellent, or praiseworthy (Philippians 4:8).

A Prayer

Deliver me, Lord, from a critical spirit. Help me not to be a wet blanket to another's joy. Let me not nitpick or find fault. Grant me a glad heart that I may encourage rather than discourage.

A NEW WAY

No one sews a patch of unshrunk cloth on an old garment. If he does, the new piece will pull away from the old, making the tear worse. And no one pours new wine into old wineskins. If he does, the wine will burst the skins, and both the wine and the wineskins will be ruined. No, he pours new wine into new wineskins.

MARK 2:21–22

SYLVAN GOLDMAN DIED in 1948 at the age of eighty-six, leaving an estate conservatively valued at more than $200 million dollars. You have probably never heard of him, but you have used his invention.

Goldman owned a grocery store in Oklahoma City and one evening in 1937 he was thinking about how to improve slow sales. Two folding chairs stood against a wall in his office, and an idea hit him.

With the help of a mechanic, Fred Young, Goldman designed the first shopping cart, based on the folding chairs. They put wheels on the bottoms of the chair legs and stacked two baskets between the chairs. Later they designed the present-day nesting carts that fold into one another.

The enterprising grocer then attempted to lure shoppers through newspaper advertisements ballyhooing a "new device." The ad read, "Can you imagine wending your way through a spacious food market without having to carry a cumbersome shopping basket on your arm?"

No one wanted to use them. So he placed another ad proclaiming, "Shoppers came, saw, and said, 'It's a wow!'" Goldman later said of the ad, "It was the biggest lie."

Finally, Goldman hired men and women to walk up and down the aisles of his store pretending to grocery shop. That proved successful. Today multiplied millions of carts go up and down the aisles of stores all over the world.

The critics of Jesus' day were like the reluctant cart users in Goldman's store. They didn't like what Jesus introduced: a new way of life. Their idea of religion was regulation—doing your best to follow hundreds upon hundreds of man-made rules.

Jesus chose not to reform that kind of system, saying that you cannot put unshrunk cloth on shrunk cloth or new wine in old wine skins. He came, not to give us more rules but to bring us into relationship with God.

Before Goldman's cart, shopping had been hard. One had to carry groceries in a basket on the arm. Goldman made it easy.

That's what Jesus did for us. We can never be good enough for God, no matter how hard we try. So Jesus came and said, "Let Me do it for you."

The new wineskin and the unshrunk cloth are metaphors for the gospel—the good news! This good news has set us free from the law of sin and death. It has brought us into relationship with God by grace through faith rather than works through law.

Salvation is a gift, not a pay check for working hard. Jesus gave us a better way to live!

A Prayer

Lord Jesus, thank You for giving me what I could never give myself: forgiveness, salvation, and eternal life. I follow you today, not because I have to, but because I want to. Your love draws so much more from me than the drudgery of duty ever could.

LAW AND GRACE

One Sabbath Jesus was going through the grainfields, and as his disciples walked along, they began to pick some heads of grain. The Pharisees said to him, "Look, why are they doing what is unlawful on the Sabbath?" He answered, "Have you never read what David did when he and his companions were hungry and in need? In the days of Abiathar the high priest, he entered the house of God and ate the consecrated bread, which is lawful only for priests to eat. And he also gave some to his companions." Then he said to them, "The Sabbath was made for man, not man for the Sabbath. So the Son of Man is Lord even of the Sabbath."

MARK 2:23–27

THE STORY IS TOLD that Dr. Harry Ironside, the late pastor of Moody Church in Chicago, once brought a young man with him on a train to Oakland, California. A few days later, Ironside found himself in a small Bible study where other young people fell to arguing about the relationship of law to grace.

Finally, the young man who traveled with him and who had not been a Christian very long spoke up: "When Mr. Ironside asked me to go to Oakland with him, I had never been on a train before. We traveled all day and finally came to Barstow out in the desert.

"I was very tired so I got off the train to walk the platform and stretch my legs. I saw a sign that read Do Not Spit Here. I looked at that sign and thought, *what a strange sign to put up: Do Not Spit Here.*

"While I looked at that sign, the next thing I knew, I spit! I thought to myself, *how strange. At the very place the sign says Do Not Spit Here many people are spitting.* I wasn't the only one.

"We got back on the train and finally arrived at Oakland. Some friends took us to a beautiful home. Mr. Ironside and I went in, and he showed me to a sitting room while he excused himself. I looked around at the soft, thick rug on floor, beautiful walls painted a lovely color, pictures hanging on the wall, and beautiful furniture.

"I looked all around that room and tried to find a sign that said Do Not Spit Here. But, of course, I couldn't find such a sign.

"I thought to myself, ironically, *too bad this lovely room is going to be ruined by people spitting on the floor.* It was obvious nobody had been spitting there.

"Then the thought occurred to me. *When the law demanded Do Not Spit Here, it made me want to spit. I spit, and many other people spit. But, when I came into grace and everything was lovely and nice, I didn't want to spit and I didn't need the law to say Do Not Spit Here.*"

This young man experienced exactly the same situation on the railway platform as Jesus' disciples, except that the law back then said Do Not Pick Grain on the Sabbath! Jesus defended His disciples from the criticism of the Pharisees by illustrating from David's example that genuine human need—whether our own or that of another (recall the healing of Peter's mother-in-law on the Sabbath, Mark 1:29–31)—trumps obedience to ritualistic demands.

A Prayer

Lord Jesus, I am saved, not because I am good but because You are good. The law that said, "Do not . . ." could never save me. But You did. You gave me grace. Help me to give others grace when I want to hold them to the letter of the law.

SHRIVELED

Another time he went into the synagogue, and a man with a shriveled hand was there. Some of them were looking for a reason to accuse Jesus, so they watched him closely to see if he would heal him on the Sabbath.

MARK 3:1-2

WHENEVER JESUS SHOWS UP, things happen.

The previous time He was in the synagogue (1:21-28), a demon-possessed man confronted Him. Part of Jesus' synagogue ministry in general involved the driving out of demons (1:39).

This raises the question as to how many seriously disturbed people attend houses of worship but remain unchanged. Why? Could it be that we go through the motions of worship but have not invited the living presence of Jesus into the house?

As Mark 3 begins, we see Jesus again in the synagogue, but this time the action is different. He previously healed in Simon's home (1:29), in the street (1:33), out in the open (1:40), and at home in Capernaum (2:1). Now His healing power was released in the synagogue for the man with a shriveled hand.

I wonder how many people who love Jesus today come regularly for worship at the appointed time, but for whom something in their lives has shriveled.

Perhaps you have never had a shriveled hand but instead have had shriveled emotions, shriveled ambitions, shriveled longings, or shriveled relationships. Your reach in life is not as far as you wanted it to go. You want to put out your hand toward a goal but you can't.

Unlike the leper or one who has cancer, you aren't on the verge of dying. You aren't possessed by evil spirits who force you to act on uncontrollable urges. You just aren't all that you could be.

The good news is that the Lord stretches out His hand to your shriveled life. His power can make you whole—so reach out your hand to Him!

But Jesus had His critics. They didn't like it when He healed on the Sabbath. Even Jesus could not and would not make everyone happy.

Criticism feeds criticism. Once you start being judgmental and negative, you will feed on it. That was true of the negative people around Jesus. They couldn't see the good because they were too caught up with the fact that He wasn't doing everything the way they would do it. So they watched him "closely."

The criticism against Jesus repeatedly lay with "the teachers of the law" (Mark 2:7, 16, 18, 23). That was the problem. They gained their title through years of schooling and proven ability to master the minutiae of religious regulations. However, they missed something better than the title "teachers of the law." Never were they called "teachers of grace"!

When we practice and teach grace rather than law we don't have time to sit around and pick at every nit and thistle. Grace reaches out to help; legalism can only judge.

Those who are shriveled in life can only be helped by grace. In Jesus, the grace of God reaches out to take our hand and restore us to fullness of life

A Prayer

Lord Jesus, show me my blind spots about being judgmental. Help me to be full of grace and not full of legalism.

NEVER A TIME NOT TO DO GOOD

Jesus said to the man with the shriveled hand, "Stand up in front of everyone." Then Jesus asked them, "Which is lawful on the Sabbath: to do good or to do evil, to save life or to kill?" But they remained silent.

MARK 3:3–4

PICTURE THE SCENE.
People jam the synagogue all through the main floor, the tier of U-shaped seating all around, and the balcony in back. Jesus holds center stage.

They expect Him to teach. His disciples, seated in front, perhaps think that He will elaborate on His earlier message in the Nazareth synagogue where He proclaimed, "The Spirit of the Lord is upon me" (Luke 4:16–21).

But Jesus spots the legalists in the crowd whose angry stares dare Him to violate the Sabbath by healing.

So Jesus lays aside what He might have intended to say and instead picks out a man from the audience who has a shriveled hand. He tells him, "Stand up in front."

This is a rather odd request. What disfigured person wants to be singled out? If you already feel you are different, you don't want anyone to make a spectacle of you. But that is exactly what Jesus does—only His motive is not to embarrass the man but to do an act for him that makes him whole.

The man is probably sitting midway to the back of the synagogue, not on an aisle. He is safely tucked into his unnoticeable seat. Jesus gets him out of the pew, down the aisle, and to the front and center. He could just as easily have taken umbrage at Jesus for the public singling out and walked out the back door—unhealed.

Maybe you feel unnoticed by Jesus, but He sees you even when you are trying to hide. In order to make you whole, He asks you to do something, to come out of your seat of anonymity. He wants to dislocate you from where you've been to take you where you must go.

Unless the man with the shriveled hand had come forward, he would have missed the good thing the Lord had for him. When we are willing to be identified as having a spiritual need, then God can do His work in us.

The man with the shriveled hand trusted that Jesus had good intentions for him. You also must trust Jesus' good intentions.

Jesus' opponents did not trust Him. Their myriad Sabbath rules permitted them to stop a physical condition from getting worse but not to help it get better.

Jesus got no answer to His question as to which is better on the Sabbath: doing good or evil, saving life or killing. At least, they should have answered, "It's unlawful on any day to do evil or to kill."

Jesus taught that there is never a time when we are exempt from doing good.

The issue is an everyday one. What are you going to do today: good or evil? You must not remain silent to Jesus' question, as did His critics. Jesus waits for a clear answer from you and me: "Yes, today and every day, I will do good and not evil, I will save life and not destroy it."

A Prayer

Lord Jesus, You put the question to me as to what I'm going to do today—not what I'm going to think or feel. Help me to do good even when I don't feel like it, even when I'm depressed or lonely. Grant me the strength to do good today.

CONSTRUCTIVE AND DESTRUCTIVE ANGER

> *He looked around at them in anger and, deeply distressed at their stubborn hearts, said to the man, "Stretch out your hand." He stretched it out, and his hand was completely restored. Then the Pharisees went out and began to plot with the Herodians how they might kill Jesus.*
>
> MARK 3:5–6

ANGER IS LIKE GUNPOWDER. Whether it is good or bad depends on how you use it. It can blast away at injustice, or it can kill and maim the innocent.

Clearly, both forms of anger were present in the synagogue when Jesus healed the man with the shriveled hand. Jesus was angry, and His opponents were mad enough to kill.

The teachers of the Law (that is, the Pharisees) had criticized Jesus for forgiving a paralytic's sins (2:6–7), for eating with sinners and tax collectors at Levi's house (2:15–16), and for His disciples plucking grain on the Sabbath (2:23). Now they dared Him to heal on the Sabbath.

Jesus was fed up with their insensitivity to those in spiritual and physical need, with their callous indifference and judgmental disposition.

Is it ever right to be angry? Yes! We have the Lord's own example! He looked around with anger and was deeply distressed!

What can the right kind of anger do for you?

It will stir you from apathy so you fight injustice.

William Wilberforce of England lived in a day when slave trading was an accepted practice. His lifetime of effort succeeded in banishing this evil from Great Britain. His righteous anger moved an entire nation to no longer ignore this terrible treatment of human beings. Surely you also can find a cause that remedies an injustice!

What makes you angry? Do you remain apathetic when someone is mistreated? Are you angry at the human trafficking that takes place all over the world? At the pornographic industry that wrecks multiplied millions of lives? At the unprincipled greedy who exploit the poor and the defenseless? At abusers who prey upon and damage children? The list is almost endless when it comes to injustice.

The human emotion of anger is meant to stir us to take action. Individually, you cannot tackle all the ills and wrongs in society, but you can do at least one thing. Get angry in the right way about something that God wants corrected.

Then release your anger in a way that heals rather than destroys. That's what Jesus did. He didn't become an angry person. He used anger rather than letting anger use Him.

Anger can fill you with energy to do the right thing. Let it be your servant and not your master.

On the other hand, destructive anger kills. You see that with the Pharisees and Herodians. They were not natural allies. They spanned opposite ends of the religious and political spectrum. The Pharisees loathed the government of Herod. The Herodians broke the rules of religious tradition left and right. However, the Pharisees and Herodians found common ground against Jesus. Their anger overrode all other passions.

The wrong kind of anger leads to destructive alliances. Its goal is not to remedy, not to help, not to heal; its goal is to destroy, to get even, and to punish.

The apostle Paul tells us, "In your anger, do not sin" (Ephesians 4:26). Constructive anger never sins. It always does the right thing in the right way with the right spirit.

A Prayer

Lord Jesus, help me to "look around" and see what You would have me be angry about. Deliver me from apathy. Rid me of anger that destroys and fill me with anger that brings good.

RETREAT AND ADVANCE

Jesus withdrew with his disciples to the lake, and a large crowd from Galilee followed. When they heard all he was doing, many people came to him from Judea, Jerusalem, Idumea, and the regions across the Jordan and around Tyre and Sidon.

MARK 3:7-8

WHAT SHOULD YOU DO when you're in a really tough situation and your physical, mental, or spiritual health is threatened? I have faced this question numerous times.

Late one evening a parishioner called me to help her. Her husband was threatening to kill her and her small son. She had fled the house, but the boy remained inside. I went immediately to see if I could help. She was frantic because her husband held a loaded pistol. I peeked inside the front door, and he appeared to be asleep on a reclining chair with a gun in his hand. I probably should have been more cautious, but I went into the home, took the boy, and carried him out to his mother. Fortunately, the husband never stirred.

Is it alright to escape when someone is trying to kill you? Jesus' action gives the answer to the question. When the Pharisees and the Herodians sought to kill him (Mark 3:6), He "withdrew."

I have also faced the issue of withdrawal for pastor and missionary friends who, despite their best efforts, encountered hard and painful dilemmas that threatened their physical, spiritual, and emotional health, and the well-being of their children. It is a great virtue to endure adversity, but sometimes it is best to walk away and get to a place of safety.

Jesus endured the cross, but He also retreated when people tried to kill Him. Only the Spirit can help us know when to stay steadfast and when to pull out.

It is vital that we not sit in judgment when someone we know feels like the pressure is so great they must extricate themselves for a while lest they be "killed."

Jesus withdrew, but that act also opened a whole new chapter. He found Himself in a place where great things began to happen.

Huge crowds came to Him from all over—in fact, this passage records the greatest geographical reach in Jesus' ministry. Gentiles came in droves from places well outside Israel proper—areas that today are named Lebanon, Syria, and Jordan. People also came from as far south as Judea and Jerusalem.

Notice that even Tyre and Sidon are presented—towns whose doom had been prophesied in the Old Testament. Yet within these places people were desperate for the Lord's touch.

All over the world today, people from every religious and secular background are coming to Jesus. Why? Because Jesus answers the deepest needs of the heart! They aren't coming to a religion—they are coming to a relationship with Jesus! What do they receive? His gifts of healing, deliverance, salvation, and eternal life! No wonder Jesus remains the most sought after person on earth!

The Pharisees and the Herodians plotted to kill Jesus, but their efforts rebounded against them. In withdrawing from them, Jesus increased His reach!

When you face a time of withdrawal, take Jesus' example to heart. It may not be a defeat to withdraw—instead, your retreat can open the door to unparalleled new opportunities!

A Prayer

Lord Jesus, even You needed times to get away—to back off from things that were stressful or dangerous. Help me not to be an escapist by always wanting to withdraw, but also help me to exercise good judgment when I need to disengage.

WHAT FAMOUS MINISTERS MAY FORGET

> *Because of the crowd he told his disciples to have a small boat ready for him, to keep the people from crowding him. For he had healed many, so that those with diseases were pushing forward to touch him. Whenever the evil spirits saw him, they fell down before him and cried out, "You are the Son of God." But he gave them strict orders not to tell who he was.*
>
> MARK 3:9-12

IN RECENT YEARS WE HAVE WITNESSED the spectacular falls of gospel ministers with high profiles. How does this happen? They forget how Jesus dealt with fame.

What did Jesus do when adoring crowds gathered around Him? This text tells us.

First, He genuinely cared for people with needs. That's why so many came to Him. He came not to get something from others but to give.

Jesus never asked, "What's in it for Me?"

I was channel surfing one day and caught a television preacher saying, "God blesses those who bless rich preachers." He told his live audience that they should come up and stuff his pockets with money. Jesus' own example tells us He abhors such greed.

Any ministry goes astray when its focus moves away from helping others. Jesus didn't heal to attract a crowd—He healed because He felt compassion for the suffering.

Second, Jesus placed limits on His use of power. When He saw that the pushing crowd posed an imminent danger to safety, He arranged an escape plan by having a boat ready.

He could just as easily have ordered an invisible barrier to drop down from heaven and separate the people from Him.

Sometimes we want the Lord to do things for us that we can do for ourselves. Jesus' provision of the boat shows that He left to human agency the things that can be done by human means.

The evangelical and charismatic landscape is littered with examples of spiritual leaders who abused their power and position for self-interest. Jesus never did that.

Third, Jesus' ministry spoke for itself. He didn't need a public relations team "promoting" Him.

Notice how Jesus dealt with the demons. The evil spirits were the only ones thus far in His ministry who knew who He really was, the Son of God. But He completely muzzled them.

Why wouldn't He accept the demons' testimony? After all, it would have electrified the crowd—especially if Jesus had let them talk about their fall from heaven and the glory of Jesus before He became human.

But Jesus didn't want or need the endorsement of evil. His church needs to learn that as well. Too often we seek the approval of politicians, academics, entertainers, and sports heroes. We somehow feel their recognition validates us within the culture.

Let the church's witness speak for itself! May our words, deeds, and examples be the means to influence others to come to Christ.

I talked with a noted public figure, a friend of mine, saying to him, "Your dad would be so proud of you."

"Oh," he said, "my dad would never use the word proud. He would say grateful."

Leaders in Christ's body have gone astray when they became proud. They let others "promote" them until they began to believe their own larger-than-life press releases.

Whether or not we are in the spotlight, let us live humbly—seeking God's approval rather than the applause of people or demons.

A Prayer

Lord Jesus, I pray that Christian leaders may truly follow Your example. Help them to keep the spotlight on You and not on themselves.

TO BE WITH HIM

Jesus went up on a mountainside and called to him those he wanted, and they came to him. He appointed twelve—designating them apostles—that they might be with him and that he might send them out to preach and to have authority to drive out demons.

MARK 3:13–15

MY FRIEND AND COLLEGE dorm mate, Phil Nichols, was the first and only Assemblies of God chaplain to lose his life on a battlefield.

During the Vietnam War, Phil had bivouacked with his troops one evening and in the early morning hours an explosion took the lives of all the men in the company.

I flew from Springfield, Missouri, to Kalispell, Montana, for his funeral service. I really didn't know what to say. How can you explain or interpret a sorrow like this to his widow and three young children?

The call of the twelve disciples came to my mind, and I saw it in a whole new way. The call had three elements: to be with Jesus, to preach, and to cast out demons.

It struck me that the last two are earth-related and not eternal. There is no need to preach in heaven since everyone is saved, and there certainly are no demons. But the first call—to be with Him—lasts for time and eternity.

That's true for us all. One day we will step outside time and space. The question is this: "Whose arms will you step into?"

The Lord Jesus waits on the other side for all who believe in Him.

So the first thing the Lord always does is call us to be with Him. He is more concerned with your presence than your activity. He is first concerned with who you are before He is concerned with what you do.

It is also fascinating to compare Matthew's account of the calling of the Twelve with Mark's. The other Gospels add some details.

Matthew notes the call came after Jesus had said the harvest was plentiful but the workers were few. Therefore, He asked them to pray for laborers (Matthew 9:37–38). Luke tells us that Jesus spent the whole night in prayer before he named the Twelve as apostles (Luke 6:12).

I have always wondered what factors led Jesus to select the Twelve from the many who followed Him. I suspect we have the answer—prayer.

Jesus had asked them to pray. Then He spent the night in prayer. Isn't it likely that the Twelve were the ones from the many who actually did what the Lord had requested? My guess is that they were the ones who prayed.

It's the same today. Jesus wants workers in His harvest fields. Whom will He send? Those who pray!

Finally, this passage marks a graduation of sorts. The disciples began the transition to being apostles. That is the new name given them for the first time. Disciples follow and apostles are sent. Jesus gave them a new status before they have even earned it. Just as salvation is by grace, so our vocation of ministry also stems from grace.

The transition from following to leading took some time for that original group of disciples, just as it takes us time to grow into the full measure of stature and maturity in Christ. But as we follow and stay close to Him, we grow into all the potential He has designed us for!

A Prayer

Lord Jesus, today again I re-enlist as Your follower. Thank You for giving me the greatest honor: to be with You now and forever. Thank You also for the responsibility You give me as You send me to witness for You by word and deed.

THE GIFT OF A NEW IDENTITY

*These are the twelve he appointed: Simon,
(to whom he gave the name Peter)...*
MARK 3:16

AUTHOR AND PASTOR Bruce Larson tells about the time when his boy was six years of age. His son began sucking his thumb compulsively. Nothing the parents did made him quit.

Finally, in sheer desperation, they gave him the nickname Thumb Sucker, hoping it would shame him out of the practice. But things only got worse. Someone who had once been a happy-go-lucky little boy now became a saddened, eyes-to-the-ground, shoulders-hunched-down son with the ever-present thumb in his mouth.

Bruce said he was praying one day when he felt the Lord ask him—not audibly but in the quiet way the Lord has of speaking to our hearts—"Is this the little boy you prayed to have? Are you happy with him?"

"Yes, Lord," Bruce answered.

"Then why are you calling him Thumb Sucker?" the Lord responded.

Bruce Larson felt he had no good answer.

He sensed the Lord speak again, "I did not give you a thumb sucker. I gave you a wonderful little boy, and I want you to call him that."

Right then and there, Bruce Larson decided on a new name, "Mr. Wonderful." He rose from his place of prayer, found his little boy sucking his thumb as usual, picked him up, hugged and kissed him, looked into his eyes and said, "Hi, Mr. Wonderful!"

Larson and his wife kept calling their son by his new name, and it was only a short time until the son stopped all thumb sucking and returned to being his happy little self.

They had given their son the gift of a new identity—a gift of grace from a greater to a lesser, a gift the son could never have given himself.

That is exactly what Jesus did when He renamed Simon as Peter (the rock!).

John tells us that when Jesus met Peter for the first time He immediately renamed him Rock (John 1:40–42). There were many factors that Jesus evidently didn't take into account when He gave such a complimentary name to Simon. Simon was impulsive, talked too much, and cracked under pressure. But the Lord saw something in Simon that no one else saw—not even Simon's mother or Simon himself. Jesus perceived that Simon took initiative and was willing to learn and obey. Rather than focus on Simon's weaknesses, Jesus determined to bring out his strengths, giving him the gift of grace—a new identity. He renamed Simon as Peter, which means "rock."

We learn something from this. Too often, we focus on our shortcomings, the areas where we fail, our vulnerabilities, and sins. Jesus is aware of all that, but He also envisions what we can become.

Before we ever had faith in Him, He had faith in us. Immediately upon our confession of Him as Lord, He calls us sons and daughters of God, saints, and heirs of eternal life. He gives us the inexpressible and inexhaustible gift of a new identity!

We are no longer sinners or thumb suckers—we are God's precious children!

A Prayer

Lord, I'm a lot like Peter. I don't deserve to be called a rock. But You bring wholeness out of the fragmentation of my life. Thank You for seeing something in me far better than I or others even imagine.

ENERGY BOLTS

... James son of Zebedee and his brother John (to them he gave the name Boanerges, which means Sons of Thunder).
MARK 3:17

WE LEARN SEVERAL THINGS throughout the Gospels about James and John.

John was actually the first brother to follow Jesus. He notes in his gospel the exact hour (4:00 p.m.) when he responded to Jesus' invitation to "come and see." Over the next three years, he saw close-up the person, works, words, and mission of Jesus. As with all disciples, the "come and see" over time became "come and die" (Mark 8:34-38)—die to self and live for Christ.

John's discipleship at first must have been occasional, but it became full time when Jesus called him and James away from the family business of commercial fishing (Mark 1:20). Jesus never called anyone who was lazy. The persons He gathered around Him were engaged in everyday life and work.

Today, we might call these two brothers "pistols" or "firecrackers." "Sons of thunder" conveys the idea of explosive energy and vitality. Indeed they could be over the top at times. When a Samaritan village gave no hospitality to Christ, their solution was to burn it down (Luke 9:54). At that time they didn't understand that Jesus' way is to call persons to Himself through love rather than through violence or force.

Jesus totally transformed them out of their prejudices—we find John later preaching the gospel in many Samaritan villages (Acts 8:25).

We also know these brothers had a great desire for position (Mark 10:35), egged on by their mother's drive (Matthew 20:20-21). Jesus didn't completely deny their quest for the top spots inasmuch as He permitted them into the inner circle for the raising of Jairus' daughter, the transfiguration, and the visit to Gethsemane the night of His arrest. The Lord took their misplaced ambition and changed it into something good. Without ambition, we fall to the bottom of the class, or out of the class of discipleship altogether.

The end for the two brothers greatly differed. James became the first of the Twelve who died a martyr (Acts 12). He, who had desired to burn down a Samaritan village, ended by being a victim of violence and not its perpetrator.

James died before we ever had a chance to see the fruitfulness of his life. From him we have no recorded sermons or writings. On the other hand, from John, we have a gospel, an Apocalypse, and three letters. Our times are in the Lord's hands. We don't determine the length of our days. Why is one taken and another left? We won't know until the other side.

John, of course, lived the longest of the apostles, ending his life as a prisoner in exile on the Island of Patmos, probably in the tenth decade of his life. He became the disciple "whom Jesus loved" (John 13:23). It wasn't that Jesus loved the others less, but simply that John did what we all must do—see ourselves as *one* whom Jesus loves.

John—who with his brother wanted to burn down a village, who with his brother antagonized the other disciples by asking for chief positions—that John became the apostle so changed by Jesus that he later wrote, "Dear friends, let us love one another, for love comes from God.... Whoever does not love does not know God, because God is love" (1 John 4:7–8).

A Prayer

Lord Jesus, help me today to yield to Your transforming power. Teach me how to transition from being turbulent to being restful; from bulldozing my way through people to loving them instead.

SPIRITUAL STEM CELLS

Andrew, Philip, Bartholomew, Matthew, Thomas, James son of Alphaeus, Thaddaeus, Simon the Zealot...
‹*MARK 3:18*

JESUS CALLED TWELVE DISCIPLES to be His apostles. Mark lists the first three as Peter, James, and John; and the last as Judas Iscariot. In between are eight others.

The New Testament gives us four different listings for the Twelve, and there are some variances in the order. In Matthew 10 and Luke 6, Simon and Andrew are listed first and second, James and John third and fourth—two sets of brothers. In Mark 3 and Acts 1, Andrew is listed fourth rather than second.

Could it be that Andrew made less of an impact in the life of the early church than James and John and, therefore, is placed fourth rather than second in two of the lists? Or could it be that Mark and Acts desired to give prominence to the first apostle martyred: James (Acts 12)? Or perhaps Mathew and Luke felt it better to place the two sets of brothers together?

We simply don't know.

We do know in all four listings of the Twelve that Peter is always first, Philip is always fifth, James the son of Alphaeus is always ninth, and Judas Iscariot is always last.

Within the three groupings of four, the names are always the same—except Thaddaeus in the last group is identified by Luke in his gospel and Acts as Judas, son of James (probably later in life Thaddaeus dropped the name of Judas so as not to be identified with the betrayer, Judas Iscariot). There is no one from numbers five through eight ever listed in the groupings of the first or last four names. No one from the first four names or the last four names is ever found in another grouping.

This may suggest that Jesus subdivided the Twelve into three groups. We know also that later He sent them out two by two (Mark 6:7)—thereby dividing them even further into six groups.

What are we to make of this?

I suspect we underrate the importance of smallness. Jesus poured Himself into a few. He organized them in a way to promote effective relationship building. He also knew it was a stretch for Matthew the tax collector and Simon the Zealot to link together in the common cause of following Him. Perhaps too much closeness would have negated their growth, so Jesus wisely put them in different groupings: Matthew with the second group of four and Simon the Zealot with the third group.

The contemporary church may too often focus only on crowds and numbers. Surely it is good that the kingdom grow extensively, but it will do so only if it first grows intensively.

Jesus devoted the vast majority of His time to a few. These were His "stem cells" for the growth of the church.

Almost every day I recall a prayer that was prayed over me when I began serving as pastor of a small church: "Lord, help them to lay foundations strong enough to bear the weight You will later place on them."

You must take time to build strong foundations—as Jesus did with the Twelve. Are you significantly investing time, prayer, resources, and training in the handful of people the Lord has put in your life?

The Lord wants to replicate His life through you even as He did through His first followers.

A Prayer

Lord Jesus, You placed each of the Twelve next to others
even as You place me alongside the people in my life.
Draw me nearer, Lord, to You—not to be ahead
of others, but to be closer to You.

THE BETRAYER

And Judas Iscariot, who betrayed him.
MARK 3:19

JUDAS IS ALWAYS NAMED last in the listings of The Twelve (Mark 3; Matthew 10; Luke 6). He is variously identified as the one "who betrayed him" (Mark, Matthew, John), or "became a traitor" (Luke). John tells us the name of his father, Simon Iscariot (John 6:71; 13:2). The term *Iscariot* most likely identifies his town of origin, probably a few miles south of Hebron—making Judas the only non-Galilean among the disciples.

Jesus identified him as a "devil" one year before the betrayal (John 6:70–71). One week before the passion, Judas protested when Mary anointed Jesus with expensive perfume. John said Judas' motive was not because he cared for the poor, but because he was a thief and "as keeper of the money bag, he used to help himself to what was put in it" (John 12:6).

All kinds of questions arise concerning Judas. Was he fated or predestined to do this? Did he have freedom of choice? Why didn't Jesus terminate his discipleship when it became evident Judas was stealing funds? Perhaps these questions will never be answered satisfactorily.

Judas' example does teach us that you can be close to Jesus, but far from Him.

Judas enjoyed proximity of relationship. Morning, noon, and night he was with Jesus walking on the road, at meal times, private conversations, and at public meetings. He heard the Lord's teachings, witnessed His miracles, and even engaged in preaching and healing missions (Mark 6).

But Judas never imbibed the spirit of Jesus. How else can you explain his stealing from the fund? How do you explain his protest over Mary's anointing of Jesus with expensive perfume? Judas flat-out lied when he said the money should have been spent on the poor. He wanted to line his own pockets with the proceeds (John 12:5–6). Nakedly put, Judas said on that occasion: "Pour out your money on me, not on Jesus."

Did his self-absorption result from disappointment with Jesus? From the realization that Jesus was not bringing in a political kingdom? Certainly Judas had a lot to lose if there were no huge messianic treasury from which he could profit.

We will never know, until eternity, his true motivations. It is sufficient to say that when any disciple begins to pull away from Jesus in one area of his or her life, this begins a decline into graver acts of rupture and betrayal.

You are either moving toward Jesus or away from Him.

Peter and the other disciples who failed and fled from Jesus' arrest, trial, and crucifixion were restored by Jesus after the resurrection. What if Judas, instead of committing suicide, had waited three days, returned to Jesus, and asked for pardon? I'm sure that the same grace given to Peter and the others would have been freely extended to Judas as well.

Judas gave up on Jesus several days too soon. He missed the resurrection.

You have a choice to be like Peter or like Judas. There will be occasions when, like them, you fail the Lord. Will you let sin and disobedience open the door for further flight from Him, or will you return, repent, and gain His grace?

Perhaps, like Judas, you are disappointed that Jesus didn't do something you thought He should do. Jesus would be much more acceptable to you if He had done things your way. Will you set aside your disappointments that life has taken some turns you didn't want or seek? Will you stick with Jesus all the way?

A Prayer

Oh Lord, help me never to become like Judas—turning away from You before I've seen the full story of what You will do. Help me to purge dishonesty and impurity from my life. Keep me faithful.

PERSPECTIVE

Then Jesus entered a house, and again a crowd gathered, so that he and his disciples were not even able to eat. When his family heard about this, they went to take charge of him, for they said, "He is out of his mind."

MARK 3:20-21

I WAS TRAVELING ON A BUS in western Turkey with a group of friends, visiting the sites of the seven churches talked about in Revelation 2 and 3.

We had already been under way several hours when I noticed an American newspaper on the empty seat next to me. I took off my new eyeglasses to read some of the finer print. When I was done, I put my glasses back on and looked out the windows to enjoy the beautiful scenery. Something was wrong. My vision now seemed blurred.

I thought that perhaps I was just tired from jet lag, so I closed my eyes for a while. But when I looked around again I still could not see clearly. I opened and closed each eye until I figured out that the vision problem was in my right eye.

Inwardly I felt panic and thought *I'm having a stroke in my right eye.* I became fearful.

The bus finally stopped for lunch. I headed through the food line and found a table in a corner by myself. I didn't want to eat or talk with anyone because I was depressed and concerned about my condition deteriorating.

Just then one of my friends, who had been seated across from me on the bus, came over smiling and said, "I noticed this was underneath your seat. Is this yours?" It was the lens to the right side of my eyeglasses. It had evidently fallen out of the frame when I picked up the newspaper. I popped the lens back into the frame and could see clearly again.

I wasn't having a stroke after all! What I had thought was happening was not what was really going on!

PERSPECTIVE

It's that way here in the gospel story. Jesus' own family thought He was crazy. From their point of view, Jesus had left off being sane.

It was probably His selection of The Twelve (Mark 3:13–19) that did it. The family had gone along and said nothing about His teaching and healing, but immediately after the selection of disciples as apostles, they weighed in. Clearly, they opposed the direction He was taking.

They had left Jesus alone so long as He was the sole actor. But now He was institutionalizing. He wasn't going to be a solo prophet/miracle worker who passed from the scene when His time was done. He intended to perpetuate Himself through others.

His family thought He had lost His mind.

I wonder how many times we misread Jesus. It's as though the lens to our spiritual glasses has fallen out. We don't see clearly, and as a result leap to false conclusions.

Jesus was not crazy. He knew exactly what He was doing. And He knows exactly what He is doing in your life and mine.

In times of distress and heartache, we often don't see very clearly. It's as though we are having a spiritual stroke in one of our eyes. We feel that God has failed us. We endlessly go through the "what ifs" and the "if onlys." Life seems like a maze in which we have lost our way.

But Jesus sees the whole picture of our lives. He has the complete overview. Let's avoid the mistake His family made. Let's not jump to wrong conclusions.

A Prayer

Lord Jesus, I'm sometimes like Your family. I don't understand what You're doing. Forgive me for not trusting You. You see the whole, and I see only a part.

NASTY RELIGIOUS PEOPLE

The teachers of the law who came down from Jerusalem said, "He is possessed by Beelzebub! By the prince of demons he is driving out demons."

MARK 3:22

I WILL NEVER FORGET an incident that happened in a small church my dad pastored when I was ten years of age.

Two deacons accosted my father one evening during the prayer time at the altar. One of them was big and the other was fat. The big deacon put his fist on my dad's chin and told him to resign because my dad, in their eyes, wasn't "spiritual."

My dad had not embraced some of the crazy and nonbiblical manifestations that a group wanted to bring into the church. Additionally, my dad preached from notes—a cardinal indication in their eyes of his lack of anointing!

That incident marked my first encounter with nasty religious people. It would not be the last.

My father graciously stood his ground and didn't resign until those people left and the church was stabilized with people of godly character. I admired the heroic way he responded—he didn't act like the Devil in resisting the Devil (see Jude 9).

Jesus also dealt with individuals who were outwardly religious but not inwardly godly. His conflict with them had been building. It started when He forgave a paralytic of his sins (Mark 2:6–7). The religious types didn't like Jesus eating with sinners and tax collectors, or the disciples of Jesus not fasting, or the disciples plucking and eating grain on the Sabbath, or Jesus healing a man with a withered hand on the Sabbath (Mark 2:15–3:6).

Religious headquarters now got involved. A delegation walked the nearly 100 miles from Jerusalem to accuse Jesus of being demon-possessed. Their goal was to discredit Him. (You really have to be upset to walk that far to make an accusation!)

They couldn't argue against the wisdom of His words or the wonders of His works, so they attacked Him by alleging the source of His power came from the prince of demons.

These weren't theological liberals who debunked the unseen world of the supernatural. No! These teachers of the Law were persons who spent their life in the "Book." But they didn't know its Author!

They had mastered theological study without knowing God. Their relationship was with the words and interpretation of the text, but their lives did not reflect the goodness and kindness of the living God.

The two deacons who nearly assaulted my dad, like the teachers of the Law, had a disconnect between their theology and their actions. Why would any person who presents himself as spiritual threaten to slug someone? Why would harsh and unkind words be said—all in the name of God?

Our culture is filled with preacher's kids, deacon's kids, and former church members who have abandoned the church—not because of the gospel but because of the poor example of nasty religious people. My heart goes out to them because the representation they saw of the gospel is *not* the real one.

Let's never become persons who are expert in doctrine but devoid of the character of Christ. What good is served if we are full of opinions and information but lacking in love and kindness?

A Prayer

Lord Jesus, let me never be a person who causes others to stumble and lose their way through my bad example. May my words and actions always be consistent with my confession of faith in You.

DEALING WITH CRITICISM

So Jesus called them and spoke to them in parables: "How can Satan drive out Satan? If a kingdom is divided against itself, that kingdom cannot stand. If a house is divided against itself, that house cannot stand. And if Satan opposes himself and is divided, he cannot stand; his end has come."

MARK 3:23–26

THE TEACHERS OF THE LAW walked about 100 miles from Jerusalem to Galilee with the accusation that Jesus drove out demons by the power of the Devil.

How did Jesus respond to their criticism? What can we learn from His example about our own reactions to people who don't like us, misinterpret our actions or motives, or say not-so-nice things about us to other people?

First, Jesus teaches us that if we make a response, it should be direct. The teachers of the Law bad-mouthed Jesus outside His presence, but Jesus did not answer in kind. He called them to Him.

Too many times, even in church circles, criticism is passed on indirectly: "Well, I've heard this about so and so, and I cannot reveal the source but it may very well be true." Later in His ministry, Jesus taught us to go directly to another person rather than roundabout (Matthew 18:15). Jesus set the example here with the teachers of the Law. He didn't let them get away with criticism not expressed directly.

Second, Jesus dealt with the issue and didn't attack the character of the persons making the charge. Of course, in the last week of His ministry, Jesus did excoriate the Pharisees and scribes (Mark 12:38–40, Matthew 23), but here, rather than blasting their motives, He treated their personhood with respect by dealing rationally with their accusation. Jesus could have written them off and sent them a message: "You are children of the Devil, and I won't even stoop to talk with you."

Instead, He drew them into His presence and courteously engaged them. He extended the opportunity of grace to those who liked Him least. As their rejection of Him later hardened further, He became far more direct and confrontational, but here He threw the seed of reason on the ground. If the ground had become good soil to receive His words, that was well and good. If the soil was hard, then the fault was with the soil and not the seed.

In His kingdom-divided and house-divided analogies, Jesus articulated a universal principle of relationships. A marriage can't stand when two are divided, nor can a home endure when there is division. A split church cannot effectively reach its community for Christ.

Jesus repudiated their charge that His power derived from Satan, but He didn't repudiate the existence of Satan. Jesus clearly held that evil wasn't an impersonal force—it had a face. It was a person. Satan stands behind the controls and forces of all that is wrong and terrible in this world.

How could Satan be casting out Satan when his goal is to cast "in" and not cast out? He wants to possess, not deliver; to inhabit, not vacate; to bind, not set free.

When someone falsely accuses you, can you be as gracious and direct in dealing with them as Jesus was with His critics? Will you make a reasonable response, or will you make an all-out attack on their character?

A Prayer

Lord Jesus, place Your personality into mine. Fill all the nooks, crannies, and crevices of my life with Your presence, Your thoughts, and Your feelings. Help me deal wisely when I am the object of false accusations.

THE UNPARDONABLE SIN

"In fact, no one can enter a strong man's house and carry off his possessions unless he first ties up the strong man. Then he can rob his house. I tell you the truth, all the sins and blasphemies of men will be forgiven them. But whoever blasphemes against the Holy Spirit will never be forgiven; he is guilty of an eternal sin." He said this because they were saying, "He has an evil spirit."

MARK 3:27–30

AS A YOUNG PERSON, I was perpetually frightened that I had committed the unpardonable sin. I wish I had understood then what the sin actually is.

Jesus clearly defines the unpardonable sin as blasphemy against the Spirit: It's denying the Holy Spirit's testimony to Jesus' own identity. The teachers of the Law attributed Jesus' activity to an evil spirit rather than to the Holy Spirit. If continued in, this was the unpardonable sin—for how can a person enter heaven if they deny Jesus is Lord? And who convinces us that Jesus is God's Son and our Savior? The Holy Spirit (John 16:7–12)!

At this point in Jesus' ministry, He didn't say that the teachers of the Law had already crossed that line—His statement was more a warning than a verdict.

In the ultimate sense, the only sin that keeps people out of heaven is a denial of the true nature of Jesus. It is the Holy Spirit who tells us through God's Word and through His witness that Jesus is Lord. The Holy Spirit recognizes no other Savior (Acts 4:12).

Therefore, the central issue related to Jesus is neither His mighty works nor His insightful words. The issue is His identity. The Spirit says, "Son of God, Savior, Messiah."

The good news of this teaching of Jesus is that all other sins may be forgiven. Furthermore, we know that Jesus has the power to forgive sins because throughout His Galilean ministry He demonstrated mastery over the Devil—Jesus had entered the Devil's territory, tied him up, and was now carrying off the Devil's possessions (us!).

Look at the sins embodied in breaking the Ten Commandments: having other gods, worshipping idols, using the Lord's name in vain, breaking the Sabbath, dishonoring parents, murder, adultery, stealing, bearing false witness, and coveting. All these sins (and far more) are forgivable! Amazing!

Jesus underlined the authority in His offer of blanket amnesty by saying, "I tell you the truth . . ." Jesus knew what His opponents did not know. He knew the Father and therefore knew the grace of the Father. He knew it was God's desire not to hold people's sins against them.

In this text Jesus said nothing about our need to ask for forgiveness. That is covered elsewhere (1 John 1:9). Here, the context for Jesus' statement lies in the charge made against Him by the teachers of the Law: that His might acts were done through the agency of the Devil. Jesus clearly regards that accusation as the one thing God cannot forgive; to underscore the seriousness of that sin He set it apart from all other sins. But all other sins are forgivable—and that means we can be beneficiaries of God's grace!

A Prayer

Lord Jesus, I may not be able to escape the stain and memory of my sins, but You have forgiven me. It's a grace so amazing I'm at a loss to understand it. I rest on Your word–even my sins are forgiven!

MISUNDERSTOOD BY FAMILY

Then Jesus' mother and brothers arrived. Standing outside, they sent someone in to call him. A crowd was sitting around him, and they told him, "Your mother and brothers are outside looking for you."

MARK 3:31–32

FOR THE FIRST TIME in Mark's gospel, we learn that Jesus had a mother.

Mark's introduction of Jesus on the scene of human history came via John the Baptist. In Mark there is no mention of Jesus' birth and childhood—no shepherds or wise men, manger or inn, angels singing "Gloria in excelsis Deo"; no Herod destroying the babies of Bethlehem, no flight into Egypt or childhood in Nazareth, and no visit to Jerusalem when He was twelve.

In Mark, Jesus comes fully formed, grown, with His ministry commenced. Now we learn He has an unnamed mother and brothers.

Prior to the arrival of the scribes from Jerusalem, Jesus' own family "went to take charge of him, for they said, 'He is out of his mind'" (Mark 3:20). The scribes had gotten to Jesus first—walking about 100 miles to accuse Him of being possessed by the Devil.

His family never leveled such a charge, but they thought Him crazy. They arrived the fifteen miles or so from Nazareth too late to prevent the heated exchange with the scribes.

It was clearly a family intervention: "Let's pull Him away and detox Him of His messiah complex before He destroys Himself and us with Him." They used a go-between in an attempt to fetch Jesus.

Notice, the family stood outside. Whenever you stand outside the place where Jesus is, you will really never know Him, even if you are family. The scribes were inside the house, but they didn't know Him either. Inside or outside, it makes no difference if your heart is in a far country.

MISUNDERSTOOD BY FAMILY

Clearly, Jesus' mother and brothers stood outside because they weren't yet insiders to His saving mission. You are left to wonder if His mother had recessed the miracles attendant to His birth too far into her memory.

His brothers had played with Him, worked with Him, gone to synagogue and school with Him. They had slept together in the same small house, shared mealtimes day after day, year after year. Yet, they didn't know Him. They only knew Him as their brother—they had no idea He could be more.

It must have been an awkward moment for everyone: the family, the crowd outside, the crowd within the house, and Jesus Himself. It was also an embarrassing moment—Jesus' family reduced to talking to Him through intermediaries. Why didn't Jesus' family make their way through the crowd and come to Him personally? The failure to do so illustrates the breach that John talks about later: "He came to His own and His own did not receive Him" (John 1:11, NKJV).

But the family's failure to understand Jesus wasn't permanent. We find His mother and brothers in the upper room on the day of Pentecost and they, too, received the Holy Spirit (Acts 1:14).

Perhaps, like Jesus' own family, you have misunderstood the Lord. He hasn't been what you expected Him to be for you. You wish that circumstances had fallen differently in your life.

Take heart! Jesus knows the whole and right now you only know a part. Trust Him even when you don't understand.

A Prayer

Lord Jesus, forgive me for the times when I feel You don't know what You're doing in my life. I, too, have misunderstood You. You never gave up on Your family, and I'm grateful You'll never give up on me.

THE NEW FAMILY

"Who are my mother and my brothers?" he asked. Then he looked at those seated in a circle around him and said, "Here are my mother and my brothers! Whoever does God's will is my brother and sister and mother."

MARK 3:33–34

IMAGINE YOU ARE SITTING in a house surrounded by admirers, but your own family cannot get in. Your mother and brothers stand outside and send an intermediary to fetch you. You then ask the circle around you a question that seems to indicate you don't know your own kin!

The mother who nursed you, taught you to walk and talk, shepherded you to school and synagogue, and invested her life and soul in you as her firstborn—you don't know your own mother! Amazing!

But that is exactly what Jesus said: "Who are my mother and brothers?" No one volunteered to answer the question. Dead silence.

So Jesus answered the question Himself. He redefined family. No longer did His family consist of blood relatives; it was made up of obedience-to-the-will-of-God relatives. And it was not just mother and brother but sister as well.

When Jesus posed the question, sister was not mentioned. In fact, His sisters were not standing outside with His mother and brothers—and we know He did have sisters (Mark 6:3). (Joseph, the husband of Mary, is also not there, having evidently died sometime in the period between Jesus' twelfth birthday and the beginning of His ministry at age thirty.)

What was Jesus doing? He was redefining our relationship to Him both vertically (mother to son) and horizontally (brother to siblings).

What does it mean to be a mother of Jesus in the spiritual sense? It is evidently an available role since Jesus includes it as a possibility for familial relationship. Does this not open the door for us to assume a nurturing role toward Jesus by lending our hearts and hands to help His body in every way possible?

And what does it mean to be the brother or sister of Jesus? Doesn't that involve camaraderie, mutual support, honesty, and a deep relational commitment that goes far beyond friendship?

I am very close to my family. I cherish the memories of my father, mother, and sister. My brother, daughter, and son, and their spouses and children are all living. I know who they are. In fact, I know them well. I am grateful for family, and I would never think to ask the question, "Who are my mother and brothers?"

Jesus came to create a family based not on bloodline but on faith in Him. Having formed that family, He calls us to belong to it.

Yes, we will always have our family formed by the flesh, by our common bonds of DNA, parentage, and ancestry. But we also have another family. It's called the body of Christ, and we are to treat that family as Jesus does.

Mistreatment of a brother or sister believer is an offense to Jesus since that individual is a mother, brother, or sister of Christ. If we wouldn't mistreat our own blood family, then we must certainly love well the family of Jesus.

A Prayer

I call You Lord. I know You are God's Son—and that title stands far above me—but "brother" or "sister" or "mother" binds me close to You. I am thrilled to be a member of Your family!

THE TEACHER

On another occasion Jesus began to teach by the lake. The crowd that gathered around him was so large that he got into a boat and sat in it out on the lake, while all the people were along the shore at the water's edge.

MARK 4:1

THIS IS THE FIRST TIME Mark records formal teaching by Jesus. All the teaching in the first three chapters resulted from activities related to miracles, dialog, or controversy.

Jesus, to this point, had taught by actions: calling disciples, driving out evil spirits, healing on the Sabbath, praying in a solitary place, healing, and confronting opposition. All this also constitutes teaching.

Jesus' method of teaching by actions and example tells us that we, as His disciples, should regard every moment in our lives as a potential learning or teaching opportunity. Teaching is not limited to those occasions when we have a prepared talk to give.

This poem by Edgar Guest best expresses teaching through what we do:

> I'd rather see a sermon than hear one any day,
> I'd rather one would walk with me than merely tell the way.
> The eye's a better pupil and more willing than the ear,
> Fine counsel is confusing, but example's always clear;
> And the best of all the preachers are the men who live their creeds,
> For to see good put in action is what everybody needs.
> I soon can learn to do it if you'll let me see it done,
> I can watch your hands in action, but your tongue too fast may run;
> The lecture you deliver may be very wise and true,
> But I'd rather get my lessons by observing what you do;
> For I might misunderstand you and the high advice you give,
> But there's no misunderstanding how you act and how you live.[1]

---

[1] Edgar A. Guest, *Collected Verse of Edgar A. Guest* (Raleigh, NC: Contemporary Books, 1977).

There is also a time for more formalized and structured teaching. Jesus didn't have a church or synagogue in which to give His message, so the prow of a boat became His pulpit, the water His natural amplification, and vast crowds on the shore His audience.

Of course the crowds didn't yet understand His mission. That's why He began to teach in a more formal way. During His ministry, the crowds didn't quite "get it." They didn't understand that His kingdom was internal and not external, spiritual and not political. But Jesus never chastised or harangued the crowds. He never railed on them for being "shallow." Instead, He constantly had compassion on them.

He has compassion on us as well. What He taught that day may not have been understood at the time, but after His death and resurrection it would become very plain. Perhaps you don't understand everything God is doing in your life—but stay with Him. You will discover the meaning and purpose.

We couldn't be on the shore that day with Jesus. Wouldn't you love to have been in that crowd? There were always crowds around Jesus (Mark 1:33, 45; 2:2–5, 13; 3:7–9, 20, 32). But there is a crowd we can join—in that day when there will be a multitude around Him that no person can number (Revelation 7:9)! Whatever you do, don't miss that gathering!

A Prayer

Lord Jesus, teach me to be a living example by word and deed so that I always reflect what You would say and do.

THE FARMER

He taught them many things by parables, and in his teaching said: "Listen! A farmer went out to sow his seed."

MARK 4:2–3

JESUS TAUGHT PEOPLE who were not taking notes. How could He teach timeless truths in a way that would be remembered and passed along to others by word of mouth? He taught in parables.

A parable is more than a story. It is a story with a point. The word *parable* comes from a combination of two Greek words *para* and *ballo*. We immediately recognize that our word *ball* comes from the word *ballo*, and it means "to throw." *Para* means "alongside." The parable is a story thrown alongside a truth.

Jesus never told stories for the stories' sake. He told them to illuminate His teaching.

Some of Jesus' first listeners only heard the story and missed the application. We must not make their mistake.

The most foundational of Jesus' parables is that of the soils—sometimes called the parable of the sower and the seed.

It begins with Jesus saying "Listen!" That one word at the start is akin to a speaker clapping his hands to gain attention before launching into an address. It underlines the importance of what he has to say. When the parable was done, Jesus underscored the importance of listening by saying, "He who has ears to hear, let him hear" (v. 9).

Think for a moment about the farmer. He doesn't sow seed unless he goes out. There can be no productive work unless the farmer gets up in the morning, gets dressed, takes the seed sack, goes out to the field, and sows.

Neither can anything productive happen in our own lives unless we set our minds and hands to it. A harvest of good things doesn't happen to lazy people.

In Jesus' story we have a sensible and diligent farmer. He not only has gotten up and gone to work, but he has seed to sow. He hasn't consumed last year's entire crop on his own desires but has saved some back.

There is an African story about a small village racked by hunger. Springtime was planting season, but the winter had been marked by scarcity of food. All the grain was gone from the prior year's harvest. A little boy wandered into his father's goat shack and saw a sack of seed suspended from the ceiling. Excitedly he ran back to his hut and brought the news to his family.

"We have grain," he said. "Please, Mommy, get the grain out of the goat shack, grind it, and make mush so our tummies will be full."

His father sadly said, "Son, we can't do that. We must take that grain and sow it into the ground so that we'll have plenty of food to eat in the coming months."

The father then took the seed sack down and with tears walked into the field, scattering the grain upon the fallow ground.

Why did he do that? He did it because he believed in the harvest. He refused to spend tomorrow's future on today's wants.

Are you like the farmer? What are you sowing from your own life? Are you investing today in things that won't appear until days, week, months, or years down the road?

A Prayer

Lord Jesus, I don't like the idea of delayed gratification. What I want, I want now. But, if there is a future of Your choosing in my life, then today I must forego some of what I want so that in tomorrow's day I and others will have the needed resources.

THE SOILS

As he was scattering the seed, some fell along the path, and the birds came and ate it up. Some fell on rocky places, where it did not have much soil. It sprang up quickly, because the soil was shallow. But when the sun came up, the plants were scorched, and they withered because they had no root. Other seed fell among thorns, which grew up and chocked the plants, so that they did not bear grain. Still other seed fell on good soil. It came up, grew and produced a crop, multiplying thirty, sixty, or even a hundred times.

MARK 4:4–8

THESE SAME SOILS are in you and me.

Sometimes we aren't receptive at all to what the Lord desires in our lives. At other times we quickly embrace God's will, but at the first sign of adversity we wither in our intentions and commitments.

On still other occasions we get distracted by "things," and we lose out.

Thankfully, there is also a part of us that is good soil and becomes productive for the Lord.

Jesus' most basic parable of the kingdom is this one—the story of the soils. We are that soil. He is the sower. His words are the seeds.

When you initially look at this story, you might think the farmer was rather careless. Our mass-farming methods today find a sower going out into fields that are thoroughly prepared for receiving seed. But in Jesus' day, before tractors and mechanized equipment, this story reflected the nature of terrace farming in Galilee.

A footpath went through the fields. Without chemicals, weeds had to be hand pulled, and often they were missed. Rocks littered the fields and were impossible to eradicate from the dirt.

So the farmer took the risk that he would lose some of his seed on the path and among the rocks, and that weeds would grow up even in the good soil and choke the grain. But the farmer was willing to risk a little in order to gain a lot.

Life is like that, isn't it? We prefer having everything in neat boxes. But life can be messy. Things aren't always clear-cut. And sometimes, in order to attain a greater good, you must risk some losses.

Jesus' ministry is like that. His words, like seed, are going out. He doesn't just sow His words in what He knows will be highly fertile soil. He sows also on the margins. Some of His words are going to get lost because they fall on hard places in our lives—the beaten down "paths" where we insist on our own way rather than God's.

Jesus also knows that we are greater at starting commitments than finishing them. At times, we are shallow and drop out when the going gets tough and we find there is a cost in continuing. We get distracted by other things that choke out what the Lord could have done had we remained focused.

A farmer sows his seed mostly on good soil. But the human heart isn't a vegetable garden. Much of Jesus' seed falls where it bears no fruit.

It's quite an irony: The efforts of the Lord of Glory often fall on unproductive or unresponsive people.

But when we embrace Jesus and His words, our lives blossom with value, purpose, and productivity.

A Prayer

Lord Jesus, help me to identify the unreceptive parts of my life. I want all of my life to be good soil for You.

THE SECRET

*Then Jesus said, "He who has ears to hear, let him hear."
When he was alone, the Twelve and the others around him
asked him about the parables. He told them, "The secret of
the kingdom of God has been given to you. But to those on
the outside everything is said in parables so that, 'they
may be ever seeing but never perceiving, and ever
hearing but never understanding; otherwise
they might turn and be forgiven!"*

MARK 4:9-12

JESUS SPOKE IN PARABLES. Why?
The answer lies in His strategy for gradual disclosure of His identity and mission.

Have you ever wanted to know everything at once? What the future holds? How you can make sure you're making the right decision now on the limited information you have available at the moment?

That's the position the disciples were in. Clearly they were attracted to the magnetism of Jesus, to the wonder of His works, and the splendor of His words. But they didn't see the whole picture.

It's the difference between being guided by a small flashlight or a floodlight.

In discerning the future, most of us would prefer that God beamed a floodlight so the whole landscape of tomorrow and tomorrow's tomorrow opened up before us. But He only lets us use a pen flashlight, a small beam aimed at the path directly in front of our feet. We only see a step or two ahead, but never the whole.

Fortunately, He sees everything. As we follow Him, we begin to have ears that hear and eyes that see.

Jesus' opponents and the adoring crowds didn't have a clue as to what Jesus' real mission was. He had come, not to bring a political and external kingdom, but to bring a spiritual and internal reign: The kingdom of God is within you.

How could Jesus slowly unpack that truth for His disciples, who expected Him to rule in place of Rome, who thought He was the One to bring national independence to Israel and free them from all oppression?

Jesus chose the parables as a way of revealing and concealing truth.

For those who had ears but didn't really hear, the parables hid what Jesus taught. For example, the parable of the sower and the soils—the most basic of Jesus' parables—was just another story to them. They didn't catch its inner meaning. The great truths of the gospel are never understood by nonbelievers. Not because they are incapable of learning but because they lack relationship with the One who unlocks the mystery of the kingdom.

Slowly, however, the disciples began to catch it. They had "ears to hear." The kingdom was like the seed—it had to be received. Seed, like the kingdom, isn't visible once it's planted. During its germination stage you cannot notice anything happening. When it falls on hard soil, the kingdom dies. When it falls on rocky places or thorny ground, it doesn't endure for long. You must become the good soil into which the seed falls.

Jesus says that those who "get" this are in on the secret: Relationship with God is a matter of choice. Your response determines whether you will receive the kingdom. Jesus says that those who make this decision are forgiven.

A Prayer

Lord Jesus, I want my ears to hear and my heart to listen.
Let me always remain in Your classroom,
knowing You more, loving You better.

THE PATH

Then Jesus said to them, "Don't you understand this parable? How then will you understand any parable? The farmer sows the word. Some people are like seed along the path, where the word is sown. As soon as they hear it, Satan comes and takes away the word that was sown in them."

MARK 4:13-15

THE DISCIPLES DIDN'T HAVE a clue what Jesus was talking about. They asked for an explanation.

Jesus responded with two rhetorical questions, "Don't you understand...? How then will you understand...?"

Here is the problem. The secret of the kingdom was given in the story of the sower and the seed, and even the insiders didn't get it. No wonder Jesus' questions show a hint of frustration: "Are you so dense? How will I teach you anything if you can't pass Kingdom of God 101?"

This entering class in the kingdom of God didn't show great promise. They began, as most students do, by stumbling. Early concepts were hard to grasp. It was a new way of thinking. We know the occupations of five of the Twelve: four commercial fishermen and one tax collector. They were all used to dealing with cold, hard facts—not secrets hidden within riddles. So they were on a steep learning curve.

But aren't we all? Jesus continually stretches us! And we must follow the example of the disciples. When we don't know something, we must ask!

Jesus began to explain the first element of His story: "The farmer sows the word." The farmer, of course, is Jesus. The word is His teaching.

But Jesus didn't limit His ministry to the receptive. He continued to speak even when His words fell on deaf ears and hardened hearts.

Enter the Devil. For the third time in Mark's gospel he is mentioned—he tempted Jesus in the wilderness (1:13), and the teachers of the Law accused Jesus of being in league with him (3:22–30).

Clearly, Jesus took as true the existence of the Devil. A real spiritual entity, he was active in opposing Jesus and His mission, either through deceit (the temptation) or by destroying the impact of Jesus by seizing away the seed sown upon unreceptive hearts.

It isn't Satan who prevents an individual from receiving God's Word. The predisposition of the person who rejects that Word is what causes the Devil to appear and snatch away that Word.

The practical lesson is simply this: any hardness of heart on your part toward the Lord instantly gives the Devil an opportunity. If you don't take the Word of Jesus into your life but let it lie neglected upon a hardened conscience indefinitely, then the Word will be snatched from you by the Devil. It won't have a chance to take root because it has been taken away.

Why is there such hardened opposition to Jesus in all sectors of society—especially the entertainment media, the secular intellectual community, the opinion molders, and even religious leaders? Jesus answers: The Devil they don't believe in is the stealthy thief of the truth they have rejected.

If you or I don't want the Devil to destroy the Word of Jesus sown in us, then we must become something other than hard soil.

A Prayer

Lord Jesus, I don't want the Devil to snatch Your Word from my life. I want to meditate on Your Word day and night. Let there be no hardened places in my conscience where sin can hide.

ROCKY PLACES

Others, like seed sown on rocky places, hear the word and at once receive it with joy. But since they have no root, they last only a short time. When trouble or persecution comes because of the word, they quickly fall away.

MARK 4:16–17

JESUS IDENTIFIES THE PROBLEM that will be systemic in His church: Starting is easy; finishing is hard.

I see this all the time. Our national statistics show that for every five persons who pray a confession of faith, only one even follows through with water baptism—the most elemental first step after conversion.

Any leader of a home Bible study knows there are far more that begin than finish. It's the same with volunteers in any ministry. More sign up than show up; more drop out than endure.

The problem isn't with the seed, the Word of Jesus, the gospel. Not at all!

In fact, when the good news of Jesus is first received it immediately results in joy. And, why not? Sins are forgiven. Reconciliation has taken place with God. A new name has been written down in heaven. Life has now taken on purpose and meaning.

The rocky-place-person is showing initial productivity in their Christian walk. The seed of God's Word has landed, germinated, and sprouted. What had once been only ugliness in his or her life now shows promise of beauty and fruitfulness. Jesus has been received with gladness!

But the seed withers away on the rocky place just as quickly as it had sprung up. The recipient of Jesus welcomed the newfound joy but not the hardship.

That's a lesson for us all. None of us likes hardships. We want every day to be enjoyable. We desire our work to be satisfying, our marriage or family to be wholesome, challenging, and fun. We want everyone to like us. So long as life is a bowl of cherries, we're content.

If we receive Jesus with gladness but falsely assume that no difficulty will follow, then we become the rocky place. Yes, trouble will come.

Jesus speaks not just of any commonplace trouble but specifically of trouble that arises from embracing Him. This has an obvious and a subtle meaning.

The obvious is when our Christian testimony stands out and we are opposed because of our witness. This happens at many levels—from ridicule to outright violent persecution. In many parts of the world today, followers of Jesus know firsthand the latter. At this moment, one of my friends is awaiting trial in a country where religious freedom is guaranteed only to those who practice the approved religion. He is charged with witnessing about his faith in Jesus.

The more subtle form of enduring trouble comes when we remain loyal to Jesus' teaching rather than doing what we want. A telling illustration is when two believers find in their marriage that they're no longer satisfied with one another. In obedience to Jesus, do they stay and work things out? Or do they do what the world does and pack up and leave?

Is there a disconnect between what you believe and how you behave? Are you following Jesus for the long haul, or just when everything is going well?

The example of the rocky places provides a sober warning to us that we must also be true to Jesus even when the going gets tough.

A Prayer

Lord Jesus, my comfort lies not in my circumstances but in knowing You. I want to follow You all the way to the end and hear You say on that day, "Well done!"

THE THORNS

Still others, like seed sown among thorns, hear the word; but the worries of this life, the deceitfulness of wealth and the desires for other things come in and choke the word, making it unfruitful.

MARK 4:18–19

THERE ARE MULTIPLE responses to Jesus.

The seed fallen on the path points to the hardened heart. The seed fallen on rocky places illustrates the heart initially receptive to Him, but not for the long haul. The seed of Jesus' words fallen into thorns presents us with the divided heart.

Unlike the seed among the thorns, the seed growing in rocky places has no plant competition. It's the only thing growing there. That would explain the joy of many new converts. Jesus has become the only positive news in their lives—no wonder He is immediately welcomed with gladness. But hardship quickly scorches the seed among the rocks.

Not so the seed among the thorns—it is simply squeezed. There is too much else fighting for attention. That person hears the Word, but that's not the only thing being heard. Life is full of many noises and distractions competing against Jesus.

Jesus says that the thorns are three things: worries, wealth, and desires. Usually, we only think of worries as thorns—the prickly things that disturb our comfort. Worries or anxiety can become so large that they choke our human and spiritual potential.

We do worry—about our health, our children, our family, our jobs, our retirement, and lots of other cares. We can become so bound up with these concerns that we lose meaning, purpose, and joy.

Wealth isn't a problem for most of us since lack of money seems to be a bigger problem. But I have noticed that those followers of Jesus who become financially well-fixed have the unique danger and temptation of exempting themselves from meaningful Christian service because their money can afford them much leisure.

Desires reach out to all of us. We want other things!

I remember receiving a prayer request once from a visitor in our church. It said: "Pray for me. I want a new home, a new job, a new wife, and a new car." It was the "new wife" I couldn't pray for!

What unholy desires do you have? Can you live satisfied with what the Lord has put in your hands today? Or are you perpetually unhappy because you're always reaching for something more, for a future that is outside your grasp?

As followers of Jesus, we must learn to balance aspiration with contentment. Desires (and wealth) can be good things, but the nature of sin is such that even the good things in life can be contaminated through misuse.

Which of these "thorns" do you have the most trouble with: worry, wealth, desires?

As a young minister, I went through a terrible season of anxiety about my work. In the middle of a nerve attack one evening, I shot up a desperate prayer to the Lord: "Jesus, I've worried about this all day. I would like to sleep. It's Your turn to worry. Good night." The Lord instantly answered my prayer. I fell asleep, and the healing from anxiety has remained to this day.

Why not give your worry, your wealth, and your desires to the Lord? Lay them at His feet. It isn't His will that the thorns grow up and choke you.

A Prayer

Come, Divine Gardener, and weed out of me that which is unlike You. Heal my anxiety with Your calm. Let my wealth serve You and others and not just myself. Replace my wrongful desires with passion to do Your will.

THE GOOD SOIL

Others, like seed sown on good soil, hear the word, accept it, and produce a crop—thirty, sixty or even a hundred times what was sown.

MARK 4:20

JESUS' WORDS HAD FALLEN on the Pharisees and teachers of the Law—but they proved to be nonreceptive, a beaten path.

The adoring crowds responded joyfully at first flush, but when tough times or difficult teaching came, they faded away. Did they even know they represented the rocky ground?

Some followed Jesus longer, but soon became distracted with other things. Their affections faded, choked out by the thorns of this world's cares and pursuits.

What if there were no fourth response, no people willing to be good soil? Jesus' mission would have failed—then and now.

Clearly, Jesus risked everything by taking disciples. If they proved to be poor learners, rebellious, careless, reckless, inattentive, lethargic, or self-centered, where would the world be today? We would never have heard about Jesus, His death on the cross, and His resurrection from the dead.

We would know nothing about His teaching—no Sermon on the Mount, no Lord's Prayer, no "love your neighbor as yourself." We never would have heard of the Good Samaritan, the Prodigal Son, the Lost Sheep, or a host of other stories that conveyed earthly and eternal truth. We wouldn't know how to live now, how to have our sins forgiven, or how to go to heaven.

But in our generation there are far more people who know little or nothing about Jesus than the population of the first-century world into which the first disciples—the "good soil" followers of Christ—came. Will you and I prove to be the "good soil" in our homes, our neighborhoods, schools, and workplaces?

When we share our faith, some of what we share will always fall on good ground.

It was that way with Ray and Helen. I met them years ago in a South American country. They had served thirty years as missionaries and single-handedly translated the entire Bible into the language of the largest indigenous people group in that land.

I asked them what it had been like in the beginning.

"Oh," they said, "it was very difficult. We moved into a village to learn the language, but the witch doctor told everyone not to talk with us. It took us two years to make our first friend. He was willing to teach us the language."

Their home church cut off their missionary support because the pastor felt they didn't have enough results. That pastor didn't understand that simply because the seed doesn't sprout up right away doesn't mean the ground is infertile.

This missionary couple not only learned the language and translated the Bible, they created the orthography for the language. Until they came, the language of this indigenous people had been oral—it had never been written down.

They told me, "Now we are retiring, but today there are thousands of believers and scores of churches."

Fortunately, they didn't make a premature assessment that the ground into which they witnessed was unproductive soil. What if Ray and Helen had stopped sowing too soon, or had never sown at all?

May we also be good soil so that we become good sowers who produce a bountiful harvest for the Master!

A Prayer

Lord Jesus, I don't want to be among those who don't have time for You, who start but don't finish, who let other things get in the way of following You with a whole heart. I want to be as productive as possible for You.

SECRET MESSAGE OR SECRET SINS

He said to them, "Do you bring in a lamp to put it under a bowl or a bed? Instead, don't you put it on its stand? For whatever is hidden is meant to be disclosed, and whatever is concealed is meant to be brought out into the open. If anyone has ears to hear, let him hear."

MARK 4:21-23

IS THERE SOMETHING in your past that is hidden? Do you pray that it will never be disclosed?

Suppose that what you did is not a criminal act but an ethical or moral failure. You sinned against God and another person. What you did never became generally known. You've gone on with your life. You repented and did your best to protect innocent persons who would be harmed if they knew the secret from your past.

Does this teaching from Jesus apply to you—that everything hidden or concealed will be brought into the open?

To answer that question we must look at the context of Jesus' ministry as recorded thus far in the book of Mark.

Jesus has been gradually disclosing His identity. He doesn't allow the demons to testify about Him—and so far they are the only ones who know His true identity (1:23-26, 34). He has also gradually disclosed the nature of His kingdom.

The parable of the soils (4:1-20) says that His reign or rule will not be imposed but must be received. It will not be an external but an internal kingdom; not political, but spiritual; not earthly, but eternal.

Jesus' opposition didn't get it. The disciples didn't understand the parable either (4:10) and, thus, Jesus had to explain it clearly to them.

In that context, Jesus talks about the lamp under the bowl or bed. For the moment, His teaching is that lamp. But it is hidden—it is known only to a few. However, Jesus knew the day was coming when His teaching would become broadly known. It was meant to be disclosed.

Thus, in this passage Jesus is not talking about secret sins. He is talking about His own teaching—"the secret of the kingdom" (4:11)—given first to the disciples and subsequently to the whole world. If the disciples from the day of Pentecost forward had not proclaimed Him, then Jesus' teaching would have remained under a bowl or bed.

Too often this passage is applied to secret sin, with a warning to anyone who commits a private sin that sooner or later what was done in secret will get out. And many times it does get out. However, the Lord was not particularly impressed with those who attempted to humiliate the woman taken in adultery (John 8). He isn't in the business of shaming sinners.

The very concept of "atonement" means "to cover." Or, as David put it, "As far as the east is from the west, so far has he removed our transgressions from us" (Psalm 103:12). God's forgiveness includes His intentional forgetfulness. He isn't interested in broadcasting your failures. Instead, He throws His robes of righteousness around you.

The true meaning of this passage is that we, His disciples in the twenty-first century, should not hide His words but openly share the life, teaching, and ministry of Jesus with everyone we can. If we have a mouth to speak, we will speak; and if they have ears to hear, then they will hear.

A Prayer

Jesus, You take away my sins even though I remember the wrongs that You have forgotten. May I openly share with others the words of life You bring so that Your message doesn't remain hidden.

THE LEARNING PRINCIPLE

"Consider carefully what you hear," he continued. "With the measure you use, it will be measured to you—and even more. Whoever has will be given more; whoever does not have, even what he has will be taken from him."

MARK 4:24-25

I SIGNED UP FOR A BEGINNING course in piano my first semester in college.

I considered myself a quick learner and thought that within three months I would play the piano with the best of them. My teacher, however, insulted me on the first day by placing in front of me a Clara Thompson beginning piano book designed for first-graders.

My teacher had it right. No one can become a concert pianist in a few weeks! I needed to start with the basics. Much to my chagrin, I had no talent for even that. I couldn't seem to make the movement of my fingers on the keyboard and my feet on the pedals line up with the squiggly notes on the score in front of me.

At the end of the semester I dropped out. I have long since forgotten all I learned, and today I can't even play the simple little ditties I learned back then.

My experience illustrates the principle Jesus was talking about—use it or lose it.

Some read these words of Jesus and falsely assume He was endorsing a form of economics: The rich get richer and the poor get poorer (which they often do). But He was really addressing issues of discipleship.

He challenges us to "hear." He says there is a relationship between listening and capacity. You can bring to Jesus the capacity of your measure: Is your desire to know Him the size of a thimble, a cup, a glass, a jar, a fifty-gallon drum?

Your capacity to "hear" lies with you. You can bring whatever receptivity you will. And to the extent of the capacity you offer, He will fill it up. "It will be measured to you—and *even more.*"

Notice the "even more." There's a lot more spillover from a fifty-gallon drum than there is from a thimble. Your willingness to grow in Christ determines the size of the spillover!

In short, Jesus says that what you do today determines what is given to you tomorrow. If you choose to become stagnant, then more cannot be given to you and you risk losing even what you have.

Jesus' learning principle applies to all areas of discipline. If you pray regularly, then prayer will grow. If you start praying spasmodically, then sooner or later you will quit praying all together.

The same holds true for reading or studying the Bible, giving, witnessing, stewardship of time and talent, or deepening of relationships.

I asked a friend of mine who had been married for over thirty years, "How is it that you have such a successful and happy marriage?"

She answered, "Oh, my husband and I work at it, and every year we read a book specifically on the subject of marriage to help us in our relationship."

What was the secret? They had not stopped growing in their relationship, and more was being added to them.

You must never reach a time in your Christian journey when you feel you have done enough, that from here on out you can coast. There's never a time in your Christian life when it's all right to stop growing, because when you quit, you go into reverse. You lose what you had.

A Prayer

Lord Jesus, help me so that I never become stagnant in my walk with You. Keep me on the growing edge. I desire to be full and overflowing.

UNDER DEVELOPMENT

He also said, "This is what the kingdom of God is like. A man scatters seed on the ground. Night and day, whether he sleeps or gets up, the seed sprouts and grows, though he does not know how. All by itself the soil produces grain—first the stalk, then the head, then the full kernel in the head. As soon as the grain is ripe, he puts the sickle to it, because the harvest has come."

MARK 4:26–29

WHEN JESUS FIRST GAVE this parable about scattered seed, only a few people followed Him.

Imagine if a pollster had surveyed the population of the Roman world and asked two questions: (1) "Have you ever heard of Jesus?" and (2) "If you have heard of Him, do you think anyone will be aware of His existence 100 years from now?"

The results would probably not be much different from those who today are predicting the decline or demise of Christianity.

But Jesus saw clearly into the future and knew that His message would have great effect. He is the One who scatters the seed (His Word). The soil is humanity in general, and you in particular.

Jesus knew nature and nurture. He understood plant processes—that nothing springs up from the ground full blown. It goes through a process of germination, growth, and development until full potential is reached.

That's the way it is in your life and mine. We don't become mature followers of Jesus Christ all at once.

I was ten years of age when the "seed" of conversion entered my life. Actually, in the middle of the night I dreamed I had missed the Lord's coming. I awakened in the darkness and shook with fear. I promised right then and there that if He had not returned, I would serve Him. And I have.

But I knew little then compared to what I know now. I didn't understand the Bible, I couldn't explain the major doctrines, and I didn't know where that childhood decision would take me in life.

Christ's followers acknowledge both miracle and development. Healings may take place immediately, but learning takes time. It's developmental. Jesus, in this parable, tells us that over time His Word will bring growth and maturity into our lives.

In the natural, none of us arrived from the womb as adults. My birth weight of seven pounds is not where I am today. My birth length of twenty-one inches has stretched to about seventy-two. If my mother were alive, she could no longer carry me in her arms.

Just as biological growth takes time, so does spiritual development.

I love the epitaph on the grave of Ruth Graham, wife of Billy Graham. One day as they drove through a work area on the highway, she saw this sign: "End of construction. Thank you for your patience." She told Billy, "That's what I want on my tombstone."

Whether we use the illustration of construction or seed growth, the result is the same. God isn't finished with you yet. You are to keep growing until "the harvest"—until the "end of construction."

Jesus' parable, however, doesn't deal only with personal spiritual growth in you. It's also about the larger kingdom.

Over the centuries, the followers of Christ have grown from the first handful of believers into multiplied hundreds of millions. And His kingdom will continue to grow all the way until He comes again for us!

A Prayer

Lord Jesus, You never put an age limit on growth.
There are areas of my life where You still seek growth.
May I continue to be fertile ground for Your life
growing in me. Keep me farm-able and fruitful!

THE MUSTARD SEED

> *Again he said, "What shall we say the kingdom of God is like, or what parable shall we use to describe it? It is like a mustard seed, which is the smallest seed you plant in the ground. Yet when planted, it grows and becomes the largest of all garden plants, with such big branches that the birds of the air can perch in its shade."*
> MARK 4:30–32

THREE TIMES IN MARK 4 Jesus compares His kingdom to a seed.

The story of the soils (vv. 1–20) tells us that His kingdom meets with different responses. It isn't externally imposed but internally received.

The parable of the scattered seed (vv. 26–29) informs us that His kingdom is developmental. None of us is fully formed on the first day we begin to follow Him.

The third story, the mustard seed, shows us the extensive reach of His kingdom. It grows from tiny to huge.

Jesus starts the parable with a question: "What shall we say the kingdom of God is like?" As the master teacher, Jesus sought to get students to think on their own. "Peter, Thomas, Matthew, the rest of you—what you do you think?" I suspect that before Jesus gave His own answer He engaged in a discussion with them and got their viewpoints.

How would you answer that question?

Kingdom is not a word we use in a democracy. But Jesus' hearers were well familiar with the term because it was the political realm in which they lived. Herod ruled as king in Galilee. Rome's kingdom extended throughout the Mediterranean world.

So it would be natural to assume that the disciples' first answer would be: "The kingdom of God is a government that has authority to impose its will and law on all its citizens. As God's kingdom, it is mightier in armament and power than any human institution.

The leader of that kingdom is God's Messiah, who will overthrow Rome, Herod, and any other human leader or power that stands in His way."

But that's the wrong answer.

Jesus compares the kingdom to the smallest of seeds.

Like the mustard seed, Jesus' kingdom didn't look like much in the beginning. He spent his days and nights investing most of His time in a small band of unknowns whom others would have discarded for their lack of potential.

In launching His kingdom, Jesus truly used the smallest seed possible—including you and me. Like the disciples, we don't appear to have much potential.

But Jesus knows the transforming power of His presence in those who follow Him. Collectively, they become "the largest of all garden plants." Jesus sees into the future and knows from the beginning that He will have more followers than any person in the history of humanity.

What began as small will end as "a great multitude that no one could count, from every nation, tribe, people and language, standing before the throne and in front of the Lamb" (Revelation 7:9).

The mustard plant is a descriptive term for the church. And to that church come "the birds of the air." These birds aren't sinister beings as some commentators have falsely assumed. They are simply looking for a safe place to land, a place to rest in the shade from the boiling sun of life's burdens and searing sorrows.

That's what the church is meant to be—a refuge and safe place for all to find shelter and shade.

A Prayer

Lord Jesus, grow Your life in me. Help me to understand that even though I am small, Your power in me is great.

CAPACITY

With many similar parables Jesus spoke the word to them, as much as they could understand. He did not say anything to them without using a parable. But when he was alone with his own disciples, he explained everything.

MARK 4:33–34

TAKEN TOGETHER, Mark 4, Matthew 13, and Luke 8 give us nine of Jesus' parables explaining the nature of the kingdom of God.

All three Gospels record the parable about the sower and the seed. Matthew and Mark give us the story of the mustard seed. Mark and Luke relate the story of not putting a light under a bushel or bed. Mark alone records the parable of the growing seed, while Matthew alone records the stories of the weeds among the wheat, yeast that influences dough, hidden treasure in a field, a merchant looking for fine pearls, and the net of good and bad fish.

All these parables focus on the fact that Jesus' kingdom is not imposed externally but grows up from within; and that the kingdom or reign of God must be voluntarily received.

Mark admits that he is giving us the Reader's Digest condensed version when he summarizes, "With many similar parables Jesus spoke the word to them." Perhaps Mark should be the patron gospel writer for all who prefer to listen (or preach) shorter sermons: messages that don't dilute essence but still get the point across!

Notice Mark's phrase, "Jesus spoke *the word* . . ." Not *a* word, but *the* word. "Word" becomes crucial throughout the New Testament, culminating in the apostle Paul's admonition to Timothy, "Preach the Word" (2 Timothy 4:2). The Word is *the* message from God and therefore wholly reliable.

The Word is not our invention, it is God's revelation. It isn't the product of human reason, but neither is it contrary to reason. Living out God's Word in our daily lives makes us rational and self-controlled persons because we are thinking, talking, and doing as the Lord intended when He created us.

But how much of God's revelation can we take? Mark answers, "As much as they could understand."

In other words, Jesus could have given the crowds a whole lot more than they were able to absorb. He possessed all knowledge; therefore, He could have led them deeper. But you cannot fill a cup fuller than its capacity.

This forces us to think about our own spiritual growth. Do we limit Jesus' ability to pour truth into our lives because we have chosen not to enlarge our capacity? Have we shut off learning more of Him because we don't open His word, spend time waiting on Him in prayer, or share our faith with others?

Our capacity can expand. Peter's last written words tell us to "grow in the grace and knowledge of our Lord and Savior Jesus Christ" (2 Peter 3:18). Peter had a far greater capacity after three decades of serving Jesus than he did when he first heard the words recorded in Mark 4.

I love the phrase that describes growth in Christ: "You are expansible, and His gift is infinite. You are capable of receiving more, and He is capable of giving more."

Mark closes this section of the kingdom parables by reminding us that the crowds listened to the stories, but the disciples learned their meaning. It is always easier to listen than to truly "hear."

May we always want to be among those who press through to a deeper knowledge of and relationship with our Lord.

A Prayer

Lord Jesus, open my heart, my mind, and my spirit to receive You in ever greater measure. Increase my capacity to love, to know, and to have faith.

JUST AS HE WAS

That day when evening came, he said to his disciples, "Let us go over to the other side." Leaving the crowd behind, they took him along, just as he was, in the boat. There were also other boats with him.

MARK 4:35-36

ALL OF JESUS' MIRACLES can be grouped into four categories. The four miracles in this span of Mark illustrate Jesus' sphere of authority in these areas: (1) nature (calming the sea); (2) demons (the Gerasene demoniac); (3) illness (the woman with a bleeding condition); and (4) death (Jairus' daughter).

Not only are we taught by Jesus' words, we also learn from His actions.

Mark tells us that evening came as Jesus finished teaching at the lakeside (4:1, 35). Mark doesn't tell us the departure location, but we can assume it was somewhere along the northwestern side of the Lake of Galilee because they arrived later, after a terrific storm, on the eastern side (Mark 5:1; Luke 8:26).

We should note several things about these verses.

First, we all like security and ease. After a long day of teaching and dealing with the crowd—get me a hotel reservation, a comfortable room, a good dinner, and a hot shower. But Jesus wanted to keep going into the night hours. At necessary times, He keeps pushing us when we find it more comfortable and convenient to stop. We want rest; He wants action.

Wouldn't you rather be in a dangerous place if Christ is with you, than a safe place where He is absent?

Second, life often gets tougher before it gets better. The disciples were glad to get rid of the mass of people. It had been a long day of listening, learning, and crowd control. Now, they could get away and have peaceful moments in a boat, then dock later at some quiet spot along the shore.

You think you are getting out of one stress-filled situation and moving into a calmer time when, *wham*, you actually get hit with something worse! The disciples didn't know a violent storm and a crazed demoniac were next on their itinerary. Had they known, they wouldn't have been so glad to get away from the crowd.

Third, what does it mean: "They took him along, just as He was"? We normally think Jesus would take them rather than vice versa. But the disciples took one look at Jesus and knew He was exhausted. The proof of that comes when He sleeps soundly during the storm.

The disciples were protective of Jesus. Here is such a great example of the full humanity of Jesus—too tired to go further. Jesus was more tired than they, so the disciples made a transportation decision for Him.

We must never forget that Jesus carried a far heavier burden than we will ever be asked to carry. We will never be called to protect Jesus by placing Him in a boat; but we protect His reputation by the quality of our lives. Let the "Christ in you" always be the real Jesus and not the fractured or shattered image that so many non-Christians see in professed followers.

Finally, although "they took him," the other boats are described not as "being with them" but "with *him*." Why?

Writing from the perspective of decades later, Mark looks back on the story and subtly tells us that the others boats wanted to be close to Jesus. The disciples are mere accessories to the story. The star is always Jesus.

A Prayer

Lord Jesus, I know not whether a day holds calm or storm.
The one thing I need is You—just as You are—
no matter what the weather.

I'M SWAMPED, HE'S SLEEPING

A furious squall came up, and the waves broke over the boat, so that it was nearly swamped. Jesus was in the stern, sleeping on a cushion. The disciples woke him and said to him, "Teacher, don't you care if we drown?"

MARK 4:37–38

DANGER OFTEN RISES SUDDENLY. It would be nice if we could ride out storms in insulated watertight boats, but we sail life's seas in fragile vessels.

"All your waves broke over me," says the psalmist (42:7)—a true figurative description of our vulnerability in peril. The storm in Mark's text is not symbolic—it is real—yet it represents all the storms in life:

They are "furious"—it is not a mild adverse wind you are dealing with.

They "come up"—you don't see them until they hit.

The wind kicks up the waves—there is a cause-and-effect relationship between the primary trial (the squall) and its consequential impact (waves). For example, a serious illness can suddenly result in financial peril. Trials tend to come in bunches.

"Swamped" is how we feel—except the gospel term is "*nearly* swamped." The adverb *nearly* tells the disciples and us that no matter what the peril, we are never *completely* swamped. In the midst of wind and waves, it's easy to assume that we've been totally overcome. But the presence of the One with us is our protection in the midst of any storm.

The disciples initially missed this truth. They assumed that Christ's presence didn't make a difference in their nearly swamped boat. Our feelings often betray us. We forget that we are not alone, that He has promised, "I will never leave you."

Even when we acknowledge the Savior's presence, so often it appears that He is asleep in our storm.

In the gospel story, He was. If ever we have a picture of the humanity of Jesus it is here. He was dead tired—so exhausted that neither wind nor waves nor water swamping the boat disturbed Him.

He was asleep on a cushion or pillow—notice that! Only an eyewitness would include that kind of detail. Early Christian tradition says Mark wrote down what Peter preached. Thus, through Mark's words we see Peter's eyes remembering the pillow.

But the disciples reached a false conclusion. They assumed that since Jesus was sleeping He didn't care if they drowned. So they woke Him up. I doubt if they expected a miracle. I think they wanted one more hand to help them bail water.

Don't we do the same thing?

A fierce wind blows into our lives. We feel overwhelmed. Despite our best efforts, things only get worse. Our frail attempts at stability and safety gain us nothing. We are losing the battle.

We go to the Lord in prayer. We find Him "sleeping." We don't sense an answer. How can He remain silent when we're in so much trouble? Our first inclination is to jump to the conclusion: "Lord, you don't care!"

So we offer our own solutions to Him: "Grab a bucket and help me bail water." We don't see it at the time, but His inaction in the present moment will provide a superior solution than what we proposed. It may take time to see it.

It is better for us to have the Savior sleeping in our boat than for us to sail along without Him. His presence in the storm will ultimately make all the difference!

A Prayer

Lord Jesus, help me not to believe that "You're not here" or "You don't care." May I not impose my solutions during my own time of desperation but trust You even when You appear to be doing nothing.

GREAT PEACE

He got up, rebuked the wind and said to the waves, "Quiet!" Be still!" Then the wind died down and it was completely calm.

MARK 4:39

DAVID CRIED PLAINTIVELY, "May God arise, may his enemies be scattered" (Psalm 68:1).

It is certainly what we cry when we want our circumstances changed—"Arise, O Lord. Can't You do something about my situation?"

In Mark's story of the storm at sea, the disciples cried out and the Lord did arise. He got up. The urgent shaking and pleading of the disciples to "wake up" stirred Him from His slumber. "We're swamped!" they said.

Isn't that how you feel on occasion? God is sleeping and you are screaming!

The eternal and universal lesson, however, is that He always hears. He always gets up—although sometimes we are disappointed by His inaction or surprised at His action.

The disciples were surprised. It is completely logical to believe that all they wanted was for Jesus to help them bail water out of the boat. They had never seen Him calm a storm. I doubt their faith had grown mature enough to think that if He could heal a paralytic, He could also calm a storm.

If ever a miracle showed Jesus as Creator, this one certainly qualifies. He who spoke the universe into existence commanded the elements with His voice. I can't get my own dog to obey me—let alone wind and waves. But there's a receptor in nature that knows and responds to the voice of the Master.

No storm lasts forever, and no storm blows at the same time over all the earth. All storms are limited both by geography and duration. But when they come, it is with ferocity and surprise.

Our problem is that we don't feel we can outlast our own localized storm, whether illness, abandonment, financial reverses, loss of a job or a friend, or the death of a loved one. That's surely how the disciples and those in the boats nearby felt—they were going to perish before the storm ended.

On a normal night, conversation can flow freely across the water boat to boat, but not in a storm. That's life. On calm days relationships flow freely, and we stay in easy communication with those around us. Yet, in storms, the words blow back in our faces, and we feel that it is useless to even try to communicate. The fury of the moment deafens all speech and hearing.

Jesus spoke. The winds and waves ceased. The older translations put it better, "Peace, be still!"

Would that all storms in life ended as quickly! But they don't. Look at another storm, one of hurricane force that raged for two weeks. It's recorded in Acts 27. In the end, the ship wrecked and cast the apostle Paul onto the beach. Why is one storm quieted and not the other? We may never figure out the answer this side of heaven.

But the Lord can give us peace from the storm or peace in the storm. You can have His peace no matter what the circumstance. The apostle Paul, writing from prison to the Philippians, assures us that peace is available at all times: "And the peace of God, which transcends all understanding, will guard your hearts and your minds in Christ Jesus" (4:7).

A Prayer

Help me, Lord Jesus, to know that I can trust fully in You. There is no storm that outlasts You, and You will either make my storm subside or carry me safely through it.

QUESTIONS

He said to his disciples, "Why are you so afraid? Do you still have no faith?" They were terrified and asked each other, "Who is this? Even the wind and the waves obey him!"

MARK 4:40–41

I WILL NEVER FORGET the first time I preached from this text. It was my senior year in seminary and I had been selected by the faculty to give the last chapel sermon of the year.

I broke this entire storm-at-sea story into three parts: (1) high winds—the adversities of life that arise quite suddenly; (2) desperate voices—the panic we feel in the storm; and (3) an unexpected word—Jesus speaks to the circumstances, "Peace!" and a word of rebuke to the disciples for their lack of faith.

When I finished I was filled with pride. I thought I had preached a masterpiece and even made a few listeners seasick with my soaring rhetoric about the wind and the waves.

All that ended when Dr. Everett Harrison, my New Testament professor, walked over to me and kindly said, "George, that's always been a favorite passage of mine. Have you noticed (I hadn't!) that perhaps the reason Jesus accused them of 'no faith' was that at the beginning He had said, 'Let's go to the other side'? In the middle of the storm they forgot His word. When we forget the word of Jesus, we will always be afraid."

In his gracious way, Dr. Harrison told me that I had preached for twenty-five minutes and missed the main point. I have never forgotten it since.

You will always be afraid when you forget the promise, the word of Jesus.

At least the disciples might have had some faith—but they had *no* faith. They weren't able to transpose Jesus' past acts into a faith that trusted Him to deal with this new emergency.

Isn't that like us? The Lord brings us through one trial, and when we hit the next one, we panic all over again. We fail to transfer the lesson that if He didn't abandon us in the past, He won't leave us now.

The disciples didn't answer Jesus' question, "Why have you no faith?" Instead they asked a question of their own, "Who is this?"

For the first time, they were afraid of Jesus. More than afraid—terrified!

They didn't fear Him during the storm—they awakened Him, as though He was just a lazy passenger unwilling to help them bail water. His presence wasn't making a difference in their situation, or so they thought.

In the wake of His miracle, they no longer regarded Him as ordinary. Even here we can learn from their example: It is far better to be terrified of Jesus than to treat Him as just another person.

This is the One who has power alone to grant eternal life, to raise the dead, to forgive sins, and to present us to the Majesty on High! He is the One alone who will lift us out of time and space into God's heaven. Do we have any idea of the magnitude of His power?

Our greatest danger is assuming Jesus has no power to help or save us; the greatest reality is that He does!

A Prayer

*Teach me, Lord, to fear You—not with fear that cowers
as a victim thrashed by a bully; but with fear that comes
from a healthy respect for Your power. Help me to see that
You are greater than my mind can ever embrace.*

LIFE'S SURPRISING TWISTS

They went across the lake to the region of the Gerasenes. When Jesus got out of the boat, a man with an evil spirit came from the tombs to meet him.

MARK 5:1–2

SOMETIMES YOU END UP at a place you didn't plan to go. It was that way with the disciples. On the northwestern corner of the Lake of Galilee, Jesus had said, "Let us go over to the other side" (4:35). They probably figured they could hug the shoreline, sail a few miles, and then end up on the northeastern edge of the lake where a number of them had their homes, Bethsaida.

But the wind blew them off course, and they hit the shore several miles southeast of Bethsaida, at Gerasa (or Gadara).

I have been blown off course myself a few times in life.

I graduated from seminary in California at the age of twenty-three. I was single and didn't know how I could "break in" to a ministerial position. The only thing I could land was a ten-week job as a youth counselor at a camp in the Poconos of Pennsylvania. I had no idea what I would do after that post.

I wrote a string of pastors between California and Pennsylvania, asking if I could show Teen Challenge movies in their churches and preach. A few responded positively, and I laid out an itinerary for my VW Beetle that took me in a zigzag fashion from the West Coast to Wyoming, down to Kansas and Arkansas, and up through Indiana and Ohio. One of the churches cancelled just before I set out, forcing me to reroute through Springfield, Missouri.

I drove onto the campus of my alma mater, Evangel University, and walked down to the dean's office to say hello. He looked at me and asked me if I wanted to teach that fall. I immediately agreed, and he hired me.

I came to work that fall, promptly met my wife, and the rest is history. The family I have today and the ministry I do all proceeded from an unwelcome cancellation. Thank God for closed doors. It means He's opening a door you don't see!

A lifelong direction resulted from a course correction I didn't engineer.

Sometimes Jesus takes us to places we didn't intend to go. We prefer to go, as did the disciples, to a familiar place where we know our friends and family. But we find ourselves in places we have never been, working in situations we did not choose, or living in a neighborhood not of our choosing.

It must have been a shock when the disciples found themselves in Gerasene land. It's likewise a shock when we find ourselves where we had no intention of going or wished we didn't have to remain.

But on the other side of the lake was a person who needed the Lord's help. From the shoreline, that man had watched the boat draw near. Then he raced to the water line to welcome Jesus.

The incident became a life lesson for the disciples. Contrary winds would sometimes take them where they had no intention of going, but the Lord knew someone desperately needed their presence, help, and the good news they carried.

A Prayer

Lord Jesus, You direct my itinerary and Your stops often surprise me. I ask, "Why did You take me here?" But if You landed me here it's because You have someone who needs me. Help me to be content today where I am.

TORMENTED

This man lived in the tombs, and no one could bind him any more, not even with a chain. For he had often been chained hand and foot, but he tore the chains apart and broke the irons on his feet. No one was strong enough to subdue him. Night and day among the tombs and in the hills he would cry out and cut himself with stones. When he saw Jesus from a distance, he ran and fell on his knees in front of him.

MARK 5:3–6

CEMETERIES ARE NOT NATURAL habitats for living people. This man lived among the tombs. He was deranged, possessed of evil spirits. He had no control over his life.

Unfortunately, he isn't the only one. Our society is full of people out of control with eating disorders, dependencies on and addictions to alcohol, drugs, sexual deviancy, pornography, or a host of other things—including demon possession. Try as hard as they might, they cannot seem to break the hold of what has hold of them. But Jesus goes to people living in "tombs" of their own making.

I'm sure on that night the disciples would rather have avoided this meeting. I know I would. Take me to people I'm comfortable with, please!

The demoniac's bondage had been of substantial duration, since he had "often" been bound. Given his wild behavior, it had taken several persons to clasp the chains on his feet. These attempts at restraint proved unsuccessful; thus we meet him wandering among the tombs, isolated from the living.

You hear his torment in the gut cries from the depths of his being. And he's a "cutter"—a not-too-infrequent practice today among young people with emotional pain so great they cut themselves.

This man was past human hope. He represents all who live

in deathful places of body and spirit. Everyone had given up on helping him. The best they could do was to tie him down or chain him up. Deliverance was out of the question because he was undeliverable.

He was strong enough to break the chains but not strong enough to free himself. Perhaps you know someone like that.

Or could that also be you? Despite your best efforts to break a bondage, you are still not free. You try and fail. You ask for forgiveness but then repeat the conduct that devastates you on the inside. You wish someone could help you, but no one can.

Then notice what this possessed man did. He saw Jesus from a distance.

The Pharisees saw Jesus close up but didn't really *see* Him. Here was a man written off by society, controlled by powers he could not tame. However, there was one thing he could control—the direction he would move when Jesus came into view.

You have freedom either to run to Jesus or away from Him. At a far distance, there may not be much of Jesus you can see. He had no firsthand knowledge of what Jesus had already done for others.

But he saw in Jesus the prospect of hope, the prospect of a better day.

Inherently, he recognized the magnitude of Jesus and fell on his knees—a proper posture for one meeting the Lord of All.

If you are tormented, start heading toward Jesus. You will encounter Him because He is already headed toward you.

A Prayer

Lord Jesus, I bring to you any out-of-control aspect in my life. I desperately need Your help. I throw myself, Lord, at your feet for I know You will deliver me.

LEGION

He shouted at the top of his voice, "What do you want with me, Jesus, Son of the Most High God? Swear to God that you won't torture me!" For Jesus was saying to him, "Come out of this man, you evil spirit!" Then Jesus asked him, "What is your name?" "My name is Legion," he replied, "for we are many." And he begged Jesus again and again not to send them out of the area.

MARK 5:7–10

WHAT MAKES YOU AFRAID?

I can tell you what scares the Devil—Jesus. Hell's dominions panic in the presence of the Lord. You see it here.

The first words Jesus spoke to Legion form a command, "Come out." The demons knew they had to obey His authority, but they were afraid that torture waited if they obeyed.

Many write off demon possession as an antiquated notion and a misdiagnosis for schizophrenia or other mental illnesses. The Great Physician knew the difference. The problem with the Gerasene man lay not within his own mind; rather, evil spirits from the outside had gotten inside him. A physician must make an accurate diagnosis if there is to be a remedy. Jesus knew exactly the problem.

This man had knowledge of Jesus' identity. Thus far, in Jesus' ministry, no one except demons knew who He was. A mentally disturbed person wouldn't know that.

Jesus didn't negotiate by telling the spirits to settle down and let the man live a normal life. Nor did Jesus treat the evil spirits like a petulant teenager, "Now, I'll give you an hour to clean up your act."

The order was, "Out! Now!" There is no compromise in dealing with evil spirits. Eviction is the only cure.

It's the same in the later instruction from James: "Resist the devil and he will flee from you" (James 4:7). Don't equivocate with the Devil or listen to his lie that you can't take authority over him.

Jesus didn't get into a discussion with the evil spirits. He didn't ask for details about where they came from, how they got into the man, or what other special knowledge they might have had. He didn't inquire about any past encounters He might have had with the Devil and his minions before the earth was formed. Jesus' focus was on the practical, not the mystical.

There's only one thing that needs to be known: Jesus has power over evil. Period.

These demons totally destroyed the quality of life this man could have enjoyed. That's the Devil's business. He comes like a thief to steal, kill, and destroy—but Jesus has come that we might have life and have it to the full (John 10:10).

Clearly the demons feared Jesus since they didn't want to be tortured, and they feared the unknown since they didn't want to be sent out of the area. Evidently, demons don't have much room to roam. Their fear of dislocation was so great that the demon doing the speaking begged "again and again."

The reluctance of demons to go outside their area is in direct contrast to the end of Mark when Jesus tells His disciples to "go into all the world." Part of that worldwide mission involves driving out demons (Mark 16:15–18).

The contrast is striking. Demons stay in localized areas while Christ's disciples have traveled the world with the gospel. Followers of Jesus are willing to go outside their comfort zones to share with others the good news about Jesus—that He is the Son of God, our Savior.

A Prayer

Lord Jesus, help me in dealing with temptation and evil. Send me away from my own comfort zones, and let me not be afraid to go wherever You might send me.

JESUS AND THE DEMONS

A large herd of pigs was feeding on the nearby hillside. The demons begged Jesus, "Send us among the pigs; allow us to go into them." He gave them permission, and the evil spirits came out and went into the pigs. The herd, about two thousand in number, rushed down the steep bank into the lake and were drowned.

MARK 5:11–13

WHAT KIND OF FOOD do pigs eat? Garbage! It had to be the town dump.

Now you have a more complete picture of the setting. The demoniac man lived in the cemetery next to the town dump. Not the kind of place to build a multi-million-dollar home.

But society always casts its most unwanted into stinky places—whether it's the slums of Calcutta or a homeless hotel in Anytown.

Jesus goes where decent and normal people don't—out where the deranged live among tombs and an army of pigs roots around in the town dump. Oh yes, Jesus goes as well to the homes of the rich (as with Zaachaeus), but He also comes to the desolate, the cast-offs, to the broken people living in awful places.

The demons knew they had to leave the man. The only two alternatives were destruction ("Have you come to destroy us?") or permission to enter pigs. Unstated in the text is that the demons themselves didn't ask for deliverance from their condition. If they were fallen angels, as some believe, then their plight was irreversible. That in itself constitutes a solemn warning for all human beings—the choice we make in this life about Christ has eternal, irreversible ramifications.

The Lord granted the demons' request by letting them enter the herd of swine. It was an impressive number: 2,000 pigs. The disciples must have stood agape as they watched the herd running into the Lake of Galilee and drowning.

The incident shows the tremendous power of the demons. Just a moment before, they all resided in the man, and now they disperse into the pigs. What does that tell us?

The Devil destroys. The demons disintegrated the personality of the man they possessed, and they stampeded to death the swine. The Devil and his legions cause personality disorder and all manner of devastation. On the other hand, Jesus delivers and makes whole.

As a boy I listened one day to an evangelist on the radio who said, "I'm going to cast out a demon and if you're not right with God it's going to enter you."

I was scared spitless.

If you study the ministry of Jesus carefully, you'll observe that He never permitted a demon to leave one person and enter another. Demons were always cast out. The only time they were permitted to enter flesh was here—into the pigs.

The good news of this story is that no demon or bondage can successfully resist the delivering power of Jesus. He has given us His authority to cast out demons. We must be so full of the Spirit that evil has to let go its grip when we pray for those who, like this demoniac man, want to be free from the bondages of demons, drugs, or whatever holds them captive.

A Prayer

Lord Jesus, I know that You have power over all evil—including any evil in me. Thank You for both freeing me from the grip of the Devil and empowering me with the Holy Spirit to live for You.

PIGS OR PEOPLE?

> *Those tending the pigs ran off and reported this in the town and countryside, and the people went out to see what had happened. When the people came to Jesus, they saw the man who had been possessed by the legion of demons, sitting there, dressed and in his right mind; and they were afraid. Those who had seen it told the people what had happened to the demon-possessed man—and told about the pigs as well. Then the people began to plead with Jesus to leave their region.*
>
> MARK 5:14–17

PIG HERDERS WERE AT THE BOTTOM of the totem pole socially and economically. The Gerasene herders not only had to tend the swine but also keep watch over the crazy demoniac man who lived nearby—perhaps on the next hill.

It's a wonder the demoniac had not already stampeded the pig herd just by the wildness of his roaming and yelling.

After Jesus' miraculous deliverance of the demoniac, these pig tenders ran off into the town and countryside—to the small pockets of population. With a huge herd of 2,000 pigs to watch over, it's a safe assumption that the herd was a community mutual fund. Many had an interest in the well-being of their animal investment.

So the owners came looking for their pigs and saw the man instead. Mark notes he was "dressed"—the assumption being that prior to his deliverance he was naked or disheveled.

And he was sitting! What joy he must have felt to have physical control of his own body. Before deliverance, he had been restless and tormented—unable to control his own actions. Just as Jesus had earlier brought peace to the wind and waves, He had given peace to a fractured soul.

The reaction of the people was twofold: first fear, and then rejection.

The fear of Jesus didn't lead the crowd to reverence Christ or bow down in worship. They quavered in the face of Jesus' power but ignored the evidence of Jesus' love in bringing the man to wholeness.

Surprisingly, they rejected Jesus. They told Him to get out of town. Why?

Suppose they had an election and could only vote for one: keep their pigs or restore the wild man to wellness. How do you suppose they would have voted?

Jesus knew; that's why He let the pig herd be destroyed. He knew this community valued property more than people. The citizens of Gerasa focused on what they had lost, not on what they had gained. Their own wallets had been hit so they couldn't rejoice that a person had been restored to humanity.

The Gerasenes were neither the first nor the last to make this kind of choice.

We see these same values at work later in the life of the early church. What happened when a demon-possessed fortune-telling slave girl was delivered at Philippi? Her owners seized Paul and Silas and had them flogged and thrown into prison (Acts 16). The same phenomenon was repeated on a larger scale when the gospel came with such power at Ephesus that the major industry of the town, idol making, was practically put out of business—the idol industry workers rioted (Acts 19).

Whenever we put our possessions above the well-being of people, we—like the Gerasenes, the slave owners of Philippi, or the idol makers of Ephesus—will be sending Jesus on His way.

A Prayer

Lord Jesus, help me to keep a loose grip on my wallet so that I might keep a tight grip on the hands of those I love and those whom You died to save.

ZOOM OUT, ZOOM IN

As Jesus was getting in the boat, the man who had been demon-possessed begged to go with him. Jesus did not let him, but said, "Go home to your family and tell them how much the Lord has done for you, and how he has had mercy on you." So the man went away and began to tell in the Decapolis how much Jesus had done for him. And all the people were amazed.

MARK 5:18–20

THE CITIZENS OF GERASA begged Jesus to leave (v. 17), but the delivered man begged to go with Jesus. So who is in their right mind now? You are only in your right mind when you want to be with Jesus!

Jesus, however, had other plans for the man. He was to go home and tell his family how much the Lord had done for him.

We don't know if the man had a wife and children or if "family" refers to extended relatives. What we do know is that he had a family at home while he had been living out of control among the tombs.

Jesus called other disciples to leave their homes but not this one. Why? It's reasonable to assume that his separation from family had been long and difficult. What joy to be restored to them after such a horrendous absence!

Perhaps you are one whom Jesus has delivered, or you belong to a family that welcomed home a member whom Jesus set free from alcohol, drugs, or bondage of any kind. Jesus came to set the captive free.

The man is not only called to go home but also to tell "how much the Lord has done for [him] and had mercy on [him]." Early on, Jesus called Himself Lord of the Sabbath (3:24). Now, for the first time, Jesus calls Himself "Lord" without any modifier.

The word *Lord* demonstrates authority, but when Jesus first used the term for Himself, He linked it with mercy. "The Lord . . .

has had mercy." We learn from this that Jesus uses His power not to impress but to relieve suffering. How wonderful that our Lord is not only moved by our infirmities but has power to help us!

The account of this miracle ends with the man going well beyond his own family to tell his testimony. The Decapolis consisted of ten Gentile cities, nine of which were east of the Jordan. It was the first time the good news of Jesus was to reach non-Jewish audiences. It's a tip off of what's to come when the disciples go into all the world to proclaim the gospel.

Notice that the man is never named. But compare Mark's account with that of Matthew (8:28–34). You'll see two key differences.

The first is inconsequential: two different names, Gerasa or Gadara—similar to a city in Poland like Gdansk that also bore the name Danzig. Same place, just different names.

The second difference: Matthew notes there were two demoniacs, while Mark mentions only one. What's going on?

If you've used a zoom lens you know. Matthew zooms out to focus on two while Mark zooms in on the one. Why? Matthew leaves out the account of the man going into the Decapolis. Mark tells us the story of the one man because of what happened after he was delivered. Only the one man begged to go with Jesus. And only the one man went out and talked about Jesus everywhere.

A Prayer

Lord Jesus, You have done so much for me. May I be like the man who not only received Your mercy but went out and told others all You had done for him!

A DESPERATE DAD

> *When Jesus had again crossed over by boat to the other side of the lake, a large crowd gathered around him. While he was by the lake, then one of the synagogue rulers, named Jairus, came there. Seeing Jesus, he fell at his feet and pleaded earnestly with him, "My little daughter is dying. Please come and put your hands on her so that she will be healed and live."*
>
> MARK 5:21–23

I WONDER IF THE DISCIPLES were afraid to get into a boat again with Jesus. A fierce storm almost sank them the last time they sailed (4:35–41). But this time there was fair weather. Life is like that, isn't it? Sometimes, terrible peril, and other times, quiet calm.

If the disciples had been hoping for some time off, they were in for a disappointment. A large crowd awaited their arrival. We can assume Jesus was at the outskirts of Capernaum, His new home town, based on the description of events in Matthew 9:1–26.

It was in the synagogue at Capernaum where Jesus delivered the demoniac (1:21–28). Jairus was one of the leaders in that same synagogue. No doubt he would have been present for the healings in the street after Sabbath ended at sunset (1:32–28). He would have been aware of the paralytic who had been healed after being dropped through the roof (2:1–12); perhaps Jairus was in the house.

Certainly Jairus knew the criticism against Jesus—that He claimed to forgive sins, which only God can do (2:7), and that He healed a man with a shriveled hand on the Sabbath, most likely an event that took place also in the Capernaum synagogue (3:1–6).

I wonder if Jairus had been on the fence regarding Jesus. However, desperate need will drive you to wherever you can get help. So, this dad comes to Jesus.

A DESPERATE DAD

Jairus is only one of a handful of miracle recipients ever named in the Gospels. Why? Perhaps he went on to become a prominent member of the early church; perhaps his daughter became known in the Christian community and shared in many places her own testimony of Jesus' raising her up when she was a girl.

We do know for sure that Jairus came with great humility, falling at Jesus' feet. He made a request of Jesus that no one else had made—namely, that Jesus put his hands on his sick daughter. To this point in Mark, the only times Jesus had touched the sick had been when He took the hand of Peter's mother-in-law (1:31) and when He was moved with compassion for the leper (1:41). Most likely, Jairus had seen Jesus heal by laying on His hands in contexts not reported in the Gospels.

The key element in all this is that Jairus had faith. Based on the miracles he had either witnessed personally or had heard about through others—the miracles in his own synagogue and town—he had faith to believe that what Jesus did for others, He could also do for his extremely sick daughter.

Jairus had no doubt that if Jesus would only come, his girl would be healed and live.

How desperate are you for the Lord's help in your life? Are you willing, like Jairus, to fall on your knees and plead for help?

A Prayer

Lord Jesus, I so easily disconnect Your past kindness from the possibility of Your present provision. In every new crisis, help me to come to You with faith for my need.

A DESPERATE WOMAN

So Jesus went with him [Jairus]. A large crowd followed and pressed around him. And a woman was there who had been subject to bleeding for twelve years. She had suffered a great deal under the care of many doctors and had spent all she had, yet instead of getting better she grew worse.

MARK 5:24–26

JAIRUS, A RULER of the synagogue, pleaded with Jesus to come to his home and heal his dying daughter. Jesus responded to the emergency. Whatever His plans were for that day, they were laid aside. Jairus had made a 911 call, and Jesus answered—not with words but with deeds, for "he went with him."

But there was an impediment—much like an ambulance trying to thread its way down a narrow street blocked by traffic on all sides. This time, however, the traffic jam came not from automobiles but from people. The crowd not only followed but "pressed around him"—that is to say, they were in the back, at the sides, and in front of Him. A circle of humanity pressed in to see Him, touch Him, and cry out to Him.

It was a slow-motion dream for Jairus. He was in a hurry to get Jesus to his little girl. That's how we feel sometimes: "Hurry up, Jesus. I'm desperate. Come to my home right now. Fly up over the crowd and all the things You're tending to and come to my aid."

As desperate as your need is, others are equally desperate. Mark's camera zooms in on a woman in the crowd. Like Jairus, she was in great distress.

We know from later in the story that Jairus' daughter was twelve years old. The desperate woman lived in a parallel universe in which she had suffered for twelve years. While the little girl was growing up in a privileged home, the woman had been isolated through her ritual impurity. No doubt others blamed her and said she was sick because there was sin in her life or she didn't have faith.

We do know her life savings had been exhausted on medical care and she had only grown worse. Dr. Luke, in defense of the medical establishment, noted that "no one could heal her" (Luke 8:35). In other words, no physician had a remedy for her condition. You can only imagine the despair in this woman as, year after year, she dealt with the false hopes raised at the beginning of each new treatment with each new specialist, and then renewed depression when the treatment ended and the disease was worse.

For twelve years she had chased a cure. Medical costs then, as now, were expensive. To preserve her life, she gradually divested herself of all her assets and, in doing so, had lost both wealth and health.

The magnificent thing about her, however, is that despite her suffering, despite spending all she had in seeking a cure, despite getting worse rather than better—she still hadn't given up!

That's the state we find her in when she presses through the crowd toward Jesus.

When you suffer for a long time, it's the easiest thing in the world to throw in the towel, to say, "I'm defeated." This woman could have remained in her house, bolted the door, shuttered the blinds, and said, "Life's over. I'm done."

We learn from her example. No matter how many setbacks you have experienced—never give up, never give in. Jesus is passing your way today.

A Prayer

Lord Jesus, the easier thing for me to do is throw up my hands and quit. I get discouraged, Lord, when the harder I try the worse I get. Help me never to give up.

THINKING, SAYING, DOING

When she heard about Jesus, she came up behind him in the crowd and touched his cloak, because she thought, "If I just touch his clothes, I will be healed." Immediately her bleeding stopped and she felt in her body that she was freed from her suffering.

MARK 5:27-29

IT WAS A DEFINITE NO-NO. She had no business being out in public. According to the Law, everyone she touched became ritually impure, thereby requiring them to take an inconvenient "time out" for isolation and cleansing before they could return to normal life (Leviticus 15:25-27).

There was a crush of people around Jesus, and she "contaminated" them all as she pressed through the crowd. But Jesus had also been breaking the ritual rules in violating the Sabbath by casting out a demon (1:21-28); permitting His disciples to pluck grain (2:23-28); and healing (3:1-6).

The lesson is simple: Religious rules are made to be broken when they get in the way of helping people, when they violate the law of love. Jesus broke the legalistic rules. So did this woman. Those rules would have barred her from approaching Jesus.

Clearly she was concerned about His reaction to being "defiled" since she came up on Him from behind.

It's interesting to compare Mark and Matthew's accounts. Matthew reports, "She said to herself, 'If only I touch...'" (Matthew 9:27), while Mark notes "she thought..."

What you say is what you think; and what you think is what you say.

This lady could have been thinking a lot of other things. Her focus could have been on the discouragements of the past, all the suffering she endured from her doctors, and her exhausted bank account. She could have been thinking that she might as well stay home and die.

But when she heard Jesus was passing by, she thought, *If I can just get to Him I'll be well.* And as she thought it, she said it. She was not going to give up. And once she said it, she did it—she got up and went toward Jesus.

She represents all who don't give up on life, even in the most hopeless and negative circumstances. For twelve years, the battle in her body never let up, but she didn't give in to the disease and become a hopeless and negative person. Her thinking and her self-talk got her up off the couch and into the street.

She approached Jesus from behind, pushing her way through the people pressed around Him. The moment she touched His cloak, her bleeding stopped.

Not only that, but "she felt in her body that she was freed from her suffering." The illness had brought more than physical impairment, isolation, and declining health. Suffering overarched it all. In that moment of time when she touched Jesus, not only did her body recover but her whole life as well.

When you are sick for an extended season, your suffering is far more than the physical ravaging of your body. It can be spiritual, as in "Why, God, have You not come through for me?" Or relational, as in "My family has moved on and left me here." Or psychological, as in "I'm no good to anyone anymore."

This woman had borne sickness and sorrow but had never let it crush her spirit. She didn't let her illness corrupt her thought life or make her a whining "poor me." Her attitude and self-talk paved the way out of her suffering.

A Prayer

Lord Jesus, I come to You today with my own suffering. Through prayer, I touch You today with faith in my heart, knowing that You will help me.

THE TOUCH AND THE FRUSTRATION

At once Jesus realized that power had gone out from him. He turned around in the crowd and asked, "Who touched my clothes?" "You see the people crowding against you," his disciples answered, "and yet you can ask, 'Who touched me?'"

MARK 5:30–31

CLEARLY THE DISCIPLES were exasperated with Jesus. Look at the scenario they have been through within the preceding twenty-four hours:

- Dealing with the crowd who listened to His parables (4:1, 36);
- Battling a night storm on the lake while Jesus slept (4:37–38);
- Landing off-course at the shore of Gerasa rather than their home in Bethsaida (5:1, compare with 6:45);
- Witnessing an encounter with the demoniac and spending a good part of the day waiting while a crowd gathered to see what happened and ask Jesus to leave—all of which took place after a sleepless night on the storm waters (5:2–20);
- Returning to the northwest side of the lake and immediately dealing with a crowd again, precluding retreat and rest (5:21);
- Changing itinerary again when Jesus is diverted by Jairus' request to come and heal his dying daughter (5:22–23).

Now a woman sneaks up on Jesus, and they haven't even been aware of her. They have no clue that she has touched Jesus and has ritually defiled them in the process. No power had gone out from them, for they were at that point powerless.

They were exhausted. No sleep. No decent warm food. No bathroom accommodations. No chance to wash up. They really want to get isolated for a while, have a sumptuous meal, and catch some sleep. And they are frustrated with Jesus—even more so than when they accusatorily awakened Him when their boat was sinking (4:38). Now, they are downright snapping at Him: "And yet you ask, 'Who touched me?'"

The lesson? When you're tired, hungry, and frustrated you get cranky and you don't see things rightly. Clearly, the disciples were ticked at Jesus. "Who touched me?" *Everyone, Jesus, everyone!* they thought. *How could You ask such a stupid question?*

We're a lot like His original followers. We, too, get upset with His agenda. He often takes us where we don't want to go, keeps us where we don't want to stay, and sometimes in our pain and exhaustion, we become oblivious to the needs of others. So we snap at Him or anyone else for inconveniencing us.

Jesus asked the question, "Who touched me?" because He knew something had happened. This is the first involuntary miracle of Jesus—it happened not with His face toward the person but when He was not even aware of the individual's approach, with His back turned.

The woman's faith had literally vacuumed the power out of Him, or like a dry sponge had soaked out all the water.

So what group do you belong to?

The woman who approached Jesus with faith, or the disciples who complained because things weren't going the way they wanted or expected?

If you follow Jesus for any length of time, His actions or inactions will at times baffle you. You just can't figure out why He is doing what He is doing, or why He allows to happen what is going on.

You don't have to figure Him out. Keep touching Him rather than griping about where He's taking you. Relax. He knows what He's doing.

A Prayer

Lord Jesus, teach me Your way so that as I touch others they may be strengthened rather than withered.

THE WHOLE TRUTH

But Jesus kept looking around to see who had done it. Then the woman, knowing what had happened to her, came and fell at his feet and, trembling with fear, told him the whole truth.

MARK 5:32-33

THIS IS THE THIRD TIME in Mark that Jesus "looked around." In the synagogue, He ordered the man with the withered hand to stand up. Some in the crowd were looking for a reason to accuse Jesus for healing on the Sabbath, and Jesus asked them whether it was lawful to do good or evil on that day. When they were silent, Jesus "looked around at them in anger . . . deeply distressed at their stubborn hearts" (3:5).

The second time Mark records Jesus looking around comes in 3:34-35 when His mother and brothers are on the outside and He looks around at those seated in a circle about Him and exclaims, "Here are my mother and my brothers! Whoever does God's will is my brother and sister and mother."

We can summarize: The first "look around" shows Jesus with steady eye contact sweeping each individual in the synagogue when He is angry and distressed. The second steady eye contact comes as He speaks foundational truth of the kingdom—that membership in the kingdom results not from bloodlines but from obedience.

Here, with the bleeding woman, Jesus looks around once more. But this time He isn't eyeballing the crowd with anger or instruction, but with compassion. He looks to find who touched Him.

Evidently some time elapsed from the moment Jesus asked, "Who touched me?" to the moment when the woman fell at His feet and told her story. How do we know that? Because He kept looking around while the disciples asked Him why He even asked the question, given the press of people around Him.

The woman delayed. Why? Her trembling shows us. She was afraid. Why did she fear? Because she knew she had ritually defiled Jesus. Could it be the deeper fear was that she would lose the healing because she had offended Him by touching the tassel of His garment?

She knew she had been healed. Perhaps she was tempted just to melt away into the crowd and not risk losing what she had sought for twelve years—relief from her suffering and healing from her disease. Her fear arose from her concern that she had gravely offended Him.

She was shaking as she fell at Jesus' feet. What happens, though, when we tell Jesus the truth?

Are you afraid that if you told Him everything going on in your life that He would also turn you away? What if you were to tell Jesus, as this woman did, "the whole truth"?

The good news of Jesus is that He already knows the whole truth and still loves you, accepts you, saves you, and heals you. It really is amazing, isn't it?

Jesus wants us to come to Him with "the whole truth" so that we can live in His light and realize that no matter what we tell Him it will not change in the least His love for us.

Just as with the woman in this story, He will not withdraw His healing or salvation when we pour out the entire story.

A Prayer

Thank You, Lord, that even though You know everything about me, You still love me and You bring health and healing into my life.

FAITH, NOT MAGIC

*He said to her, "Daughter, your faith has healed you.
Go in peace and be freed from your suffering."*

MARK 5:34

MATTHEW, MARK, AND LUKE all record that Jesus addressed the woman as "daughter." He never used the title "daughter" for anyone except this woman who had suffered a bleeding condition for twelve years.

If He had called her by the title of "mother" we could assume she was older than He was (in terms of His earthly life). If "sister," then the same age range. But "daughter" conveys the sense of being younger.

Had she suffered from this bleeding condition since puberty? If she was a young woman, it rearranges our idea of this event, for it shows a woman in her early to mid-twenties who had exhausted all her resources, knew she was getting worse, and had lost all hope but one.

She had lost faith in doctors—and anyway, they had given up on her health. Her cure lay beyond their expertise.

Perhaps her condition prevented her from being married; or if married, kept her from having children.

Or it could be that "daughter" is just a term of endearment from Jesus to her, and the word may have been much on His mind as He wended His way through the crowded and narrow streets to Jairus' little girl.

The woman's wealth and health were exhausted. She was spent in every way. This moment, when Jesus came passing by, was her last hope. She pressed through the crowd to touch His clothes, thinking that in doing so some power in Him would radiate out to her.

Jesus immediately let her know that it wasn't the magical touching of His garment that had brought the healing.

Uninformed or misinformed faith often attaches itself to some talisman of hope: "If I can just brush up against this holy artifact, or get to this shrine, or have a point of contact with this person who claims power—then my miracle will also come." That's misplaced faith.

Jesus let her know that He understood the attitude that caused her to touch His clothes—the attitude of faith. He took the time to help her understand that her healing didn't result from some act of magic, the touching of His garment, but from what she believed. Her healing wasn't the result of magic but of faith.

By transferring the source of her miracle to her own faith, Jesus diminished His role. He simply could have said, "I healed you." Surely she knew that, but He wanted her to know that His action couldn't have taken place without her action.

A friend of mine who prays regularly for the sick and has witnessed many healings said to me, "If we don't pray for healing, there's a 100 percent chance none will occur."

Jesus told the woman to go in peace and that she was freed from her suffering. He removed any doubt or anxiety that the healing was only momentary or that it was illusory. He assured her that the repair in her body was permanent. She was free to live to the fullest.

The loving concern Jesus showed for the one He called "daughter" is no different than the loving care Jesus has for you.

A Prayer

Lord Jesus, I reach out today to touch You in faith.
Your gentle word comes also to me, "Go in peace
and be freed from your suffering."

JUST BELIEVE

While Jesus was still speaking, some men came from the house of Jairus, the synagogue ruler. "Your daughter is dead," they said. "Why bother the teacher anymore?" Ignoring what they said, Jesus told the synagogue ruler, "Don't be afraid; just believe."

MARK 5:35–36

IT SO OFTEN HAPPENS. We pray, but the answer we seek is delayed. In the interim, disaster strikes.

It was so here. For Jairus, events unfolded like a slow-motion dream. He had urgently pleaded with Jesus to come to his home because his little twelve-year-old daughter was dying. Every good parent can identify with this dad.

But a less urgent need interrupted—the woman with the twelve-year bleeding condition. Surely she could wait an hour longer and catch Jesus at another time. Or surely the Lord could say to her, "I'm on an emergency call right now, and your need is not quite as pressing. I'll get back to you later."

Instead, Jesus stopped. He asked the crowd, "Who touched me?" and then He took time to speak to the woman. While He talked, death walked into the daughter's bedroom. News came to Jairus, "It's too late. She's gone."

Evidently, Jairus had not given up. He was still "bothering" Jesus. That's why the men who brought him the news told him, "It's no use. The teacher cannot help you now."

If Jesus is only a teacher, then the case is always hopeless.

Jesus ignored the counsel of those who came from Jairus' house, telling Jairus to believe rather than fear. Fear eviscerates faith—it tells us there's no remedy. It leaves us in despair.

Mark 4:35 through 5:43 records four significant miracles showing Jesus' authority over nature, demons, illness, and death. Faith is involved in three of the miracles.

Jesus chastised the disciples after He quieted the storm because they had no faith. The woman with the bleeding condition had great faith, believing that even touching the hem of His garment would cure her. Jairus had come to Jesus in great faith to request a visit to his house, but now his faith was leaking out.

How could he possibly have faith in such a circumstance?

How many times have loving Christian parents lost a child even though they had faith for healing? How do we explain that what Jesus did for Jairus, the widow's son (Luke 7:11–17), or Lazarus (John 11) is the exception rather than the rule?

What kind of faith is Jesus calling Jairus to? The faith He calls you to. Is it not a faith that trusts Him?

What stops faith from leaking? Trust. If a loved one I have prayed for lives or dies, I am still called to trust Jesus. There's a resurrection to eternal life that's just around the bend—and that resurrection will be far greater than that experienced by Jairus' daughter, the widow's son, or Lazarus, for it will be a resurrection to a glorious new body that will never again experience sickness or death.

Jesus says the exact same thing to you that He said to Jairus, "Trust Me. Don't fear. When I'm done, all will be well."

A Prayer

My faith so quickly evaporates, Lord, when I'm hard-pressed or stumped by the reality of situations I can't change. Help me, Jesus, to trust You—whether I'm in a storm, facing illness, grief, or death.

DEATH AS SLEEP

He did not let anyone follow him except Peter, James, and John the brother of James. When they came to the home of the synagogue ruler, Jesus saw a commotion, with people crying and wailing loudly. He went in and said to them, "Why all this commotion and wailing? The child is not dead but asleep."

MARK 5:37-39

MARK USES THE TERM "synagogue ruler" four times in describing the position Jairus held in the town (vv. 22, 35, 36, 38). Why this emphasis?

Mark wrote some thirty or so years after the event. He wanted to let the whole world know that "synagogue ruler" and "follower of Jesus" were not incompatible terms. Jairus was both. The need in his family brought him to the One who could help him, even as our needs bring us to Jesus.

This incident records the first time Jesus separated three of the disciples from the others. There are two other occasions: the transfiguration and Gethsemane. I suspect the reason for leaving the nine behind was crowd control. The streets were narrow and the nine quickly formed a road block. Besides, it's not a good idea to take twelve grown men into a small room where a group of disconsolate mourners are gathered around a little dead girl.

The atmosphere in the home was nothing less than heartrending. You can understand if you've ever lost a child. Mark calls our attention to the commotion, crying, and loud wailing. There's a special grief in the death of a young person, of a little girl twelve years of age. It seems so unfair. All the bright promise had been snuffed out before the child ever had a chance to savor life or realize her potential.

Jesus' statement, "The child is not dead but asleep," raises the question as to whether the death diagnosis had been inaccurate.

Was the child merely in a coma?

Not so.

This comment of Jesus gives us His first stated reflection on death—that death doesn't represent the cessation of existence, but sleep. I suspect this miracle impacted the early church so greatly that they chose the word *sleep* to better define the death of a believer. Stephen—the first Christian martyr, put to death by stoning—simply "fell asleep" (Acts 7:60). In one of his earliest letters, three times in one paragraph the apostle Paul referred to deceased believers by the term "fall/fallen asleep" (1 Thessalonians 4:13–15).

Sleep as a reference to Christian death doesn't mean our souls go to sleep when we die, for the testimony of Scripture is clear: To be "away from the body" is to be present with the Lord" (2 Corinthians 5:8). Rather, "sleep" is a euphemism given to us as believers when we face the death of a fellow believer. Death is the harsh word. We know instead that nothing can ever separate us from Christ and that a reunion day is coming. Therefore, death is also not the last word.

So take heart! The day approaches when all of us must pass from time and earth into eternity and heaven.

You will never cease to exist. There is One in the room with you, even as He was in the room with the twelve-year-old daughter of Jairus. He has power to ensure that the lamp of your life will never be extinguished.

A Prayer

Lord Jesus, You've given me more than twelve years. Life is Your wonderful gift. But, some day, unless You return first, I too will "fall sleep." Thank You for letting me know that when You are in the room, death is never a hard reality.

BETTER TO BE INSIDE

But they laughed at him. After he put them all out, he took the child's father and mother and the disciples who were with him, and went in where the child was. He took her by the hand and said to her, "Talitha, koum!" (which means, "Little girl, I say to you, get up!").

MARK 5:40–41

FOR JAIRUS, it must have seemed like a dream unfolding in slow motion. He had come to Jesus urgently asking help for his twelve-year-old daughter.

But the procession through the crowd took "forever." They were stopped by a woman with a twelve-year illness. Next, word came to Jairus that it was too late. But Jesus resumed the walk with Jairus—now, not to a dying but a dead daughter.

Upon the Lord's arrival, He declared her sleeping. That provoked laughter from the same people who had just been weeping and wailing. It's the only time in Jesus' recorded ministry when people laughed at Him. So distinct is the memory of the derision that Matthew, Mark, and Luke all take note of it.

Jesus put them all out of the house except the mom and dad, and Peter, James, and John.

Jesus will not operate in a home or a life filled with cynicism, derision, despair, disrespect, or ridicule. He functions in an atmosphere of hospitality, trust, and faith. Unbelief will always put us outside the door of His presence. We must remain inside the room that unfolds His delivering power.

A short time earlier, Jesus had been ritually defiled by the bleeding woman who had touched Him. Now He ritually defiled Himself by touching a dead body, by taking the little girl's hand.

Of the three recorded resurrections done by Jesus for others (this one, the Nain widow's son, and Lazarus), this is the only one in which He touched the dead body. Unlike the other resurrections, this one was in the privacy of a bedroom. You can sense the family intimacy and the tender pastoral care and compassion of Jesus as He takes the daughter's hand.

This is one of only two times in Mark that the Aramaic of Jesus comes straight across into the text—*Talitha, koum*. The other time is on the cross—*Eloi, Eloi, lama sabachthani* (15:34). It's as though these words to the little girl made such a powerful impression on the disciples that in telling the story years later they recorded the mother tongue of Jesus before translating the words.

In fact, Peter must be hearing echoes of *Talitha koum* when several years later he says almost exactly the same Aramaic words to the dead Dorcas—*Tabitha, koum* (Acts 9:40). I suspect that in the raising of Dorcas, Peter's faith flowed out of the memory of the healing of Jairus' daughter, because Peter not only used practically the same words but he also put all the mourners out of the room.

These verses teach us at least two things: (1) Cynicism will never get you close to Jesus. If you want to draw near Him, you must come with an open and honest heart. (2) We learn from Peter's raising of Dorcas that the past acts of the Lord influence our present approach to any impossibility. What the Lord did for us yesterday is meant to fill us with faith in the challenges we face today.

A Prayer

Lord Jesus, never put me outside the door because of my unbelief. Let me always remain in the room with You. And, what You did for Jairus' little girl You will also one day do for all of us who trust in You. You will raise us to eternal life.

ORDERS NOT TO TELL

Immediately the girl stood up and walked around (she was twelve years old). At this they were completely astonished. He gave strict orders not to let anyone know about this, and told them to give her something to eat.

MARK 5:42-43

IMMEDIATELY IS A WORD used over forty times in Mark. Sometimes it is used simply as a connective like the word *and*. Here, it signifies time—the response to Jesus' command to "get up" meets with an instant response.

Jesus didn't restore the girl gradually. She didn't slowly awaken, blink her eyes, and remain for a time in a semi-comatose state. The life in Him filled her up, while not exhausting the life that was in Him.

She stood and walked. Then, finally, Mark tells us her age: twelve. Her age connects her to the bleeding woman who had suffered for twelve years (5:25-34).

The bleeding woman was healed through her faith; but the little girl had no faith since she was dead. It was the faith of her father that brought Jesus to her.

You would think, in the wake of such a great miracle of raising Jairus' daughter from the dead, that Jesus would want the news spread far and wide. Why, then, the order not to tell anyone?

Jesus already was pressed by huge crowds. News of a resurrection would have brought a mass of desperate beseechers asking Him to empty cemeteries. (One day He will do that—but not yet!) Jesus was determined to remain focused on teaching and inculcating kingdom principles. He couldn't allocate all His time to performing miracles.

Further, Jesus didn't want to lead the disciples or the crowd into false assumptions about the nature of His messiahship or kingdom. The "secret" of the kingdom—that the kingdom was internal and must be voluntarily received—would never be learned if His ministry consisted only of miraculous acts.

We can see the practicality of Jesus in this incident when He ordered that food be brought to the little girl. The order shows how complete the healing was—the little girl was able to resume normal life immediately. We never hear of her again. Perhaps she was known years later in the early church. People would say, "There's Jairus' daughter." She would have been around fourteen when Jesus was crucified. Did she go on to become one of His witnesses throughout her life? We won't know until the full story is told on the other side.

With the raising of this girl, the section from Mark 4:35 to 5:43 is ended. It contains a sampling of the four spheres in which Jesus showed power and authority: over nature, demons, illness, and death.

One day, nature will be no more. The heavens and earth will vanish in fervent heat. One day, demons will be forever doomed, never again to oppose or afflict God's people. One day, illness and death will be banished eternally.

What we have in these four great miracles is a glimpse of what the eternal kingdom will be like. In performing these four miracles, Jesus moves the kingdom future into the kingdom present. It's a tip-off for what things will be like in that Day.

Is His kingdom living in you today? If so, then you will be living in His kingdom in the age to come!

A Prayer

Lord Jesus, I'm grateful You have power to raise all Your followers up at the last Day and for all eternity.

THE NAZARETH MENTALITY

Jesus left there and went to his home town, accompanied by his disciples. When the Sabbath came, he began to teach in the synagogue, and many who heard him were amazed. "Where did this man get these things?" they asked. "What's this wisdom that has been given him, that he even does miracles! Isn't this the carpenter? Isn't this Mary's son and the brother of James, Joseph, Judas, and Simon? Aren't his sisters here with us?" And they took offense at him.

MARK 6:1–3

DID YOU EVER HAVE a time in grade school when the teacher left the room unsupervised and one of your classmates sneaked to the blackboard, drew a stick-figure person, and wrote the word "teacher" at the bottom?

We call that stick-figure a caricature. In all likelihood the teacher was an attractive young woman with a great love and zest for life, but the student saw her as a mean, demanding old grouch. The caricature was a total misrepresentation of who she was.

That's where a lot of people are in relation to Jesus. Their image of Him may come from negative contacts with the church, those professing to follow Him, or the attitudes of those who don't know Him. So, they have embraced a view of Jesus that's far different than reality.

That is what happened at Nazareth.

Jesus originally left Nazareth and adopted a new hometown of Capernaum because Nazareth was a small place tucked in the hills, off the beaten path, while Capernaum was a major city located on the northeastern shore of the Lake of Galilee. It was a city thriving with commerce through which passed a major road.

Jesus took the long climb from 650 feet below sea level up to the hill top town of Nazareth, a small town with a precipice overlooking what we now call the valley of Armageddon. With Him were his disciples—quite an entourage for a small village.

The reaction by many in the synagogue was amazement. They hadn't seen this side of Jesus in the thirty years He had lived among them. So they initially wanted to know two things: the source of His knowledge ("Where did this man get these things?") and the explanation for His miracles—which, interestingly, they attributed to His wisdom.

But that wasn't all that was on their minds. They asked three more questions.

The first question had to do with His vocation: "Isn't this the carpenter?" The underlying Greek word is *teknon,* and its most frequent use is related to a stone mason rather than a woodworker. Their question tells us that Jesus didn't spend His "hidden" years in isolation as a monk would, nor in the solitude of study as would a theological student. He worked a trade and earned a living. There was nothing in His vocation as a mason or carpenter that intimated He held the potential of teaching and doing miracles.

The second and third questions had to do with His mother (the absence of reference to Joseph probably means that he was deceased), his four brothers, and at least two sisters (plural is used for sisters). This lays to rest the idea that Mary was a perpetual virgin. Clearly, she had at least six more children after Jesus.

The citizens of Nazareth took offense at Jesus because they weren't willing to admit new evidence. They preferred to stay with their caricature of Jesus rather than open their hearts and minds to the evidence He presented.

A Prayer

Lord Jesus, may I never lock You in the box of my small mind or interpret You by the filter of my preconceptions. May my view of You never be small, and may I never take offense at You.

PROPHET WITHOUT HONOR

Jesus said to them, "Only in his hometown, among his relatives and in his own house is a prophet without honor." He could not do any miracles there, except lay his hands on a few sick people and heal them. And he was amazed at their lack of faith.

MARK 6:4–6A

JESUS RETURNED TO NAZARETH following a series of great miracles: calming a storm, delivering a wild demoniac, healing a woman with a long-term illness, and raising from the dead a twelve-year-old girl. You would think His hometown would welcome Him as a hero.

Not so. Not only did His hometown reject Him—the people closest to Him did the same: His relatives and even His own home. That must have stung. John later reflected on this when he stated: "His own did not receive him" (John 1:11).

The rejection of Jesus by Nazareth also shows, however, how much Jesus had remained hidden until He began His public ministry. No one who knew Him well expected that such powerful miracles and life-transforming words would flow from Him.

It is often the case that those closest to us don't see our value. We can be highly praised and regarded by others, but those nearest us may often cut us down. The praises from others are more than matched by the stinging criticism of those who should have been our best encouragers.

Mark notes that Jesus "could not do any miracles there, except lay his hands on a few sick people and heal them." Note that Mark didn't say Jesus "would not." He said "could not." Mark, therefore, is explicit in saying that the attitude of the homefolk actually prevented Jesus from doing His works. It is a sobering lesson on the need for faith (the kind of faith illustrated by the bleeding woman and Jairus in Mark 5).

It was at Nazareth that Gabriel told Mary in the announcement that she, a virgin, was to give birth to a Savior: "For nothing is impossible with God" (Luke 1:37). Now, thirty years later, the message of heaven has been turned on its head in the very place where "nothing is impossible" was first spoken. The refrain from most in Nazareth has become: "Nothing is possible with God."

Miracles don't come out of a negative environment. You can't have a constant attitude that demeans and criticizes and then expect wonderful things to happen. Let's not tie the Lord's hands with our unbelief.

However, a few people in Nazareth did believe in Him. They came for healing while most of the sick people stayed away.

Earlier in the Nazareth synagogue, many at first had been amazed when they listened to Jesus (v.2). Now, He is amazed at them. There are only two times in the Gospels where it is recorded that Jesus was amazed. In Luke 7:9, Jesus was amazed at the faith of the centurion in Capernaum who sent friends to come and ask Him to heal his servant. Jesus was amazed that the Roman officer said that Jesus didn't need to come personally, but only speak the word of healing from a distance.

But at Nazareth, Jesus was amazed at His hometown's unbelief.

The people who knew Him best for thirty years didn't believe, and Jesus was amazed. A Gentile, an officer of an occupying power, who knew Him not at all, greatly believed and Jesus was amazed.

Would you rather Jesus be amazed at your unbelief, or be amazed at your faith?

A Prayer

Lord Jesus, may I not write off as beyond help the very areas in my life where You want to do a miracle. May my faith cooperate with Your power.

MICROWAVE AND OVEN

Then Jesus went around teaching from village to village.
MARK 6:6B

JESUS LEFT HIS HOMETOWN, Nazareth, following their rejection of Him. He couldn't do mighty works there except for the few who believed.

So the Lord turned His attention next to an itinerant ministry from village to village—focusing on teaching rather than miracles. It's easy to skip over this small reference in Mark, but it should grab our attention.

There was another occasion in Jesus' ministry when He also turned from the ministry of healing and miracles to teaching. Remember the Sermon on the Mount (recorded in Matthew 5 to 7)? Immediately preceding that sermon is the most extensive summary description of Jesus' power. Crowds came to Him from all over the region and far away and brought with them those with various diseases, severe pain, paralysis, seizures, and demonic possession and He healed them (Matthew 4:24–25).

But Jesus abruptly broke away from doing miracles, went up on a mountainside, called His disciples to Him, and taught them. Why?

Why would He break away from doing something with such evident visible results? Even today crowds will come out for healing services but stay away if only teaching is on the agenda.

Too often we seek for the Lord to do something *for* us rather than *in* us. We pray more for a change in our external circumstances than for transformation of our internal attitudes. But Jesus is more concerned with the kind of person we are on the inside than how things are going on the outside. He is far more interested in our bodies being His temple in which He dwells than what kind of house our bodies live in.

It is always tempting to think that a ministry of miracles is superior to a ministry of teaching—but Jesus did both. The early church did as well—for the story of those first believers is that Jesus continued both to *do* and to *teach* through them (Acts 1:1).

The ministry of the gospel is most potent when the Word and power work together.

I compare some works of God to a microwave, where the result is rather instant, and others to an oven, where the process takes time. The microwave represents healing, deliverance, and miracles, while the oven represents wholeness, discipleship, and maturity. Our microwave view of prayer says to the Lord, "I want it now." The oven may answer, "It takes time." The microwave involves the gift of faith, and the oven births perseverance.

Both the microwave and the oven are integral parts of Jesus' ministry, as they must also be today in the lives of His people. Our task is not to set one against the other.

In the villages of Galilee, Jesus focused on teaching. He knew that the miracles He did for individuals would benefit them during their own lifetimes, but His teaching would last for untold centuries. Today, we know by name only a handful of the people He healed, but we know the words He spoke.

The miracles of Jesus arose out of His compassion for human need and served to authenticate His identity as the Son of God. Knowing who He is, then, provides the greatest credence possible for what He taught. Thus, when Mark ended His gospel He noted that the preaching of the disciples—like the ministry of Jesus—was confirmed by the signs that accompanied it (Mark 16:20).

A Prayer

Lord Jesus, may I hunger as much for You to work in me as I do for You to work for me. Let me not minimize Your power to change my circumstances nor underrate the importance of the words You speak.

AUTHORITY AND POWER

Calling the Twelve to him, he sent them out two by two and gave them authority over evil spirits.

MARK 6:7

DO YOU REMEMBER the name of the fifteenth president of the United States? No?

How about the sixteenth president? Sure! Abraham Lincoln!

Why don't we remember the president before Lincoln, James Buchanan? The answer has to do with authority and power.

Buchanan and Lincoln had the same constitutional authority. They held the same office. So, the difference between them didn't relate to authority. Rather, only one of them fully exercised the power of his office.

Jesus had authority and power. Look at how Mark's gospel has shown us His delivering power over the demoniac in the Capernaum synagogue (1:21–28) and the wild, maniacal Gersaene demoniac (5:1–20).

However, Jesus didn't reserve the exercise of His authority and power to Himself alone. When He first appointed the Twelve as apostles He did so that He "might send them out to preach and to have authority to drive out demons" (3:14–15).

There it is—they had been given the authority; but until now they had not exercised it.

Therefore, this sending out of the Twelve shows us the first operational aspect of the authority given earlier in Mark 3:14–15. Now the Twelve were to actually go out and do what Jesus had said they would do.

There is often a gap in Christian ministry and life between the authority to do something and the implementation of that authority. Authority must be exercised or it remains latent. The Holy Spirit is given that the life, teaching, and power of Jesus may be exercised through us, His people. If we become spiritual James Buchanans—

holding the "office" of Christian but not exercising its power—then those around us will never know that Jesus is Lord.

This passage from Mark also shows how the deliverance of those with evil spirits is an integral component to ministry. The wording here is very terse: "And gave them authority over evil spirits." It's foreign to any modern way of thinking. We relegate all life-controlling addictions or abnormal acting-out to the solutions of medication, therapy, and counseling. There's truly a place for this when the diagnosis justifies.

However, evil spirits also exist and may possess individuals. Nothing less than exorcism will cure. If evil spirits were real to Jesus, shouldn't they also be real to us? All Christians have the authority to deal with evil spirits, but that authority is Buchanan-like unless there is the exercise of power. That's why Jesus later told the disciples that driving out evil spirits could only be done through prayer (9:29), and why He instructed them after the ascension to wait in Jerusalem until they had received power from on high (Luke 24:49).

Jesus also sent the Twelve out two by two. There is strength in that because such a coupling both encourages and corrects. If one gets discouraged, the other can encourage; if one steps out of line, the other can pull him back in.

In sending out the Twelve, Jesus clearly was expanding His mission. That mission continues today as we, His twenty-first century disciples, go out to do His work. There is evil around you somewhere today, and the Lord wants you to address it.

A Prayer

Lord Jesus, help me to clearly identify the areas I face where evil spirits or where just plain evil lies behind the visible. Grant that I may be empowered by Your Spirit to exercise both power and authority. Work with Your strength through me.

IS YOUR VISION SMALL ENOUGH?

These were his instructions: "Take nothing for your journey except a staff—no bread, no bag, no money in your belts. Wear sandals but not an extra tunic. Whenever you enter a house, stay there until you leave that town. And if any place will not welcome you or listen to you, shake the dust off your feet when you leave, as a testimony against them."
MARK 6:8–11

I GREW UP IN SMALL CHURCHES. Each Sunday morning I couldn't wait to enter the sanctuary and see the numbers go up on the Sunday school attendance board. Our board had information something like this:

- Attendance Today   43
- Attendance Last Sunday   39
- Attendance a Year Ago   48
- Record Attendance   124
- Attendance Goal   125

I knew we would never hit the goal. The record attendance had been set at a special occasion in the far distant past. No one took seriously the goal of 125. It would have been far better if we had had a goal of fifty for three Sundays in a row.

Jesus knows that we need a small vision before we're ready for the big one.

His ultimate goal was to send disciples into all the world (Mark 16:15), but He didn't start there. He first gave the Twelve a limited commission with three distinct restrictions.

First, He limited their geography. They were not to go to the Gentiles or Samaritans. Why this restriction? At that moment in time, the disciples were too prejudiced against peoples of other cultures or ethnicities. When the Samaritans proved inhospitable to Jesus, the disciples wanted to burn down their town (Luke 9:54)! Jesus recognized the narrowness of their worldview, so he restricted their geography until they could begin to comprehend that God loves everyone (John 3:16).

Second, He limited their baggage. He told them not to take a bag (suitcase or backpack!) or extra tunic. They could take sandals and a staff but no gold, silver, or copper.

Of course, it was practical to take the tunic (outer garment) for cold nights, sandals to protect the feet, and a staff to ward off wild animals—just nothing beyond that.

Later in the missionary journeys of Paul, his ministry team did take along resources, and so do our missionaries today. Why then this restriction? They needed to learn the baby steps of faith. They had to master the hard lesson that He is the Lord of the supply!

The denial of food, money, and extra clothing served as an extra incentive for them to do something with their ministry. They couldn't just hole up somewhere and wait for things to happen. They had to get out and make contacts and do the work of the ministry. If they didn't, at the end of the day they would be hungry and homeless.

Also, staying in the first hospitable home enabled them to concentrate on what they were supposed to do in that community rather than wasting time seeking out finer "digs."

Third, He limited their words. He forbade them to get into arguments with people, telling them to shake the dust off their feet if people wouldn't listen to them. Why? They didn't know enough to answer objections. In fact, at this point in the gospel narrative, they hadn't grasped what kind of Messiah Jesus was—that didn't come until later (Mark 8:27–30). However, they had been around Him enough that they could (1) testify to what they had seen and (2) demonstrate His works in the powerful deeds He did through them!

A Prayer

Lord Jesus, help me to do little things well, to live in the present rather than the future, to take care of small things rather than becoming idle while waiting for bigger opportunities.

IN WORD AND POWER

*They went out and preached that people should repent.
They drove out many demons and anointed many
sick people with oil and healed them.*
MARK 6:12-13

THUS FAR IN HIS GOSPEL, Mark has given us only a few words spoken by the disciples.

Their first recorded words were said to Jesus when He had gone to a solitary place, "Everyone is looking for you" (1:37). That's a wonderfully prophetic word that holds true for all time!

The second time, they asked Jesus the meaning of the story of the sower and the seed (4:10). Their third word expressed reproach to Jesus, "Teacher, don't you care if we drown" (4:38). But immediately after Jesus calmed the storm they cried out, "Who is this? Even the wind and waves obey him!" (4:41). So, in one moment they were afraid of the storm and in the next moment they were in awe of Jesus!

The fifth time the disciples spoke showed their incredulity when Jesus asked, "Who touched me?" They said, "You see the people touching you, and yet you ask, 'Who touched me?'" (5:31).

Thus far in following Jesus their speech had not suggested them to be world-changers. The nearest they came was their first utterance.

But in this passage, Jesus sends them out to talk. He had initially called them to preach (3:14). Now they get to do it. All their talk thus far had been addressed to Jesus; now they are sent to speak to others.

It's clear they don't have a great store of doctrine to disseminate. So they start preaching where Jesus and John the Baptist started—with the command to "Repent!" (1:4, 15). The word means to change your mind.

We know more now than the disciples did at that moment. When they first started, Jesus had not yet died on the cross or risen from the dead. For us, therefore, repentance has an even fuller meaning. Peter said it best on the day of Pentecost: "Repent and be baptized, every one of you, in the name of Jesus Christ, so that your sins may be forgiven.... Save yourselves from this corrupt generation" (Acts 2:38, 40).

The Twelve's ministry was not only in word but also in power. They replicated the ministry of Jesus in driving out demons (1:34). The use of the word "drove" implies strong action even as Jesus drove out the money-changers in the temple (11:15). Exorcism may not be a quiet experience but one that requires commanding spiritual authority.

In the Western world, the idea of demon possession is often discounted as a misdiagnosis of schizophrenia, bipolar disorder, or some form of mental illness. Not so! Medicine cannot cure demon possession, and just one dose of medication does not instantly and permanently cure those mental disorders. Not so with deliverance from demonic possession. The cure is instant and permanent. The evil spirit that had lived in the person makes a complete exit because of the authority of Jesus and those who minister in His name.

There is also a clear distinction between demon possession and illness. The demon-possessed are never anointed with oil, but the sick are. We see no instance in the Gospels of Jesus anointing others with oil, but it's clear He intends this to be a practice not only on the first preaching tour of the disciples, but throughout His church for all time (James 5:14–15).

A Prayer

Lord Jesus, Your order for disciples to speak and act with supernatural power is not limited to the Twelve. It includes Your followers today. May I be a person today through whom You speak and through whom You work.

THE WRONG VIEW OF JESUS

King Herod heard about this, for Jesus' name had become well known. Some were saying, "John the Baptist has been raised form the dead, and that is why miraculous powers are at work in him." Others said, "He is Elijah." And still others claimed, "He is a prophet, like one of the prophets of long ago. But when Herod heard this, he said, "John, the man I beheaded, has been raised from the dead!"

MARK 6:14–16

WHO IS JESUS?
That's the biggest question in the world, the biggest question you will ever answer. Get it right and all heaven opens up to you. Get it wrong, and hell waits for you.

Herod got it wrong. His name appears for the first time in Mark's gospel, but by the time Mark actually wrote his gospel, Herod was no longer king—he was dead.

Herod had a troubled and afflicted conscience. His murder of John the Baptist had come back to haunt him all the more when he heard about Jesus. Not only that, the mention of Herod alerts us that Jesus was accumulating danger. The political party allied with Herod had already plotted with their opposites, the Pharisees, to kill Jesus (3:6).

Now, Herod was wondering, *Who is this Jesus, really?*

Mark tells us that up to this point in Jesus' life there were divided opinions. The theologically educated believed that He was possessed by the prince of demons, Beelzebub (3:22). These teachers of the Law would never have entertained the view that Jesus was John the Baptist. They totally rejected the idea of reincarnation.

However, there's always a *National Enquirer* mentality in any culture that believes what they hear regardless of fact. These people thought that John the Baptist or Elijah had come back from the dead in the person of Jesus. The revelation of God in both the Old and New Testaments clearly rejects reincarnation. "Man is destined to die once, and after that to face judgment" (Hebrews 9:27)

Others had a more enhanced view of Jesus—that He was a prophet.

To this point, the disciples were uncertain of His true identity (4:41), although they were making progress. Jesus' hometown viewed Him with disdain (6:3), and His family hoped the whole hullabaloo would quickly die away (3:31).

Herod embraced the reincarnation view—that Jesus was John the Baptist come back to life.

Let's put it this way. If you had ordered a man decapitated and then thought that individual was now walking around with his head on, teaching powerfully, doing mighty works, and attracting a vast following, how would you feel? If you were wicked and corrupt like Herod, you would be far more than amazed. You would be afraid!

We won't meet Herod again in Mark's gospel. It's left to Luke (23:6-12) to tell us that Pilate delivered Jesus to Herod. He wanted Jesus to do a miracle, but Jesus didn't respond in word or deed. Herod wasn't worthy of further revelation since he had already rejected the revelation he had been given through John the Baptist. Jesus refused to be an exhibitionist of miracles to satisfy Herod's curiosity or to save Himself.

How do you answer the question, "Who is Jesus?" Your eternal destiny depends on your response.

A Prayer

*Lord Jesus, I confess You as Lord, Son of God,
Messiah, Savior. You are everything to me.*

GENERALITIES OR SPECIFICS

For Herod himself had given orders to have John arrested, and he had him bound and put in prison. He did this because of Herodias, his brother Philip's wife, whom he had married. For John had been saying to Herod, "It is not lawful for you to have your brother's wife."

MARK 6:17–18

A STORY IS TOLD about a new preacher in a Western logging town downriver from a forest. The loggers would cut down the trees, brand into the tree the insignia of ownership, and then launch the logs into the river to float downstream to the town mill.

The preacher was told that some of his parishioners were going down to the river at night, grappling the logs to the bank, cutting off the notches of ownership, and putting their own identification on them. He snuck down to the river, and sure enough, that's what they were doing.

The next Sunday he went to the pulpit and preached about keeping the eighth commandment, "Thou shalt not steal." That next week he went out again to the river and observed that his church people were doing as they had done before.

The following Sunday he went back to the pulpit and preached on the theme: "Thou shalt not cut off the ownership brand of thy neighbor's logs." The church people ran him out of town.

That was basically John the Baptist's problem.

Had he preached in general terms against adultery, no one would have bothered him. But he dared to be specific.

Here is where being specific gets dicey for those who address moral wrongs. John's ministry focused on repentance. He had singled out several groups coming to him that he warned to repent (Matthew 3:7; Luke 3:7–14). However, Herod was the only one he singled out individually, because Herod had married his own brother's wife, Herodias.

This Herod of Galilee was a son of Herod the Great who killed the babies of Bethlehem (Matthew 2:1–18). John the Baptist clearly knew he was taking on a corrupt leader with a violent ancestry.

Had John simply preached in generalities, he might have enjoyed a longer life.

Several years ago a prominent Christian television network continued to use in ministry leading "charismatic" personalities who had divorced their spouses and married others for no reason other than they simply didn't want to be married to the first spouse and the other person was more attractive.

When I raised the issue I was told that I wasn't a forgiving person. I suspect John the Baptist would have gotten the same answer.

There's a price to be paid when you get specific in confronting sin. Not everyone is like King David, who had a heart change when confronted by a man of God (2 Samuel 12). John the Baptist would pay with his life for confronting Herod.

Strikingly, the Lord didn't intervene to protect John. John was seized, bound, and imprisoned. No angel sprang him loose.

Many times there's no immediate reward for doing right. Those who confront injustice are often treated unjustly.

When you see moral wrong, how do you respond? Do you let it pass? Are you willing to be wrongfully treated if you do confront it? Will you remain true to the Lord even if He doesn't intervene to protect you?

A Prayer

Lord Jesus, help me to know when to generalize and when to be specific as I deal with wrongs around me, but always help me to be specific about the wrongs within me.

THE PERIL OF INDECISION

So Herodias nursed a grudge against John and wanted to kill him. But she was not able to, because Herod feared John and protected him, knowing him to be a righteous and holy man. When Herod heard John, he was greatly puzzled; yet he liked to listen to him.

MARK 6:19–20

SEVERAL YEARS AGO I was dragging out a decision I needed to make. Seeing my procrastination, a close friend took me aside and said, "George, not to decide is to decide."

Herod chose not to decide regarding John and events would overtake him.

Herod's wife, Herodias, nursed a very large grudge. John the Baptist had openly denounced her marriage to Herod because she had been married to Herod's brother Philip. While others had remained disapprovingly silent, John went public.

Herodias turned bitter. She wanted John dead, but she didn't have the authority to order it. She remained suspended between desire and ability.

Instead of taking responsibility for her own actions in leaving Philip and going to Herod, she took umbrage at the criticism. Instead of repenting, she stewed. A grudge is simply simmering anger—getting hotter and hotter. It seeks a release, and that release either comes through repentance or doing a terrible deed.

We must not repeat her mistake. When another rightfully identifies wrong in our lives, we must be careful not to kill the messenger. How different from Herod and Herodias is King David, who repented when the prophet Nathan confronted him over his adultery with Bathsheba.

Let's also learn from Herodias the danger of holding a grudge. Trying to get even or retaliate against someone is like throwing a cactus. Your throw may be accurate and injure the other person, but your own hands will be scarred in the process.

Herod had a more ambivalent reaction to John than Herodias. On the one hand, Herod had John arrested; on the other hand, he regularly listened to him. Herod believed John to be a righteous man and holy, yet he kept him imprisoned. He liked to listen to John, but he didn't take to heart what John said.

There's great spiritual peril when we fail to act on the truth of God's Word. Going to Bible studies, attending church, listening to sermons, and performing all kinds of religious activities is all in vain if we don't deal decisively with sin in our lives.

The clock was ticking down for Herod. Sooner or later he would be forced to make a decision. At the moment he didn't see it. He thought he could keep dragging out the choice to sentence John or release him. He chose to not make up his mind. He knew that what John was saying was right. His conscience had been awakened through John's preaching, but he wouldn't come to a conclusion. The same mistake is repeated decades later by his great-nephew, Herod Agrippa II, who listened to the apostle Paul without being persuaded (Acts 26:26–29).

Herod's indecision determined his destiny. What will your record show? Are you acting on the truth you know? Are you listening to and obeying what the Lord is telling you to do?

A Prayer

Lord Jesus, I don't want to be like Herod. Give me a heart to act rightly on what I hear. And, Lord, I don't want to be like Herodias either. I release any grudge I have against another. I want a clean heart and a right spirit.

RASH PROMISES

> *Finally the opportune time came. On his birthday Herod gave a banquet for his high officials and military commanders and the leading men of Galilee. When the daughter of Herodias came in and danced, she pleased Herod and his dinner guests. The king said to her, "Ask me for anything you want, and I'll give it to you." And he promised her with an oath, "Whatever you ask I will give you, up to half my kingdom."*
>
> MARK 6:21–23

SOMETIMES WHAT WE ANTICIPATE to be a great time becomes a disaster instead. This was the case with Herod.

Lots of planning had gone into his birthday party. The grounds of the palace had been freshened and festooned. The servants and catering crews had worked for days. The secretarial and office staff had sent out party invitations all across Galilee. From miles around the guests had traveled to Herod. If the party was held at Machaerus—down by the Dead Sea—then the guests from Galilee would have come quite a distance, many of them traveling for days.

Herod had a great celebration in mind for himself. But underneath the veneer of celebration, an injustice was boiling. He had wrongly arrested and imprisoned John the Baptist. He had not dealt rightly with that injustice—and now that unrighteousness would come back to bite him at the very moment he had hoped all the attention would be on himself.

Imaginations typically run wild as to what kind of dance the daughter of Herodias performed. If it were an all-male audience, as Mark seems to indicate, it could have been a lewd and provocative one. On the other hand, if the "leading men of Galilee" included religious figures, Herod may not have wanted to offend them. And, there is no mention in the Gospels of anyone being inebriated.

It may just have been a graceful and elegant dance. The girl was his wife's daughter, therefore Herod's stepdaughter, and most likely the daughter of his brother Philip.

We aren't told the age of the daughter. If she was a minor, Herod may have thought his promise was safe—the little girl would never be able to administer a political empire. Besides, a child would be satisfied with a new doll, new clothes, or a trip to an amusement center. If she was a teen or a young woman, why would she want the burden of political power? She would surely choose affluence, leisure, or travel.

Nothing will touch a woman more deeply than loving her daughter. The likelihood is that Herod's offer served as an attempt to cement his relationship to the girl whom he had torn away from her own father, thus deeply pleasing his wife, Herodias.

So Herod promised the daughter half his kingdom and affirmed it with an oath. It would not be possible for him to back down and thereby lose face. He completely miscalculated what the girl would do.

While we aren't told the reason for Herod's offer or the kind of dance she did, we do know it set into motion unintended consequences. He had given the stepdaughter a blank check and her mother would cash it.

What is the lesson? Be careful what you say. Be careful what you promise. Words have consequences.

A Prayer

Lord Jesus, may I watch carefully what I say so I will have nothing to regret. Keep me from foolish promises and unwise speech.

THE CHILD DESERVED BETTER

She went out and said to her mother, "What shall I ask for?" "The head of John the Baptist," she answered. At once the girl hurried in to the king with the request: "I want you to give me right now the head of John the Baptist on a platter." The king was greatly distressed, but because of his oaths and his dinner guests, he did not want to refuse her.

MARK 6:24–26

HEROD, RULER OF GALILEE, was not only a vassal king to Rome; he was a stepfather.

Millions of young people today are growing up in blended homes. The man their mother lives with or is married to is not their real father.

Herodias, the girl's mother, had been married to Herod's brother Philip. Herodias had been a willing accomplice with Herod in stepping from one marriage to the other—probably giving little thought to the impact on her daughter. The decisions made by adults do affect children for a lifetime.

There are consequences when a home is broken up through adultery or other sinful behavior. The children suffer. In this case, the daughter of Herodias became trapped in a desperate situation when she tried to please both her stepfather by dancing well and her mother by asking for the head of John the Baptist.

Most likely the daughter was young since she didn't know what to ask for when Herod gave her a blank check, so she rushed out to ask her mom what to do.

In her desperate desire for parental acceptance, the girl had no moral compass of her own. When her mother said, "Ask for the head of John the Baptist," the girl didn't protest. She didn't say, "I could never do that." Instead, she immediately acquiesced to her mother's desire.

Her parents were adulterers. The girl can't be faulted for that, but their bad example paved the way for her to become complicit in the murder of the great prophet.

The apple seldom falls far from the tree. If you want to raise disturbed children, then violate your marriage covenant.

Herod and Herodias cared only about their own pleasure. Herod wanted his brother's wife. Herodias wanted to move up the social ladder and leave her husband, Philip. The daughter grew up not learning right from wrong.

We are left to wonder what ultimately happened to this daughter. At some point in time, did she hear the good news about Jesus and become His follower?

We know there was a Manaen who was brought up with Herod the tetrarch (Acts 13:1) and became a leader in the Antioch church. Did Manaen ever become a friend to this girl? We also know that Joanna, one of the women who followed Jesus and helped provide for Him, was the wife of Cuza, Herod's administrator (Luke 8:3). Did Joanna have any influence on her?

Did this girl hear the gospel when she grew up—through Manaen or Joanna or some other believer in the first century?

We do know this—Jesus has transformed the lives of countless people who grew up in an evil or dysfunctional family.

Perhaps you grew up in a home that was less than ideal. The good news is this: You don't have to pass on your parents' bad example to your children. Jesus will truly transform your life if you let Him!

A Prayer

Lord Jesus, You welcomed children into Your arms. Help me to never harm a child by my actions or attitudes.

PURE EVIL

The king was greatly distressed, but because of his oaths and his dinner guests, he did not want to refuse her. So he immediately sent an executioner with orders to bring John's head. The man went, beheaded John in the prison, and brought back his head on a platter. He presented it to the girl, and she gave it to her mother. On hearing his, John's disciples came and took his body and laid it in a tomb.

MARK 6:26–29

SOMEWHERE IN THE WORLD today a follower of Jesus Christ is laying down his or her life to an unjust executioner. Believers are killed for no other reason than their fidelity to the Lord.

The poet James Russell Lowell put it this way: "Truth forever on the scaffold, wrong forever on the throne." Herod of Galilee sat on such a throne of wrong.

There was no legal charge against John, no trial, no appeal. Herod dispatched an executioner to sever John's head and bring it back into the banquet hall.

The gospel writers never play on our emotions in telling this story. They don't delve into feelings; instead, they let the readers form their own conclusions. And we have. These people were pure evil. Herod was a cruel despot. The daughter was complicit in murder. Herodias may have gotten John's head—but she lost her heart in the process.

John's disciples are another story. They showed courage and loyalty. These unnamed disciples who stuck with the Baptist couldn't accept that their prophet's body would be thrown out somewhere in a dump as trash. They showed courage in risking their lives to take his headless corpse and bury it.

I pray daily for a young widow serving the lord faithfully in a country where her husband, a minister of the gospel, was summarily executed with a shot to the head at point blank range with a pistol. His crime? He followed Jesus. This widow, with her young daughter, continues to serve Jesus faithfully in the very town where her husband was shot down. Like John's followers, she is filled with courage and loyalty.

How do we face injustice? Do we throw up our hands and say, "God has abandoned us!" Do we become bitter or withdrawn? Do we blame God?

No! We live with the long view. A day of justice is coming. Wrong may be on the throne and truth on the scaffold today, but not tomorrow. The next line in Lowell's poem says: "Yet that scaffold sways the future, and, behind the dim unknown, stands God within the shadow, keeping watch above his own."

When terrible things happen to us, we are called to do exactly what John's disciples and the young widow of a martyred husband did. In the face of pure evil, we look behind the visible to the invisible. We don't interpret God by our circumstances. We know that even if evil has scored a touchdown it can never win the game. When we have no control over what has happened to us, we can still control what happens in us. We can choose to live with loyalty and courage.

A Prayer

Lord Jesus, when I experience injustice and evil may I respond like You. You allowed others to nail You to the cross, but You never crucified anyone. Let me not be overcome with evil, but rather, let me overcome evil with good.

DO YOU NEED TO TAKE A BREAK?

The apostles gathered around Jesus and reported to him all they had done and taught. Then, because so many people were coming and going that they did not even have a chance to eat, he said to them, "Come with me by yourselves to a quiet place and get some rest."

MARK 6:30–31

SOMETIMES YOU JUST NEED to get away from it all. You can't function well if you are always under stress. Jesus understood that.

He had sent the disciples out to preach, heal, and cast out demons (6:7–13). During their itineration, Herod began to think that John the Baptist had risen from the dead (6:14–29).

Jesus' disciples returned to Him—no doubt weary and exhausted as well as apprehensive and fearful that what happened to John might next be the fate of Jesus.

They reported to Jesus what they had done and taught. I would love to have heard their stories—probably some humor, some hardship, some dull and dry days; but also, some wonderful accounts of hospitality, unexpected provision, and jaw-dropping accounts of miracles and exorcisms.

Mark doesn't tell us what Jesus was doing or where He was while the disciples were on their first mission. Perhaps He had withdrawn into solitude for a time, or maybe there were some personal matters back in Nazareth that He tended to.

However, once the disciples returned He was again mobbed. This incident is the tenth time Mark records Jesus as being surrounded with a press of people. Consider the previous nine:

- Sundown healings (1:33)
- A crowded house and a rooftop paralytic (2:2)
- A large crowd by the lake when He called Levi (2:13)

- Another large crowd from all over gathered by the lake (3:7)
- A crowd in the house while His mother and brothers were outside (3:32)
- The crowd by the lake while He taught in parables (4:1)
- The crowd by the lake as He and His disciples set sail (4:36)
- The people of Gadara and environs (5:14)
- A pressing crowd by the lake when Jairus and the bleeding woman met Him (5:21, 24)

These ten incidents demonstrate the popularity and attractiveness of Jesus. Unlike the religious leaders who harped on technicalities of the Law, Jesus made it His priority to meet human needs by healing bodies through His power and nurturing souls through His teaching.

Jesus was sensitive to people and to the fact that people had traveled from all over seeking Him. He was also sensitive to the needs of His exhausted and stressed disciples. They needed some rest, quiet, and a good meal. Jesus didn't push them past the level of their endurance.

Sure, the sick were waiting to be healed, people needed deliverance, lessons needed to be taught—but Jesus broke away from it all to give His disciples a needed break.

There's a lesson for us in this. There will always be things pressing at you, more things to be done in the day than you can do. You can't get your own "to do" list done because others are intruding into your schedule with their concerns.

It's okay for you to take a break, to get some rest. You have no less an authority than Jesus to show you that getting away for a season is the right thing to do.

A Prayer

Lord Jesus, I leave the busyness of this day with all its demands to have some solace with You. Restore my strength and heart in quiet moments.

SLOW BOAT, FAST CROWD

So they went away by themselves in a boat to a solitary place. But many who saw them leaving recognized them and ran on foot from all the towns and got there ahead of them. When Jesus landed and saw a large crowd, he had compassion on them, because they were like sheep without a shepherd. So he began teaching them many things.

Mark 6:32-34

THE DISCIPLES NEEDED REST after their intensive tour of ministry in Galilee (6:6-13, 31-32). They had no sooner linked up with Jesus than a crowd massed around them, and they didn't even have time to eat.

They were evidently on the northwestern shores of the Lake of Galilee since Luke (9:10) tells us that their destination was Bethsaida on the northeastern side of the lake.

There's also a very strange phrase: "but many who saw them leaving recognized them." How could you not recognize Jesus and the Twelve getting into the boat? It could be that they slipped away very early in the morning while it was still dark.

I wonder if, when Jesus told His disciples to get into the boat, they thought twice about the risk of traveling with Him on water. The last time they got into a boat while dead tired, a fierce storm almost sank them (4:35-41). Would another storm arise?

In everyday life, some days are storm-filled and others are not. This one was not. A trial of a different nature waited them—this time not on the lake, but on the land.

The crowd outran them! It must have been a slow boat and a fast crowd. The trip was anywhere from four to seven miles, and the people reached the spot ahead of the boat.

If I have pieced together the timeline correctly, Jesus and the disciples got into the boat sometime before the dawn's light. The morning would have been spent on the lake, while the people were running through the countryside and towns, keeping an eye on the trajectory of the boat. By the time Jesus and the Twelve pulled to shore, it was early afternoon and the crowd was already there.

All the Gospels only count the number of men present—5,000—although Matthew alone notes women and children were also there (Matthew 14:21).

I had always wondered why the women and children were not counted. When you look at the scenario you can understand why. People in the crowd ran for hours to get to the spot. Men were in better condition to make such a jaunt. Men were counted because that's mainly who was there. The women and children would have lagged behind, thus their proportion of the crowd would have been greatly reduced.

Several things stick out. First, Jesus didn't see the crowd until He landed. Second, He didn't get back into the boat and escape. Third, the motivation that prevented Him from leaving was compassion. Fourth, what motivated the compassion was the spiritual state of the people—they were shepherd-less.

Although Luke tells us that healings occurred (Luke 9:12), the main focus of the afternoon was Jesus "teaching them many things." Think of the occasion as a Men's Retreat with Jesus. He was helping them become men of God, better persons, more loving husbands and fathers, and more responsible citizens.

That's what He does for us as well. His words nourish our souls.

A Prayer

Lord, have compassion on me. Feed me Your Word today and help me to digest it so that it remains in me. Teach me, Lord, many things today.

THE INCONVENIENCE OF MINISTRY

By this time it was late in the day, so his disciples came to him. "This is a remote place," they said, "and it's already very late. Send the people away so they can go to the surrounding countryside and villages and buy themselves something to eat." But he answered, "You give them something to eat." They said to him, "That would take eight months of a man's wages! Are we to go and spend that much on bread and give it to them to eat?"

MARK 6:35-37

I RECENTLY READ Kay Warren's book, *Dangerous Surrender*. Her routine as a pastor's wife, mother, and grandmother was interrupted one day when she couldn't put down a magazine that told the gripping story of people dying from HIV/AIDS. She didn't know that the majority of persons with the dread disease were women and that multiplied millions of children were orphans because of AIDS.

David Wilkerson, founder of Teen Challenge, had a similar epiphany in 1958 when he saw a drawing of New York City gang members on trial for murder. The Holy Spirit so impressed upon his heart their need for the Lord that he drove to the Big Apple, where he had never been, in an attempt to witness to them. Like Kay Warren, he was "gloriously ruined" by the plight of others in need of Jesus. Five decades later, over 24,000 men and women daily receive deliverance from life-controlling issues in Teen Challenge centers around the world.

Kay and David discovered what we all must—that serving people in the name of Jesus means stepping outside of our comfort zones and into the danger zones of others.

It was that way in the situation described in Mark. A huge crowd gathered around Jesus. They had chased Him by land along the seashore as He traveled across the lake by boat.

THE INCONVENIENCE OF MINISTRY

The disciples must have been irritated. They had just returned from their first training mission (6:6–13) and wanted some downtime with Jesus. Instead, Jesus met the crowd and spent the rest of the day teaching because He had compassion on people. Now, it was nightfall and the Twelve had had it.

"Send the people away," they begged Jesus. Their ostensible reason? "The people don't have food." Perhaps the unstated reason was more accurate: *We want some time to ourselves.*

Jesus, however, wanted them (and us) to be inconvenienced by people with needs. So, He told the Twelve to feed the crowd—something He surely knew they didn't have the resources to do. They answered that it would take two-thirds of a year's salary just to feed the crowd once—while Philip said (sarcastically) that even that amount of money "would not buy enough bread for each one to have a bite" (John 6:7)!

What's going on here? Jesus does with them what He does with us. "So you want to be My disciple?" He asks. "Then I'm going to throw things at you that seem impossible to do. You don't have the necessary training, you don't have the necessary resources, and you're going to think Me unreasonable in asking you."

Yes, if you want to be used of the Lord, then get prepared to be inconvenienced and overwhelmed.

A Prayer

Lord Jesus, I'm like the disciples. Just when I feel I deserve a break, you put others in my path who need help, and I want to send them away. But, if I did that I would miss the miracle You want to do. So, I offer myself to be inconvenienced at Your call.

WHAT'S IN YOUR HANDS?

*"How many loaves do you have?" he asked. "Go and see."
When they found out, they said, "Five—and two fish." Then
Jesus directed them to have all the people sit down in groups
on the green grass. So they sat down in
groups of hundreds and fifties.*

MARK 6:38–40

THE DISCIPLES WANTED TO SEND the people away. Like the disciples, our priority often is to think of our own comfort. Jesus wants us to focus on helping others.

The impetus for locating food came from Jesus. When He asked, "How many loaves do you have?" they didn't know. They evidently had no provisions with them—perhaps as they walked that day they had already consumed whatever food they had.

It could be that they didn't search very hard when Jesus asked. After all, there were 5,000 men plus some women and children. The disciples wouldn't have wanted to stand up and make an announcement: "Anyone got food? Come up to the front!" That would only have been a signal for the crowd to stay, and the disciples wanted to send them away.

Only John's gospel reports that Andrew found the source: a little boy with five loaves and two fish. But even Andrew reflected the futility of his find when he told Jesus, "But how far will they go among so many" (John 6:8–9)?

In presenting Jesus with the boy's small resources, I suspect the disciples hoped this would be all the evidence Jesus needed to send the crowd away as they had suggested earlier.

We're not too much different than them. When the Lord asks us to do something over our heads, our first reaction is, "Lord, I don't have enough to work with." We don't understand that He works miracles with whatever resources we have in our hands. Our solutions are often not His solutions.

The fact that Jesus directed the crowd to sit down on *green* grass tells us it was spring. John's gospel corroborates the dates more exactly by telling us the Passover was near (John 6:4). So, this incident occurred one year before Jesus' death and resurrection at the next Passover. Two-thirds of His three-year ministry was complete at this point.

Luke's gospel adds a detail that, in addition to teaching the multitude, Jesus had also "healed those who needed healing" (Luke 6:11). This would explain why people had been standing—perhaps waiting in line for Him to touch them, or observing Jesus as He healed. Thus, Jesus directed the crowd to sit in groups of fifty and one hundred.

In my own church fellowship, one third of the churches are fifty or fewer in attendance, and another third have between 100 and 650. Twenty centuries later, many followers of Jesus still gather in groups of fifty and one hundred. Even the megachurches have to break the large congregation into smaller units in order to provide community.

Thus, when the Twelve began distributing food they weren't serving everyone all at once—they were moving from person to person, one group at a time. Jesus didn't rain down bread as happened with the manna in the wilderness. His pattern is that we use whatever is multiplying in our hands as we go from person to person, need to need, day by day, hour by hour, minute by minute.

A Prayer

Lord Jesus, I too have not much in my hands. What can You do with that? If I trust You and obey what You tell me to do, I'll find out what You can do!

THREE DON'TS FOR SUCCESS

Taking the five loaves and the two fish and looking up to heaven, he gave thanks and broke the loaves. Then he gave them to his disciples to set before the people. He also divided the two fish among them all. They all ate and were satisfied, and the disciples picked up twelve basketfuls of broken pieces of bread and fish. The number of the men who had eaten was five thousand.

MARK 6:41–44

THIS IS THE ONLY MIRACLE of Jesus, other than His resurrection, recorded in all four Gospels. That fact underscores the impact this miracle had upon the early followers of Jesus.

One year after the feeding of the 5,000, Jesus sent His disciples out to spiritually feed the world, and they faced an even more formidable challenge.

Three lessons of this miracle illustrate three actions to avoid if we are to fulfill the Great Commission.

First, don't look at the size of the task. The Gospels tell us there were 5,000 men, plus women and children. One year later, the task of reaching the world would grow exponentially. There were an estimated 250 million people living in the Greco-Roman world. On the day of Pentecost there were only 120 Spirit-filled people. That's one Christian for every 2,083,333 persons, and the disciples had no modern means of transportation or communication to reach them!

When the Lord lays some assignment on your heart, the likelihood is that at first it will be daunting. You will think it too big, and you will be tempted to not even try.

Second, don't look at the little you have. They had only five small loaves and two small fish. As Andrew said whimsically, "But how far will they go among so many" (John 6:9)?

The Enemy will always attempt to maximize the difficulty and minimize your resources so that you feel it can't be done.

If your response to being asked to do something for the Lord is, "But I don't have the time," or "I don't have the ability," you're the person the Lord wants to use because you know you can't do it in your own strength. You're going to need the help of the Lord because the task is too big and you are too small.

Third, don't leave the Lord out of the picture. You will fail if you forget that Jesus works through you and takes whatever you place in His hands and multiplies it.

If you refuse to focus on the size of the task or the little you have, and you ask the Lord for help—you reverse the laws of failure.

Had I been one of the Twelve, I would have asked Jesus to do the miracle in advance. I would have said, "Lord, if You're fixing to do a miracle here—then do it in advance. Make a big pile of bread over here, and another pile of fish over here. I'll fill up my basket, serve the first row, return for more and serve the second row. I'll keep doing that until everyone has eaten and there is no more bread or fish in the pile."

But Jesus builds His kingdom differently. We want to start out full and end up empty. He always starts us with nearly empty baskets so that we end up with full ones. We want the miracle in advance before we start out; He wants us to obey Him and let the miracle take place as we do what He has asked.

A Prayer

Lord Jesus, too often I have used excuses instead of doing what You ask. At Your word, I lay aside my lack of faith. I trust You to work above and beyond my ability.

SAFE

Immediately Jesus made his disciples get into the boat and go on ahead of him to Bethsaida, while he dismissed the crowd. After leaving them, he went into the hills to pray. When evening came, the boat was in the middle of the lake, and he was alone on land. He saw the disciples straining at the oars, because the wind was against them. About the fourth watch of the night he went out to them, walking on the lake.

MARK 6:45–48A

TWICE BEFORE in Mark's gospel the disciples had sailed the Lake of Galilee (4:35f. and 5:21). The first ride terrified the disciples when they felt they were drowning in the storm at sea. The second trip went smoothly.

I wonder if the disciples thought there was a fifty/fifty chance of trouble on this third trip. We know now what happened. Did the Twelve even think, *This time He's not in the boat with us—what if something really bad happens?*

Perhaps any apprehension was assuaged by the fact that Jesus told them to go to Bethsaida. Since Peter, Andrew, and Philip were from Bethsaida (John 1:44), they may have just been happy to get home—even if Jesus wasn't coming with them.

This is the only time Jesus was left alone with a crowd. Help from His disciples to assist Him in dealing with the crowds was evidently unnecessary. He had met the people's needs, and when the throng saw the disciples get into the boat and depart, they knew the event was over. They, too, needed to go home. Night was coming.

This is the second time in Mark that Jesus sought out a private place to pray (1:35–39). On the earlier occasion, Jesus rose early in the morning while it was still dark. Here, He headed off to a solitary mountainside in the late afternoon, early evening.

What did Jesus pray for in those moments? Was it primarily fellowship with the Father? Were there things on His heart? Was

He praying for His disciples? After all, He only had a year left with them, and they still failed to understand the nature of His kingdom and His role as Messiah. Was He praying down through time for us as well?

From the vantage point of the mountainside, He had a clear view of the lake. I have stood in that vicinity many times, and you can see all the way across the seven plus miles of the lake's width.

Things didn't go well for the disciples. The fourth watch of the night was between three and six in the morning—they had been rowing for hours and were still stuck in the middle of the lake.

What a picture! The disciples were straining, and Jesus was praying. They were on the water, and He was on the land.

Like them, we are often in trouble while He is safe on the shore! He doesn't come immediately to our rescue and offers no excuse for His delay. He didn't let the "emergency" of the disciples interrupt His time in prayer.

But we have a Lord who is always safe, never threatened. Just as He continued in prayer while the disciples were fighting a storm, so today from heaven's throne He prays for us (Romans 8:34). We are safe because He keeps watch over us just as He did for them!

A Prayer

Lord Jesus, sometimes I feel that I, too, am in the middle of getting nowhere and life's winds are blowing against me. But You always see me, even when I don't see You. I'm safe in Your care.

"IT IS I!"

> *He was about to pass by them, but when they saw him walking on the lake, they thought he was a ghost. They cried out, because they all saw him and were terrified. Immediately he spoke to them and said, "Take courage! It is I. Don't be afraid." Then he climbed into the boat with them, and the wind died down. They were completely amazed, for they had not understood about the loaves; their hearts were hardened.*
>
> MARK 6:48B–52

WHAT DOES IT MEAN, "Jesus was about to pass by them"? Did Jesus intend to walk past them undiscovered? If so, what purpose would that serve?

Maybe the point is that Jesus often passes by when His people are in trouble. He doesn't immediately stop to help. This is the terrible mystery of suffering—that Jesus is near but not immediately active. That He has the power to help us but does not. He passes by.

Is He indifferent? Does He not care? Is it a matter of conserving His power so that He is not continually intermeddling with the laws of nature?

At first the disciples didn't see Him walking on the water. Often that's also our first reaction when we hit a rough spot. We don't see Him because we are so focused on the bad news swamping us.

But for the disciples and for us, Jesus is there—whether we see Him or not.

The reaction to His presence was twofold: incredulity and terror. Their first reaction was incredulity as they dismissed Him as an apparition, a ghost. Their thinking shows us that Jesus had not yet theologically cured them of believing in folklore. Ghosts don't exist!

Their subsequent reaction of terror is somewhat mystifying because by now the disciples had already gone through an earlier storm. They should have had confidence that if Jesus brought them to safe harbor before, He would do it again. However, the difference now is that He is outside the boat rather than in it with them.

But whether in or out of the boat—both times they were terrified (4:41).

This reaction to Jesus is rarely talked about. We see Him as the gentle, loving, open-arms Jesus. Do we also see Him as so Almighty that His presence terrifies us? He is both The Lamb of God and the Lion of Judah, so we draw near to Him in love, but we also bow down before Him in awe.

Jesus spoke three short sentences to them: The first and last sentences relate to their fears, and the middle sentence relates to His identity, "It is I." If we keep Jesus in the middle of our beginnings and endings during whatever trauma or difficulty comes our way, we too will be safe.

Jesus stepped from the water into the boat. The disciples didn't expect Him to show up because "they had not understood about the loaves"—that is, they didn't make a connection between His most recent miracle and their present need. When we forget what He has already done for us, we walk in fear in the present moment.

You will note that Mark omits the account of Peter's walking on the water (Matthew 14:22–23). Why? It is believed that Mark wrote at the influence of Peter. If Peter really told this story through Mark, we see evidence of a truly humble servant.

A Prayer

I get so caught up in heartbreaks and disappointments, tedium and unresolved issues of life, that, like the disciples, I am fearful. Help me, Lord, to always realize that "It is I" is sandwiched between "Take courage" and "Don't be afraid."

RECOGNIZING JESUS

When they had crossed over, they landed at Gennesaret and anchored there. As soon as they got out of the boat, people recognized Jesus. They ran throughout that whole region and carried the sick on mats to wherever they heard he was. And wherever he went—into villages, towns or countryside—they placed the sick in the marketplaces. They begged him to let them touch even the edge of his cloak, and all who touched him were healed.

MARK 6:53-56

HAVE YOU EVER GONE in the opposite direction from where you intended?

That appears to be the case here. Late the previous afternoon Jesus had sent the disciples sailing to go ahead of him to Bethsaida. I've been by the ruins of Bethsaida many times—it's on the northeastern part of the Lake of Galilee.

So, if they were headed for Bethsaida, how did they end up at Gennesaret, the fertile plain on the northwestern shore of the lake? Verse 48 gives the clue: "The wind was against them."

Sometimes the winds of life take us to places we didn't plan to go. But that doesn't mean we are out of God's will. Getting blown to unintended locations may be God's pathway to open doors.

Consider again the exhaustion of Jesus and the Twelve. One day earlier the disciples had listened to Jesus teach most of the day, and then served to control and feed the crowd of 5,000 men along with women and children. Next they spent all night rowing in the face of a strong wind—getting nowhere. Jesus Himself had been up on a hillside praying through the night.

So, lots of work and prayer—and no sleep or rest.

Have you ever had that experience? You deserved a break from what had exhausted you. Just at the moment you thought it was coming, something else intervened and you had to draw upon reserves of strength physically, emotionally, and spiritually that you didn't know you had?

That was the case with the disciples of Jesus. With no sleep, they were back dealing with crowds that thronged Jesus everywhere He went. It didn't matter where—in town, out of town, in the country, in small places, and in bigger places. Everyone was trying to get to Jesus!

The people didn't gather to see the disciples, they came because of Jesus. That's a lesson for the church today. Do people recognize Jesus is present? Or do they hear the church sermonizing, lecturing, politicking, encapsulated in its own programs and activities?

Our mission is to help people get to Jesus!

Look at the contrast between the beginning of Mark 6 and the end. As we entered the chapter, Jesus' own hometown rejected Him. As we end the chapter, people from everywhere are welcoming Him.

The crowds thronging to Jesus show us that people respond when their needs are met. Living in a day when there was no decent medical help, Jesus presented their only option for a cure.

The long and short of it is that when word gets out that the church of Jesus Christ, His body, meets the needs of people, they will flock in. People with needs respond to Jesus. They may not always stay with Jesus once their needs are met—but that doesn't prevent Jesus from helping them.

A Prayer

Lord Jesus, You didn't have a smart advertising campaign to draw people. You just went about doing good—using the power God had given You on behalf of others. Help me to use the abilities You have given me to help others also.

CONFLICT

> *The Pharisees and some of the teachers of the law who had come from Jerusalem gathered around Jesus and saw some of his disciples eating food with hands that were "unclean," that is, unwashed. (The Pharisees and all the Jews do not eat unless they give their hands a ceremonial washing, holding to the tradition of the elders. When they come from the marketplace they do not eat unless they wash. And they observe many other traditions, such as the washing of cups, pitchers and kettles.)*
>
> MARK 7:1–4

WHAT QUESTION WOULD YOU ask Jesus if you had walked a hundred miles to get to Him? I doubt you would ask Him, "Why don't Your disciples wash their hands before they eat?"

These religious leaders aren't the only ones who ask the wrong question. I've seen it happen in the church.

I was once called upon to meet with a small group of people who were upset with a pastor's decision. I drove 150 miles to meet with them. They were led by a longtime church member who was now in his eighties.

The church sanctuary sat about 1,000 people, but the congregation had dwindled down to about 100. They had been so divided that a new pastor was appointed to lead them, and the church in the next two years had grown to around 300. Good progress!

Now this group wanted me to listen to their grievance. I asked, "What's the problem?"

Their elderly leader answered, "The pastor moved the church nursery without our permission." The nursery had been at the back of the church and so many new families were coming that the pastor had wisely relocated the nursery near the front. This group was upset because they hadn't been consulted.

Unfortunately, there are a lot of people like them who are more interested in their own agenda than in people coming to Christ.

So many conflicts in the body of Christ result not from division over doctrine, but division over preference.

We can be as bad as the Pharisees in picking the wrong issue!

The likes of the Pharisees and teachers of the Law have never gone away. There are still those today who look at the small things they deem wrong rather than the wonderful things God is doing! They nitpick at those who are doing the work of God because the way that work is being done doesn't please them.

The Pharisees' faultfinding with Jesus came at the very time the sick were being healed in villages, towns, and the countryside (6:56). They should have rejoiced rather than criticized.

Mark takes time to explain the custom of handwashing. His parenthetical aside shows us he is writing to a non-Jewish audience who wouldn't be familiar with the customs of the Pharisees.

Is it wrong to wash your hands before you eat? By no means! There are hygienic reasons for that. We are careful in handling food lest we contaminate our body with unwanted germs. But the Pharisees had substituted a ritualistic legalism for matters that were best left to individual judgment. Jesus let His disciples violate these rules because such proscriptions had no bearing on one's relationship with God.

Let's not repeat their mistake. Jesus is more interested in clean hearts than clean hands.

A Prayer

Lord Jesus, help me not to be a person whose initial tendency is to find fault with what someone else is doing. Help me first to look for the good, and if any fault remains, then grant me wisdom to know how to address it lovingly.

WHAT QUESTION WOULD YOU ASK?

So the Pharisees and teachers of the law asked Jesus, "Why don't your disciples live according to the tradition of the elders instead of eating their food with 'unclean' hands?" He replied, "Isaiah was right when he prophesied about you hypocrites; as it was written: 'These people honor me with their lips, but their hearts are far from me. They worship me in vain; their teachings are but rules taught by men.'"

MARK 7:5-7

WE ARE OFTEN DEFINED in life by the questions we ask or the issues we raise. If you had a chance to ask Jesus a question, what would it be?

There are a lot of things I would ask Him:

- Why do good people suffer?
- What is heaven like?
- When will the world end?
- How can I overcome temptation and sin?

Of course, the Scripture itself holds answers to these questions, but it would have been wonderful to listen to the Lord answer in direct conversation.

The rich young ruler asked the greatest question of all: "What must I do to inherit eternal life" (Mark 10:17)? The Pharisees and teachers of the Law never came close to asking anything of that importance.

But legalists always concentrate on the letter of the Law. They aren't interested in the big questions. Their worldview is so fixed that all they can see are the minutiae—the tiny deviations from their prescribed orthodoxy. Any who live outside their box are deemed heretics. There's no grace in legalism.

These critics of Jesus totally missed out on the greatest opportunity ever given on planet earth—the chance to interview the Son of God on the biggest issues of life—eternity, salvation, suffering, and death.

As a result of their nitpicking they never got a picture of who Jesus really was.

Their bad example teaches us not to miss the most important things in our own walk with God. We must never get focused on the trivial and unimportant, or let our preferences be elevated to matters of principle. We need to give ourselves to people and issues that are on the Lord's heart rather than spending our time on tangential and marginal matters that may attract us, but have no eternal value.

How did Jesus respond to them? Interestingly—by not stating His own opinion—although as the Son of God He had the complete right to do so. He relied on Scripture. His basis for dealing with His critics was the written Word.

Eight centuries earlier Isaiah had his own critics to deal with—so Jesus took Isaiah's words and applied them to His contemporary opponents. Jesus' words from Isaiah form a searing indictment against the Pharisees and teachers of the Law. He described them as people whose "hearts are far from me," who "worship me in vain." In effect, Jesus said to them: "You are nowhere even close to God despite all your pretense."

Let's be careful to never place observance of ritual over our relationship to the Lord and others. It's an easy temptation to think that our performance of religious duties, whether it is church attendance, tithing, prayer, Bible study, or any other means of grace, is acceptable without a vital relationship with Christ. No! Those means of spiritual growth are the outcome of our walk with Him, not a substitute. They are a means and not an end.

A Prayer

Lord Jesus, help me to keep the plain things as the main things and the main things as the plain things. When I'm tempted to major on minors, may Your Holy Spirit pull me back to the essentials of what it means to truly follow You.

TRADITION

> *"You have let go of the commands of God and are holding on to the traditions of men." And he said to them: "You have a fine way of setting aside the commands of God in order to observe your own traditions."*
>
> MARK 7:8–9

FIDDLER ON THE ROOF has proven to be one of the most popular and enduring musicals in our culture.

The story is set in Czarist Russia in 1905. Tevye, the peasant dairyman, is father to five daughters. He attempts to maintain his family and religious traditions in the face of outside influences. He tries to cope with the edict of the Czar evicting Jews from their villages while also dealing with challenges from the strong-willed actions of his three oldest daughters.

In one of the most famous songs from the musical, Tevye forcefully defends tradition and ends singing: "Tradition. Without our traditions, our lives would be as shaky . . . as a fiddler on the roof!"

When Jesus talked about tradition it wasn't because He had a problem with tradition. After all, He instituted the tradition of Communion at the Last Supper. His objection came when tradition set aside God's commandments.

I grew up in an atmosphere that mixed warm spirituality with a lot of rules that mostly had the word "don't" in front of them.

I could never understand, for example, why male ministers preached against women wearing red lipstick while they wore bright red ties. Historically, the reason evidently was that in the early part of the twentieth century lipstick was an identifier of an immoral woman. I was a teenager at a camp meeting when the evangelist compared women wearing lipstick to an old barn. He said, "When you farmers paint that barn red and it later catches on fire, the first thing that begins to crackle and peel is that red paint, and the same with you women when you get on fire for the Lord!"

The key always is learning to distinguish God's commandments from human traditions.

I think of it this way. Suppose I want to ride my bicycle across town. You come to me and say, "But you can't do that because riding your bicycle across town is a sin. It's forbidden in God's Word."

I then go the Bible and read it through and through, and I can't find such a prohibition anywhere in Scripture. So I get back on my bicycle. You come to me again and say, "I know it's wrong for you to do that."

So I get off my bike and again examine the Bible to see if there is any underlying principle that would prevent me riding my bicycle across town. Finding none, I get back on.

Then you come to me a third time: "If you ride your bicycle across town, people will see you and some of them will lose their faith because of your bad example." So I have to get off my bike for the third time and determine whether that's a true or false statement. If I would cause others to lose their faith, then I will forego riding my bike. But if I determine that others just want something to criticize, I will get back on my bicycle and ride happily across town.

When I think this way about what I should and shouldn't do, I keep a healthy perspective on commandment and tradition.

A Prayer

Lord Jesus, may I never let observance of a tradition substitute for loving You with all my heart, soul, mind, and strength; and loving my neighbor as myself.

CROSS YOUR FINGERS

"For Moses said, 'Honor your father and your mother,' and 'Anyone who curses his father or mother must be put to death.' But you say that if a man says to his father or mother: 'Whatever help you might otherwise have received from me is Corban' (that is, a gift devoted to God), then you no longer let him do anything for his father or mother. Thus you nullify the word of God by your tradition that you have handed down. And you do many things like that."

MARK 7:10–13

JESUS WAS RESPONDING to criticism by the Pharisees and teachers of the Law that His disciples had violated tradition by eating food without first performing the religious ritual of hand washing. He accused His opponents of majoring on minors, of substituting their traditions in place of keeping God's laws.

He then illustrated their hypocrisy by describing how they violated their responsibility to parents as mandated by the fifth commandment to honor your father and mother.

Jesus' words to these hypocrites remind me of the childhood practice of crossing your fingers behind your back while telling a lie. The idea was that the crossed fingers cancelled out the words spoken.

In Jesus' day, a person could shelter their assets by putting them in a "religious trust" called Corban. Anything Corban was technically owned by God and could only be used for holy purposes. However, the individual still retained full control over the use of the money.

The commandment to honor mother and father included the responsibility of an adult child to care for their parents if they needed help in their old age. It was long before the days of Social Security and governmental assistance (which even now do not cancel out our obligations to assist our elderly parents as need and resources dictate).

Jesus evidently had direct knowledge of occasions when a needy parent had gone to an adult child of financial means and asked for help paying their rent or providing groceries, medicine, or other necessities. The legalistic and financially able son or daughter could avoid the responsibility to help by saying, "You know I would really like to be able help you, but everything I have is dedicated to God and it wouldn't be right for me to take what is God's and give it to you."

The parent would leave disappointed and destitute while the adult child went ahead and spent the Corban for themselves on whatever way they wanted, justifying their actions by crossing their fingers and saying, "Everything I do is really for God even though I'm the beneficiary."

Jesus knifed through this kind of twisted and tortured logic. He opposed rationalizations. Right is right, and wrong is wrong. No crossed fingers or lip service when it comes to moral and ethical obligations!

I am intrigued with Jesus' summary phrase: "And you do many things like that." In other words, Jesus had given only one example of His opponents' crossed-fingers misbehavior. If you are careless in one area of your life, the chances are that's not the only line you cross.

Ethical and moral dishonesty bleeds into the whole of life. It becomes easier and easier to give excuses for not fulfilling moral and spiritual duties, to justify our own wrong actions. Self-honesty is one of the hardest, but most necessary, self-disciplines.

A Prayer

Lord Jesus, may I honor You by being a good child and a good parent. Grant that I live with integrity and never disappoint or disillusion my family through my words and deeds.

KOSHER IN THE HEART

Again Jesus called the crowd to him and said, "Listen to me, everyone, and understand this. Nothing outside a man can make him 'unclean' by going into him. Rather, it is what comes out of a man that makes him 'unclean.'"

MARK 7:14–15

SEVERAL YEARS AGO, the orthodox in Jerusalem threatened to burn down the new McDonalds if it served cheeseburgers. Why?

It had to do with the law of kosher (clean and unclean)—the dietary laws established in Leviticus 11 and Deuteronomy 14.

Certain animals, fish, and insects could not be eaten, and even the animals permitted were to be killed in a specified way.

Deuteronomy 14:21 instructs: "Do not cook a goat in its mother's milk." The interpretation flowing out of this prohibition means that in eating you never mix a dairy with a meat product. Thus, if you are dining in a hotel in Israel or in an observant Jewish home, you will not have butter with your bread or cream with your coffee because meat is on the menu. Creative substitutes take the place of dairy products.

Is there anything wrong with observing kosher? Not at all. These dietary laws have helped the Jewish people maintain their identity over millennia of dispersion in the countries of the world. Where today are the Hittites, the Jebusites, or the other "-ites" of the Bible? They morphed into other cultural identities, but the Jewish people retained their identity through diet and ritual, and by God's keeping.

So, if kosher is okay—why does Jesus set it aside?

His religious critics had a false view of what pleases God. They performed their outward religious duties with corrupt hearts.

Jesus taught that righteousness before God was first a matter of inward disposition. If your attitudes, your thinking, your desires are wrong—then you can't make things right by performing religious rituals.

I came across a young college girl working the switchboard at her Christian campus. She was crying. I was her campus pastor, and I asked, "What's wrong?" She sobbed that an older lady had just come by and reamed her out because her skirt came only to her knees. The girl's dress was not immodest in any way. I replied, "The next time that woman comes around, tell her that you will lengthen your skirt if she will shorten her tongue."

I think that's the point Jesus was making here. Legalism always wants sharply defined rules and, over time, these rules become more important than anything else.

We face the same issue with the tendency to "dress-down" now occurring in many of our churches. I personally like to wear a suit and tie to church. What happens though when pastors—in an attempt to create a welcoming atmosphere for the unsaved and their own parishioners—wear more casual clothes to the pulpit? Some of the saints don't hear the sermon because they're upset with the clothes.

Do some pastors get carried away with trying to be "relevant"? Certainly! But, the opposite is also true—we can get carried away with trying to be "traditional."

Let's take Jesus' words to heart and truly listen. He is more concerned with a kosher heart than a kosher diet.

A Prayer

Lord Jesus, help me to guard my own heart so that what comes out of me is pleasing to You.

THE HOME AND THE LESSON

After he had left the crowd and entered the house, his disciples asked him about this parable. "Are you so dull?" he asked. "Don't you see that nothing that enters a man from the outside can make him 'unclean'? For it doesn't go into his heart but into his stomach, and then out of his body." (In saying this, Jesus declared all foods "clean.")

MARK 7:17–19

JESUS' MINISTRY TOOK PLACE out in the open, in synagogues and also in homes.

At this point in Mark's gospel, we are now in home number six. Look at what happened in the previous homes.

First, there was the home of Simon and Andrew, into which Jesus came and healed Peter's mother-in-law (1:29–30). Next He preached in a home where four men tore a hole in the roof and dropped down their paralyzed friend, whom Jesus forgave of sin and healed (2:1–12).

The third occasion found Jesus in Levi's (Matthew's) home, where He ate with sinners and tax collectors (2:15–17). After the appointment of the Twelve, Jesus entered another home, but He and His disciples were unable even to eat because too many people heard He was there (3:20). The teachers of the Law accused Him of being in league with the Devil, and His own family thought He had lost His mind.

At Jairus' home, Jesus raised a twelve-year-old daughter from the dead (5:37–43). Now in this passage (7:17–19), He was in a home explaining to His disciples that food doesn't defile but what comes out of the heart does.

Notice that in three of the six homes, miracles of healing and resurrection took place. In the other three homes, Jesus ate with sinners, sought refuge with His disciples, and then taught them.

There's a lesson in this for us. What are our homes for? They are designed by the Lord to be places of healing, refuge, evangelism, and training. That's how He used the home.

There's more. Remember the statement, "Jesus declared all foods clean"? Then why was it that years later, in Acts 10, Peter was still keeping the kosher law (Acts 10:14)? He had not applied Jesus' teaching to his own life, and his failure to do so made it impossible for him to consider going to a Gentile's home and eating there.

He needed the experience of a large sheet being let down from heaven full of all manner of non-kosher and kosher food, along with a command to "get up, Peter, kill and eat," before he actually experienced the truth of what Jesus had taught him years earlier.

Isn't that the same with us on occasion? How many truths lie dormant because we don't practice or experience them?

Take, for example, the stewardship of finances. We know the Scriptures teach that the first portion—the tithe—belongs to the Lord. But, like Peter's nonresponsiveness to the Lord's teaching that "all foods are kosher," we may not put into practice the Bible's teaching on giving. That's just one example. There are so many more: how we are to relate to our spouse, our children, our parents, our neighbor; our responsibility to fulfill the Great Commission; praying in words we know as well as praying in the Spirit.

Jesus actually called His disciples "dull" because they didn't apply His teaching. Let's make sure He never has reason to call us "dull"!

A Prayer

Lord Jesus, may my home become more than a place of personal refuge where I'm insulated and isolated from others. Come into my home and transform it into a center for healing, evangelism, and instruction.

THIRTEEN BAD THINGS

He went on: "What comes out of a man is what makes him 'unclean.' For from within, out of men's hearts, come evil thoughts, sexual immorality, theft, murder, adultery, greed, malice, deceit, lewdness, envy, slander, arrogance and folly. All these evils come from inside and make a man 'unclean.'"
MARK 7:20–23

MARK 7 OPENS with Jesus' critics challenging Him because His disciples have eaten with unwashed hands. The dialog grows more heated as you listen to Jesus excoriate His opponents for focusing on all the wrong things.

Instead of concentrating on unwashed hands, they should have been concerned with unwashed attitudes. Instead of using tradition to mask their moral obligation to parents, they should have honored their commitment.

Rather than being concerned about the kosher law regarding food, they should have been concerned about developing a kosher (or clean) heart.

The opponents of Jesus looked better from the outside than the inside. A photograph would have made them look good. An X-ray would have given the opposite result.

Jesus drew the dialog to a close with a strong statement about what really defiles a person, what truly makes them ugly: It's what comes from within. His list of thirteen evils is very similar to the fifteen acts of the sinful nature articulated by the apostle Paul (Galatians 6:19–21)—referred to also as the works of the flesh.

Have you considered seriously what sin does to the human personality? It brings disintegration rather than wholeness. Look at the difference with the fruit of the Spirit (Galatians 6:22–24). Fruit is singular, "works" is plural. Thus, the person living the Christ-life enjoys an integrated personality that blossoms with love, joy, peace, patience, kindness, goodness, faithfulness, gentleness, and self-control.

In other words, the fruit of the Spirit all come together in a package. You don't say, "Well, I'll take joy, but I really don't want patience or kindness." But the "works" of the flesh or the "acts" of the sinful human nature don't all come together in a bunch. An adulterer, for example, may not be a murderer. Or a deceitful person may not be a slanderer.

What unites wrong behavior is the attitude arising from the heart—evil thoughts. Thus, Jesus puts it first in His list of thirteen things that defile the insides.

Where do sexual immorality, theft, murder, adultery, greed, malice, deceit, lewdness, envy, slander, arrogance, and folly come from? They arise from evil thoughts.

What you think . . . is what you do . . . is what you say!

What a different world we would have if evil thoughts and actions all disappeared. However, the reverse is happening. In the past few decades, there's been an alarming increase of all the bad things Jesus said cause personal defilement. And personal defilement reproduces exponentially into societal defilement. Right now we are witnessing the breakdown of morality and a sense of righteousness in the culture; we are becoming a civilization on the brink of collapse.

The poet William Butler Yeats described the breakdown as "the center cannot hold." In other words, sin ultimately makes us fall apart—both as individuals and as a nation.

What's the solution? Bringing our brokenness to the Lord and asking for a clean heart, for right attitudes that lead to right actions. It is Christ who fixes us with salvation, deliverance, and healing from the inside out.

A Prayer

Lord Jesus, I confess that I, too, have been defiled with evil thoughts that have led to sinful actions. Create a clean heart in me. Renew a right spirit within me.

A MOTHER'S DESPERATE PLEA

Jesus left that place and went to the vicinity of Tyre. He entered a house and did not want anyone to know it; yet he could not keep his presence secret. In fact, as soon as she heard about him, a woman whose little daughter was possessed by an evil spirit came and fell at his feet. The woman was a Greek, born in Syrian Phoenicia. She begged Jesus to drive the demon out of her daughter.

MARK 7:24–26

HAVE YOU EVER BEEN so busy night and day that you just wished you could get away from it all for a few days?

That sentiment does not belong to you alone! Even Jesus knew the value of a retreat. He had been constantly traveling, teaching, healing—everywhere He went people thronged Him. Not only that, the opposition to Him had intensified (7:1–23). He wanted a break from the grueling schedule.

He headed north, outside the boundaries of Israel, to the area we know as southwest Lebanon. For the second time in Mark's gospel, He was in Gentile territory. On the last occasion, He delivered the Gerasene demoniac (5:1–20). This time, He was again dealing with a demon. (We'll write more about that in a moment.)

Jesus entered a private house, desiring that no one know His whereabouts. It's the seventh time in Mark that we see Him in a home. On three of the prior six occasions, wonderful miracles had taken place.

When Jesus is in the house, however, His presence can't be kept secret. When He resides in your home, in your life, others will soon know it. The word will get out!

A desperate mother found Him and fell at His feet begging.

Can you picture her? Face to the ground, tears falling around Jesus' feet, sobbing out her story, describing the symptoms in her daughter? She said nothing about her husband—perhaps, like so many in this world, she was raising a child as a single parent.

Somewhere and somehow this child had been exposed to an evil spirit; perhaps in a pagan temple or through contact with someone in the occult. Why did the demon seek residence in the child rather than the mother? We simply don't know—there's so much about the spirit world we don't understand.

Are demons loose in the world today? Just read the daily newspaper, and you will see evidence of demonic activity in the senseless and savage acts perpetrated against the innocent. How else can you explain the horrendous evil of sexual violation against children, rampant violence, senseless shootings, and a host of almost unimaginable atrocities? Evil is not impersonal; it has a source. The Devil has come to rob, destroy, and kill.

Sometimes the Devil works through humans with a depraved heart. On other occasions an actual evil spirit inhabits the body of a man, woman, boy, or girl.

That was the case here. But this mother was a lot like Jairus. (5:37–43). Both parents refused to accept their daughters' dilemmas as hopeless. They had faith that Jesus had power over death and demons. Although she wasn't Jewish, this mother trusted that Jesus would help her.

A Prayer

Lord Jesus, when I have done everything I can humanly do, I have one last resort. I can come to You. Help me to have the large-sized faith of this mother.

A WINNING RESPONSE

"First let the children eat all they want," he told her, "for it is not right to take the children's bread and toss it to the dogs." "Yes, Lord," she replied, "but even the dogs under the table eat the children's crumbs." Then he told her, "For such a reply, you may go; the demon has left your daughter." She went home and found her child lying on the bed, and the demon gone.

MARK 7:27–30

AT FACE VALUE THIS IS one of the strangest things Jesus ever spoke.

A desperate mother came to Him, fell at His feet, and begged Him to deliver her demon-possessed daughter. He appeared to put her down—comparing her Gentile ethnicity to a dog and referring to Jews as children.

Was Jesus raising the age-old barrier that separates people from people, ethnicity from ethnicity, culture from culture? At first blush, His words seem cruel. He appears to denigrate her rather than help.

That's how it may seem, but that's not how it was.

Here is where we could have used a voice recording to better interpret the text. Tone is everything. If Jesus' words were spoken harshly or brusquely, then He was being cruel. But what if He said it playfully, with a twinkle in His eye? What if He said it to draw out her faith, to help her realize that He came for Gentiles as well as Jews?

She responded to Him with absolute confidence.

First, she called Him Lord. Although not Jewish, she already had a clearer understanding of Jesus than many around Him. This is the first time in Mark's gospel that anyone has called Him Lord. Although a Gentile, her identification of Jesus stands in sharp contrast to the opinion of the religious experts who opposed Him (7:1–23)

Further, she wasn't at all hesitant to come back at Him with a playful rejoinder by saying even the dogs eat the crumbs from the children's table.

Third, she had great faith that Jesus would indeed deliver her daughter—even though the girl wasn't present. She wouldn't take no for an answer, thereby demonstrating a faith that persists even when Jesus' first response seemed negative.

Observe one other thing. New Testament scholar William Barclay notes there are two Greek words for *dog*—one to describe wild savage dogs, the likes of which are excluded from the New Jerusalem (Revelation 22:15), and the other to describe the small household pet used here in Jesus' dialog with the mother.[2]

Clearly, Jesus responded to her faith. The question remains as to what would have happened had she not rebutted the Lord's first statement. Is it possible to miss the great acts of God on our behalf because we get discouraged too easily, because we don't keep pressing, because we don't understand the essential goodness and willingness of the Lord to help us if we persevere?

This passage also tells us that Jesus knows what's happening in the spirit world without Him being spatially present. He knew the demon was gone. Physical distance proved no barrier to prevent Him from making the demon leave. The demon had to obey even when Jesus wasn't in the same room or even the same house.

Jesus has the final say over all evil, no matter where it's located!

A Prayer

Lord Jesus, Your Word says we ought always to pray and not to faint. I too easily faint. Let the faith of this Syro-Phoencian mother inspire me to press harder and not give up!

---

[2] William Barclay, *The New Daily Study Bible* (Louisville, KY: John Knox Press, 2001), 206.

HELP FROM FRIENDS AND FAMILY

Then Jesus left the vicinity of Tyre and went through Sidon, down to the Sea of Galilee and into the region of the Decapolis. There some people brought to him a man who was deaf and could hardly talk, and they begged him to place his hand on the man.

MARK 7:31–32

AFTER DELIVERING THE DAUGHTER of the Syro-Phoenician mother in Tyre, on the coast of present-day Lebanon, Jesus crossed from the Mediterranean coastland through the high range of Galilean hills, and descended to the lake nestled at 650 feet below sea level.

We don't know for sure the road juncture He next took. He could have kept going straight south to the one Decapolis city on the western side of the Jordan River, Scythopolis (ancient Beth Shean).

More likely, Jesus headed to the remaining nine cities of the Decapolis that lay to the east of the Lake of Galilee and Jordan River. Either way, He was in Gentile territory.

His venture into a non-Jewish area was a precursor to sending His disciples to the entire world. The message Jesus brings can't be limited to one ethnicity or one small geographical territory.

In the Gentile area of the Decapolis, His whereabouts again became known. People brought a deaf person to Jesus, begging Him to place His hand on the man.

As you follow Mark's gospel, you can't help but note how instrumental family and friends were in bringing people with desperate needs to Jesus.

- Others told Him about the high fever of Peter's mother-in-law (1:30).
- Four men dropped a paralytic through a roof (2:3).
- Jairus' pleaded for his dying daughter (5:22–23).

- The Syro-Phoenician mother pled for her demon possessed daughter (7:26).
- People brought the deaf and nearly mute person to Jesus (7:32).

On these five occasions, three involved relatives bringing the need to Jesus and two involved friends. These instances from the gospel of Mark encourage us that we are also welcome to bring Him the needs of others that weigh heavily on our hearts.

We should also notice that Jesus' healing and deliverance ministry reached beyond the borders of ethnicity to include the Gerasene demoniac (5:1ff.), the Syro-Phoenician daughter (7:24ff.), and this deaf man. His love and power reaches out to people who are outside the faith. He gives to all from His amazing grace.

Finally, we should also note that the people who brought the deaf man "begged" Jesus to place His hand on him. The term *begged* is also used of the Syro-Phoenician mother (7:26). What's going on?

I suspect that Mark is letting us know that as Jesus' ministry progressed, persistent faith on the part of the recipient or the recipient's family and friends became a more important factor in healing and deliverance. If you skip ahead to Mark 8:22, you will see again this word *begged* in reference to those who brought the blind man for Jesus to heal.

Certainly, we don't understand all the mysteries involved in our prayers for the sick. But this we do know—Jesus also asks us to come with earnest faith as we bring Him the needs of our family and friends.

A Prayer

Lord Jesus, I come to you today with my list of family and friends who need Your help. Lay Your hands upon them today and grant them Your mercy.

BE OPENED

After he took him aside, away from the crowd, Jesus put his fingers into the man's ears. Then he spit and touched the man's tongue. He looked up to heaven and with a deep sigh said to him, "Ephphatha!" (which means, "Be opened!").

MARK 7:33-34

FOLLOWING HIS CONFLICT with the Pharisees and teachers of the Law (7:1-23), Jesus wanted to get away from Galilee for a time of respite and solitude. Thus, in Mark 7:24-37 we find Him in what are now the countries of Lebanon and Jordan.

Think of the ocean tides. A huge wave breaks in, followed by moments of calm, and then another huge wave crashes into the shore.

Jesus was less than a year away from His own death in Jerusalem. His great Galilean ministry was drawing to a close. As He prepared for the next wave of activity that would drive Him even closer to His destiny on the cross, He took time to withdraw to Gentile territories.

Even there needy people found Him. A deaf and mostly mute man was brought to Him. Jesus dealt with this man differently than with any other. The Lord did four things uniquely in this healing.

First, He separated the man from the crowd. Why did He do this? Most likely, in this instance, he did it to keep news of the healing as private as possible (7:36). Remember, Jesus was on retreat from conflicts and crowds.

Second, Jesus did something not associated with any other healing—He put His fingers in the man's ears, spit, and then touched the man's tongue. Jesus could have simply spoken a command. Why didn't He? We'll have to ask Him on the other side. The normal pattern He has given for us in praying is to lay hands on the sick and anoint with oil (Mark 6:13; 16:18; James 5:14). Symbolic actions are meant to accompany the prayer of faith.

Third, Jesus sighed deeply. Normally, sighing is a symptom of tiredness, concern, or sadness. We know when Jesus healed the hemorrhaging woman power went out from Him (Mark 5:30). Jesus' sigh tips us off that healing this man took something out of Him. He paid a personal price to heal us from our sins and diseases.

Finally, we listen to Jesus speak in His mother tongue of Aramaic, "Ephphatha!" From early Christian tradition, we are told that Mark wrote his gospel under the influence of Peter. When you read Mark, that makes sense because in this second gospel you have unique moments that strongly show the presence of an eyewitness—such as Jesus sleeping on a pillow during the storm (4:38), speaking Aramaic to Jairus' dead daughter (5:41), the crowds sitting on green grass in the feeding of the 5,000 (6:39), and the Aramaic again spoken here to the deaf and mute man.

He not only said "Be opened!" to this man. He came to set free what is bound in us, to heal both body and spirit.

He speaks, "Be opened!" to closed hearts and closed minds. He wants to open the closed doors that have walled us off into windowless rooms of unforgiveness, shame, and regret. He is the One who opens the prison doors of bondage and captivity to sinful and destructive habits.

A Prayer

Lord Jesus, open my ears that I may truly respond to Your voice, Your will. Open my heart so that I may truly follow You and become the person You intended when You beheld my unformed substance.

THE AMAZING JESUS

At this, the man's ears were opened, his tongue was loosened and he began to speak plainly. Jesus commanded them not to tell anyone. But the more he did so, the more they keep talking about it. People were overwhelmed with amazement. "He has done everything well," they said. "He even makes the deaf hear and the mute speak."
MARK 7:35-37

IT ONLY TOOK A MOMENT for a man's world to be changed. Life had been difficult for him without the ability to hear or speak. At this moment in history, sign language had not been developed, so he had communicated as best he could.

However, adversity hadn't made him bitter. People don't befriend one who has a surly disposition. Jesus only needed to heal his body, not his attitude.

Instantly the man could both hear and speak—two of the greatest gifts in life that most of us take for granted every day. How do we use these gifts? Do we listen to the right things? Are our hearts open to the Lord to hear from Him? Do we hear His word daily from the Bible, and do we listen to the Spirit speaking to our hearts?

What about our speech? What good is it to have a voice if from our mouth come words of darkness, bitterness, blame, criticism, and cursing? Better to have a closed mouth than one that spews bile.

Early in His ministry, Jesus asked a leper to keep the news of his healing to himself (Mark 1:44). But the man disobeyed, and as a result Jesus' ability to move about freely was curtailed. This time, Jesus repeatedly asked the formerly deaf man and his companions to not spread the news. But they couldn't stop talking about it. How could anyone stop talking who had never been able to speak before!

Was Jesus, therefore, serious in giving the prohibition? Absolutely! He was still seeking privacy, wanting some retreat time in the Gentile area of the Decapolis. Jesus surely knew that any healing activity on His part would engender a crowd if the news got out, but He took the risk of losing His privacy to meet another person's need. It's a great lesson for all of us who often put our own privacy ahead of responding to the interruptions of those with needs.

People were amazed at Jesus. In the book of Acts, we also find people were amazed at what the Lord continued to do through His servants (Acts 3:10).

A question: Is anyone amazed at Jesus today because of what is happening in His church? Or are they bored? Indifferent? Angry? Is it possible that there can be a disconnect between the amazing Christ and an unamazing church?

As followers of Jesus, we must do everything possible to reflect the glory and splendor of the character and power of our Lord!

It was in the Gentile area of Decapolis where Jesus was acclaimed as having "done everything well." It's a wonderful testimony when His church goes into its secular community and represents Him with excellence so that the people living there give the same testimony of the church that the Decapolis citizens gave to Jesus—that we do everything well.

A Prayer

Lord Jesus, I can too easily take for granted all You do for me, Your great love for me, the salvation and healing You have given me, the home You are now preparing for me. May I truly be thankful.

COMPASSION

> *During those days another large crowd gathered. Since they had nothing to eat, Jesus called his disciples to him and said, "I have compassion for these people; they have already been with me three days and have nothing to eat. If I send them home hungry, they will collapse on the way, because some of them have come a long distance."*
>
> MARK 8:1–3

IF YOU HAD BEEN THERE that day as one of the disciples, what response would you have made to Jesus' concern?

It is easy now to answer because we know what happened. You and I would say, "Well, Lord, just a few weeks ago You fed a very large crowd that had only been with you for one day, and these folk have camped with us three days, listening to You teach hour upon hour even though they have been hungry (Mark 6:34–44). They have certainly demonstrated their sincerity, and You don't want them to faint or even die on the long walk back to their homes. So, Lord, we'll go looking for another little boy with some small loaves and fishes!"

That is what we think we would say!

But I'm afraid we're more like the disciples who don't connect the Lord's past miracles to the present situation. That's why Jesus posed the problem rather than just announcing He was going to do another feeding miracle. He was testing His disciples to see if they could come up with a right solution.

We will look at their response in a subsequent devotional, but for now let's focus on Jesus.

You can't fail to be struck by His magnetism. We know from Mark 7:31 that Jesus was in the area of Decapolis, in Gentile territory. He had initially withdrawn from Galilee to be alone, but that proved impossible. People found Him. The word of His presence spread and great crowds gathered.

This time, thousands of people had clustered around Jesus for three days, listening to Him teach and probably bringing their sick folk as well.

I was recently in a country that has only a tiny fractional minority of Christians. If you walk into one of the church buildings of the historical denomination, with its "smells, bells, and icons," you immediately understand why non-Christians aren't attracted. There is no life in the place. The symbols of Jesus are there, but He is not.

The absence of Jesus can just as easily be seen in nearly empty Pentecostal or evangelical churches in North America. What good is the building, organization, or program if Jesus is not the main attraction?

What makes Jesus so attractive? Certainly His teaching. Certainly His works of healing and deliverance. But is that all? There's something underlying all He does. It's His love. He teaches, heals, and delivers because He loves people.

And that is seen here. He had compassion on people. They knew it. They felt it. He is more than a great lecturer or wonder worker; He is the Good Shepherd who cares for us, His sheep.

When we, His people—His church—act with compassion as He did, then those who don't know Christ realize we aren't interested in them as growth statistics for our church, but because we love as did our Lord.

When we care about people who are tired and without food, sooner or later the word gets out: "Jesus is in the house."

A Prayer

Lord Jesus, let me not be indifferent to the hungry, the homeless, or the helpless. Give me a heart to care, eyes to see, and hands to help.

LEST WE FORGET

His disciples answered, "But where in this remote place can anyone get enough bread to feed them?" "How many loaves do you have?" Jesus asked. "Seven," they replied. He told the crowd to sit down on the ground. When he had taken the seven loaves and given thanks, he broke them and gave them to his disciples to set before the people, and they did so.
MARK 8:4–6

HOW QUICKLY WE FORGET the Lord's past miracles. Weeks, perhaps months, have gone by since the feeding of the 5,000 (Mark 6:30–44). The disciples don't connect the Lord's past acts with the present need.

In dealing with the hunger of the 5,000, He asked the disciples the same precise question He asks now, "How many loaves do you have" (Mark 6:38; 8:5)? You would think they would say among themselves, "Remember when He asked us that last time? He's repeating the question as a test to see if we learned the lesson—that He can meet a great need even if we have tiny resources. If He did it then, He is able to do it now."

But their question to Him focused instead upon the impossibility of the situation, "Where in this remote place can *anyone* (including Jesus) get enough bread to feed them." They had no more faith here than they had during the storm at sea (4:40).

Their failure to connect God's past provision with their present need is one we face continually in our own lives. We run up against situations that perplex us, where solutions aren't even on the horizon. And we ask in bewilderment, "What can be done here? We don't have any answers."

The real problem is that our need always appears to be greater than our resources or ability to deal with it. Fortunately, when we are out of options, He is not!

The crowd had run out of food, but the disciples still had some bread stashed—seven loaves in all. The cupboard was nearly bare.

The Lord instructed them to give out all the loaves, to hold nothing back. There is to be no hoarding in His kingdom. The seven loaves cannot be kept for a later day. They must be disposed of now. Jesus, the Creator, can make food out of nothing, but He chooses to start with something—our something.

What do you have to give to the Lord today to meet the need you face? Do you also have some loaves, something stashed away that you don't want to let go of? Are you willing to let Jesus do with it what He wants?

Jesus had the crowd sit down—there would be no stampeding for the food or crushing gawking to see what He was doing when He multiplied the loaves.

In both the feeding of the 5,000 and here, Jesus gave thanks (6:41) before He broke the loaves. He also gave thanks at the Last Supper. I can assume, therefore, that these feedings of the 5,000 and 4,000 foreshadow the Passover meal in which Jesus' body and blood become food and drink for all who will believe. He gave thanks before the bread was broken, and He gave thanks before the cup was drunk.

The disciples distributed the bread—"setting it before the people." After Pentecost they will set the living Bread before the world. And today, all who minister in His name are still giving the Bread of Life to all who are hungry.

A Prayer

Lord Jesus, help me to remember what You have done for me in the past so that I may trust You with all my present and future needs.

SATISFIED

They had a few small fish as well; he gave thanks for them also and told the disciples to distribute them. The people ate and were satisfied. Afterward the disciples picked up seven basketfuls of broken pieces that were left over. About four thousand men were present. And having sent them away, he got into the boat with his disciples and went to the region of Dalmanutha.

MARK 8:7–10

THE STORY OF THE FEEDING of the 4,000 begins with discontent.

The crowd of men had been with Jesus in a remote place for three days. They were hungry because the food had run out. The disciples didn't have a solution to the dilemma Jesus posed—that if He sent the famished crowd away, some would collapse.

The disciples didn't know what to do. We are just like them. Perhaps you are facing a situation that is far larger than you have resources to address. You are physically, financially, emotionally, or spiritually at wit's end.

Take a moment and look at what Jesus does to address the need—both then and now.

First, He sent the disciples out into the crowd in two stages: first to distribute the seven loaves, and next the small amount of fish.

It was the Lord's way of showing us how He will always address the needs in our lives and others. He tells us to use what is already in our hands. We would like all the resources in advance, but He instructs us to start with the little we already have.

Our resources are always too small; but we must not sit around in idleness waiting for more of what we think we need. Our task is to use what we have; it's the Lord's task to provide.

Second, the Lord gave thanks. In fact, He gave thanks twice—before the breaking of the loaves and the distribution of the fish. We carry over the Lord's example in saying grace before our meals.

We should not skip the fact that Jesus gave thanks to God for such mundane things as eating bread and fish. It is a lesson for us to show gratitude even in the small matters of life that we take for granted.

Third, when we obey Jesus and give what we have, then the needs of others are met. The 4,000 men were sent away satisfied.

How many opportunities to witness, to serve others in the name of Jesus, are lost because we don't feel we have enough or know enough? We become afraid to witness to an unsaved friend, coworker, or neighbor because we think they're not interested or we don't have enough information to answer all their possible objections. All Jesus wants us to do is start with what we have—our own testimony. When we give our own experience away, the Lord multiplies that in the hearts of those around us.

It's the same principle when we know someone else has a greater need than our own. When we give away what we have, then we truly see how God richly blesses.

Finally, Jesus was not wasteful. He ordered a cleanup of the site, and the disciples gathered seven baskets of fragments—the visible evidence of the Lord's abundant provision.

When we follow Jesus, we always end up with more than we had when we began.

A Prayer

Lord Jesus, help me not to focus on the little I have—
rather, give me the courage to give away what You have
placed in my hands. I, too, want to be an eyewitness
of the miracles You do through my own life.

NO SIGN

The Pharisees came and began to question Jesus. To test him, they asked him for a sign from heaven. He sighed deeply and said, "Why does this generation ask for a miraculous sign? I tell you the truth, so sign will be given to it." Then he left them, got back into the boat and crossed to the other side.

MARK 8:11–13

THE ROLES ON JUDGMENT DAY will be reversed. Jesus is the One who will ask the questions then.

But in the here and now, the religious leaders were upset with Him. It wasn't the first time. They took exception to His . . .

- forgiving the sins of the paralytic (2:5–7)
- eating with tax collectors and sinners (2:15–16)
- permitting the disciples to pluck grain on the Sabbath (2:23–24)
- healing the man with the withered hand on the Sabbath (3:1–5)
- permitting the disciples to eat with unwashed hands (7:1–8)

They also rejected Him as coming from God—saying He was possessed of the Devil (3:22–30). At one point they even joined their arch-enemy rivals, the Herodians, and plotted to kill Jesus (3:6).

In this passage from Mark 8 the Pharisees tried to put Jesus on the spot by demanding He do "a sign from heaven." From their point of view, the healings, exorcisms, teachings, and miraculous feedings were insufficient evidence of His divine identity.

Jesus refused. He never performed His miracles to impress anyone or to coerce anyone into believing. He chose not to gut free will through overwhelming an individual's ability to say no to Him.

The sign from heaven the Pharisees missed is that Jesus showed us the nature of God—that He is love. Jesus loved, and that's why He healed, why He taught, and why He cast out demons. He loves us even when we are unlovely. Out of love, He went to the cross for us because there was no other way to expunge our sin.

Jesus does no show-boating miracles. He doesn't snap His fingers and draw lightning down from heaven or summon hosts of angels to become visible to skeptical religious or irreligious people. He doesn't write "Jesus saves" in the clouds.

That's not to say He refrained from giving us signs. The gospel of John explicitly notes seven signs Jesus performed—from transforming water into wine to raising Lazarus from the dead. Mark shows us the signs of His feeding the 5,000 and the 4,000, plus the healings and deliverances; and at the end, His resurrection from the dead.

I had a college friend who locked himself in his dorm room for three days and demanded Jesus do a miracle in the room. Three days later, my friend walked out of the room an agnostic. He made the same mistake as the Pharisees. He didn't act on the signs already given to him: that the created order, like a wristwatch, didn't happen by accident; that Jesus' resurrection is the only viable historical evidence for why the tomb was empty; that lives today are still being delivered, healed, and transformed by Jesus.

The signs Jesus gives are enough to lead us to a faith that rests in the sufficiency of the evidences. His signs satisfy our deepest needs, not our curiosity.

A Prayer

Lord, when they were done testing, You left them. Only Your disciples got into the boat with You. I don't want to be left apart from you. I want to be wherever you are.

YEAST

The disciples had forgotten to bring bread, except for one loaf they had with them in the boat. "Be careful," Jesus warned them. "Watch out for the yeast of the Pharisees and that of Herod." They discussed this with one another and said, "It is because we have no bread."

MARK 8:14–16

JESUS HAD JUST FED a crowd of 4,000 men even though the total resources at the beginning were seven loaves and a few small fish (Mark 8:6–7). At the conclusion, the disciples picked up seven basketfuls of the broken pieces.

Fast forward a few hours and the disciples are all worried again about food. They had forgotten to bring the leftovers and were down to one loaf for the Twelve plus Jesus. So they were worried!

Isn't that just like us! We, too, forget things. Did you ever lay down your cell phone, leave the house, and then have to double back to pick it up? That's the disciples, except they're already on the other side of the lake, and it's too late to go back and get the plentiful leftovers. So, they're down to one loaf and worried about where their next meal is coming from. Already they had seen the Lord feed huge crowds with a handful of resources twice, and yet they are tensed up about their next meal! How like us! No matter what the Lord has done for us in the past, the present need worries us.

Not only that, but I suspect the disciples played the blame game with one another. Someone failed in his responsibility to bring the basketfuls of bread on board the boat. You can almost see them pointing fingers at one another.

The disciples were focused on the temporal and physical. Jesus drew them to the spiritual and eternal. They were concerned about bread. He was concerned about yeast.

Recognizing they were distraught, Jesus seized their moment of consternation to teach them. He transformed their discussion about bread into a lesson on yeast in order to anchor an important truth into the warp and woof of daily life.

Yeast transforms dough. "Watch what yeast you're putting into your life," Jesus said. The yeast of the Pharisees was rigid adherence to external rules without inward transformation of character. The yeast of the Herodians was the pursuit of power and privilege regardless of moral and spiritual responsibilities or conformity to God's desires.

The Pharisees lived legalistically, the Herodians lived hedonistically. Jesus said, "Stay away from either lifestyle. Don't let that yeast get into you!"

The disciples clearly were slow learners. They didn't get His point. Their minds weren't fast enough to keep up with Jesus. This shows us that Jesus wasn't working with world-class intellectuals. But denseness is not a quality belonging to them alone.

How often do we not get the point as we read the Bible or apply God's Word to our daily lives? We often make the same mistake of focusing on the temporal and the external rather than the spiritual and the eternal.

There are all kinds of yeast lying around waiting to invade your life. Identify them so that they don't corrupt you!

A Prayer

Help me, Lord, to hear You clearly so that I don't stumble along purposelessly in life.

MISSING THE POINT

Aware of their discussion, Jesus asked them: "Why are you talking about having no bread? Do you still not see or understand? Are your hearts hardened? Do you have eyes but fail to see, and ears but fail to hear? And don't you remember? When I broke the five loaves for the five thousand, how many basketfuls of pieces did you pick up?" "Twelve," they replied. "And when I broke the seven loaves for the four thousand, how many basketfuls of pieces did you pick up?" They answered, "Seven." He said to them, "Do you still not understand?"

MARK 8:17-21

JESUS USED EVERYDAY events as teaching moments. The disciples were evidently very concerned about their next meal when they realized they had left the food behind that they had gathered from feeding the 4,000. They were down to one loaf for the twelve of them plus Jesus.

Jesus jumped into the conversation by connecting bread to leaven, warning His disciples against taking in the leaven of the Pharisees and of Herod.

It is as though Jesus stepped on the accelerator and went from zero to 100 mph in ten seconds, leaving the disciples at the starting line. Their minds didn't follow Him. They were still all wrought up over the lack of bread, and He had left them miles behind.

They thought He was talking about the bread that went into their stomachs when He was talking about the leaven that went into their minds.

So, what exactly was Jesus saying and how does it apply to us?

The Pharisees and Herod were on opposite sides of the political and religious spectrum, but they had something in common: the leaven of wanting temporal power. Each wanted to run everything.

But Jesus didn't come to establish a new political party. He wasn't interested in political power. He later told Pilate, "My kingdom is not of this world. If it were, my servants would fight to prevent my arrest by the Jews. But now my kingdom is from another place" (John 18:36).

At this point in Mark 8, the disciples had not grasped what Jesus would later say to Pilate. So, Jesus probed them with a series of questions. Twice He sternly asked, "Do you not see or understand? ... Do you still not understand?"

They were concerned about running out of bread. Jesus wasn't. He had demonstrated that, if need be, He could multiply bread. He reminded them that both times when He had broken the loaves they had gathered up plenty of leftovers.

The reason for the stern questioning lies in the fact that shortly after this, Jesus would ask the disciples, "Who am I?" (8:29). When they answered correctly, He began to tell them about His approaching death (8:31). Peter didn't want to hear it (8:32–33), so Jesus rebuked him and then invited the disciples to deny themselves, take up their cross, and follow Him.

The leaven of the Pharisees and Herod rejected self-denial, cross-bearing, and losing one's life to gain it.

I wonder if Jesus would bring the same rebuke to us as He did to His disciples. What if we prayed more and politicked less? What if we paid far greater attention to building His kingdom than which party will win the next election? What if we focused on converting our neighbors to Jesus rather than converting them to our political point of view?

A Prayer

Lord Jesus, help me to live with Your priorities. It's so easy for me to be partisan on issues that don't matter for eternity. Help me to avoid the leaven of the Pharisees and Herod.

AMONG THE "SOME"?

They came to Bethsaida, and some people brought a blind man and begged Jesus to touch him. He took the blind man by the hand and led him outside the village. When he had spit on the man's eyes and put his hands on him, Jesus asked, "Do you see anything?"

MARK 8:22-23

PETER, ANDREW, AND PHILIP were all from Bethsaida, the small town tucked away on the northeastern side of the Lake of Galilee (John 1:44). A network of relationships existed in the town through families and friends connected with these three men.

In addition to the stories told about Jesus by these hometown disciples, the Bethsaida folk also would have heard firsthand and secondhand accounts of Jesus' ministry throughout Galilee.

But only "some" had the faith to bring their blind fellow-citizen to Jesus and beg for his healing. Why didn't all the people turn out? Bethsaida wasn't that big a place.

We get a clue as to how Bethsaida as a whole responded to Jesus when we read Matthew 11:20-24. The city was one of three that proved unresponsive to Jesus despite the mighty miracles He did in its midst. Jesus condemned it.

Interestingly, if you visit Israel today, you will find all that remains of these three towns are ruins.

Which group in Bethsaida would you rather identify with: the "some" who came to Him or the many who ignored Him?

Note the sensitivity of Jesus in taking the man by the hand—it's an appropriate gesture of help toward a blind person. Jesus led him outside the town because the Lord didn't require the electricity of an audience to enable Him to perform a miracle. He never showboated with crowd-pleasing histrionics. Jesus exercised the care of a physician respecting the privacy of His patient.

Then something most unusual happened. Jesus spat on the man's eyes. Why? We aren't told. Perhaps the man's eyes were dried out, and Jesus re-enacted the work of creation when dry dirt was breathed upon and man became a living being. Here, Jesus took the lifeless material of the eyeball and apparently added moisture that it might see.

Obviously Jesus could just as easily have spoken healing. I suspect the Lord tailored the method of healing to the man's need. Then Jesus provided time for the man to assess the results. Jesus asked, "Can you see anything?" Jesus didn't ask, "Can you see clearly?" Jesus already knew that this was a healing in process. It's the only healing miracle recorded in Mark that wasn't completed instantly.

That's an encouragement for us because sometimes the healing we receive from illness occurs over time. There is initial progress, but the healing is not yet complete.

In the town of Bethsaida, where a man was receiving his sight, most of the people remained spiritually blind to who Jesus really was.

There is a blindness more debilitating and destructive than the loss of physical sight. It is blindness of the heart: blindness to see the needs of others in our family or among the needy, blindness that fails to observe personal faults and correct them, blindness to discover God's will and purpose for our lives, and blindness that prevents us from seeing Jesus as He really is.

Will you be among the "some" who come to Jesus either for yourself or for another and ask Him to give you 20/20 vision in the eyes of your heart?

A Prayer

Lord Jesus, help me to see You, others, and myself clearly. I don't want to be blind to what You want me to see.

I CAN SEE CLEARLY NOW!

He looked up and said, "I see people; they look like trees walking around." Once more Jesus put his hands on the man's eyes. Then his eyes were opened, his sight was restored, and he saw everything clearly. Jesus sent him home, saying, "Don't go into the village."

MARK 8:24–26

I KNOW EXACTLY HOW this formerly blind man felt after Jesus had partially restored His sight.

Several weeks ago I had cataract surgery. First, the left eye; then a week later, the right eye. Both times the affected eye was covered with a bandage for a day. What a relief to get the patch off and know that the doctor had not blinded me!

There was a remarkable change in my vision. Before cataract surgery I, too, saw men as trees walking. After the surgery, my vision dramatically improved. Today I see clearly with just a minimal boost from my eyeglasses.

In the healing of the Bethsaida blind man, after Jesus had spit on his eyes and laid hands on them, the man answered truthfully that he still could not see clearly. Credit him with being honest. He might have chosen instead to try to please Jesus by acting like he had good eyesight, "Oh, thank You, Jesus! I now can see! Oh, it's so wonderful!" But he didn't fake his healing; nor did he confess that he could see clearly when he could not.

This time Jesus chose not to spit on the man's eyes, but simply to place His hands on them again. Full sight was restored.

This is the only progressive healing recorded by Mark—all the others occurred instantaneously. Why this miracle required two actions by the Lord isn't clear. But there is a clue.

In just a few days (Mark 8:27–29), the disciples would begin also to see clearly who Jesus was. Their spiritual sight had taken more than two years to develop. The healing of the Bethsaida blind man in two stages shows also that sometimes coming to spiritual sight takes time.

One of my friends came to Christ out of a pretty dreadful past of bondage to destructive attitudes and actions. He found that he didn't gain deliverance all at once over these things that had had such a strong hold on him. He said to me, "It took me awhile to fall into these habits, and it's taken me awhile to fall out of them."

It would be wonderful if all bad thoughts and deeds were cured instantly at conversion. And Jesus often does grant complete and immediate deliverance. However, just as with the healing of the blind man at Bethsaida, Jesus may use a process instead of giving deliverance all at once.

We must avoid the danger of trying to program the Lord, of holding Him to a rigid expectation of what He should do in all circumstances. We can see only the moment. He sees the distance, and because He sees farther, He knows best what to do in the present.

The citizens of Bethsaida, as a whole, rejected Jesus (Matthew 11:21). That explains why Jesus told the healed blind man not even to go back into town, but to go to his own home. The folk at Bethsaida missed the chance of a lifetime when they turned their backs on Jesus.

A Prayer

Lord Jesus, Your first touch is salvation and Your final touch is the resurrection of my body. In between those two healings, I often see through a glass darkly or partially. But the Day is coming when I shall see, even as I am seen by You!

OPINIONS OF JESUS

Jesus and his disciples went on to the villages around Caesarea Philippi. On the way he asked them, "Who do people say that I am?" They replied, "Some say John the Baptist, others say Elijah; and still others, one of the prophets."

MARK 8:27–28

WE ARE NOW AT THE TURNING POINT in Jesus' ministry. More than two years earlier, Jesus had selected twelve men to follow Him closely. They were eyewitnesses to His words, works, and personal presence. If Jesus' mission was to succeed, then everything depended on whether they now saw Him for who He truly was.

Jesus took them away from the Galilean crowds that adored and followed Him. He headed up to an area we now know as the Golan Heights. In the foothills of Mount Hermon, in the villages of Caesarea Philippi with their pagan populations and temple, He began the all-important assessment regarding His identity.

Jesus inched into the discussion by asking, "Who do people say that I am?" This doesn't mean He was unaware of public opinion. He certainly knew what others were saying about Him, and He knew that opinions were divided. He also knew that the general population had not assessed Him as the Messiah—and that, indeed, was confirmed by the disciples' answer.

However, Jesus wanted to engage the disciples in a conversation of discovery, so He approached the subject of His identity from a more oblique angle. Isn't that also how He works with many of us? There are some who have an instant blinding-light conversion experience as Saul of Tarsus, but for most of us there's a process in coming to Christ—as though we were watching the sun slowly rise until the light of the gospel shines fully in our opened eyes.

Rather than immediately saying to the Twelve, "Who do you say that I am?", He began by lubricating their thought processes. He forced them to consider others' assessment of Him.

When Jesus also asks this question of us, He knows what people are saying of Him. For some people today, Jesus is a legend. For others, He is a liar. A handful may even see Him as a lunatic. A vast number place Him in the pantheon of other religious figures, shrug their shoulders and say dismissively, "Who is right?" Jesus' goal is to move us from all those positions toward affirming His true identity as Lord.

The disciples' response tells us that while Jesus was highly regarded in public opinion, the people didn't see Him as the Messiah.

When Jesus was called John the Baptist or Elijah, that didn't mean the masses of Jewish people believed He was a reincarnated John or a translated Elijah come back to earth. Their perspective was that Jesus was John-like or Elijah-like—a preparer for One who would come after Jesus.

John the Baptist had come as the Elijah promised in Malachi 4:5, but in the popular opinion Jesus had now succeeded to that role of Way Preparer.

In the parallel account in Matthew (16:14), one other possibility named by the people was Jeremiah. The linkage of Jesus with Jeremiah might accord with the idea of some that God's people now faced judgment from the foreign power of Rome just as Jeremiah had seen Babylon as God's visitation of judgment; or, that Jesus' ministry—like Jeremiah's—was one of tears (Hebrews 5:7).

Do you know what the people around you are saying about Jesus? How are you helping them to know who He truly is?

A Prayer

*Lord Jesus, help me today to influence others
to see You for who You truly are.*

LIFE'S GREATEST QUESTION

"But what about you?" he asked. "Who do you say that I am?" Peter answered, "You are the Christ." Jesus warned them not to tell anyone about him.

MARK 8:29-30

IT'S THE MOST IMPORTANT QUESTION you will ever answer: "Who do you say Jesus is?"

For nearly three years, Jesus had laid the foundation for asking this question. His messiahship was not the one expected by the religious teachers or the general population of the day. Both groups hoped for a ruler who would physically sit on David's throne and expel the Romans, initiating the day of God's rule on earth.

Instead, Jesus brought a kingdom that must be voluntarily received, a rule that is not imposed from without but grows up inside. There will certainly be a kingdom He brings in the future where all sin, disease, and death are banished—but, for now, His kingdom is like seed sown into soil that is met with a variety of responses (Mark 4:1-20).

Had Jesus' ministry fallen on any good ground? Did His disciples "get it?" Did they understand now that the Messiah, which literally means Anointed One, had come in the person of Jesus? Jesus' question was the big test. It was an examination with only one question, and it didn't require a long answer.

Unless this question is answered correctly, Jesus must delay His journey to the cross. He cannot begin walking to Jerusalem unless they have settled this matter in their hearts. And if the Twelve never answer the question correctly, Jesus' whole mission with them has been in vain. He would need to start over with another group.

You may be thinking that I'm minimizing the Lord in saying that His mission depended on others. But that's the truth isn't it? How would we ever have known Him if we hadn't been told?

J. B. Phillips once imagined an account of a wondering angel in heaven who asked Jesus after His return from earth, "How will the world know?" Jesus answered, "I'm depending on my disciples to tell the story." The angel replied, "But what if they don't?" Then Jesus responded, "I have no other plan."

Indeed there are some who will never know Jesus unless you tell them.

Who is Jesus? That's the most important question you will ever answer. Not only is your eternal destiny at stake, but His purpose and plan for your life on this earth also hang in the balance. When you surrender to His identity you find your own.

After Peter said, "You are the Messiah," Jesus warned them not to tell anyone. Why? Others in hearing the term *messiah* would apply a different meaning to it. It would take Jesus' own death and resurrection for others to fully understand what it meant for Him to be Messiah.

You'll notice that Mark omits the statements made to Peter about his being the rock, etc., as recorded in Matthew 16:17–19. Why?

If, as early tradition indicates, Mark wrote down what Peter preached, then it isn't surprising that Peter would minimize his own role. It is a characteristic in Mark that where Peter looks good in other Gospels (such as walking on water in Matthew 14:28–30), it is left out by Mark.

It's a good lesson for us not to boast of anything. The apostles focused on telling Jesus' story and being humble about their own roles.

A Prayer

Lord Jesus, along with Peter I say, "You are the Christ." You are my Savior, King, Prophet, Priest, and blessed Son of God. You are forever Lord.

A STUNNING ANNOUNCEMENT

He then began to teach them that the Son of Man must suffer many things and be rejected by the elders, chief priests and teachers of the law, and that he must be killed and after three days rise again.

MARK 8:31

WHEN WE BEGIN to follow Jesus, He doesn't show us the full picture. He doesn't tell us all that the future will hold. He discloses Himself to us gradually as we follow Him.

That was certainly the case here with the Twelve. They had now been with Jesus for more than two years. When they first began to follow Him they thought they knew who He was. On that first day of discipleship, Andrew excitedly exclaimed to Peter, "We have found the Messiah" (John 1:41).

But now at the villages of Caesarea Philippi, far removed from the adoring crowds of Galilee, the defining moment came. The disciples passed the test when Peter said, "You are the Messiah" (Christ—the Anointed One).

Early in His ministry, Jesus gave a hint of what was to come: "But the time will come when the bridegroom will be taken from them, and on that day they will fast" (Mark 3:20). The disciples didn't catch it then—even as we often are insensitive to subtle signals the Lord gives about our own destiny.

Now comes the jolt! For the first time, Jesus explicitly states how His life will play out. We know it's the first time because Mark says, "He *began* to teach them." We know also that this was not a one-time announcement since the word *teach* is used. Mark is only giving us the summary of Jesus' extended explanation of the completion of His mission on earth. It's summed up in these four stages:

First, Jesus must suffer many things. Certainly Isaiah 53 and Psalm 22 provide a rather clear picture of the suffering Jesus would go through. No doubt Jesus walked the disciples through those passages and tried to open their minds to understand the Scriptures, even as He did later to the two disciples on the road to Emmaus after the resurrection (Luke 24:27).

Second, Jesus must be rejected. The Lord clearly identified the three centers of rejection: elders, chief priests, and teachers of the Law. He didn't list the general population, His family, or even His disciples. At this point, He didn't even identify Judas. Clearly, Jesus targeted the religious establishment of His day as the ones who will be responsible for rejection.

Third, Jesus must be killed. Jesus didn't detail the manner by which He would be killed, nevertheless *killed* is a chilling and foreboding word.

Fourth, Jesus must rise again after three days. Death would not be the end. For Jesus, and for all who follow Him, death is not the terminus. Death will be swallowed up by life (2 Corinthians 5:4).

In just moments the disciples had gone from the exhilaration of identifying Jesus as the Messiah to stunning and sobering news they had not anticipated. The only cushion to Jesus' announcement of His impending death is the promise that He would also be raised.

You and I also are going to die—a death much different from our Lord (unless He returns first). But what He promises for Himself, He also promises for us! Death and the grave can neither hold Him nor those who believe in Him!

A Prayer

Lord Jesus, continue to reveal Yourself to me. Help me to learn again from Your example that suffering is never Your last word—that, like You, I am destined to live!

CROSS AVOIDANCE

*He spoke plainly about this, and Peter took him aside and
began to rebuke him. But when Jesus turned and looked at
his disciples, he rebuked Peter. "Get behind me, Satan!"
he said. You do not have in mind the things
of God, but the things of men."*

MARK 8:32–33

FOR THE FIRST TIME, Jesus plainly told His disciples that He was going to be killed and rise again three days later. Peter didn't want to hear it.

Just moments before, Peter had gone to the head of the class by being the first person to confess Jesus as Messiah. Now, he goes to the bottom of the class. The idea of Jesus being killed didn't fit into his expectation of Jesus' identity.

That is often the case with us. We love Jesus. We make a correct confession as to who He is, but then He points us down a path we don't want to take. We object and say to Him, "Surely, this isn't part of the deal. You can't be serious. I don't want to take that direction."

At least Peter had the courtesy to take Jesus aside and talk with Him privately. Actually, it was more than a "talk"—Peter rebuked Him. In other words, Peter vehemently protested and essentially said to the Lord, "You are the Messiah, but You are mistaken about what You're supposed to do."

Jesus turned the tables on Peter and responded with a rebuke of His own. Although Peter rebuked Jesus privately, the Lord rebuked Peter publicly in the presence of the other disciples. Not only did Jesus confront Peter, Jesus went a step further and identified the source of Peter's rebuke—it came from Satan. Jesus essentially said to Peter: "You have just been the mouthpiece of the Devil."

In our "feel good" culture, we might have expected Jesus to gently take Peter aside, lay an arm on his shoulder, and tenderly tell him, "You know, Peter, that's not what I have in mind. But I so appreciate your suggestion because it shows how much you love me. I just want you to know I'm concerned for you, and that maybe in the ultimate scheme of things you'll understand about My death. For right now, let's just have a moment of prayer together, and we'll talk about this later. Your concern means a lot to Me, and I value the comfort you give Me."

Oh, no! Jesus wasn't going to have anyone tamper with His fundamental mission. Being tender with Peter at this point would neither help Peter nor the rest of the disciples grasp the severity of what was about to happen. Jesus would have none of Peter's persuasive efforts and didn't chalk up his counsel to good intentions.

If the cost of doing God's will involves pain and suffering, the Devil will always be whispering in our ear to avoid it—that God couldn't possibly be in the pathway that costs us so much. Peter wanted Jesus to escape. Jesus knew He must endure.

That choice frequently confronts us. We pray for escape rather than endurance. We want the easy way out. But sometimes the cross calls us as well. Our culture calls for self-fulfillment, and Jesus calls for self-denial.

A Prayer

*Lord Jesus, may I be willing and ready to lay down
my own self-interests to seek first Your
will and Your kingdom.*

COME AND DIE

Then he called the crowd to him along with his disciples and said: "If anyone would come after me, he must deny himself and take up his cross and follow me. For whoever wants to save his life will lose it, but whoever loses his life for me and for the gospel will save it."

MARK 8:34–35

WHEN THE DISCIPLES first met Jesus, He gave them an invitation to come and see (John 1:39). The journey of discipleship ultimately brings you to the place where Jesus says, "Now that you have seen, come and die."

The death He speaks of isn't necessarily martyrdom, although it may include that.

The history of Palestine in the Roman era carried memories of insurgents who were nailed to crosses as punishment for their acts of rebellion. Perhaps many in the audience that day may have initially thought Jesus was calling them to take up weapons against the occupying power.

We know differently, of course. Jesus wasn't inviting people to bear arms. Instead He asked four things:

1. *To come after Him.* This means you relinquish leadership in your own life and follow His direction.
2. *To deny self.* We live in a day that focuses on self-fulfillment. Jesus calls you to divestment and relinquishment.
3. *To take up your cross.* Some people say of a difficult circumstance or a relative who is hard to live with: "Well, that's my cross to bear." That's not the cross Jesus was talking about. Rather, the cross is something you endure solely because of your loyalty to Christ.

4. *To follow Him.* Little did the disciples or the crowd at that moment know that following Jesus meant going to Golgotha. But, ultimately, after the cross our itinerary leads to resurrection and eternal life. We follow Him all the way to glory!

During one of the battles of the American Revolution, a general quoted from Thomas Gray's poem, "Elegy Written in a Country Churchyard," which says "The paths of glory lead but to the grave." Jesus taught and exampled for us that the paths of glory lead *from* the grave! That's why He talks to us about losing our lives rather than saving them.

Here is where the martyrs help us understand. Why did a recent pastor in a country lay down his life for Jesus—why didn't he just deny the Lord and save his life? Or why did another pastor not take up an opportunity when he was given a chance to deny Jesus with his words even if he didn't deny him in his heart?

It's because these martyrs knew that human death is not the end. Jesus is waiting on the other side of death—just as He was when the first Christian, Stephen, died. Jesus stood to greet him on heaven's shore (Acts 7:56).

What does self-denial and cross-bearing mean if you are not a martyr? You are faced with choices every day. Will you choose a more enjoyable path, a sinful act, disobedience over what Jesus wants from you? Do you choose self-fulfillment over doing His will?

Jesus says that sooner or later our choices catch up with us, and those choices have eternal consequences.

Come and die is the pathway through which we come and live!

A Prayer

Lord Jesus, I want with all my heart to follow You and embrace whatever difficulty comes my way as a result of serving You.

WHAT DO YOU WANT MORE THAN ANYTHING?

What good is it for a man to gain the world, yet forfeit his soul? Or what can a man give in exchange for his soul?
MARK 8:36-37

JESUS ASKED TWO of the most important questions you will ever answer.

Imagine a scale. On one side is the whole world—on the other, your soul. You can have one or the other, but not both.

There has never been a human who owned the whole world—not Caesar, not Napoleon, not Warren Buffet, Bill Gates, or Donald Trump. The richest people on earth may own billions of dollars, but that's a grain of sand compared to the composite wealth of the whole world.

Jesus says, "Suppose you had it all. Everything you've ever wanted—money, fame, position, family, health, influence—everything. All together, they aren't as valuable to you as your soul."

Your soul is you—the *you* that lasts forever. Jesus says you are more important than anything you could ever have. If that is the case, then you must pay attention to who you are.

The question Jesus asks comes within the context of His call that you deny yourself for His cause. He says that when we choose this world, with all its passing values, rather than Him and His gospel, we forfeit our eternal souls.

Instead, Jesus says: "Deny yourself, take up your cross and follow Me." In other words, you are to live by His terms. It isn't your agenda that counts. If you think that following Jesus will bring you wealth, fame, and comfort—think again. You are likely to experience suffering. The cross is not fun and games. Self-fulfillment is much easier than self-denial.

But if you lose your life for Him, then you save it for eternity.

Jesus, in so many words, asks: "What will you trade for your soul?" Will you trade it for what is temporary: wealth, things, title, sex, approval from others, security, personal ambition?

You are of more value than all the things of this earth. In fact, you are so valuable that Jesus came to earth to lay down His life for you. He took the punishment for your sin so that you could stand before God without fault or blame of any kind.

When I was younger, I heard preachers say: "When you quote John 3:16, put your own name in place of the word 'world.' God so loved (your name) that he gave his one and only Son that whoever believes in him shall not perish but have eternal life."

I used to think, *I'm not that valuable. He wouldn't have come just for me. There had to be a critical mass of people—perhaps hundreds of thousands or even millions—before He would have thought it worthwhile to lay down His life as a substitute for sinners.*

But my view did not square with the reality of Jesus' own teaching. He looks for even one lost sheep, one lost coin, one lost son (Luke 15). The amazing love of God is that Jesus would have come for you alone if you were the only person who needed the gift of salvation, the gift of eternal life.

He values you so much that He laid down His life for you! Will you give Him your life in return?

A Prayer

Lord Jesus, I don't want to forfeit my soul. I don't want to spend my life living for things that don't matter. I place all that I am and have in Your hands.

HIS COMING

If anyone is ashamed of me and my words in this adulterous and sinful generation, the Son of Man will be ashamed of him when he comes in his Father's glory with the holy angels.

MARK 8:38

THE OWNER OF A CHAIN of Christian radio stations, in the months leading up to May 21, 2011, predicted that date as the one on which Jesus would rapture His church. He made his prediction despite Jesus' clear statement in Matthew 24:36 that "no one knows that day or hour, not even the angels in heaven, nor the Son, but only the Father."

The gullible who followed this radio station owner now know that his prediction was just another in a long line of false prophecies that have attempted to set the date for the Lord's return.

Even the secular culture seems to sense that an end date is near. The popular movie *2012* (which I did not see), portrays the fulfillment of an ancient Mayan belief that the world would end in that year with titanic catastrophes.

Clearly, however, the Lord is going to return to earth! We have His words as validation!

Mark's gospel has taken us through the gradual self-disclosure of Jesus as to His identity (8:27–29) and mission (8:31–32). Now, for the first time in Mark, Jesus discloses the glorious future. There will be a day in which He comes in His Father's glory with all the holy angels!

Jesus' promise contains four sub-themes.

First, there's going to be shame for those who were ashamed of Him and His words. Often you hear people say, "Well, Jesus was a great teacher," and then they proceed to ignore what He said. For example, His stringent requirements on moral and ethical purity, care for the poor and the distressed, and confession of Him as the only means of salvation. These persons, including even leaders in churches that have forsaken core Christian beliefs, openly disagree with Jesus' words, rejecting what He had to say about sinful behavior. To be ashamed of His words is to be ashamed of Him.

Second, this is a sinful and adulterous generation. If that was true in Jesus' day, how much more so now? A recent Academy Awards show included an actress five months pregnant without benefit of marriage, another actress who had evidently practiced using a four-letter expletive for her acceptance speech if she won, yet another actress thanking her lesbian partner, and a producer expressing gratitude to his homosexual lover.

We live in the midst of a culture rife with immorality, pornography, and degenerate behavior. Paul's description in Romans 1:18–32 fits exactly with what we see today on every hand.

Third, Jesus affirms that He is coming again to the world in glory! Referring to His first coming, John says, "We have seen His glory" (1:14). How much greater will be His glory when He appears again, this time not as the suffering Savior, but as the triumphant Lord!

Fourth, He will come with the holy angels. Clearly Jesus teaches the existence of beings beyond what we know. Even as angels sang in the night sky over Bethlehem at His first coming, so they will return in strength of numbers with Him when He comes again!

What a day that will be!

A Prayer

Lord Jesus, I don't want to miss that day. I never want to be ashamed of You or Your words. I want to be close to You at all costs, both now and at Your coming!

WHEN THE KINGDOM COMES IN POWER

And he said to them, "I tell you the truth, some who are standing here will not taste death before they see the kingdom of God come with power."
MARK 9:1

THIS IS ONE OF THE MOST problematic of Jesus' sayings. What, exactly, did He mean?

The answer is found in how you understand Jesus' definition of the kingdom of God and how you interpret the word *power*.

Let's look at the various ways Bible scholars have sought to understand these words of Jesus.

First, some take these words as referring to the remarks Jesus made immediately prior to these in which He talked about the Son of Man coming in the Father's glory with all the holy angels (8:38). This view certainly fits best the immediate context, but it doesn't take into account the phrase "some of you will not taste death before. . . ." All Jesus' original disciples died, and Jesus did not return in their lifetime.

Second, some take this saying as referring to His resurrection from the dead. Truly, the kingdom of God came with power when Jesus rose again. However, this view also fails to adequately explain "some who are standing here will not taste death before. . . ." To our knowledge, Judas was the only one who died prior to the resurrection; and Jesus seems instead to be inferring that a good number of His followers would die prior to the kingdom coming with power, with only "some" being left.

Third, some scholars take this saying as referring to the day of Pentecost, when the promise of Acts 1:8 was fulfilled, "You will receive power when the Holy Spirit comes upon you." However, the problem with this view is the same as with the second. At the day of Pentecost the bulk of Jesus' disciples (120) were still alive, not "some."

A fourth view relates this saying of Jesus to the event that immediately followed—the transfiguration of Jesus, when Peter, James, and John saw Jesus in His divine glory. In this view Peter, James, and John are the "some" who saw Christ in glorious form before they saw death. The problem with this view is that the transfiguration didn't necessarily mean that the kingdom of God had come with power.

Fifth, others take this saying as referring to the explosive growth of the early church. By the time the apostolic age was concluded, the gospel of Jesus that is the power of God for salvation (Romans 1:16; 1 Corinthians 1:18) had been carried throughout much of the then-known world (Romans 15:18-19). Some of Jesus' disciples lived long enough to see the kingdom of God come with power through this worldwide proclamation of the gospel.

In this view, the kingdom of God isn't defined as the end-time kingdom when He will rule over all, but the present kingdom—the rule of God within (Luke 17:21). It comes in power when you receive Him and your life is transformed.

It is wise not to be dogmatic on how this saying of Jesus is to be interpreted. Before saying the kingdom comes with power, Jesus talked about laying down His life and His followers laying down theirs. The laying down is not the end of things. The effort of self-denial, of taking up your cross, isn't futile or vain because the kingdom of God comes in power both in this age through transformed lives and in the age to come through His eternal rule.

A Prayer

Lord Jesus, may Your kingdom come with power in my life today and in those whom my life shall touch.

METAMORPHOSIS

After six days Jesus took Peter, James and John with him and led them up a high mountain, where they were all alone. There he was transfigured before them. His clothes became dazzling white, whiter than anyone in the world could bleach them.

MARK 9:2–3

WE CALL THIS EVENT the transfiguration of Jesus. More about what that means in a moment.

The preceding week Jesus had disclosed to the Twelve His approaching death and resurrection. His announcement was followed by Jesus inviting His disciples to a life of self-surrender and self-denial, with the promise that reward waited for them when He returned in glory (8:31–38). Those same promises apply to us as well.

Jesus moved from the villages of Caesarea Philippi, in the area we now know as the Golan Heights, into the range of Mount Hermon, the highest mountains that straddle the modern nations of Syria, Lebanon, and Israel. He left behind three-fourths of His closest disciples, taking only the inner core of three: Peter, James, and John.

These three appear to have had a special relationship with Him as their names are first in the list of the Twelve (3:16–19). They accompanied Him into the room where lay Jairus' dead daughter (5:37), and in the Garden of Gethsemane Jesus asked them to watch and pray with Him (14:33).

The selection of these three holds important implications for leadership and discipleship in that it rebuts the idea that a leader must not show discrimination or play favorites. The fact is that Jesus drew some closer to Himself than others, probably because they were the ones who moved closest to Him. It's a great lesson for us as well—that we draw near to Him.

METAMORPHOSIS

Somewhere on a high mountain, Jesus was transfigured before the three. The Greek word used here comes straight across in the English language as "metamorphosis."

Morphe means form or structure. *Meta* means to change.

We understand this term better by looking at Romans 12:1-2, where we are told not to conform to this world but to be transformed. The word *conform* has as its root the word *schema*, from which we derive the words *scheme* or *fashion*. Here's the difference between the two words. My *morphe* doesn't change. I have been male all my life. However, *my schema* or appearance is much different today than when I was 6, 16, or 69.

We are told in Romans 12 to *not* simply add the gloss of being a Christian to an otherwise worldly life, but to truly undergo a complete metamorphosis—a fundamental change in who we are, our own transfiguration.

For Jesus, the word *metamorphosis* meant that His radiance on the mountain was not just a thin layer of glow on His humanity. Rather, in those moments the three disciples were eyewitnesses to His divine nature. Peter never forgot it. Decades later he said, "We were eyewitnesses of his majesty" (2 Peter 1:16).

It is that same glory we will be privileged to see at Jesus' return, "the Son of Man coming in clouds with great power and glory. And he will send his angels and gather his elect from the four winds, from the ends of earth to the ends of the heavens" (13:26-27).

Are you living today in expectation of that Day? Peter, James, and John were taken to a high mountain where for a few hours they saw Christ in His glory! Will you see Him in His glory for all eternity?

A Prayer

Lord Jesus, receive me into Your presence today and every moment of my life so that when the great Day comes I will see firsthand Your majesty and splendor.

VETERANS AND ROOKIES

And there appeared before them Elijah and Moses, who were talking with Jesus. Peter said to Jesus, "Rabbi, it is good for us to be here. Let us put up three shelters—one for you, one for Moses and one for Elijah. (He did not know what to say, they were so frightened.)
MARK 9:4-6

IT WAS A SCENE that would make one's hair stand on end. Not only were Jesus' garments dazzling white and His face shining like the sun (Matthew 17:2), but two great leaders from the past were talking with Him on the Mount of Transfiguration.

What did they discuss? Luke tells us: Jesus' departure in Jerusalem. Mark left out that detail as well as the fact that the disciples were very sleepy (Luke 9:31-32). In the Greek New Testament the word "departure" is *ek hodos* (the way out), from which we derive the word *exodus*.

Moses and Elijah were both talking with Jesus about His exodus—an exodus of a different nature than the one Moses led. Moses brought his people out of bondage and to the edge of the land of promise; Jesus' exodus brought us out of the bondage of sin, death, the Devil, and the grave into the eternal land of promise!

The fact that Moses and Elijah were talking with Jesus about His exodus shows that the two great leaders of the Old Testament—Moses, representing the Law and Elijah, the prophets—fully endorsed the mission of Jesus to go the cross and die for our sins.

What a moment it must have been for Moses. Fourteen hundred years earlier he had been denied entrance into the Promised Land. Now he stood in the land with the Son of God. Don't worry if something you want doesn't happen in your lifetime! God has all eternity to make it up to you! Moses' appearance further shows us that after death we do not soul-sleep, but are alive.

Wouldn't you like to have been an observer to this scene? Jesus said to the rookies of the new covenant, "Come over here. I would like you to meet the veterans of the old covenant: Moses and Elijah." It was a moment that called for being dumbstruck. But not Peter!

What should you say when you don't know what to say? Nothing! However, Peter—not knowing what to say—spoke anyway!

Eight days earlier he had correctly identified Jesus as the Christ (Messiah). Now, he simply called Him Rabbi. Peter had awakened quickly from sleep and reverted to his old title for Jesus.

I would love to have listened to Peter later in life when he recounted this story. I think it would have gone something like this: "I blurted it out. We were so scared and sleepy. I spoke without thinking. But the Lord has patience with impulsive people like me. He didn't rebuke me. That's just the way He is with you. He's so very kind even when we say or do dumb things."

At least Peter was willing for the rookies to spend the night without shelter, because his offer was only to build the three shelters for Jesus, Elijah, and Moses. Credit Peter with humility, a trait we could all use more of.

A Prayer

Lord Jesus, I thank You for the moments in my life that stand out as special in my relationship to You. Just as Peter wanted to serve You rather than himself, may I follow his example.

MY SON, WHOM I LOVE

Then a cloud appeared and enveloped them, and a voice came from the cloud: "This is my Son, whom I love. Listen to him!" Suddenly, when they looked around, they no longer saw anyone with them except Jesus.

MARK 9:7–8

THE MOMENTS OF THE transfiguration are nearly complete. Jesus' appearance was as dazzling as lightning and His clothes whiter than any bleach could get them. Moses and Elijah stood with Him, giving their endorsement of His person and mission.

As spectacular as those moments were, the event builds towards its climax. A cloud appears and the heavenly Father speaks. What the Father says is the core of the good news, for He affirms the identity of Jesus ("This is my Son"), describes the quality of their relationship ("whom I love"), and backs His Son's mission ("Listen to Him!").

Before the Father spoke, Jesus received the approval of the Law and the prophets through their representatives, Moses and Elijah. But the Father's approval is far more important. God Himself backs who Jesus is and what He will do.

I also have a son whom I dearly love. I know how I feel toward him and toward anyone who would either love or mistreat him. Those who love him, I will love; but those who mistreat him, I will not honor. The heavenly Father feels that way toward His beloved Son.

For the second time in the gospel of Mark the Father is recorded as speaking from heaven. The first instance was at Jesus' baptism, where the Father said, "You are my Son, whom I love; with you I am well pleased" (Mark 1:11). The words of the Father in that moment communicated the endorsement of the years Jesus had spent in obscurity.

By contrast, the Father's words at the transfiguration provide an endorsement of Jesus' ministry to that point. A new phrase is spoken that was not mentioned at His baptism: "Listen to Him." That admonition is now necessary because Jesus has set His face to go to the cross. The temptation of the disciples would be to dissuade Him and to seek other alternatives. Instead the Father says, "You must listen!"

On a theological level, we clearly see here a dynamic in the nature of "God is One" that is only hinted at in the Old Testament. While the word *trinity* is not used in the Scripture, clearly the identity of God is being revealed as Father and Son, and, subsequently, the focus will also include the Holy Spirit (as had happened at Jesus' baptism). We are dealing with mystery here: how God can be One . . . yet Father, Son, and Holy Spirit.

We can no more fully plumb the depths of God's nature than a mouse can be genetically engineered to solve a calculus problem. The secret things do belong to God, but the things He has revealed belong to us (Deuteronomy 29:29).

The transfiguration comes to a close. The lawgiver is gone as is the prophet's representative. Their momentary appearances stand in contrast to the permanence of Christ.

Moses and Elijah, as great a mark as they left, were mere mortals. They could never make the promise Jesus would later make; "I am with you always" (Matthew 28:20).

When friends or finances fail, when reverses come, when you lose all that is near and dear to you, Jesus still remains a faithful Friend, trusted Counselor, loving Lord, and Savior.

A Prayer

Heavenly Father, I will listen to Your beloved Son.
I can never love Him as much as You, but I love Him.

THE SECRET

As they were coming down the mountain, Jesus gave them orders not to tell anyone what they had seen until the Son of Man had risen from the dead. They kept the matter to themselves, discussing what "rising from the dead" meant.

MARK 9:9–10

PETER, JAMES, AND JOHN experienced what no other disciple saw—the transfiguration of Jesus. If you had seen Jesus' countenance and clothes glowing and had met Moses and Elijah, you would want to tell everyone. I'm sure these three disciples, who were privy to the event, couldn't wait to recount their adventure on the mountain.

But Jesus told them to keep it secret. And they did! Why?

There are several reasons.

First, Jesus knew that all His audiences, whether disciples, religious leaders, or crowds, had their own conception of who the Messiah would be and what He would do. The event of the transfiguration was so overpowering that, if known prematurely, it would only feed the idea that the Messiah was a spectacular figure. Instead, Jesus' pathway was to take the role of the suffering servant and to journey to the cross. The transfiguration story could only be told when He was on the other side of the cross. It contrasts what the Father thinks of Jesus ("my Son, whom I love") with the human verdict ("crucify Him").

Second, Jesus didn't do miracles for show. He did them to help people. Earlier in Mark, Jesus had shut up the demons when they testified of Him (1:25, 34). He told a leper not to share the goods news of his healing (1:44), and Jairus' family was given strict orders not to tell anyone of their dead daughter's deliverance from death (5:43). Jesus wasn't into a showbiz, commercialized ministry where He blatantly advertised miracles in order to get a crowd. If Jesus sometimes ordered people not to tell of His

THE SECRET

acts of power, it's not surprising that He instructed the three disciples to keep quiet about this overwhelming revelation of His divine identity.

Jesus' orders to keep this event secret came from His intention to tamp down the popular belief that the Messiah would be an earthly ruler. Further, if the three disciples had begun to broadcast their experience it would only have created jealousy among the other disciples who weren't privy to what happened on the mountain. They were prone already to contest who was the greatest (9:33–34).

The order not to tell would be lifted after Jesus rose from the dead. Peter, James, and John clearly didn't understand what "rise from the dead" meant—even though after Peter's confession, Jesus said plainly that He would be killed and rise again three days later (8:31–32).

Like the disciples, we may not see clearly the first time around what truth the Lord wants us to lay hold of!

The three disciples witnessed His many miracles, but Jesus was setting them up for something more powerful than anything they had seen—His resurrection. This wouldn't be a resurrection on the order of Jairus' daughter (5:41–42), the Nain widow's son (Luke 7:15), or even Lazarus (John 11:44). All those subsequently died.

Jesus' resurrection was far greater. His death was not the result of sickness, but of crucifixion; and He would never again die.

That same kind of resurrection waits for all of us who believe!

A Prayer

Lord Jesus, Your demand for secrecy is a reminder to me that it's not always appropriate to say what's on my mind. Help me to discern when it's the right time to speak or to stay silent.

ELIJAH COMES FIRST

And they asked him, "Why do the teachers of the law say that Elijah must come first?" Jesus replied, "To be sure, Elijah does come first, and restores all things. Why then is it written that the Son of Man must suffer much and be rejected? But I tell you, Elijah has come, and they have done to him everything they wished, just as it is written about him."

MARK 9:11–13

THEOLOGICAL ISSUES must be dealt with. When disciples ask questions it isn't necessarily due to a lack of faith. The Twelve had a big intellectual problem that was hindering them from full commitment to the mission of Jesus. They had been taught all their lives that Elijah would come before the Day of the Lord. Why then had he not shown up?

Evidently the opponents of Jesus had been throwing this question at the disciples, and they had no answer. When you don't have an answer, it's always best to ask someone who does. They came to Jesus.

The question couldn't be dismissed. After all, the weight of the prophet Malachi lay behind it—he had said flatly that Elijah would come before the Messiah to prepare the way (Malachi 4:5-6).

Jesus responded to their question by saying that the prophecy was correct. Elijah did come first. However, Jesus knew what Malachi couldn't see four centuries previously. Malachi saw one part; Jesus saw the whole. The prophet's focus was on "restore all things." Jesus knew that restoration depended on "The Son of Man must suffer much and be rejected."

It's as though Malachi, looking from a distance, only saw the mountain peak of the eternal age, not recognizing that the mountain peak of the cross and resurrection was in the foreground—and a long valley of time separated the two peaks.

Malachi saw the age of restoration (which Jesus begins when He heals our hearts and forgives our sins), but other prophets saw the suffering the Messiah would endure (Isaiah 53, Psalm 22). Jesus brought both strands of the prophetic word together.

In answering the disciples' question, He turned them away from the long future to the immediate present where suffering lay before Him.

Then, Jesus said that Malachi's prophecy of Elijah to come had been fulfilled in the person of John the Baptist (Matthew 16:13). Jesus took what many regarded as a literal Elijah and instead brought a spiritual fulfillment to it. His whole ministry was that way—the general expectation was for the literal earthly reign of the Messiah, but Jesus repudiated that view in His announcement of death and resurrection, and in His teaching that the kingdom in this age is internal and not external.

It's just as easy for us disciples today to focus on the grand promises of Scripture without regard to the perils that the Scriptures also indicate await us. Would that every day would be one of fulfillment, happiness, health, safety, and success. But, alas, there are also days of storm, trouble, nightmare, difficulty, and deep distress. We cannot focus on one to the exclusion of the other until that Day when there is no more night!

A Prayer

Lord Jesus, I like fulfillment better than frustration, success rather than stress, healing rather than hurt, and good news rather than bad. Help me, Lord, to hold on to the promise of good things on the one hand, but with the other hand receive if necessary the nail that causes so much pain.

FROM ARGUMENT TO WONDER

When they came to the other disciples, they saw a large crowd around them and the teachers of the law arguing with them. As soon as all the people saw Jesus, they were overwhelmed and ran to greet him.

MARK 9:14–15

SOMETIME EARLIER JESUS LEFT BEHIND nine disciples and took the inner three—Peter, James, and John—to a high mountain where they were alone. There Jesus' appearance was transformed before their eyes, and they listened to a conversation Jesus had with Moses and Elijah.

Upon returning to reunite with the others, Jesus found the nine disciples surrounded by a crowd listening to an argument between them and Jesus' critics.

Credit the nine! They had been left at the foot of the mountain, but they had not left Jesus. They remained loyal rather than dispersing. They were arguing passionately in His defense even though He had left them behind.

It's not an easy thing to be excluded, to be outside the inner circle. Did they have feelings like, "Why was I not included?" "What's wrong with us?" "Does Jesus have His pets and we're not among them?"

Haven't you felt left out at times? Others have their prayers answered yes and your answer is either no or delay. Someone else gets a great new job, and you're terminated from employment. Someone you know testifies they've been healed. You try to rejoice in their miracle but find it difficult because you haven't been healed.

This feeling of being left out happens a lot. The Lord is moving on with others but leaving you behind—or so it seems. They get to see the glory while you are left with a mess.

And a mess it was for the nine! As Jesus walked back into the scene they were losing a heated argument with religious experts.

What the nine and we need most to understand in such a moment is: (1) Jesus is sovereign and we must respect His choices as to who goes with Him on the mountain, and (2) He will always reappear in our valley!

Only later do we understand why He took the three. The disclosure of Himself in radiant glory and talking with Moses and Elijah had to be kept secret. The number of witnesses was kept small lest the news leak out before the time. Premature disclosure would only have reinforced the false expectation that Jesus came as a politically powerful ruler. Also, Peter, James, and John would subsequently suffer much. James was the first apostle to be martyred. Peter was crucified upside down on a cross in Rome. John lived his final years as an exiled prisoner on Patmos. No doubt the Lord knew that taking them with Him to the transfiguration would become ballast for each of them in the midst of their own coming storms.

Then, notice a remarkable shift. The crowd was drawn to an argument like children are drawn to watch a fight in the schoolyard. But when Jesus showed up their attention went to Him.

There's a lesson in that. People are not persuaded by argument. Too often argument only reinforces our own opinions. The more we argue the more disagreeable we become. But Jesus is attractive! The church always does well when it remembers that.

May we always be overwhelmed with wonder in the presence of Jesus and run to greet Him!

A Prayer

Lord Jesus, there are so many things I need to do today.
But, the most important thing I do is come to You.
Be present, Lord, to me today—be with me,
in me, for me, through me.

THEY COULD NOT

"What are you arguing with them about?" He asked. A man in the crowd answered, "Teacher, I brought you my son, who is possessed by a spirit that has robbed him of speech. Whenever it seizes him, it throws him to the ground. He foams at the mouth, gnashes his teeth and becomes rigid. I asked your disciples to drive out the spirit, but they could not."

MARK 9:16–18

WHEN JESUS CAME DOWN from the Mount of Transfiguration with Peter, James, and John, He found a distressing scene in the valley. A huge argument had broken out between the nine disciples left behind and the teachers of the Law, with a large crowd looking on.

The crowd, on seeing Jesus, turned its attention away from the fracas to Him. Any normal cleric might have taken time to bask in the glow of adoration, but Jesus was no ordinary spiritual leader. He ignored the crowd and queried His disciples regarding the argument, "What's this about?"

Before they can answer, or perhaps because they are hesitant to answer, a father does it for them. His statement about having a son possessed by a demon, at first blush, seems to have no bearing on what the argument was about.

Early on in Jesus' ministry, His opponents accused Him of driving out demons by the power of the Devil (Mark 3:22). Later, when Jesus sent out His disciples on their first mission, they also drove out many demons (6:13). This is the first time exorcism doesn't occur and it gives the critics of Jesus powerful ammunition to argue that prior occasions were a demonstration of Jesus' connection with the occult—that what He and the disciples did was through demonic agency. And since the Devil has limited powers, exorcism can only be done sporadically and not at all times.

This story really tells us about a powerless church. When the mighty works of God are not being done, then all that's left is argument. The church must have more than an argument if the world is to be won.

This account also contains a powerful paradigm at what the Devil does to people. (1) He seizes them. They are no longer able to control themselves—another power is in control of their lives. They think, say, and do the wrong things. (2) He throws them to the ground. The Devil doesn't come to build up, but to tear down. The ultimate end is down even for those who consider themselves successful and have no need of God.

The effect of the Devil is seen on what happens to persons whose life he influences: (1) foaming at the mouth—embarrassment before God and people. (2) Gnashing of teeth—a foretaste of hell, and a present act of despair. (3) Becoming rigid—rigor mortis is the spiritual condition of incapacity and inability to change. Jesus came to reverse all these effects of the Devil.

A powerless church is no help to those dominated by the Devil. When Jesus sent out the Twelve, He gave them authority over evil spirits, and they indeed "drove out many demons" (6:7, 13). Somewhere along the line, their power had leaked out. Their bad example is a lesson for us.

A Prayer

Lord Jesus, I cannot be effective with yesterday's anointing, yesterday's blessings, yesterday's spiritual reserves. I need present power if I am to overcome the deeds of the Devil, if I am to live a life that is right before you, and if I am to help others. May my supply of the Spirit be full today!

WHEN JESUS IS NOT PLEASED

> *"O unbelieving generation," Jesus replied, "how long shall I stay with you? How long shall I put up with you? Bring the boy to me." So they brought him. When the spirit saw Jesus, it immediately threw the boy into a convulsion. He fell to the ground and rolled around, foaming at the mouth.*
> MARK 9:19–20

THIS MAY BE THE MOST explicit example of Jesus being frustrated with His disciples.

Even though He had given them power over demons (3:15) and they had previously exercised that authority (6:13), they were now powerless to help a boy a father had brought to them.

Jesus' rebuke was scathing. He called them unbelieving and asked two "how long" questions. The first, "How long shall I stay with you," relates to the shortness of time that Jesus had left in His mission. The second "how long" found Jesus rhetorically wondering if He should fire them all: "How long shall I put up with you?"

We know the answer to both questions as we journey on with Jesus. We learn that He didn't give up on His disciples even though, at this point in His ministry, He was very frustrated with them. That's helpful encouragement because the Lord doesn't give up on us either—even when we severely disappoint Him.

If Jesus was upset then by His disciples, I can't begin to imagine how He must feel sometimes about His church today—a church that is often powerless in addressing the pressing needs of others. It really disappoints Jesus when His people are no help to those weighted down with adversities and dominated by evil.

But it's more than frustration with His church—it's also frustration with you and me. We must take this personally! What in your life or mine really disappoints the Lord? What causes Him to ask, "How long shall I put up with you?"

Jesus ordered the boy brought to Him and the demon manifested itself.

In Jesus' ministry you will never find Him diagnosing a person with demon possession. The demon always manifests itself in His presence. When we have clean hands a pure heart, when we are in communion with the Lord, we also clearly see when evil manifests itself. One of the reasons for powerlessness over evil is that there is too much sin in us. The Devil in others cannot be driven out when there is an aggregate of evil and good in our lives. Yielding to temptation, prayerlessness, and giving in to spiritual laxity diminish our efforts to confront evil effectively.

Clearly the boy didn't have epilepsy even though to the casual observer that may have appeared to be the case. In epilepsy there is no controlling evil spirit that shrieks and comes out (9:26). The boy was deaf and mute due to the indwelling presence of a demon (9:25).

Until the father brought his son to Jesus, there was no cure. Family, religious leaders, well-intentioned friends had not been able to help. The disciples should have been able to help since they had delegated authority from Jesus.

There are countless children whom the enemy is throwing down and tossing out—they are the lost boys and girls of our generation. Will we stand by helplessly and do nothing? Or, will we act in Jesus' name to rescue them and confront the evil that harms them?

A Prayer

Lord Jesus, help me not to walk away from a desperate adult or child who needs help. I can't help everyone, but I can do something about those You put within my reach.

HELP THE CHILDREN

Jesus asked the boy's father, "How long has he been like this?" "From childhood," he answered. "It has often thrown him into fire or water to kill him. But if you can do anything, take pity on us and help us."
MARK 9:21–22

JESUS HELPS CHILDREN. You see that in the Gospel of Mark. He raised from death the twelve-year-old daughter of Jairus (5:35–43), and healed the little daughter of a Greek woman (7:24–30). Now, for the third time in this Gospel, a desperate parent has come to Jesus with concern for his child.

Jesus' question to the dad is a curious one: "How long has he been like this?" Didn't Jesus already know? I suspect He did. The onlookers however did not. When the father identified the possession as one of long standing, the crowd realized the severity of the problem. Additionally, the father volunteered that the demon had tried to kill the boy by throwing him into fire and water.

What a nightmare this must have been for the dad. He had to constantly watch over his son, helpless when the boy went into convulsions but ever vigilant to rescue him from burning or drowning. The fact that the father said his son had suffered this condition from childhood suggests that now this boy may be in his teenage years or older.

The father's love is compelling. It speaks volumes to all parents who have severely disabled children, children who require constant, watchful care. Here before us is a parent who loves his child deeply even though the son's condition severely impinged on the father's own daily life and schedule. Absent from the story is the mother. Is it possible that, like so many parents, she could no longer deal with the disabled son and left the home and marriage?

The father doesn't know if Jesus can do anything. His question is a pitiful plea, "If you can do anything . . . help us."

Jesus is not physically present today, but we, His church, are.

How do we respond to the terribly hurtful adversities children suffer? The neglect and abuse of children has reached epidemic proportions in our culture.

Can we help even one foster child, one son or daughter of a prisoner, one malnourished or poverty-stricken child, a disabled boy or girl, a child used for human trafficking? Are we willing to help a single parent?

We can so easily allow our crowded schedules and busy routines to wall us off from the needs of children. We must hear their cries and the plea also of a distressed parent, "If *you* can do anything ... help us."

I like the story of the old man walking the beach at daybreak. He was throwing back into the surf starfish that had washed up on the sand. A smarty teenager followed him and said, "Old man, what are you doing? There are millions of starfish on this beach, and they're going to die when the sun comes out. What difference does it make what you do?"

The old man held a starfish in his hand and, as he tossed it back into the water, replied, "It matters to this one."

Indeed, we may not be able to do everything, but we can always do something! It matters to this *one*.

A Prayer

Lord Jesus, the father's plea haunts me. It calls me to listen to the heart cries of others. May I not remain passive or impotent in meeting the needs of others, especially children, who come to me this day.

GROWING IN FAITH

"'If you can'?" said Jesus. "Everything is possible for him who believes." Immediately the boy's father exclaimed, "I do believe; help me overcome my unbelief!"

MARK 9:23–24

A FATHER BROUGHT HIS demon-possessed deaf and mute son to the disciples of Jesus. They were unable to help. Jesus came on the scene. The demon threw the boy into convulsions.

We know a lot more about epilepsy today than people did then, and the temptation for some modern readers is to say that Jesus either misdiagnosed the boy's condition as demon possession or accommodated Himself to folk belief.

However, note that earlier Jesus didn't treat the deaf and mute man as being possessed of an evil spirit (Mark 5:31–35) but as suffering from a physical condition. Further, in healings there are no evil spirits "coming out" of the person. In the accounts of demonic deliverance, there is an evocative response from the demons clearly identifying themselves as distinct from the person they inhabit (1:26; 5:7; 9:26).

The father had asked Jesus, "If you can do anything . . . help us." Jesus responded rhetorically, "If you can?" meaning, "Are you really asking Me if I can?" Jesus then answered His own question, "Everything is possible for him who believes."

Obviously, Jesus believed. He came from the other side of time and space where disease can't live and death doesn't exist. He knew that all it took to banish evil was His word.

Unfortunately, we mortals have not yet made it to that world, so our faith fails and fades. We want to believe that evil will be banished, but despite our best efforts it remains. Our faith is feeble.

But, the Lord tells us in this passage to stretch our faith muscles, to reach out and expect good to happen against the very presence of evil. "It is possible," Jesus says, "but you have to believe." In other words, "Don't go passive. Don't accept things the way they are. Your faith can make a difference."

The father could have disputed the statement of Jesus. He might have responded, "No, in my own life experience, that is not true. I've believed for many things that have not happened." Or, the father could have ignored Jesus' statement and made no response, perhaps thinking to himself, *That's preposterous!*

However, the father picked up on Jesus' declaration and responded affirmatively, "I do believe." Then, recognizing that he really hadn't told the whole truth, he added, "Help me overcome my unbelief."

You have to love the honesty here, "I believe . . . but I have unbelief."

Sometimes we falsely thing that we must have perfect faith in order for the Lord to work, when all He really wants is for us to make the effort to have faith.

Jesus' interchange with this man helps us as we pray. There are some who falsely tell us, "When you pray or ask for something, if you have any doubt at all, you will not get it." Thus, if we do not receive the answer we wanted, the blame falls on us.

It's far better to be honest with the Lord, as was this father; and to say to Him, "I do believe but I'm not all the way there yet. You're going to have to make up whatever I lack."

Jesus would much rather we be honest with Him than try to bluff our way in His presence.

A Prayer

Lord Jesus, I have faith but I also waver and fall short. I'm grateful that the results to my prayers depend on Your power and not my imperfect trust.

LIFTED UP

> *When Jesus saw that a crowd was running to the scene, he rebuked the evil spirit. "You deaf and mute spirit," he said, "I command you, come out of him and never enter him again." The spirit shrieked, convulsed him violently and came out. The boy looked so much like a corpse that many said, "He's dead." But Jesus took him by the hand and lifted him to his feet, and he stood up.*
>
> MARK 9:25–27

JESUS RETURNED FROM THE Mountain of Transfiguration only to find His disciples helpless in casting out a demon from a boy. Jesus took father and son apart from a large crowd to talk privately.

Within moments, the crowd reconnected visually where Jesus was and raced toward Him. Jesus was no grandstander. He chose not to do the exorcism with a horde of witnesses, casting out the demon before the throng arrived on the scene.

Jesus' voice had been obeyed by wind and waves (4:35ff.). Demons and sickness fled at His orders. The word of Christ is all-powerful and everything must yield before His spoken word. That's true for your life as well. Demons and elements must obey His voice, but He has given us the choice to disobey. But to all who say yes to Him, life changes for the better forever!

The deliverance Jesus brings is not a temporary one. He commanded the demon to never enter the boy again. What great hope for the sufferer! Jesus is the only One who brings permanent deliverance from sin, sickness, hell, and the grave.

I remember as a child hearing an evangelist say, "When I cast out a demon if you're not right with God, it will enter you." I was scared spitless. I notice however in the Gospels that when Jesus cast out a demon He never said anything like that. We never see Jesus permitting demons to enter someone else.

The demon acted upon this boy like the Devil acts upon each human being. The Evil One causes us to behave other than our true selves, other than the image of God in which we were created. He shakes us, and when he's sucked everything out of us, we're left for dead.

The verdict of the crowd, in fact, was that the boy was dead. But appearances are deceiving. Actually, as the boy lay there motionless, he was more alive than he had been because he had been set free.

When Jesus touches our lives we no longer are out of control. We do not shriek or convulse violently. He brings peace rather than disruption.

There may be occasions when you falsely assume that someone or some work of God is "dead." It appears lifeless, and your tendency may be to write it off as did this crowd. But it could be that at the very moment you thought things were hopeless, the tide has turned.

The enemy throws down and disables. He leaves us as dead. It's more difficult to pull someone up than down. But Jesus has strength. It was not just the physical lift that Jesus gave to the boy; it was the power that infused his body with life. Once Jesus' hand grabbed him and lifted him to his feet, the boy could be limp and lifeless no longer.

It's the same with you and me. Jesus lifts us up and stands us on our feet!

A Prayer

Lord Jesus, I was knocked down and out by the Enemy. I didn't have the strength to rise. I was crushed beyond all measure. But Your strong hand reached down and lifted me up! I am grateful!

WHY?

After Jesus had gone indoors, his disciples asked him privately, "Why couldn't we drive it out?" He replied, "This kind can come out only by prayer."

MARK 9:28–29

THE FATHER HAD BROUGHT his demon-possessed son to Jesus and left rejoicing. The disciples were left asking a question that begins with the word, "Why?"

That question not only perplexed them. It perplexes us to this day. We do our best to live for Jesus and to advance the kingdom, but despite our best efforts, sometimes things don't work out. Bad things happen. We don't get the results we want. Our emotional and spiritual gasoline tanks are on empty.

So we ask inside ourselves and even to the Lord, *What's wrong? Why can't we do as Jesus did? Why did that happen or not happen?* We are perplexed, and we stumble for an answer.

Notice the disciples asked their question "indoors." Like them, we don't want to admit our failures in the presence of others. So we seek a quiet opportunity to ponder and question. It's best we do it that way. Why perplex others with our own struggles? Besides, they don't know the answer to the "why" question either.

Jesus isn't afraid of our questions. In this particular situation in the Gospels, His answer was "This kind can come out only by prayer." Note first that He didn't rule out that some things can be accomplished without prayer. It's just "this kind"—the situation that can't be resolved with human will or resources. That kind of situation can't change without prayer. Some things can only be resolved with God's help.

In responding as He did, Jesus graciously pointed out to the nine disciples that they had not been praying. At the beginning of the incident (9:14), we found them arguing instead. Argument and prayer are incompatible.

Additionally, the nine had been left for a week without Peter, James, and John. No doubt that was upsetting to them. Why had they been left behind? Why were they not among the favored? It's hard to be productive for Jesus when you question Him and envy other believers. Prayer and spiritual power easily fly out the window when we are jealous.

Credit the nine, though, with sticking up for Jesus against the teachers of the Law despite the fact He had gone off with the three.

The nine represent the stress of working for Jesus. Left without His presence (or the sense of His presence), dealing with difficult circumstances that do not change despite our best efforts, defending the Lord and ourselves from criticism—no wonder we get burned out. We want to say to the Lord, "Where is the 'my yoke is easy and my burden is light'?"

In the midst of all that, we fail to pray. We are just too busy dealing with the stuff of life, struggling with conflict and even spiritual impotence. Our communion with the Lord leaks out of our daily routine.

Absent prayer, we are left helpless and hopeless. We become just like the nine—taking little or no time to pray and lacking the will or the desire to pray.

May we take heart from Jesus' answer to the nine that a life of prayer is essential if we are to spiritually overcome. May we also take heart that Jesus is the One we go to when we have questions. There are questions only He can answer.

A Prayer

Lord Jesus, help me to remain in constant communion
with You through the day, for without Your presence
I lack power to overcome the challenges I face.

REFRESHED AND CONFUSED

> *They left that place and passed through Galilee. Jesus did not want anyone to know where they were, because he was teaching his disciples. He said to them, "The Son of Man is going to be betrayed into the hands of men. They will kill him, and after three days he will rise." But they did not understand what he meant and were afraid to ask him about it.*
>
> MARK 9:30–32

IMAGINE THE NINE DISCIPLES were glad to get out of there. While Jesus had been with the "inner three" on the Mount of Transfiguration for a week, the disciples left behind had to deal with feelings of their own about exclusion, along with the crowds pestering them as to where Jesus was. The tipping point in their difficult week had been their inability to cast the demon out of the boy.

Like them, we do leave places, even difficult places. Nothing stays the same forever. It passes. Jesus is with them again. We sense also that He is with us again, so we go on.

They "passed through Galilee." That means from their starting point of the area of Caesarea Philippi they headed in a southwesterly direction down from what we know today as the Golan Heights toward their destination of Capernaum (9:33). During this time, Jesus skirted the population centers so He could have time alone to continue disclosure of the key element of His mission: His approaching death and resurrection.

We all need a break at one time or another to recharge our batteries. Jesus was providing that as He pulled the disciples apart for a season from the crowds who always looked for Him. But Jesus had more on His mind than giving them a break. He had to get them ready for events that would shortly happen to Him.

After Peter had confessed Him as the Christ (8:27–30), Jesus began to teach the Twelve about His approaching passion. After the transfiguration, He picked up on this theme a second time.

The phrase "He was teaching" tells us that this was no two-minute conversation. Day after day, He attempted to focus them on what was coming.

In this season of teaching, Jesus added details not given earlier. He used the word "betrayed." The betrayal will be "into the hands of sinners." In the earlier announcement following Peter's confession, Jesus said He would be rejected by the religious leaders. Now, the list is expanded to "sinners"—Gentiles such as Pilate and the Roman soldiers who would kill Him. Absent from both the first and the second announcement is the manner used to kill Him. Jesus saved that detail for later.

It's very clear the disciples aren't getting this. When they began to follow Jesus, they had dreams of the dawn of a messianic age in which Jesus would rule the world and evict Rome from the land of Israel. They would be the administrative leaders of a powerful political kingdom.

Now, Jesus was telling them things they didn't want to hear—that He was going to be killed. The "after three days He will rise" was simply beyond their comprehension.

Sometimes we block difficult lessons the Lord wants us to learn. Like the disciples, we don't ask questions because we really don't want to deal with the answers. We become confused. The good thing is this: The Lord is walking with us, and He is never confused!

A Prayer

Lord Jesus, some things are hard to understand. We don't get it the first time around. But we're grateful as we continue walking with You that, in time, we will understand it all.

FIRST OR LAST?

They came to Capernaum. When he was in the house, he asked them, "What were you arguing about on the road?" But they kept quiet because on the way they had argued about who was the greatest. Sitting down, Jesus called the Twelve and said, "If anyone wants to be first, he must be the very last, and the servant of all."

MARK 9:33–35

SEVERAL DAYS BEFORE Jesus returned to Capernaum, His disciples had asked Him a question for which they had no answer, "Why couldn't we drive it [the demon] out?" (9:28). A few moments later, after Jesus again announced His approaching betrayal and death, they were afraid to ask a question of Him (9:32).

But Jesus was not afraid to ask them a question. He wants to know what they were fussing and fuming about as they walked on the road. He knows the peace of the community had been disturbed—as it always is when believers get into verbal fisticuffs. He certainly knew what they were arguing about. He didn't ask them because He didn't know but because they needed to verbalize in His presence their competition with one another.

In starting with a question rather than an accusation, condemnation, or correction, Jesus modeled excellent conflict resolution. Good leadership draws people out by providing a context and opportunity for tough issues to emerge into the open.

It's obvious the disciples didn't want to answer since they refused to answer His question. They were embarrassed. And with good reason! We should always be mortified in the Lord's presence when we're trying to favorably compare ourselves with someone else.

It's easy to see why the Twelve argued. Three of them enjoyed the special privilege of going with Jesus and witnessing His transfiguration. Nine of them were stuck in the valley below, impotent to deal with the demon possessed boy while beleaguered by Jesus' critics. I suspect the three asserted that their selection, instead of the nine, demonstrated they were the top dogs.

The three made the mistake of assuming blessing meant status. Just because they were blessed in a particular way did not mean they were at a higher level than the others. The same is true for us. There's no place in the Lord's kingdom for those who want to be the big cheese.

Jesus had watched in heaven while the angel Lucifer tried to elbow his way to the front. Therefore, Jesus knew the destructive power of inordinate ambition and self-promotion. He knew that such an attitude leads straight to expulsion from the kingdom of heaven.

So He warned His disciples that the greatest one must be the very last and the servant of all. This is easier said than done, but it is exactly what the Lord Himself did, and it's what He expects from us!

In other words, whether you are a boss at work, a leader in the home, or occupy a position of influence in church or community, you must see yourself fundamentally as serving rather than leading. Leadership is not about bossing others around (including dictatorial attitudes and behavior toward spouse and family members). It's not about acquiring status for yourself.

If you want to be first, then take care of the needs of others before your own. Replace pride with humility, and arrogance with a servant's heart.

A Prayer

Lord Jesus, You didn't condemn the desire to be first; You just sanctified ambition by redirecting me from the path of self-fulfillment to others-fulfillment. Help me, Lord, to be a better servant to others.

LESSONS FROM A LITTLE BOY

*He took a little child and had him stand among them.
Taking him in his arms, he said to them, "Whoever
welcomes one of these little children in my name
welcomes me; and whoever welcomes me does
not welcome me but the one who sent me."*

MARK 9:36-37

AS THEY WALKED with Jesus to Capernaum from the Mount of Transfiguration, the disciples argued among themselves as to ranking. Who was the greatest?

When Jesus asked them what they had been debating, they were too ashamed to answer Him. But, Jesus always knows what's going on, even when we don't want to tell Him. He responded to them by saying that those who desire position in His kingdom must be servants.

Too often religious leaders adopt an opposite attitude. They try to lead from a standpoint of "My way or the highway," saying "I'm God's anointed and if you don't like the way I'm leading, then you know where the door is." Jesus clearly told His disciples not to lord it over others (10:42).

In his classic children's book, Dr. Seuss spins out the story of *Yertle the Turtle*. Yertle lives in a pond and cannot see much. He wants to be higher, so he calls turtles to stack up so he can be on top. The pile of turtles keeps getting higher and higher and Yertle keeps demanding more so that his throne can be higher yet. The poor turtle at the bottom of the pile, named Mack, groans each time another volume of turtles is added to the stack. Yertle is happy but Mack is miserable. Finally, Mack burps. Yertle falls off his throne and splats into the mud. All the turtles are happy again.

Overbearing leaders cause misery in those they lead. Instead of desiring to be supported at the top by others, Jesus says, "Oh no. I'm not putting you in a position so that others can support you. I'm giving you leadership so that you might support others."

To illustrate this principle, Jesus used a small boy and stood him in the midst of the disciples. At first blush what Jesus did and said here seems to bear no resemblance to the issue at hand—who is the greatest? What does welcoming a child have to do with being servant of all?

I think Jesus was saying that if you are in leadership then you had better pay attention to the little people. Greatness is how you care for the people who don't have position, wealth, title, or office.

Additionally, there is value in seeing Jesus folding a child in his arms as a lesson we all need to follow. Christ gives us an example of the importance of taking the next generation into our arms.

In our culture it's easy, even for adult Christians, to elect to do the things that bring personal fulfillment and recreation. Why is it that local churches often have such difficulty in securing volunteers who will faithfully work with children and youth? Every church could be filled with children and young people if adults were willing to take on the responsibility.

Jesus was saying that when you don't take the next generation into your arms, you're not receiving Him; and if you are not receiving Him then you are not receiving the Father who sent Him.

Pretty tough words about our duties to boys and girls, young men and women!

A Prayer

Lord Jesus, help me to open my arms and my time to children. Help me concentrate on how best I can serve others, especially the young.

NO FRANCHISE

"Teacher," said John, "we saw a man driving out demons in your name and we told him to stop, because he was not one of us." "Do not stop him, "Jesus said. "No one who does a miracle in my name can in the next moment say anything bad about me, for whoever is not against us is for us."

MARK 9:38–40

THIS IS A HARD LESSON for us to learn. It's often easier to unite around a common enemy than to unite around a common cause.

We live in a polarizing society. Commentators on news networks and radio talk shows advance their positions by attacking persons of the opposite viewpoint. Politicians often get elected by funding more negative ads than their opponents. The mission is to destroy the opposition.

Sometimes Christians get caught up in this spirit. They look for the chink in armor of another believer or pastor, and then go on the attack. The idea is, "If you don't agree with me 100 percent, then you're not really one of us."

This exclusiveness did not begin in the twenty-first century. The same thing happened in the presence of Jesus with His disciples. They wanted to exclude others who are not in their camp, their select group, and their chosen dozen.

They brought to Jesus their complaint that a man was casting out demons and he was not part of their group. The humorous side of their indignation is that just days earlier they had been unable to drive out a demon from a boy. Now, they are complaining about someone else's success in the very thing at which they had failed!

John spoke for the group when He used the plural pronoun "we." They were upset because they thought they had the exclusive right to use the name of Jesus. The answer Jesus gave should be a warning to everyone in the body of Christ to be careful lest we draw the circle of relationship to Jesus smaller than He Himself draws it.

It's evident John and the others were less concerned with end results than with means. They would rather have the man stop using the name of Jesus than see people delivered from demonic possession. And therein is a lesson for church folk. Whenever we require something to be done in a particular way, rather than being concerned with the end result we call attention to the wrong thing.

Unfortunately, there are demolition experts in the church who make it their vocation to point out what's wrong with other believers. They are far more eager to blow up bridges than to build them.

Jesus says that if another is acting in His name, they're not denigrating Him. His inference to us is clear: "Don't denigrate them." The reason? They're with us, not against us! Jesus draws a circle big enough to take people in, not a circle small enough to rule out others who believe in Him and in the power of His name.

No one person or group owns the franchise on Jesus. He tells us, from this dialog with His disciples, that we are to be charitable with His followers who are outside our circle of association, who don't see everything the exact same way we do.

A Prayer

Lord Jesus, keep me from the narrowness of spirit and attitude that looks to criticize and tear down rather than encourage and build up.

REWARD AND PUNISHMENT

> *"I tell you the truth, anyone who gives you a cup of water in my name because you belong to Christ will certainly not lose his reward. And if anyone causes one of these little ones who believe in me to sin, it would be better for him to be thrown into the sea with a large millstone tied around his neck."*
>
> MARK 9:41–42

THE DISCIPLES WERE UPSET because a man not in their group had been driving out demons in the name of Jesus.

The first part of Jesus' response was to tell them that the man's actions placed him on their side. If he wasn't against them, then he was for them.

Then Jesus furthered His response by using illustrations of a cup of water and a millstone.

What does a cup of water have to do with their complaint about the man? Simply this. What you sow, you reap. They were sowing inhospitality to others, but Jesus knew they were going to need hospitality from others. If they were going to exclude the man from doing good things in the name of Jesus, then others could be excused for excluding them when they came in the name of Jesus.

We sometimes forget the context for these remarks of Jesus. His followers will need to rely on the hospitality of others as they travel with the good news. Unlike today, where we have hotels and motels and a plethora of restaurants (along with credit cards to pay for them), first-century disciples had to rely on the good will of those who hosted them in their homes.

Thus, Jesus promised a reward to anyone who is kind to His people.

The parallel passage in Matthew 10:40–42 provides the fuller explanation in which Jesus talks about three rewards for those who are hospitable to His followers. Those who receive a prophet will receive what a prophet can give—that would be a word from God. Those who receive a righteous man will receive what a righteous man can give—influence to walk rightly.

The nature of the reward for providing a cup of water is not described; however, from the total context of Scripture the reward is not related to the after-life. If that were the case, then entrance into heaven would be granted on the basis of hospitality rather than saving faith in Christ.

The cup of water reference occurs immediately following the complaint about the man casting out demons in Jesus' name. The cup of water is being given "in his name." By putting these "in his name" comments together in sequence, Jesus was saying, "Don't make enemies of those who are predisposed to be with us. You may need their help one day with something as simple as a cup of water. Be gracious so that you can give a gracious reward to those who help you."

All the time He was speaking, Jesus evidently had been holding a little boy (9:36). So, He next directed His concern to the influence we have on children.

The disciples' narrow attitude toward the man casting out demons in Jesus' name could easily rub off on the child. Adults do influence the young. They are watching us. They'll parrot our attitudes and our speech. Bigots have a tendency to produce bigots. Saints have a tendency to produce saints. Better that we be destroyed than someone else be destroyed through our bad example.

A Prayer

Lord Jesus, may I never create a pitfall for others.
Help me to keep pure motives and a pure heart.

HAND, FOOT, EYE

"If your hand causes you to sin, cut it off. It is better for you to enter life maimed than with two hands to go into hell, where the fire never goes out. And if your foot causes you to sin, cut it off. It is better for you to enter life crippled than to have two feet and be thrown into hell. And if your eye causes you to sin, pluck it out. It is better for you to enter the kingdom of God with one eye than to have two eyes and be thrown into hell, where 'their worm does not die, and the fire is not quenched.'"

Mark 9:43–48

LET'S START BY GETTING STRAIGHT the manner of speech Jesus used.

He is not giving you permission to do self-amputation! If He were, then the early church and the church throughout the centuries to the present time would be full of one-handed, one-footed, and one-eyed members!

Jesus was using a figure of speech called hyperbole. Two Greek words give the meaning of the word. *Hyper* means "over" and is used as a prefix. It's carried directly over into the English languages in words like hypersensitive and hypertension. *Bole* morphs into our language as "ball" and literally means "to throw." When *hyper* and *bole* are put together as one word, it means "to overthrow," a deliberately exaggerated statement given for effect.

What was Jesus getting at in using such terms? What do we need to cut out of our lives in order to avoid hell and demonstrate that we are citizens of the kingdom of God?

The hand represents what we do that we shouldn't, or what we don't do that we should. I can make my hand a fist to hit others or I can use my hand to help. Put a hammer in your hand and you can either destruct or construct, you can destroy or build. You can use your hand to shake your finger at God or you can lift your hand in praise to the One who made and redeemed you. What will you do with your hand?

The foot represents direction. It's not as dexterous as the hand but it charts the path we take, walking us step by step through life. It leads us to the right places, the wrong places, or no place at all. There are eternal consequences for the directional choices we make. Where is your foot heading?

The eye represents vision. What is your eye seeing? Is it pleasing to God or displeasing?

We err if we think this teaching relates only to sexual temptation. Jesus, for example, accused the Pharisees of looking at others by externals rather than with compassion. They were quick to see what was wrong and blind to what was right. Instead of stretching their hand to Jesus, directing their feet to follow Him, and fastening their eye on Him; they lifted their hand to smite Him, propelled their feet to pursue Him to the cross, and saw Him as a blasphemer.

Remember Eve in the garden of Eden? She saw with her eyes the forbidden fruit, took it with her hands, and walked with her feet to Adam. Look at the mess the first couple created for the human race because they didn't guard their eyes, hands, or feet. You create the same mess for yourself and others when you follow their bad example.

Misery, and ultimately hell, follows those who make wrong choices.

A Prayer

*Lord Jesus, may what I do, where I go,
and what I see please You.*

BE AT PEACE

"Everyone will be salted with fire. Salt is good, but if it loses its saltiness, how can you make it salty again? Have salt in yourselves, and be at peace with each other."

MARK 9:49–50

THE LANDSCAPE OF THE CHURCH has been too often littered with the wrecks of divisions. The church lost its salt—the flavor that attracts the non-Christian.

Jesus used an illustration that's difficult to understand in the reference to being salted with fire. However, in the preceding verses He talked with His disciples about the fire of hell. We also need the fire of His purging in this life. If we are truly to retain our "salt" for Him, then we must let the fire of His words scorch away impurities in our lives.

The disciples were in danger of losing their salt. In fact, if you look back over the entire length of Mark 9, you can clearly see the decline of saltiness among the Twelve. There are four main events in the chapter, chronicling four stages descending from spiritual heights to spiritual depths.

The first stage was revelation (9:2–13). On the Mount of Transfiguration, the inner three disciples had an overpowering revelation of Jesus' glory. Revelation is the moment when we are overwhelmed in the presence of the majestic Christ, caught up in a powerful spiritual experience beyond what the rational mind can fathom. We encounter God in such a way that even language cannot describe the experience, nor can we articulate our emotions.

Revelation is followed by argument (9:14–32). When the disciples were powerless to cast out the demon from the boy, they were reduced to disputing with their opponents. When we don't have spiritual power, we argue. But our arguments don't solve the pressing needs of those looking to us for help. Prayerlessness leads to contentiousness.

Argument is followed by arrogance (9:33–37). The disciples broke into a dispute as to who among them was the greatest. Jostling for position tears asunder the peace of community. You cannot love the brother or sister whom you are trying to climb over or pull down. Periodically, in my town, I hear a church ad that says, "Try us. We are the friendliest church in town." I'm sure they mean well, but how do they know that? What makes us feel we are better than someone else?

Jesus talked to His arrogant disciples about being a servant and takes a little boy in His arms. He essentially said, "You won't be so narcissistic if you care for the little people. My way is not one of self-fulfillment, but self-denial."

Finally, the fourth stage in their decline is *exclusivity* (9:38–50). The disciples, who couldn't cast out a demon themselves, told others to stop who were succeeding. If it weren't so serious, it would be funny. They thought they had the exclusive franchise on Jesus. We must avoid narrowness of heart and spirit.

By the end of Mark 9, the disciples were at the low point in their progression to be like Christ. They were in danger of losing their "salt." But, Jesus didn't give up on them. They would later find themselves all together in one place, in one accord (Acts 2:1).

By the grace of God, the Holy Spirit is making Jesus real in us so that we too can be salt to a needy world.

A Prayer

Bind us together, Lord, bind us together with chords that cannot be broken. May there be saltiness in my life that attracts others to You.

A "GOTCHA" QUESTION

Jesus then left that place and went into the region of Judea and across the Jordan. Again crowds of people came to him, and as was his custom, he taught them. Some Pharisees came and tested him by asking, "Is it lawful for a man to divorce his wife?"

MARK 10:1–2

THE MINISTRY OF JESUS shifted from Galilee as He began the long journey to Jerusalem. At the present moment, He had returned to the area where John the Baptist ministered (1:5).

We might have expected Mark to say that Jesus was healing "as was His custom." Not so this time. He is *teaching* "as was His custom." Healing happens in a moment, and it's done. The reformation of life—learning new patterns of thought and behavior—takes time. Jesus was concerned not only for the well-being of the body, but also for the inner life, and that's why He taught.

But not everyone wanted to learn. Some only wanted to see if they could ask a "gotcha" question.

The Pharisees weren't the only ones who did this. I see it today among those who look at a pastor, a Christian author, or a ministry and do their best to find the one or two things they don't agree with. Then they blow those areas of disagreement all out of context and trumpet the one "nugget" they have found to smear the entire life and ministry of an otherwise good Christian leader. Like the Pharisees, they aren't interested in learning; they are only interested in destroying the person who may differ with them.

I call them "watchers on the wall." They are always looking for a fault somewhere, and when they find it, they trumpet it far and near. They could better spend their time witnessing to the lost than tearing down the found.

The Pharisees continually looked for some way to trip up Jesus. They charged Him with blasphemy when He forgave the paralytic's sins (Mark 2:6-7); faulted Him for eating with sinners and tax collectors (2:15-16); criticized Him for letting His disciples pluck grain on the Sabbath (2:24); plotted to kill Him for healing on the Sabbath the man with a withered hand (3:1-6); accused Him of being possessed by the Devil (3:22); walked almost 100 miles to challenge Him for letting His disciples eat without first ritually purifying their hands (7:1-23); and demanded from Him a sign from heaven (8:11).

No matter how hard you try, you just can't satisfy some folk.

So they came to Jesus, not to learn but to find out whether they could trap Him with a question about divorce. They really weren't interested in truth or in what God thought. They only wanted another reason to go after Jesus.

The Pharisee spirit is never dead in so-called religious people. Some are never satisfied no matter what evidence you present that differs from their perception. They would rather be critics than open their hearts to embrace the evidence of God's presence and blessing.

Can we learn from their bad example? Instead of imitating the politics of personal destruction that we see all around us, can the body of Christ be different? Can we fulfill the desire of Jesus, "May they also be in us so that the world may believe that you have sent me" (John 17:21)?

A Prayer

Lord Jesus, may I never have a spirit that looks for ways to find fault. Help me to ask honest questions rather than look for ways to accuse or attack my brothers and sisters in Christ.

MARRIAGE BREAKUP AND HARDNESS OF HEART

"What did Moses command you?" he replied. They said, "Moses permitted a man to write a certificate of divorce and send her away." "It was because your hearts were hard that Moses wrote you this law," Jesus replied.

MARK 10:3–5

OUR LORD WAS without sin, yet He endured much criticism—all of it from religious people.

Thus far in Mark's gospel, Jesus' critics had challenged Him seven times (2:7, 16, 18, 24; 3:2, 22; 7:5). On this eighth occasion, the Pharisees came to test Jesus' answer regarding divorce. Jesus responded by asking what the Law required.

He thus forced them to articulate what they understood to be the teaching of Moses. Jesus may have asked the question because He wanted to draw out which school of the Pharisees they belonged to—the conservative school of Shammai or the liberal school of Hillel. Those two schools of thought differed on the grounds for divorce: Shammai held that divorce could only be obtained if there was adultery; Hillel, for any cause.

The answer to Jesus indicated that this group belonged to the liberal camp. They held that the man could just write a certificate of divorce and send away the wife. Had this group of Pharisees been from the conservative side, their answer would have been: "Moses permitted divorce only in instances of adultery."

Jesus hit the nail on the head as to the cause of divorce: hardness of heart.

That's why marriages don't last. Tenderness is gone. Self-interest and self-fulfillment have become more important than the spouse's welfare. "I want to be happy" is simply a cover for hardness of heart. But the "I want to be happy" person who leaves the marriage can never really be happy because the problem lies not with their spouse, but in themselves. Their heart is hard.

MARRIAGE BREAKUP AND HARDNESS OF HEART

The opposite of a hard heart is a soft one—a heart that is supple and lives the virtues articulated in 1 Corinthians 13.

How do you keep from having a hard heart when your marriage is in trouble? There are scriptural keys. Keep a daily life of prayer and reliance upon the Holy Spirit to give you wisdom and a right heart. Subordinate your feelings to your knowing. If you live by your emotions rather than doing what's right, your inner life can become full of poison. Forgive easily. In fact, Jesus calls us to forgive an infinite number of times ("seventy times seven," Matthew 18:22, KJV). This doesn't mean you become a doormat for abuse. You must balance forgiveness with strength to stand up to injustice.

A wife was so upset with her husband that she went to a counselor asking, "What's the meanest thing I can do to my husband?" He told her to treat her husband like a king for thirty days and at the end of that time, he would have so fallen in love with her that she could then break his heart with the words, "I'm getting a divorce." At the end of thirty days she went back to the counselor and said, "In these thirty days I've done nothing but good to him. I've actually fallen in love with him, and I cannot get a divorce."

She had learned the valuable lesson that actions precede feelings. If you let your emotions determine your actions, then hardness of heart is a distinct possibility. But when you do the right things, you prevent your heart from becoming hard.

A Prayer

Lord Jesus, I want to have a tender heart. Help me to act according to Your will regardless of my circumstances.

GOD'S DESIGN FOR MARRIAGE

> *"But at the beginning of creation God 'made them male and female.' 'For this reason a man will leave his father and mother and be united to his wife, and the two will become one flesh.' So they are no longer two, but one. Therefore what God has joined together, let not man separate."*
> MARK 10:6–9

WHEN NATIONS, CULTURES, ORGANIZATIONS, or churches begin to decline, it's often because of mission creep. Slowly, they move away from their original mission. Those who come many years after the founding forget or ignore the reason why their entity began.

Jesus was there at the beginning of creation. Therefore, He knows God's plan for marriage and sexuality. God Himself created male and female as sexual persons, making them anatomically different while also amazingly similar.

If He had made two males and no females, or two women and no men, the human race would have been extinct in one generation. Clearly, in creation, God made the first two humans heterosexual. Nothing in God's intention for man and woman has changed since the day Adam and Eve took their first breath.

There is a culture war raging in the Western world to accept gay marriage. As Christians, we stand in opposition to this redefinition of marriage—not because we are narrow-minded or bigoted, but because we know what God intended when He made male and female and gave them to one another in marriage.

Furthermore, God intended the union of a man and woman to be for life. Jesus designed each marriage to be a re-enactment of creation. Once the husband and wife come together in marriage, no other options exist. They are now "Adam and Eve," and there is no third party. In fact, they are "no longer two, but one."

The couple is to establish a new unit, separate also from in-laws. The "man will leave his father and mother." God allows the opportunity for a new identity to emerge separate from the identity with parents. There would be no mother-in-law or father-in-law problems if everyone understood this. The newly married must establish their own life, cutting the cords of dependence and control from their parents. This doesn't mean that warmth and social relationships are severed; it does mean that interference from parents should not occur.

In responding to the Pharisees' question on divorce, Jesus clearly returned to God's original intention in creation: One man plus one woman equals marriage. No other alternatives exist because there are no other people. When they become one, they are as inseparably bound to each other as the hand is to the arm. Just as the body is one, the couple is one. God didn't make parts of our body detachable, nor did He make marriage detachable.

It's a rather radical view and totally opposite of contemporary culture that espouses living together or the severability of the marriage covenant.

Perhaps if people went into marriage with the commitment that marriage, once entered, doesn't have an "opt out," they would be more careful in the first place.

The marriage between a man and a woman isn't only their choice, it is God's. He designed male and female to be joined together as one.

A Prayer

Lord Jesus, help me again today to reflect on Your original intention for everything about my life. You created me. Help me to be all You want me to be.

JESUS LOVES THE LITTLE CHILDREN

People were bringing little children to Jesus to have him touch them, but the disciples rebuked them. When Jesus saw this, he was indignant. He said to them, "Let the little children come to me, and do not hinder them, for the kingdom of God belongs to such as these."

MARK 10:13–14

THE DISCIPLES JUST didn't get it. When they quarreled about who was the greatest, Jesus took a child in His arms and said that when they welcomed a child they welcomed Him (9:33–37). Now, they were shooing children away.

The disciples thought there were bigger and more important things to do than to take time to bless children. Whenever the church thinks that way, it declines.

The lifeblood of the church is taking the next generation in its arms and blessing them.

Not only that, the coming of parents to Jesus with their children is juxtaposed directly following Jesus' teaching on the sanctity and nonseverability of marriage. When you protect the marriage, then you bless the children. There are far too many fatherless or motherless children in this world, made so because parents opted out for so-called self-fulfillment rather than duty and fidelity.

Jesus took time away from a very busy schedule to spend it with children. He set a great example for us. And He is indignant when we don't regard children as important.

I like the angry Jesus. He never gets angry out of personal pique or because He has been inconvenienced by someone. But He does get angry at injustice and the way less-fortunate people are treated.

In the synagogue, His anger was in full flower at the hardness of His critics' hearts that dared Him to heal on the Sabbath the man with the shriveled hand (3:5). You can feel the bite in His voice when He inveighs against the hypocrites for criticizing His disciples for eating with unwashed hands (7:6).

But this is the first time Jesus was angry with His own disciples. What was the reason? They were ranking people in order of importance and regarding "little people" as not worthy of access to Him.

I don't know if there are children in heaven because I don't know what age we will be in our new bodies. For example, if a Christian dies at ninety-five years of age with a multitude of ailments, surely those will be gone in heaven and the resurrected body will not look like an earth body of ninety-five years. Perhaps the other end of the continuum applies—that a child will have a fully mature body as a result of resurrection transformation.

We really don't know except "we shall be like him" (1 John 3:2). But, just for fun, let's imagine the receiving line in eternity with all the ecclesiastical heads, patriarchs, political leaders, kings and queen and princes. And let's use the idea that children will still be children in heaven. Whom would Jesus meet first? Would the dignitaries and officials be at the front of the line? Or would He first welcome the children who run to Him?

I think the little kids would race to Him without inhibition, and He would open His arms to them. If that's the case, then it serves us all well to have the heart of a child.

The kingdom of God belongs to those who run to Jesus, desiring to be embraced by Him.

A Prayer

Lord Jesus, I want to have the trusting heart of a child.
Help me also to be alert to every opportunity
to bless a child.

AFFECTIVE KNOWLEDGE

"I tell you the truth, anyone who will not receive the kingdom of God like a little child will never enter it." And he took the children in his arms, put his hands on them and blessed them.

MARK 10:15–16

THE DISCIPLES WEREN'T HAPPY that Jesus was spending time with children. Didn't He have more important things to do, more important people to meet, more important places to go?

Jesus rebuked them for wanting to dismiss the children. He then used the occasion to teach them how to receive His kingdom.

How does a child receive a gift? The same way we should receive the kingdom: with excitement, anticipation, joy, and gratitude!

The kingdom of God is the greatest gift we will ever receive because it means we have citizenship, with all the rights and privileges, in the realm of King Jesus. As King, He rules where there is no death, sin, night, pain, disease, separation, war, broken promises, hatred, disappointment, sorrow, dashed hopes, depression, bankruptcy, aging, disasters, famine, crime, natural disasters, weariness, or false hopes. His kingdom isn't for a number of days, weeks, months, or years. It lasts forever!

How do we receive this kingdom? As a child would!

Years ago I was driving my then three-year-old daughter to preschool. She began writhing in pain in the backseat of the car.

I said, "Evangeline, what's wrong?"

She replied, "Daddy, Jesus is kicking me in the tummy."

For a few moments I couldn't figure out what she meant, and then it dawned on me. She had invited Jesus into her heart several days earlier. She now had a stomachache, and she assumed that if Jesus was in her heart then He must be kicking her.

I smiled and kept on driving while my thoughts rambled one to another. First, I thought of the phrase from Jesus. *Except you become as a child you cannot enter the kingdom of God.* Up to that time I had never understood what He was saying. I next thought of Martin Luther's ruminations on that text. Luther had six kids who could make quite a racket, and one day he muttered of Jesus' comment, "Dear God, do we have to become such idiots?"

Next I thought, *What, really, did Jesus mean that we must receive the kingdom as a child?*

A bolt of clarity hit me, a lesson from my philosophy class in college. There are two kinds of knowledge: cognitive and affective. Cognitive is knowledge of facts: things like what, where, when, who, and why? Affective is relational knowledge as in "Adam knew his wife, Eve."

At three years of age, my daughter didn't have much cognitive knowledge about me. However, she knew me better than a lot of people who had more facts. Why? Affective knowledge—she knew me based on relationship.

"So that's it!" I said to myself as I drove. Jesus was talking about affective knowledge. Children don't know a lot of facts; Jesus was saying that the doorway to the kingdom is through relationship.

"You must be born again" (John 3:7). Cognitive knowledge is worthless in the Christian realm without affective knowledge. It's one thing to know about God, quite another thing to know Him.

Just as Jesus laid His hands on the children, He seeks to bless us as well if we will approach Him with the open heart and unrestrained love of a child.

A Prayer

Lord Jesus, I want to be a citizen of Your kingdom. I'm grateful that I know You, and more importantly, that You know me.

TWO GREAT QUESTIONS

As Jesus started on his way, a man ran up to him and fell on his knees before him. "Good teacher," he asked, "what must I do to inherit eternal life?" "Why do you call me good?" Jesus answered. "No one is good – except God alone."

MARK 10:17–18

WE KNOW THIS MAN as the rich young ruler. Matthew, Mark, and Luke all identify him as having great wealth. Matthew tells us he was young (19:20), and Luke that he was a ruler (18:19).

He came at a time when Jesus had "started on His way." What way was that?

It was the way to the cross. Jesus had begun the journey out of Galilee. Shortly, we find Him in Jericho (Mark 10:46) and then in Jerusalem (11:1). The fact that Jesus was headed toward the cross textured His later response to this man (10:21) since Jesus would only ask him to do what He Himself was doing—lay down his life.

We can learn from this man's approach to Jesus.

- *We should run to Jesus.* We shouldn't delay or hold back. We shouldn't be casual in our approach. We shouldn't run *from* Him.
- *We should fall on our knees.* We should reverence Jesus, bowing before Him as an inferior does to a superior. Falling on our knees is a mark of humility. It's the act of a supplicant. We aren't big shots around the Lord. This man had title, wealth, and commanded others, but in Jesus' presence he was on his knees.
- *We should respect Jesus for who He is in character.* While it becomes apparent that this man didn't understand the meaning of the term *good* when he addressed Jesus, nevertheless his use of the word indicates he thought well of Jesus. In his eyes, Jesus was of good reputation.

> - *We should ask the big questions.* There's no more important question than how to obtain eternal life, and Jesus alone has the answer to that question.

Jesus, however, began to answer with a question of His own, "Why do you call me good? No one is good—except God alone."

What's happening here? Was Jesus denying His divinity?

No! He engaged in a teaching moment. The wealthy young man had not thought through his designation of Jesus as good. Jesus made him stop and think, *Do you really know what it means to be "good"?*

For Jesus, goodness meant the absence of any impurity or sin. No human can match that. As Paul later said, "There is no one righteous, not even one" (Romans 3:10).

Only God is good. Jesus later clearly affirmed His identity when asked by the high priest, "Are you the Christ, the Son of the Blessed One?" "I am," Jesus said (14:61–62).

The very first stirrings of opposition to Jesus came when He forgave the sins of the paralytic. His opposition clearly understood that in forgiving sins Jesus was asserting a right that belonged only to God, for they said, "Why does this fellow talk like that? He's blaspheming! Who can forgive sins but God alone (2:7)?"

Jesus knew the young man didn't consider Him to be divine. However, Jesus knows His own identity. He knows that He is good, and that He alone is good—that through the cross His goodness will become a blanket under which we all can crawl. We are covered by His righteousness.

A Prayer

*Lord Jesus, You have the answer to all my questions.
I call You good because I know who You are:
the Son of the living God.*

IS BEING GOOD ENOUGH?

> *"You know the commandments: 'Do not murder, do not commit adultery, do not steal, do not give false testimony, do not defraud, honor your father and mother.'" "Teacher," he declared, "all these I have kept since I was a boy." Jesus looked at him and loved him. "One thing you lack," he said, "Go, sell everything you have and give to the poor, and you will have treasure in heaven. Then come, follow me."*
>
> MARK 10:19–21

THE RICH YOUNG RULER asked Jesus, "What must I do to inherit eternal life?" Jesus began the dialog by quoting the second part of the Ten Commandments.

The Ten Commandments flesh out our two main responsibilities: The first four tell us how we are to love God, the last six relate to how we are to treat one another. Jesus quoted the sixth, seventh, eighth, and ninth commandments in order and put the fifth commandment—to honor parents—last.

Why did Jesus omit any reference to the first four commandments? Was it because He knew the young man had kept the last six, and that now Jesus was going to give him an opportunity to follow Him and thereby keep the first four?

Very few people could answer as this young man that they have kept the last six commandments. If ever a case could be made that goodness entitles a person to eternal life, then this man qualified. He was the quintessential moral man. He had kept the second part of the Decalogue. He had honored his parents and not defrauded anyone through violence, infidelity, perjury, dishonesty, or theft.

Can a good person, by nature of his or her goodness, have eternal life?

Jesus' answer is stunning.

First, Jesus looked at him. With this young man, there was much to be seen that was favorable. That's not always the case with us.

But Jesus looks at us anyway. He doesn't turn His eyes away from us. He not only sees the outsides of us, He looks into our hearts. He sees everything.

Second, Jesus loved him. There is no person whom Jesus puts in an undecided category. He doesn't need time to make up His mind as to whether or not He loves you. Before He asks anyone to follow Him, He assures them of His love.

Third, Jesus called him. He told the young man and us what we need to do if we are to follow Him. He laid His finger on what may be holding us back.

For this young man, what held him back was his way of life. He lived negatively. He could say that he didn't do this or that, but he had no "did." He wasn't hurting others, but he wasn't helping them either. So Jesus called him out of passive existence into active service: "Liquidate all your assets and give to the poor and you will have treasure in heaven, then come and follow Me."

Jesus asked this rich young ruler to do what He Himself was doing—that though He was rich, yet for our sakes He became poor (2 Corinthians 8:9).

Jesus was on His way to die in Jerusalem. He had divested Himself of His eternal glory. He asked this man to divest himself of his earthly gain. Jesus will always put His finger on what we need to surrender if we are to follow Him.

A Prayer

Lord Jesus, today You look at me, love me, and call me.
May I surrender everything in my life that would
keep me from responding to You.

IF ONLY

At this the man's face fell. He went away sad, because he had great wealth. Jesus looked around and said to his disciples, "How hard it is for the rich to enter the kingdom of God!"

MARK 10:22–23

WE CALL HIM THE rich young ruler. Have you noticed? We don't know his name.

We do know the names of Peter, James, and John as well as the other disciples. Probably in his community this man's name was well known, but it is lost to history. He chose wealth over significance. If only he had followed Jesus, he would have gained identity.

In coming to Jesus, he came to the right Person. Only Jesus knows the answer to the question, "What must I do to inherit eternal life?"

He came to Jesus at the right time. He was young and had a potential lifetime of service before him. Would we have known him as a foundation stone in the church had he made a different decision that day? If only! And it was the right time for Jesus; He was on the way to the cross. He was willing to add an eleventh-hour worker to His band of disciples.

He asked the right question. The opponents of Jesus had consistently asked questions to trap Him, but this rich young ruler asked the most important question anyone can ask: "How can I live eternally?"

He got the right answer. Jesus laid His finger on what held the man back. He always identifies to us what we must surrender if we are to follow Him. Discipleship comes with a cost.

But the rich young ruler made the wrong decision. He went away.

The German preacher Helmut Thielicke tells the story of the child who was raising a frightful cry because he had shoved his hand into the opening of a very expensive Chinese vase and then couldn't pull it out again.

Parents and neighbors tugged on the child's arm while the poor kid howled loudly. Finally, there was nothing left to do but break the beautiful, expensive vase. As the pile of shards lay there, it became clear why the child had been so hopelessly stuck. His little fist held fast to a penny, which he had spied in the bottom of the vase and would not let go.[3]

This young ruler wouldn't let go either. He had a chance to follow Jesus, and he blew it. Mark notes that he not only went away, but went away "sad." Was he sad because he knew he had made the wrong choice, or because Jesus didn't give him the answer he wanted?

Three times in the verses about the rich young ruler, Mark notes that Jesus "looked." He looked at the man and loved him (v. 21); He looked around at the crowd after the man left Him (v. 23); and He looked finally and specifically at the disciples (v. 27). Jesus is always looking, probing to see where we stand.

He penetrates right to the heart. Where do we stand? What are our values? Are we sincere? What matters most to us? What defenses have we erected against His Lordship? How ready are we to follow Him? Will we pay whatever price He asks?

A Prayer

Lord Jesus, as with the rich young ruler, You just want me. Not part of me, but all of me. May I always say yes to you so that no decision in my life will ever cause me to walk away from You.

---

[3] Helmut Thielicke, *A Thielicke Trilogy* (Grand Rapids, MI: Baker Book House, 1980).

THE CAMEL AND THE NEEDLE EYE

The disciples were amazed at his words. But Jesus said again, "Children, how hard it is to enter the kingdom of God! It is easier for a camel to go through the eye of a needle than for a rich man to enter the kingdom of God."

MARK 10:24-25

THE RICH YOUNG RULER chose to retain his earthly wealth rather than gain eternal riches in following Jesus (10:17-22).

Jesus used the man's departure as a teaching opportunity about the high cost of discipleship. The disciples were amazed at what Jesus said. Why? After all, they had left all to follow Him. Could their amazement be that they were still clinging to political expectations that Jesus would enthrone Himself as King and they would gain positions of wealth and influence? Very late into Jesus' ministry, they were still jostling for places of prominence (9:33-37; 10:35-44).

Perhaps they felt like some would-be followers of Jesus today—that Jesus is just an add-on. If you are rich, He will make you richer; if healthy, He will make you healthier; if successful, you will be even more successful.

Jesus' answer was hard to take. So, in one of the rare moments in His teaching, He simply repeated Himself for emphasis. He drove the point home: It is hard to get into the kingdom.

How do we evaluate His words in a culture where we want it to be as easy as possible to follow Jesus? Have we substituted a false gospel of relevance and convenience for the true gospel of repentance and self-denial?

What makes it possible for us to enter the kingdom of God? If the rich young ruler had sold everything to follow Jesus, would he have obtained eternal life? Not if Jesus was making a false claim. Our obedience is only one side of the equation. Jesus must be able to deliver what He promises. No one gets into the kingdom except through the vast resources gained through Christ's life, death, and resurrection from the dead.

To underline His point about the difficulty in entering the kingdom of God, Jesus used the illustration of the impossibility of a camel going through the eye of a needle.

It's fascinating to watch how various commentators try to explain away the plain speech of Jesus.

Some say that Jesus was referring to a small gate set within the larger city gate. At night time, the large gate was closed, but entry could be obtained through the small gate. In that case, a camel could get through if all its baggage had been removed. The camel would then, with difficulty, crawl through.

An alternate view is that Jesus was referring to a rope going through the eye of a needle rather than a camel, since in the original language the spelling of the two words is similar. However, with this view, the rope could still get through if the eye of the needle were large enough.

A camel going through an inner gate would not have amazed the disciples; there is considerable doubt that such an inner gate even existed in the first century. Perhaps a large rope going through would have amazed them if the needle were tiny.

But both these attempts to understand Jesus miss the point. His focus is on "impossible." Neither a camel nor a rope can go through an eye of a needle. Salvation is unattainable unless the Lord makes it happen!

A Prayer

Lord Jesus, I don't have what it takes to get into your kingdom. I'm too sinful. You must make it possible, or I will perish.

ETERNAL LIFE MADE POSSIBLE

The disciples were even more amazed, and said to each other, "Who then can be saved?" Jesus looked at them and said, "With man this is impossible, but not with God; all things are possible with God." Peter said to him, "We have left everything to follow you!"
MARK 10:26-28

THE RICH YOUNG RULER who posed the question, "What must I do to inherit eternal life?" left Jesus in disappointment. He wasn't willing to pay the price of divesting himself of all his possessions to follow Jesus.

At the rich young ruler's departure, the Lord commented that it was easier for a camel to go through the eye of a needle than for the rich to enter the kingdom of God. While various explanations have been offered as to what Jesus meant by this statement, the best way to understand it is to take it literally. It is totally impossible for a camel to go through the eye of a needle. Taking the statement literally best explains why the disciples were amazed and asked among themselves, "Who then can be saved?"

Had the "eye of the needle" been the small gate inset into the larger city gate for access at night, the idea of a camel going through it would not have amazed the disciples. That is something possible since, with a little effort, the camel can get through that smaller opening. Others have said that the word Jesus used was *rope* rather than *camel* since the two words are spelled so similarly in the original language. But it wouldn't have amazed the disciples that a rope could go through a proper sized needle.

No, the disciples were dumbfounded by Jesus' statement. Hearing their conversation, Jesus turned around and reiterated the human impossibility of entering the kingdom of God. That is the bad news. On our own, we are powerless to grant ourselves forgiveness of sins or eternal life.

But the good news is this: With God it is possible! That's why Jesus came. We couldn't save ourselves and gain heaven as our eternal home! Only Jesus has the keys to the kingdom of God.

Peter's response that "we have left everything to follow you" is sobering because it forces us to consider the depth of our own discipleship. What have you left to follow Christ?

Perhaps He hasn't required you to leave everything as He did the rich young ruler or His own disciples. But there are still things that you have to lay aside to follow Him. Have you ever been at a crossroads in life when you had to make the decision whether you would please yourself or obey Him?

I look back on my own life and review crossroads moments when I made decisions out of obedience against every screaming emotion to choose differently. I may not have left everything in terms of material goods, but I did have to leave everything that would have kept me from following Jesus. If you will obey whatever the Lord asks of you, then He will open the kingdom of God to you, because with Him, it is possible!

There is a current gospel chorus that says, "He gives and takes away . . . blessed be the name of the Lord." We all like the giving better than the taking away. But in the last analysis, wouldn't you rather, from eternity's viewpoint, be identified with Peter than with the rich young ruler?

A Prayer

Lord Jesus, I begin another day following You. May I truly divest myself of everything that hinders me from being Your loyal and faithful disciple.

FIRST AND LAST

*"I tell you the truth," Jesus replied, "no one who has left
home or brothers or sisters or mother or father or children
or fields for me and the gospel will fail to receive a hundred
times as much in this present age (homes, brothers, sisters,
mothers, children and fields—and with them, persecutions)
and in the age to come, eternal life. But many
who are first will be last, and the last first.*
MARK 10:29–31

THE RICH YOUNG RULER had just walked away, unwilling to divest himself of everything and follow Jesus.

The disciples had watched the entire exchange. Peter spoke for them all when he proclaimed that they had done what the young man had not, "We have left everything to follow You!" Could it be that some of them, if not all, were having second thoughts about their commitment? After all, Jesus increasingly was focusing on the dark days ahead, for Him and for them. *Should we have left family and vocations to follow Him?* I hear them wondering.

Whenever we are tempted to think of what we have given up to follow Jesus, we must turn our attention to His response. He tells us that we gain far more than we have relinquished.

To the original Twelve, Jesus said, "So you gave up family to follow Me? I'm giving you a new family in return."

It's His promise—that in Christ we have a community in the church not composed of strangers, but of fathers, mothers, brothers, and sisters. The local church must always remember this. The goal isn't to collect an audience where people come and go as in a concert, where relationships between people in the seats aren't essential since the focus is on the stage. In the church, we aren't meant to be holders of tickets for a seat at the Sunday morning "show." We are meant to be in relationship with one another.

In addition to gaining a new family, we also gain property, which Jesus calls "fields." Fields produce food, the necessary sustenance for life. Thus, in Christian community we care for one another and are never to go without provision because we are family, and we don't let our family members starve, become homeless, or lack clothing. These are the "fields" we gain through the community of believers.

We get three big wins: family, field, eternal life—and one downside—persecutions.

We live in a time when perhaps there have never been more martyrs for the gospel and more persecution. Even in the democratic Western countries of Europe and America, culture and politicians seek to marginalize, demonize, and ridicule Christians. There is a price to be paid for following our Lord.

Jesus closed this incident with the rich young ruler and the follow-up conversation with His disciples by talking about the first being last and the last, first.

The rich young ruler in this life was always first. Everything was at his beck and call. He never had to wait in line, always sat at the head table, and servants ensured his easy entrance and exit.

The tables are turned in the age to come. Many who thought they had it made in this age will find they have nothing in the age to come. But those who endure persecution will find that their trial is momentary in comparison to the weight of glory that is coming.

A Prayer

Lord Jesus, thank You for the family I have in Christ.
Strengthen me to face suffering. May I live
today with eternity in view.

IN THE LEAD

They were on their way up to Jerusalem, with Jesus leading the way, and the disciples were astonished, while those who followed were afraid. Again he took the Twelve aside and told them what was going to happen to him.

MARK 10:32

USUALLY WE SAY ONE is going "up" when they're headed north. Not so in Israel. It is always "up" to Jerusalem no matter where you are coming from.

Jesus was headed south from Galilee, moving toward Jericho before the ascent to Jerusalem. In that nearly one-hundred-mile walk through the Jordan Rift Valley, His pathway was up. For us, He journeyed up to the cross, up to the garden tomb, up from the dead on Easter morning, and up to heaven forty days after His resurrection.

And we are all taking that journey with Him. Like the Twelve, our ultimate journey is also "up"—and He leads the way.

I doubt if the original disciples were in the mood to go to Jerusalem. They understood the danger that Jesus faced and they also faced. The group with Jesus is described in two categories: the disciples (that is, the Twelve), and those who followed. They had two reactions to Jesus' itinerary.

The Twelve were astonished He was doing this, while the others following were afraid. Why the difference in perspective?

In all probability, the disciples were close enough to Jesus to have confidence in His leadership so they weren't fearful of what might happen. They had been with Jesus in Jerusalem on other journeys (recorded in John's gospel) and had returned safely to Galilee. If there was danger this time, didn't Jesus have the ability to dodge disaster? At Nazareth, He had walked through a crowd that sought to push Him off a cliff (Luke 4:28–30), and previously in Jerusalem, the opposition had tried to seize Him but no one laid a hand on Him because His time had not yet come (John 7:30).

I suspect the Twelve were astonished that Jesus would go up to Jerusalem again and walk head-on into the lion's den of danger. But the Twelve weren't fearful because they had seen Jesus escape unscathed on prior occasions. Their astonishment arose out of respect for Jesus' bravery.

Not so those following. They hadn't been with Jesus on the prior occasions in Nazareth and Jerusalem. They realistically sensed danger. Given their fear, Jesus could not disclose to them what was really going to happen. So He took the Twelve aside and gave them a special message not obtainable by the rest.

Jesus demonstrated in this act of separation of the Twelve from the others that wisdom provides for timely disclosure. If the Twelve could barely handle the information He would give them, the rest couldn't have absorbed it at all. We might do well to remember that when we are tempted to spill more information than another person is prepared to receive.

Jesus talked to the Twelve only about what was going to happen to Him—not to them. That's almost always the case. Jesus doesn't tell us what is going to happen to us next. We would like to know, but He remains quiet.

We'll only find out where we're going and what we're to do if we follow Him one day at a time. But we can be assured that no matter where we go He has been there ahead of us. Our Lord and Savior is always in the lead!

A Prayer

*Lord Jesus, lead me day by day. I don't
ever want to get ahead of You.*

NECESSARY

"We are going up to Jerusalem," he said, "and the Son of Man will be betrayed to the chief priests and teachers of the law. They will condemn him to death and will hand him over to the Gentiles, who will mock him and spit on him, flog him and kill him. Three days later he will rise."

MARK 10:33-34

IN THE LAST YEAR of His ministry, Jesus began the process of unfolding to the Twelve how it all would end. He didn't tell them everything at once.

This is the third and final announcement or teaching that Jesus gave regarding His approaching death and resurrection in Jerusalem.

The first time He revealed His plan to die was immediately after Peter confessed Him as the Messiah (Mark 8:31-32). At that time Jesus summarized what lay ahead by saying He would (1) suffer many things; (2) be rejected by the elders, chief priests, and teachers of the Law; (3) be killed; and (4) after three days rise again.

The second time He spoke of the future (9:30-32), Jesus repeated the essential elements He gave in the prior teaching and added a new detail: He would be betrayed. He didn't say that the betrayal would come from one of the Twelve; He left off that piece of information. Had He told them at that moment the betrayal would come from one of them, it would have created tremendous relational tension in the group as they would all begin to suspect one another. In that climate of mistrust, Jesus could not have continued to teach them effectively all they needed to learn in those last months He was with them.

In this final announcement (10:33-34) Jesus provided even more detail: (1) the chief priests and teachers of the Law would condemn Him to death; (2) they would hand Him over to the Gentiles; and (3) the Gentiles would mock Him, spit on Him, flog Him, and kill Him.

Why did Jesus think it was necessary to do this? Why was the cross essential in His plan?

It is because you and I could never make it to heaven if He didn't make it possible. Our sins simply and completely disqualify us from ever living in the presence of a holy God.

You wouldn't think of entering an operating room wearing dirty and contaminated clothes, or with a communicable disease. In the same manner, heaven is sin-free. It's a perfect environment, and God refuses to destroy that environment with soul-pollution.

How can we, who are so impure on the inside, ever exist in an external realm where there is nothing but purity? On our own, we can never get sufficiently decontaminated from sin to qualify to enter God's presence.

That's why Jesus knew He had to go to the cross. He did it for us. He didn't do it to set Himself up as some great martyr or hero for a cause, or to show He was a better person than the opposition, or to become a poster example for all those who choose a nonviolent path to protest injustice. Although those may be sufficient goals for some, that wasn't His goal.

He went to the cross for you and for me! He had you in mind as He journeyed up to Jerusalem. Think of Him saying your name, "Father, I'm going to the cross so the one I love can come into My eternal kingdom. I'm doing this for him, for her!"

A Prayer

Lord Jesus, I am overwhelmed that You love me so much.

WHATEVER WE ASK

Then James and John, the sons of Zebedee, came to him. "Teacher," they said, "we want you to do for us whatever we ask." "What do you want me to do for you?" he asked. They replied, "Let one of us sit at your right and the other at your left in your glory."

MARK 10:35-37

YOU AND I HAVE DONE the same thing as these two disciples. We want Jesus to do for us whatever we ask.

I usually tell Jesus specifically what I want. James and John were smarter. They first kept what they desired to themselves, choosing instead to see if Jesus would write them a blank check. Maybe they thought they could slide a request by Jesus since they knew He loved them, or perhaps the fact that the Lord had just talked about His death made them think He might be vulnerable to a large request.

The good thing here is that they had confidence the Lord could do whatever they asked.

If you could ask Jesus one thing, what would it be? Do you believe He has the power to grant it?

Jesus responded to James and John with a question rather than an answer. If He had been a mere man, He could have said, "I don't know if I can do anything for you, but tell Me, what's on your mind?"

Had He been a self-centered person, Jesus could have responded: "You are asking the wrong question—it's not what I can do for you, but what *you* can do for Me."

Implicitly, however, Jesus' question indicates He could grant anything. James and John could ask, largely because they knew from following Jesus that He possessed immense power.

His question still penetrates to this day, for He is searching our hearts and asking us, "What can I do for you?" The real issue is whether we ask rightly—James and John didn't.

We all roundly criticize these two disciples for trying to edge their way to the front. They have sharp elbows. You can see what's going on if you look at the listing of the Twelve.

In the gospels of Matthew and Luke, the names of Peter, Andrew, James, and John are given in that order: the two sets of brothers belonging together. That's how Jesus first called them—in pairs. In Mark and Acts, the order is Peter, James, John, and Andrew. The latter order is consistent with the fact that Peter, James, and John were the inner three with Jesus at the raising of Jairus' daughter (5:37), Jesus' transfiguration (9:2), and Gethsemane (14:33).

In making this request to Jesus, James and John weren't only trying to jump ahead of Andrew, they were also trying to bounce Peter, who is always listed first.

So, there you have it! Even Jesus' first disciples were not exempt from striving for position. No wonder we see this problem replicated in the church through the centuries.

But let's also consider the positive side of James and John's request. Let's give them some credit.

First, they wanted to be close to Jesus. Don't we all want that? In the age to come, wouldn't you rather be near Him than up somewhere in a remote gallery looking on?

Second, Jesus had just made the third announcement of His approaching death. Their request tells us that they remained unshaken in their belief that Jesus indeed had a kingdom and glory to offer! Do we also believe that about Him?

A Prayer

Lord, help me to balance my desire to be near You against the selfish ambition to leap over someone else.

REQUEST DENIED

"You don't know what you are asking," Jesus said. "Can you drink the cup I drink or be baptized with the baptism I am baptized with?" "We can," they answered. Jesus said to them, "You will drink the cup I drink and be baptized with the baptism I am baptized with, but to sit at my right or left is not for me to grant. These places belong to those for whom they have been prepared."

MARK 10:38-40

IT'S CLEAR THAT JAMES AND JOHN didn't have a clue. When they asked to sit at Jesus' right and left hand, they didn't know that the thorn of suffering first awaited them before the throne of glory.

When Jesus asked them if they were ready to drink His cup and be baptized with His baptism, they blithely and too quickly answered, "Yes."

Their grandiose request for places of prominence teaches us a valuable lesson about praying for things we want. You may not know what you are asking for. The whole idea may seem good to you and that is why you bring it to the Lord, but your request, if fulfilled, may have some unintended consequences. To get where you want to go may involve some great suffering, stress, or distress.

Jesus connected their request for the prominent positions at His right and left hand in heaven to the fact that one only gets there after passing through great adversity. Heroes are never made in circumstances where no difficulty presents itself. So Jesus asked them if they could stand to drink the cup and be baptized with His baptism (of suffering).

It's so true in life—anything worth questing after involves suffering and sacrifice of some kind. High goals are never attained by people who are unwilling to pay the price to get there.

Jesus chose to answer the question of James and John with a question of His own. He refocused them from the next life to this life. They had no idea at the moment that their "baptism" would mean that James would be the first of the Eleven to die (Acts 12:2) and John, the last (John 21:23).

When Jesus first called them, they could have remained at home and escaped the destiny of a life cut short or a long life marked in the end by exile on the island of Patmos. But when you start out to follow Christ, when you heed the invitation to "come and see" (John 1:39), you'll also ultimately hear Jesus invite you to lay down everything to follow Him (Mark 8:34).

If He doesn't call us to a life of glamor, we know that ultimately He invites us to a life of glory. Jesus clearly reveals that there is a future after this life. There will be places at His right and left. They just aren't His to give.

The places of prominence are still open. Who will sit next to Him? The seats aren't reserved—until He comes. Anyone may still qualify to sit on His right or left; or perhaps the Father will rotate and give each of us a chance. However, I suspect that on the other side we won't even care about that. Sinful human pride and striving for position will all be gone. The fact is this: We shall reign with Him!

A Prayer

Lord Jesus, I have also said stupid things to You. You suffer my naiveté as You did with James and John. But, thankfully, You also read my heart and know my future ultimately leads to You.

JOSTLING FOR PROMINENCE

When the ten heard about this, they became indignant with James and John. Jesus called them together and said, "You know that those who are regarded as rulers of the Gentiles lord it over them, and their high officials exercise authority over them. Not so with you."

MARK 10:41–43A

MARK RECORDS THAT James and John asked for positions at the right and left hands of Jesus when He came into His glory. Matthew adds another detail: their mother was a co-conspirator in the request (20:20–21)!

The question we might ask is this, "How did the other ten disciples hear about this, since Mark 10:41 makes it clear they learned about it later?" It had been a private conversation with Jesus, the mother, and her two sons. So who leaked the news?

It's the first instance I know of regarding the Christian grapevine. There's really not very much that happens in Christian community that can be concealed for too long. It's almost a miracle when a conversation, incident, transgression, or confession stays permanently private.

So someone leaked this incident to the other ten. I doubt it was James and John because they probably were too embarrassed to reveal what Jesus had told them—that they were not guaranteed the seats of prominence. I wouldn't be surprised if it was their mother who told friends, and the whole matter got back to the other disciples.

The other ten were angry and rightly so, but not for altruistic reasons. They were ticked because they hadn't beat James and John to the punch. They *all* wanted to be first. At that point, none of them had a great sense of community, that "we are in this together," that it doesn't matter who is in first or second place so long as the Lord is honored and His work built.

They were the first, but not the last, of Jesus' followers to be upset because someone tried to get ahead of them in the kingdom of God.

Whenever there is jostling for prominence, people aren't together. They are either alone or in separate enclaves plotting, gossiping, complaining, and venting their frustration and animosity.

In dealing with dissension among His followers, Jesus called them together so He could talk to all of them at the same time. Rather than give a stern scolding directed specifically at James and John, He omitted naming them and gave some general principles of what life in His community is intended to be. The gentleness of Jesus in resolving this conflict should be noted. He set forth principles rather than degrade James and John.

Too many times in Christian community, when conflict happens, the attacks become personal and people don't deal coolheadedly with the underlying issue. We must hear Jesus saying to us: *Are you going to resolve conflict like the world wants you to or like I want you to?*

Jesus dismissed the worldly way wherein "the rulers of the Gentiles lord it over them." He wants His followers to avoid two things: (1) an attitude of lording it over others. He doesn't want us to be haughty, boastful, or use whatever status we have to project that we are better than someone else. (2) He doesn't want actions that "exercise authority" in such a way that we become dictators, arrogantly bossing others and using our positions as justification for the mistreatment of those we lead and serve.

A Prayer

Lord Jesus, may I not use position in family, church, work, or community to advance my own agendas or try to be "the boss." Help me, Lord, to serve others with humility.

SERVANT LEADER

"Instead, whoever wants to become great among you must be your servant, and whoever wants to be first must be slave of all. For even the Son of Man did not come to be served, but to serve, and to give his life as a ransom for many."

MARK 10:43B-45

WHEN JESUS FIRST SAID "Follow me!" (1:17), what did the disciples think? That following Jesus led down a path toward fame, reward, and glory? Now, after nearly three years with Jesus, they were learning differently.

James and John's request for greatness came in Jesus' ministry. Jesus certainly knew that underneath the surface, competitive jostling for position among the disciples was taking place. But He didn't deal with that issue prematurely. He waited until it came to a head. It's a good lesson for us—sometimes it is best to wait until a more opportune moment to deal with a difficulty or conflict.

If you long for greatness and a lead position, then Jesus has advice for you. Leadership is not being on top with everyone supporting you. It's working your way to the bottom to support everyone else. In that succinct lesson, be "slave of all," Jesus tells us how to lead others—in marriage and family, church, work, and community.

Sadly, the church hasn't always listened to Him. I have seen too many instances in the local church and in national bodies of believers where selfish ambition, cloaked in spirituality, has flatly ignored Jesus' teaching. You can always tell self-seeking leaders—they put their own interests ahead of the unity of the body of Christ. They would rather split believers from one another than humble themselves to take a subordinate and supportive role.

Jesus points us to His own example. For the ninth time in Mark's gospel He refers to Himself as the Son of Man. No one else called Him that. It was His self-designated term. Many falsely suggest this title was a reference to His humanity. Not so! Jesus drew upon Daniel 7 imagery wherein the Son of Man comes with the clouds of heaven and is given eternal authority and dominion by the Ancient of Days (God the Father).

If Jesus, the divine Son of Man, takes the role of a servant, how can we do less? And that is His point: "The Son of Man came not to be served, but to serve."

But serving is only part of His mission. We are at a hinge moment in the gospel of Mark. Everything preceding this has focused on His serving, but from chapter 11 onward the focus shifts to His giving His life "as a ransom for many."

Jesus saw His life as a substitute for ours. Ransom is paid to free a captive. Here is what we can never have without Him: forgiveness of sin, right relationship with God, and eternal life.

Many regard Jesus simply as a good moral teacher. But Jesus saw Himself as far more than that. Living a good example, teaching the principles of God's kingdom were only part of the picture. They are incomplete without His substitutionary death. He cannot save us by His teaching alone—He understood the necessity of voluntarily laying down His life for you and me. His mission would have been forever incomplete without the cross.

A Prayer

Lord Jesus, You did not hesitate to lay aside Your glory to come and serve, to be a ransom for me. It is not for me to become a ransom, but I can follow Your example and serve.

HE HAD A NAME

Then they came to Jericho. As Jesus and his disciples, together with a large crowd, were leaving the city, a blind man, Bartimaeus (that is, the Son of Timaeus), was sitting by the roadside begging.

MARK 10:46

BEFORE WE MAKE any devotional application to this story, let's look first at what appears to be discrepancies in the three Gospel accounts of this incident.

First, Matthew (20:29–34) tells the story of two blind beggars whom Jesus healed.

Second, Matthew and Mark state that the incident took place as Jesus was leaving Jericho, but Luke states that it happened as Jesus approached the city.

Third, only Mark names the beggar: Bartimaeus, the son of Timaeus.

If we believe the Scriptures do not contradict themselves, how do we explain the differences among the accounts in Matthew, Mark, and Luke?

The account of the two beggars in Matthew and the one beggar in Mark and Luke are similar to the account of the Gerasene (Gadarene) demoniac. Matthew (8:28–34) gives the account of two, while Mark (5:1–20) and Luke (8:26–39) relate the story of one. Reconciling these accounts is easy if you think of a camera. Looking at the same scene, the camera can either take a panoramic shot or refocus and zoom in on something that stands out.

What stands out to Mark and Luke is what the one man did after his deliverance—he went and told others. Evidently the other man did nothing after his deliverance. Matthew is content to give us the panoramic shot of the healing; Mark and Luke, the close-up because of the follow-through. That principle applies here as well with the Jericho beggars. Matthew simply gives the panoramic, Mark and Luke the close-up.

The greater difficulty is the sequence. The key to understanding the difference may be that Luke alone records the encounter with Zacchaeus (19:1–9), placing it in Jericho after the healing of the beggar. Did Jesus not intend to stay in Jericho when He entered and, according to Matthew and Mark, was in fact "leaving"? Did Jesus turn around after the healing of the beggars, changing His itinerary so that Jericho became a stop? Thus, from one point of view Jesus was leaving the city and from another point of view approaching it.

Our main focus however should be on the fact that the man has a name. Excluding the mention of Jairus, in all the healings of Jesus this is the only recipient with a name—and only the gospel of Mark gives us his name, Bartimaeus. Why is this?

Early church tradition tells us that Mark's gospel first came to the Romans. Mark is the only one to tell us that the one who carried Jesus' cross, Simeon of Cyrene, had two sons, Alexander and Rufus. Paul's letter to the Romans contains greetings to Rufus and his mother (16:13).

Could it be that just as Paul calls attention to a member of the Roman church whose father had the distinction of carrying the cross, Mark also points out another person known to the Roman church—Bartimaeus, the son of Timaeus?

Of the two blind beggars healed that day, Bartimaeus is singled out for the "zoom shot" because he later became known in the Christian community, even to those in Rome. Perhaps Bartimaeus himself helped found the church in Rome.

So many are helped by Jesus but never go onward to serve Him. Bartimaeus did, and thus he is known.

A Prayer

Lord Jesus, You have done so much for me.
May I also go onward to serve You.

SON OF DAVID, HAVE MERCY

When he heard that it was Jesus of Nazareth, he began to shout, "Jesus, Son of David, have mercy on me!" Many rebuked him and told him to be quiet, but he shouted all the more, "Son of David, have mercy on me!" Jesus stopped and said, "Call him." So they called to the blind man, "Cheer up! On your feet! He's calling you."

MARK 10:47-49

THE TERM *SON OF DAVID* is clearly messianic. The New Testament begins with "a record of the genealogy of Jesus Christ, the Son of David" (Matthew 1:1).

However, in Jesus' three years of ministry leading up to Passion Week, only five people called Him that: two blind men in Galilee (Matthew 9:27); a Canaanite woman in the region of Tyre and Sidon (Matthew 15:22); and the two blind men at Jericho (Matthew 20:29) of whom Bartimaeus was one (Mark 10:46).

The disciples closest to Jesus had not yet called Him Son of David even though they had said, "You are the Christ." Does it strike you that the people less likely to know Jesus' identity—four blind men and a pagan woman—nevertheless knew Him? Could it be that our close proximity to the Lord sometimes keeps us from inquiring more deeply as to His identity? You may be with Him every day, like the disciples, but there are depths in Him you don't yet know.

One of the blind men who called out was Bartimaeus. Actually his name means "Son of Timaeus" and therefore we don't know his given name. Was he young? Middle aged? Old? Married? Single? Blind from birth? Had he been called "Son of Timaeus" because the identity others gave him in life was "that poor boy, the son of Timaeus"? So they knew him not by his real name but by his relationship to his father. He was an object to be pitied, not worthy to be called by his own name.

Perhaps that's how we often tag people with disabilities. We're afraid to come near, to learn who they really are. So we keep them at a distance. We say of them, "Oh, you know . . . that's the person in the wheelchair," or "that's the person with Down syndrome," or "that's the person who is . . ."

Bartimaeus had been sitting when he called out to Jesus. We know that because people told him to stand up. In sitting and asking Jesus for mercy, was he simply hoping that "mercy" meant a generous donation? Maybe not, since he continued to shout and that seems out of the ordinary. I believe he was shouting because he had just one chance to be rid of the blindness.

Observe how the crowd suddenly changed its mood. Just a moment earlier they were telling him to shush. After Jesus beckoned, they switched gears and told Bartimaeus to cheer up and get on his feet.

Bartimaeus immediately did so. He didn't let the discouragement of a lifetime, or even the active discouragement of the people around him telling him to be quiet, keep him from trying to attract Jesus' attention.

We should follow his example and never let others discourage us from bringing to Jesus the deep desires of our hearts.

A Prayer

Lord Jesus, Son of David, I also cry out to You! You are the One who can bring relief to my distress. Just as a king or benefactor can grant a request out of his authority or riches, so I trust You to grant me mercy from Your authority as Lord.

HOW MUCH DO YOU ASK?

Throwing his cloak aside, he jumped to his feet and came to Jesus. "What do you want me to do for you?" Jesus asked him. The blind man said, "Rabbi, I want to see." "Go," said Jesus, "your faith has healed you." Immediately he received his sight and followed Jesus along the road.

MARK 10:50–52

WE KNOW HIM as Bartimaeus, the blind Jericho beggar sitting by the roadside as Jesus passed by. He sensed this was the opportunity of a lifetime. It turned out he was right—Jesus was passing his way only once, headed up to Jerusalem to lay down His life for us.

Even though others tried to shush him up, Bartimaeus continued to cry, "Jesus, Son of David, have mercy on me." Jesus did, as He also does with us. The Lord called to him.

May we ever be equally excited when the Lord calls us to Himself. No hesitation, no reserve!

Bartimaeus evidently had been sitting with a wrap around him. It was springtime and a bit chilly. Whenever Jesus calls us, we must also be willing to throw off stuff.

But Jesus didn't heal him on the spot. Instead, He asked a question: "What do you want me to do for you?" I suspect Jesus queried him as to whether he wanted a handout or something bigger. Jesus would have given the man alms, but He was ready to give more. It's vital that, like Bartimaeus, we stretch our faith and reach for more from Jesus, rather than settling for less. "You are coming to a King, large petitions with you bring, for his grace and power are such, none can ever ask too much!"

Earlier, to attract Jesus' attention, Bartimaeus had called Him "Son of David." Now, in direct conversation, he simply called him teacher (rabbi). Perhaps Bartimaeus felt he had overplayed his hand. Jesus, however, didn't chastise him for calling Him by a diminished title. Our Lord is not easily offended.

Can you see Bartimaeus? As a blind person, no doubt he was weaving and bobbing with nervousness as he stood before Jesus. Nevertheless he clearly knew what he wanted—sight!

In healing him, Jesus took no credit. He gave Bartimaeus a huge dose of affirmation, "Your faith has healed you." What? The Lord Himself takes no credit!

Yes, certainly the credit does belong to Jesus, since Bartimaeus could have had all the faith in the world and it still wouldn't have cured him of his blindness. We must be careful about the object of our faith. We don't have faith in faith itself, but in our Lord! However, unless Bartimaeus had cried out while sitting by the roadside, refusing to be silenced by others, he never would have been healed. So in this case the source of healing was shared: the faith of one and the power of Jesus. Graciously, the Lord took no credit.

The fact that Bartimaeus then began to follow Jesus on the way up to Jerusalem is testament to the idea that later he became well-known in the early church. After his healing, he continued to follow Jesus. Some may be healed and simply revert to their old ways, to their old lives. Not so Bartimaeus.

The lesson from Bartimaeus is that we should never ask Jesus for less when He is capable of giving us more. He hears our persistent cries for mercy.

A Prayer

Lord Jesus, You have all power, but You hold that power in reserve, waiting for me to ask, to invite You to do what I cannot do for myself.

WHAT DOES THE LORD NEED?

As they approached Jerusalem and came to Bethphage and Bethany at the Mount of Olives, Jesus sent two of his disciples, saying to them, "Go to the village ahead of you, and just as you enter it, you will find a colt tied there, which no one has ever ridden. Untie it and bring it here. If anyone asks you, 'Why are you doing this?' tell them, 'The Lord needs it and will send it back here shortly.'"

MARK 11:1–3

THE WALK FROM Jericho to Jerusalem involved an arduous climb of over twenty miles from 1,200 feet below sea level to 2,500 feet above. We assume Jesus walked it because only when He neared the top did He ask for a donkey. He had begun the ascent the day before, joining no doubt with other pilgrims in singing the Psalms of Ascent (Ps. 120–134). After a rest stop for the evening, sometime in the morning He approached the villages of Bethphage and Bethany, atop the eastern slope of the Mount of Olives.

In following His steps from Jericho, we see again the humility of our Lord. He didn't ask anyone to carry Him, nor did He ask for any special means of transportation. Given that He was walking toward the cross to die for our sins, surely He was entitled to special treatment. But for our sake He became a servant. He set an example for all in His kingdom that special status doesn't mean special privilege. He declined to live an entitled life.

He knew that in the next village a colt on which no one had ridden was tied. How did He know this? We aren't told. It's possible He could have made prior secret arrangements with His friends Lazarus, Mary, and Martha who lived in Bethany, even as later in the week He made arrangements for the upper room without the disciples' prior knowledge (14:13–14). More likely, He knew it supernaturally, since if He had made prior arrangements, the colt would have been brought to Him and bystanders wouldn't have asked why the colt was being taken.

What is known is His intention. Matthew's account (21:5) of the colt was Jesus' way of fulfilling Zechariah 9:9:

"Say to the Daughter of Zion,
'See, your king comes to you,
gentle and riding on a donkey,
on a colt, the foal of a donkey.'"
(Matthew 21:5)

The Lord anticipated that His two disciples would be queried when they began to untie the colt. Jesus thought one step out in front. He considered the consequences of actions—a necessary trait in all great leaders. So He prepared the disciples with an answer in the event they were questioned.

This is the first time Mark records Jesus as saying He needed something.

Amazing! The Creator who owns all things, who made the cattle on a thousand hills, doesn't even own one animal. He has to borrow a colt in order to have transportation.

It's a lesson for us. Jesus looks at you and me today. Theoretically, He doesn't need anything. After all, He is ascended and at the right hand of the Majesty on High; nevertheless, He looks to us. He says: "I need your life. Will you give it to Me?"

Or He may say, "I need you to do this for Me. I need you to clothe the naked, feed the hungry, visit those in prison, care for the sick, and be My witness to those who are lost. Will you do that? I need you."

A Prayer

Lord Jesus, my life is at Your disposal today.
Take what You need from me!

UNDER AUTHORITY

*They went and found a colt outside in the street, tied at
a doorway. As they untied it, some people standing there
asked, "What are you doing, untying that colt?"
They answered as Jesus had told them to,
and the people let them go.*

MARK 11:4-6

RECENTLY, SOME FRIENDS and I were discussing the life of a prominent person who lays claim to being a Christian. We were confused that the testimony from his lips didn't correspond to his actions. With his words he spoke of his personal salvation, but with his actions and policies he clearly was at odds with Jesus.

I suspect this dichotomy exists fairly frequently. The problem comes when we want to own Jesus as our Savior, but not as our Lord—when we want the benefits He brings, but not the obedience He asks.

Jesus had ascended the long climb from Jericho to the top of the Mount of Olives. First, He stayed at the home of friends in Bethany (John 12). When He was ready to enter Jerusalem, He sent two of His disciples on an improbable mission to obtain a colt (which they had not seen), tied at a doorway outside in the street (where they knew not the exact address), and to remove it (and take the chance of being apprehended for theft).

If you had been one of them, would you have gone so willingly? What can we learn from their example?

First, the Lord always knows what is going on. Thus, when He directs us, we should do what He asks even if we don't know what it means. The disciples had no idea at that moment why Jesus wanted the colt. Matthew's gospel, written after the event, tells us that He needed the colt to fulfill the Scripture (Matthew 21:4-5). At the time, however, the two disciples didn't know that. They simply trusted Jesus and followed His directions.

As a pastor I taught new converts to be baptized in water. Sometimes they would ask, "But, why? Do I really need to get all wet? Isn't believing enough?" My response was that no one would enlist in the army and begin his or her military career by disobeying the first order of the drill sergeant. That being the case, why would any new Christian want to begin their Christian walk by disobeying—not the order of a drill sergeant, but the order of the Commander in Chief! The Christian life is all about obedience!

Second, there will always be those who don't understand what Jesus sends you to do. That was the case here. The bystanders were mystified as to why two strangers, who didn't own the animal, were untying it. Had I been there that day, I might have immediately called for the authorities!

Third, when others don't understand our obedience to Jesus we should respond to their questions. We are not to get huffy, or threatened or argumentative. We shouldn't give them the cold shoulder or silent treatment. Honest questions deserve honest answers.

The two disciples responded truthfully and with good hearts. The villagers accepted their response because they knew how good Jesus had been to the two sisters and brother living in Bethany: Mary, Martha, and Lazarus (John 11–12). The bystanders trusted the word of the two disciples because, first and foremost, they trusted Jesus.

A Prayer

Jesus, be not only my Savior but also my Lord. I purpose to obey you today. May I have confidence in all the everyday decisions of my life to say, "I'm doing as the Lord wants me to do."

SAVE NOW!

When they brought the colt to Jesus and threw their cloaks over it, he sat on it. Many people spread their cloaks on the road, while others spread branches they had cut in the fields. Those who went ahead and those who followed shouted, "Hosanna!" "Blessed is he who comes in the name of the Lord!" "Blessed is the coming kingdom of our father David!" "Hosanna in the highest!"

MARK 11:7–10

THIS IS THE MOMENT we recognize as Palm Sunday, when Jesus came down from the Mount of Olives, across the narrow Kidron Valley, and up to Jerusalem.

Amazingly, He was riding on a colt never ridden before. Just as He had showed His mastery over nature in calming storms at sea (Mark 4 and 6), now He demonstrated His authority by not only riding an unbroken colt, but riding it through a shouting crowd that was throwing branches on the path before Him.

Matthew tells us that the colt was with his mother—typical of Matthew, who gives us the panoramic view of the whole event, while Mark does the close-up and focuses only on the colt.

In agreeing to enter Jerusalem in this manner, Jesus clearly was making a statement, presenting Himself as the entering King prophesied by Zechariah (9:9).

Sometimes we have heard it said that on Sunday they were shouting "Hosanna," and on Friday, "Crucify Him." But that is to misread the situation. The crowd with Jesus when He entered into Jerusalem was made up of pilgrims. The people of Jerusalem would not have walked up the Mount of Olives en masse to meet Jesus. Rather, it was a pilgrim crowd coming from Galilee and elsewhere who had made the long trek up to Jerusalem. Sabbath had come, so they rested in the villages atop the Mount of Olives before completing their journey.

Now, they were ready, on the first day of the week, to enter Jerusalem and complete their week of pilgrimage. It was a different crowd, composed of Jesus' Jerusalem opposition, who shouted "Crucify Him" five days later.

The adoring throng with Jesus clearly believed their promised Deliverer was entering Jerusalem that day. You can hear it in the four distinct shout-outs from the group during the procession.

The first recurring shout was one word, "Hosanna!" The word means "Save!" It's both a shout of praise and a cry appealing for God's immediate help. Indeed, Jesus will bring God's help, but not in the way they expected. One week later, on the following Sunday, Jesus would rise from the dead on the third day following His crucifixion. His death and resurrection would open heaven for us because through Him our sins are forgiven and we receive eternal life.

The second and third recurring shouts were, "Blessed is he who comes in the name of the Lord!" and "Blessed is the coming kingdom of our father David!" Unlike the first shout where the people asked for help, these shouts asked for blessing on Jesus and the kingdom He brings.

The final recurring shout intensified the first one—not just "Hosanna" but "Hosanna in the highest!"

Don't you wish you could have been there that day, to be among those welcoming Jesus into Jerusalem? We can welcome Him this day into our hearts. We can cry, "Hosanna!" and lift up our voice to call Him "Blessed!" We have so much more now to praise Him for than the crowd did on that day.

A Prayer

Lord Jesus, from my heart today I lift my voice to praise You. I always want to be among those who honor You.

HE LOOKED AROUND

Jesus entered Jerusalem and went to the temple. He looked around at everything, but since it was already late, he went out to Bethany with the Twelve.

MARK 11:11

EARLIER THAT DAY, surrounded by an adoring and shouting crowd, Jesus rode a colt down the Mount of Olives, across the narrow Kidron Valley, and up to Jerusalem. Outside the temple, He would have dismounted and then entered one of the gates leading up to the vast platform known as the court of the Gentiles.

If the adoring crowd expected Jesus to do something dramatic to bring the kingdom of David, they were sorely disappointed. Jesus did nothing except look around. His gaze took in everything—the temple with its restricted access for priests only, the wall that separated the Gentiles from entering the inner courts, and the smoke arising from the altar of sacrifice. But mostly His focus centered on the outer court, especially the southern part where the money changers converted regular money into temple currency. He took it all in but took no action.

This is the fifth time in the gospel that Mark recorded Jesus as having "looked around." The phrase connotes a slow, elliptical movement of the eyes that carefully takes in every detail, a kind of patient, moving stare.

The first "looked around" (3:5) occurred when Jesus, in anger and deep distress, visually challenged those who didn't want Him to heal a man with a withered hand on the Sabbath.

The second "looked around" (3:34) focused on the circle of those seated around Him when His mother and brothers came to take Him away. He disowned their attempt to divert Him from His mission and instead defined His true family by saying those who do the will of His Father are His mother and brother.

The third "looked around" (5:32) came when Jesus sensed that power had gone out from Him. He looked for the person who had touched His clothes. His look wasn't one of anger, but of assurance to the woman that her faith had made her well from her twelve-year illness.

He "looked around" the fourth time (10:23) after the rich young ruler spurned the Lord's offer of discipleship. At that point, Jesus spoke difficult words to His disciples, "How hard it is for the rich to enter the kingdom of God!"

Now, in the court of the Gentiles, Jesus looked around for the fifth time recorded in Mark. He sized up everything. It was late in the day. He observed, but did nothing. In that moment, had He acted to turn over the tables of the money changers, a riot would have ensued. The adoring pilgrim throng that escorted Him into Jerusalem would have joined in a melee. But Jesus held back and returned to Bethany.

These five occasions illustrated Jesus' penetrating gaze. He was emotional at the hardness of heart from those who dared Him to heal, emotional that His mother and brothers didn't understand Him, emotional when a woman had been cured through her faith, emotional when a would-be disciple rejected Him, and emotional when the temple was prostituted for financial gain.

If Jesus looked around at you and me, what would He see? Would He look at us with anger and distress or disappointment? Or would He look at us with commendation for our faith?

A Prayer

Lord Jesus, may Your look at me be as the look of approval You gave to the woman who was healed, and not a look of grief or sadness at my wrongful behavior.

HUNGRY

> *The next day as they were leaving Bethany, Jesus was hungry. Seeing in the distance a fig tree in leaf, he went to find out if it had any fruit. When he reached it, he found nothing but leaves, because it was not the season for figs. Then he said to the tree, "May no one ever eat fruit from you again." And his disciples heard him say it.*
>
> MARK 11:12–14

THIS IS THE ONLY TIME in Mark that Jesus is described as being hungry. It attests to His humanity. He had been angry on occasion, but now He was hungry. The One who fed crowds of 5,000 and 4,000 was hungry! Amazing!

Unlike the times when He miraculously multiplied bread and fish, He made no food for Himself. In fact, He never performed a miracle for His own benefit. He always performed them for others.

What an example for us to live our lives in self-giving and not in self-serving!

Had Jesus' hosts failed to provide Him breakfast? Or, perhaps they had and He had lingered through the morning at Bethany and set out just before noon without having lunch.

Today Jesus has a different kind of hunger. Now, in heaven, He hungers for the fellowship and love of His people. He longs for you and me to draw close to Him.

Jesus turned toward a fig tree to assuage His hunger. It is fascinating that a day earlier He knew that a colt was tied at a doorway and sent His disciples to fetch it. In this instance, He apparently didn't know whether the fig tree had fruit.

It is a most perplexing text. On the one hand, Jesus surely knew that it was not the season for figs. Why then did He even bother to check the tree for fruit? Various reasons have been offered— including the idea that a fig tree in leaf, if it was going to bear fruit, already had small fig buds. The analogy would be that of an apple tree with small sour unripe apples needing further maturation. The premature fig, like the apple, would be bitter to the taste but could be edible.

On the other hand, since the text says Jesus was hungry, it doesn't make sense that He would be looking for a sour fig to satisfy His hunger.

When a fig tree was in leaf but didn't have premature figs, that meant the tree would have no fruit that year.

The Danish theologian Søren Kierkegaard used this text to illustrate the danger of the profession of "leaves" without the evidence in the "fruit" of a Christlike life. What good is the appearance of being a follower of Jesus without the evidence of godly character and choices?

Could the Lord have used His hunger not to fulfill His own human need but to give us a vital life lesson instead? The unfruitful tree becomes a sign for us that He comes looking for fruitfulness in our lives. He has a deeper hunger than for food.

Replace the fig tree with yourself. Imagine Jesus is hungry—hungry for your presence, your praise, your friendship, your service. He comes to you looking for you to satisfy His hunger. What will He find? Leaves with or without fruit?

A Prayer

Lord Jesus, I'm hungry for many things—some of which will only be satisfied on the other side. But above and beyond my hunger is Your hunger for me. May my life satisfy You deeply!

CLEANING HOUSE

On reaching Jerusalem, Jesus entered the temple area and began driving out those who were buying and selling there. He overturned the tables of the money changers and the benches of those selling doves, and would not allow anyone to carry merchandise through the temple courts.

MARK 11:15–16

FOLLOWING HIS TRIUMPHAL ENTRY into Jerusalem the previous day, Jesus entered the temple area and simply "looked around at everything" (v. 11). Now, we know the reason why. Had He taken action then to purge the temple of the money changers, the crowd with Him would have pitched in and a riot would have ensued. Jesus didn't want mob action to accomplish His purposes.

We know from John's gospel that Jesus first cleansed the temple of the merchandisers at the beginning of His ministry (John 2:13–22). Later, His disciples remembered His statement at the time: "Zeal for your house will consume me." Now, three years later in this second cleansing of the temple, Jesus' zeal remained undiminished.

How true it is that over time many go back to their old ways. Revivals come and then they ebb. Persons once "on fire" for the Lord seem passionless years later.

In the intervening three years, the temple had gone back to its old ways. The court of the Gentiles was massive, spreading out over the equivalent of almost fifteen football fields. The merchandise was located on the south side, where pilgrims and worshipers entered following their ritual cleaning in the many baths outside.

From all nations they came to worship God—Jew and Gentile alike. The sellers weren't there to worship but to profit. All money had to be exchanged for the special temple currency, the half-shekel tax. For the poor who couldn't afford a lamb, doves were sold to those who wanted to sacrifice. The temple sellers were profit-driven, not prophet-driven.

The strength of Jesus' personality is seen in that He stopped the whole vast enterprise single-handedly. He didn't do it courteously, either. He didn't give the money changers time to bag their currency. Instead, He overturned their tables, scattering coins everywhere.

While Jesus never struck a person, He didn't have the same regard for property. He permitted demons to enter the swine at Gerasa (5:13), destroying a herd of 2,000 and all the income that went with it. He cursed a fig tree because it had no fruit (11:14). Here, He crippled the temple economy—at least for a day.

In His action, Jesus leaves an example for His followers. Those who serve in leadership capacity must resist the temptation to see people as profit centers. We must be careful never to make money the main thing but to use funds as the servant of ministry.

Jesus' attitude toward "snake-charming" pulpit personalities who promise you riches if you'll send them money would bring the same response from Him as His attack on the money changers. Such activity makes Him angry.

Jesus clearly didn't condemn support for the temple since He paid the half-shekel tax Himself (Matthew 17:27), and approved the widow who gave all she had to the temple treasury (Luke 21:1-4). Rather, Jesus opposed solicitation of money for selfish enrichment, and He stands against any abusive way that might be employed to raise money for His cause today.

A Prayer

Lord Jesus, may my passion for You be as strong when I am older as when I was younger. Cleanse my life from anything that hinders the purity of my worship and service to You.

THIEVES IN THE HOUSE OF GOD

And as he taught them, he said, "Is it not written: 'My house shall be called a house of prayer for all nations'? But you have made it a 'den of robbers.'"

MARK 11:17

WE MISTAKE THE MEANING of Jesus' cleansing of the temple if we assume He forbids resources to be made available to worshippers.

For example, churches that ban the sale of books and music on their premises on the basis of Jesus' cleansing of the temple misunderstand what the event was all about.

The money changers and dove sellers of the temple did their business in the court of the Gentiles, the only place of access for non-Jewish pilgrims. The transformation of that court into a commercial center for profit prevented the Gentiles from an opportunity to worship. How could they praise the one true God when all around them were the sounds of sellers hawking their wares, turning the temple area into one of crass commercialization!

Several years ago I climbed Mount Sinai, the spot where tradition holds that Moses received the two tablets of the Ten Commandments. It was very early in the morning when I reached the top. I expected to have a few moments of prayer and sacred reflection. Imagine my disappointment when my eyes fell on nothing but vast amounts of litter left by others who had climbed before me.

The experience was a huge disappointment. I had come to relive the moments when Moses received the Law; instead I couldn't focus on anything but the trash.

That's the context for the Gentiles coming into the court of the Gentiles. They wanted to meet with the God of Israel but instead were assaulted by the noise of the profit centers.

Jesus quoted from Isaiah 56, which foretold the day when foreigners would come with joy to Jerusalem and the temple would be called a house of prayer for all nations. When the exiles of Israel returned, God also promised through Isaiah, "I will gather still others to them besides those already gathered (Isa. 56:8). In cleansing the court of the Gentiles, Jesus essentially said: "The day Isaiah looked toward has come—the day in which God is gathering the 'others.'"

In calling the merchandizers "a den of robbers," Jesus took the phrase out of Jeremiah 7:11. That verse closes with the Lord saying through Jeremiah, "But I have been watching! declares the LORD."

Jesus indeed had been watching. On Palm Sunday when He entered the temple, He had "looked around" (11:11); now, He acted.

Jesus' actions are a lesson for His church as well. Too often the church becomes an in-club. It doesn't assess its meetings by how they might affect non-Christians. We must be sensitive whenever we gather that we provide an atmosphere where non-Christians know and feel they are welcome. The Lord never called us to be an exclusive club that makes difficult the inclusion of those who seek Him.

We must also recognize that there are among us those who use the gospel to enrich themselves, who live extravagant lifestyles supported by the offerings of widows who falsely think they are giving to extend the gospel. Instead, their offerings simply provide for another mansion or luxury automobile for the "ministry" they sacrificially support. Just as Jesus cleansed the temple, so also a day of judgment will come for those who abuse the trust God's people place in them.

A Prayer

Search me, O God. Cleanse me from every wicked thought and way. May I serve You with pure heart and noble purpose.

THE GATHERING STORM

The chief priests and the teachers of the law heard this and began looking for a way to kill him, for they feared him, because the whole crowd was amazed at his teaching. When evening came, they went out of the city.

MARK 11:18-19

JESUS' CLEANSING OF THE TEMPLE lit the fuse of the opposition. Mark has already noted ten different occasions of the gathering storm against Jesus (2:6-7; 2:16; 2:24; 3:6; 3:22; 7:1-2; 8:11; 8:31; 10:2; 10:35).

Until now, the opposition of the chief priests, who were Sadducees, had not been in the equation except by Jesus' own reference that they would participate in killing Him. The opposition heretofore had been led by the religious right—the Pharisees and teachers of the Law.

In cleansing the temple, Jesus alienated the religious left—the temple establishment run by the Sadducees. His opposition was now complete on the left and right.

Nothing much has changed even today. On the left in "Christian" circles, we have the Sadducee-like churches that have abandoned core biblical doctrine and morality. I recently visited several churches in New England that were the fountainhead of the Great Awakening and the modern missionary movement. Those churches now encourage participation in gay pride marches in their bulletins and publications. They are far from the faith of their Puritan fathers and mothers.

On the opposite end are the "Christians" whose spirit is as imbibed with legalism and self-righteousness as any Pharisee or teacher of the Law in Jesus' day.

It was now Tuesday evening and Jesus left the temple precincts for the hour-long walk back to Bethany. Mark doesn't tell us specifically that Jesus was staying in Bethany, making reference instead to Jesus coming on Palm Sunday to Bethphage and Bethany at the Mount of Olives (11:1). Matthew notes He spent the night at Bethany, while Luke simply notes He was on the Mount of Olives.

Bethany is on the eastern slope near the top of the Mount of Olives. It's John's gospel that colors in the details by telling us that the evening before the triumphal entry, Jesus came to Bethany, where Martha and Lazarus served Him a dinner while Mary anointed Him (12:1–11).

I have walked the route Jesus took. The temple mount is on a plateau in which you could fit fifteen football fields. Jesus would have descended through the southern steps, walked down to the bottom of the Kidron Valley, and then started His ascent up the Mount of Olives at Gethsemane and over the crest to Bethany. He spent five nights there, from Saturday through Wednesday.

How fitting that Jesus would spend the evenings with people He loved: Mary, Martha, Lazarus, and His disciples. The only glimpse we have of what they discussed during those evenings is Mary's anointing of Jesus, which came the night before the triumphal entry.

Little did the disciples realize the impending crisis awaiting them. I wonder if they could have slept had they truly understood these were their last evenings with Jesus before the cross. Even after the resurrection, we don't read of Jesus spending an entire night with them. Perhaps He did, and it is simply not recorded. The gospel writers, moved upon by the Holy Spirit, saw fit not to tell us. Perhaps one of the delights of heaven will be our opportunity to have all the blanks filled in.

A Prayer

Lord Jesus, may my spirit never be in opposition to You;
and may I never believe other than what You teach.

TEACHER AND RABBI

> *In the morning, as they went along, they saw the fig tree withered from the roots. Peter remembered and said to Jesus, "Rabbi, look! The fig tree you cursed has withered!"*
> MARK 11:20–21

IN MARK'S GOSPEL, Jesus is called teacher twelve times and rabbi four times. Let's take a moment and learn from Jesus, our teacher and rabbi.

What does Jesus teach us? We know the answer when we examine all the occasions He was called teacher.

He cares if we're drowning. His solutions may seem late to us, but we are to trust Him in our storms (4:38). We can continue to bother Him even when our situation looks hopeless (5:35). Jesus hears the cry of a distraught parent and has power to help (9:17). He includes more people in His work than we might allow (9:38), and He does have the answer about how to attain eternal life (10:17). He loves the person who may falsely feel they have done everything right (10:25). He answers our striving for self-promotion with a question that seeks our servanthood (10:35), and He reminds us of our duty to the government (12:14). What will our immortal bodies be like? He knows (12:19). He affirms there is but one God (12:32). He knows the destiny of planet earth (13:1). Jesus desires times alone with us (14:14).

As a teacher, He never gave useless information. We can build our lives and our eternal future on what He said.

Rabbi serves as a more intense term than *teacher*. Probably in shock from beholding His glory in the transfiguration, Peter blurted out "Rabbi" (9:5). Blind Bartimaeus earnestly called to Jesus, "Rabbi, I want to see" (10:51). Here, in the cursing of the fig tree, Peter again was in shock and marveled as he called Jesus "Rabbi" (11:21). While ardently kissing Jesus at the betrayal, Judah also addressed Him as "Rabbi" (14:45).

On all four of the occasions when Jesus was called Rabbi, we see profound emotion or wonder in those who addressed Him. Look, however, at the difference between Peter and Judas in calling Him Rabbi. By this time in Jesus' ministry, Peter knew He was far more than a rabbi. Months earlier, Peter had called Him the Christ (or Messiah; see 8:29). Is Peter wavering in his understanding of Jesus? Judas also called Jesus Rabbi—yet if Judas really believed that about Jesus he would never have betrayed Him.

Even today there are those who, like Peter, should know that Jesus is more than what He is called. There are others who call Him by a high title like Lord or Savior and don't really believe—by their words or actions—that He is either.

Jesus cursed the fig tree, and Mark's gospel notes it was "withered from the roots." The overnight change in the fig tree symbolizes the transfer Jesus makes from the old covenant to the new. He didn't come to make cosmetic changes to the old covenant, but to replace it from its roots.

It's the same with us. Just as Jesus withered the tree at its root, so He attacks our sinful nature at the root within us. He wants to eradicate everything in us that doesn't bear fruit.

A Prayer

Lord Jesus, You are interested in the root issues of life. Destroy the rottenness in my human sinful nature just as You destroyed the unproductive fig tree.

FAITH IN FAITH, OR FAITH IN GOD?

"Have faith in God," Jesus answered. "I tell you the truth, if anyone says to this mountain, 'Go, throw yourself into the sea,' and does not doubt in his heart but believes that what he says will happen, it will be done for him."

MARK 11:22-23

D**ID JESUS GIVE US** a blank check for our prayers? Shall we just fill in the amount of whatever we want and sign our name—and, so long as we do it in expectation, it will be done for us?

These verses seem to indicate a hearty yes to those questions. But wait a minute! Context is always vital to understanding the text.

What is the context of these verses? Jesus cursed the fig tree, and a day later the disciples noticed it had withered from the roots. In response to their amazement, Jesus used the incident as an opportunity to teach about faith. In the rest of the New Testament we see how the disciples understood Jesus' teaching on faith.

It's a two-sided coin. The side we like best is the faith that changes our circumstances. We certainly see that in the healing of the man who was lame from birth (Acts 3:1-10), the many miraculous signs and wonders done by the apostles among the people (Acts 5:12), the raising of Dorcas from the dead (Acts 9:36-42), and Peter's supernatural release from prison (Acts 12:3-17).

The side of faith we may like least is the kind of faith where our circumstances do not change, but we are called upon to trust the Lord anyway. Examples from Acts show this side of faith as well: James' untimely death (Acts 12:1-2); the stoning of Paul at Lystra (Acts 14:19); his beating at Philippi (Acts 16:22-24); and his shipwreck at Malta (Acts 27:27-44).

Faith is not faith in faith, but faith in God. We are not at liberty to lift one or two sentences from Jesus and set them in opposition to what He taught elsewhere about prayer: we are to pray "Thy will be done" (Matthew 6:10), and our requests are conditioned by asking in His name (John 14:14).

Jesus refrained from asking wrongly—choosing to embrace the cross when He could have asked for help from twelve legions of angels (Matthew 26:53).

The illustration Jesus gives of the mountain cast into the sea is a form of speech called hyperbole—an exaggeration for effect. The disciples never took it literally (even as they didn't take literally, "cut off your hand" or "pluck out your eye" in Matthew 5:29–30) since they never commanded a mountain to disappear.

Jesus' teaching on prayer is a direct contrast to the prayers of the religious leaders. Those prayers lacked expectation. They were often done for show. Such prayers testified to the idea that God is not interested in us. They manifested no expectation.

Instead, Jesus wants us to pray with faith—a faith that first asks Him to change our circumstances. Why else would the early church have been praying fervently for the release of Peter from prison (Acts 12:5)? On the other hand, there is the fervent prayer that doesn't change our circumstances. Instead, the Lord says to us as He did to the apostle Paul, "My grace is sufficient for you, for my power is made perfect in weakness" (2 Corinthians 12:9).

We are not called upon to have faith in faith, but faith in God.

A Prayer

Lord Jesus, forgive me for going through the motions of prayer without awareness or expectation that You listen and answer.

FORGIVENESS

> *Therefore I tell you, whatever you ask for in prayer, believe that you have received it, and it will be yours. And when you stand praying, if you hold anything against anyone, forgive him, so that your Father in heaven may forgive you your sins.*
>
> MARK 11:24-25

A VERY EMBITTERED MAN who had suffered greatly at the hands of others said, "If you could lick my heart you would die of poison."

When we don't forgive, our hearts become the repository of anger and bitterness. Jesus knows this. That's why He connects faith to forgiveness.

Remember the context for these verses that invite us to pray and ask daringly. Jesus had cursed the fig tree on one day, and when the disciples saw it withered the next day they were amazed. Jesus used their astonishment as a teaching moment.

First, He invited them, and us, not to see prayer as something rote and mechanical but to believe that our prayers will be answered. However, not every prayer is answered because not every prayer should be prayed. We could misuse prayer to seek the punishment of others: "Lord, You know so-and-so has hurt me deeply—so please visit them with divine chastisement." *No!* That is not the kind of wide door that Jesus opens when He says, *Whatever you ask in faith will happen.*

Forgiveness is the necessary twin of faith. You can't pray to God and harbor unforgiveness toward another. Why? Because it's in the character of God to forgive. How can the Lord forgive you if you are unwilling to forgive others? Why would He put His nature—the Christ-filled life—into you if you are unwilling to follow in His steps?

Make no mistake. Forgiveness isn't easy. If I break something valuable of yours and you forgive me, then you are picking up the tab on what I broke. It means you are releasing me from the debt I owe you. Therefore, forgiveness is only for strong people.

On the cross, Jesus picked up the tab for the sin of the whole world. In fact, His first statement from the cross was, "Forgive them."

Is there anyone you have not forgiven? Anyone from whom you would still like to extract "a pound of flesh" for what they did to you?

The modern translations of Mark omit a verse found in the King James Version because that verse isn't supported by the best Greek manuscripts. But it logically applies the implications of Jesus' teaching on forgiveness: "But if ye do not forgive, neither will your Father which is in heaven forgive your trespasses" (Mark 11:26, KJV).

That's really very good news because Jesus teaches us that we can have assurance of God's forgiveness as we forgive others.

You may be struggling with forgiveness because of the depth of pain another has caused you. May I suggest you engage in a process? First, start with a desire to forgive. Second, pray for the Lord to help you forgive. Third, tell the other individual through a note or in person that you forgive them. If that person is deceased, tell your forgiveness to the Lord. Finally, let go of expectations that the other person will understand or accept what you have done. Leave that individual in the Lord's care.

A Prayer

Lord, as I make inventory of my life, I come to You knowing that there is no one whom I have not forgiven. Forgive me also of the wrongs I have done and the things I should have done that I did not do.

THE QUESTION OF AUTHORITY

They arrived again in Jerusalem, and while Jesus was walking in the temple courts, the chief priests, the teachers of the law and the elders came to him. "By what authority are you doing these things?" they asked. "And who gave you authority to do this?"

MARK 11:27–28

WE DEFINE HOLY WEEK as the span of eight days between Jesus' triumphal Palm Sunday entry into Jerusalem and His resurrection from the dead the following Sunday.

On the Monday after the entry, Jesus cleansed the temple by overturning the tables of the money changers. In the evening, He returned to Bethany, on the eastern slope of the Mount of Olives. We find the events of the next day, Tuesday, in Mark 11:27–13:37. That day divides into two components: (1) in the temple courts, Jesus was asked four test questions, and He also asked His opponents a test question (11:27–12:44); (2) leaving the temple, crossing the Kidron Valley and sitting on the Mount of Olives opposite the temple, Jesus laid out the course of human history (13:1–37).

The first question Jesus faced related to His authority and came from the religious establishment that controlled the temple. Their question is also a current one for us to consider because the authority of Jesus is very much under attack in our culture and throughout the world.

As I write, the newspaper this morning carried a full page ad from The Freedom from Religion Foundation urging readers to leave the Catholic Church because, among other things, Catholic teaching is opposed to abortion, gay marriage, and homosexual practice. While we, as Protestants, don't agree with Catholics on a range of issues, we nevertheless recognize that we share common ground on matters of life and sexual morality. We don't hold to our position on morality because of tradition but because of the authority of Jesus, who speaks on these issues. In reality, the newspaper ad attacked more than the Catholic Church—it attacked the authority of Jesus and all who are bound to obey His authority. The ad exemplifies the language of Psalm 2:3, "Let us break their chains . . . and throw off their fetters."

Jesus' opponents, unlike contemporary critics, recognized He had authority since they asked Him, "By what authority are you doing these things?" His works of power spoke for themselves. His words were persuasive and penetrating. His cleansing of the temple the day before had been done with authority—so much so that the opposition wanted to know who gave Him that authority. They certainly had not given it to Him.

The opposition knew that only two possibilities existed: because His miracles were beyond human ability, Jesus either acted under the authority of God or the Devil.

Their minds were made up. Three years earlier these same teachers of the Law walked nearly 100 miles from Jerusalem to Galilee to pepper Jesus with the accusation that He was in league with the Devil (3:22–30). Jesus responded that the Devil cannot drive out the Devil and a house divided against itself cannot stand.

When the chief priests and teachers of the Law questioned Jesus' authority, it was not because they wanted to know. They had already reached their own conclusion. They asked the question because they wanted to trap Him.

Is Jesus' authority from God? How do *you* answer that question? And how does your answer affect how you live?

A Prayer

Lord Jesus, may I willingly and joyfully submit to Your authority in every area of my life. Your words are true because You come from God.

LITTLE LIES LEAD TO BIGGER ONES

Jesus replied, "I will ask you one question. Answer me, and I will tell you by what authority I am doing these things. John's baptism—was it from heaven, or from men? Tell me!" They discussed it among themselves and said, "If we say, 'From heaven,' he will ask, 'Then why didn't you believe him?' But if we say, 'From men'..." (They feared the people for everyone held that John really was a prophet.) So they answered Jesus, "We don't know." Jesus said, "Neither will I tell you by what authority I am doing these things."

MARK 11:29-33

JESUS COULD HAVE answered the religious leaders' question about the source of His authority directly, but He turned the tables on them, asking their opinion of John the Baptist as a condition for His own answer.

The Lord's response shows us that we need not always answer criticism head on, that sometimes it is best to answer a question with a question of our own.

That strategy is not as easy as it looks. When we are attacked, our temptation is to strike back. Jesus' way of dealing with the question about His authority provides another example of His amazing wisdom. We saw that wisdom on an earlier occasion when the Pharisees brought a woman caught in adultery to Him and He replied, "Let anyone of you who is without sin be the first to throw a stone at her" (John 8:1-7).

Were the chief priests, teachers of the Law, and elders truly undecided about John the Baptist? I suspect not.

Had they believed John was from God they would have repented and embraced his message. Their dilemma was that they couldn't risk alienating the mass of people who had believed in John.

When these leaders told Jesus, "We don't know," they lied. They did "know," and their conclusion was that John was not from God.

You can never trust religious leaders who don't tell the truth. If responses are parsed and words are measured or calibrated by the temperament of the listeners, then leaders have no moral authority to speak. Integrity is missing. This same problem occurs in the political realm when leaders say anything to get elected.

The religious leaders allied against Jesus lied in their dialog with Jesus on this Tuesday, and they will tell bigger lies against Him later in the week when they bring Him before the Sanhedrin and Pilate.

Several years earlier in His ministry, Jesus taught the principle that "to him who has will more be given, but to him who has not, even what he has will be taken away" (Mark 4:24–25). We see that principle lived out in this exchange with Jesus and His opponents.

He had presented so many signs of His authority—His miracles, His teaching—but His enemies discarded the signs. On top of that, they were disingenuous regarding the identity of John the Baptist in not answering Jesus' question honestly.

When they dissembled to Jesus, He refused to answer their question.

Our hearts are like butter or clay. Sun melts the butter and hardens the clay. Hearts that open to Jesus become even more open. The opposite is true. For three years, the religious leaders consistently opposed Jesus, and in that process their hearts became ever more hardened.

What will you choose to be: butter or clay?

A Prayer

Lord Jesus, may my heart never be hardened toward You. Help me this day to draw closer to You, to respond to Your leading, and yield to Your will.

OWNER AND TENANTS

Jesus then began to speak to them in parables: "A man planted a vineyard. He put a wall around it, dug a pit for the winepress and built a watchtower. Then he rented the vineyard to some farmers and went away on a journey. At harvest time he sent a servant to the tenants to collect from them some of the fruit of the vineyard. But they seized him, beat him and sent him away empty-handed."

MARK 12:1–3

JESUS REFUSED TO GIVE a direct answer to the religious leaders when they asked Him, "By what authority are you doing these things" (11:28)? First, Jesus put them on the spot by asking them whether John the Baptist was from men or God; then He set about describing through a story who He really was and what they would do to Him.

The story Jesus told about the owner and the tenants drew on agricultural observations His audience knew. A land owner wanted to make some money from non-producing acreage. Jesus noted the four steps taken:

- Planting a vineyard is no easy task. It involves removing the rocks from the soil, tilling and planting, driving in the stakes for the startup vines to wrap around so that the tendrils will have support and regular watering.
- Building a wall takes effort. It would be a stone wall and was necessary to protect the vines from intruding animals or humans who could either steal or trample the grapes.
- Digging a pit involved hard work. A hollow had to be dug into the ground, and then a stone inserted as a catch basin. The pit couldn't be an earthen one lest the juice from the grapes seep into the ground.

- Erecting a watchtower meant the owner was concerned about security. The wall wasn't sufficient protection. A watchman needed to be on duty twenty-four hours a day, seven days a week.

Having improved his property, the owner rented it to tenants.

Of course, Jesus was telling the story of Israel. God called His people out of Egypt into a land He had promised and prepared for them. He gave them what they needed to cultivate their faith—the Law of Moses and the prophets. He let them live on His land and didn't even require an upfront deposit.

Over the course of time, the tenants came to feel that they owned the land. The servant of the owner came to collect some of the fruit of the vineyard at harvest time. They acted as though the land was theirs and the servant was the intruder. If the tenants felt they could not or would not pay, then they could have simply sent the servant back with the message of default. However, they turned violent against the servant—seizing him and beating him.

The servant did nothing to deserve the bad treatment. He was only acting on behalf of the owner, as had the prophets of Israel acted on God's behalf.

If we bring this story forward to today, then those who share the good news of Jesus are the servants. God is the owner, and the world holds the tenants. God is looking for a response from the tenants who are all on leased land and leased time. We own nothing at all. Everything is from God.

In the story, the owner wanted something from the tenants. In the gospel, the only thing God wants from us is our love, trust, and obedience. Are we giving Him what He wants?

A Prayer

Lord Jesus, I open my heart today to return to You my praise and gratitude for the life You have given me.

AMAZING RESTRAINT

Then he sent another servant to them; they struck this man on the head and treated him shamefully. He sent still another, and that one they killed. He sent many others; some of them they beat, others they killed.

MARK 12:4–5

THE RELIGIOUS LEADERS asked Jesus, "What is the source of your authority?" He answered their question with one of His own: "John's baptism—was it from heaven, or from men" (11:30)? When they said they didn't know, He told them a parable of a vineyard owner who leased his property to tenants.

When the time came to collect the first payment, the owner sent a servant whom the tenants beat up and sent away empty handed (12:1–3).

If you were the owner, at that point what would you have done?

For sure, I would *not* have sent another servant! I would have called the sheriff to come with armed deputies and evict the tenants from the land.

But this is a most unusual owner. After his first servant was treated violently and disgracefully, he sent a second one with no rifle, sword, or truncheon demanding, "Pay up!" The second servant was treated worse than the first. They struck him on the head and treated him so dishonorably that it is not described in detail but is summarized only by the word "shamefully."

With the deplorable treatment given two successive servants, surely it was time to call in the heavy artillery! What was the owner up to? He needed to send in the militia and evict these people. They were not to be fooled with. They were evil and had forfeited possession of the property by refusing to pay rent.

In forbearance, the owner sent yet a third servant. This one was killed. Enough! Time to drop the bombs on these ungrateful and violent tenants!

The owner still didn't give up. He continued to send other servants in succession—an unspecified number—some of whom were roughed up badly and others killed.

The story Jesus told is enough to get your blood boiling. The owner had every legal right to prosecute the lease holders to the full extent of the law. He had the right to go to court and secure a notice of eviction that carried with it the authority of law enforcement agencies to forcibly remove the tenants, indict them, and convict them for assault, battery, and murder.

Amazingly, he didn't do this!

Of course, Jesus was talking about the history of His own people that was stained with backsliding and the persecution of the prophets. Time after time God sent messengers like Isaiah, Jeremiah, Ezekiel, and others. On occasion there were momentary repentances that lasted a generation or two. But sooner or later, backsliding set in.

How did God deal with the rebellion and recalcitrance of His people? He sent His prophets with words and not weapons, with an invitation to repent that would result in mercy.

Jesus was telling about the incredible patience and long-suffering of God who instead of acting like a jilted lover who strikes back petulantly, keeps coming to us with roses and a promise that "all is forgiven" if we will just give Him what is due—our love.

This is how God treats you. He doesn't compel you with force to serve Him. He is remarkably patient with us, seeking always to win us with love.

A Prayer

Lord Jesus, You are incredibly patient with me.
You keep wooing me even after all the times I have
rebuffed You. You show amazing restraint, amazing grace!

AMAZING LOVE

He had one left to send, a son, whom he loved. He sent him last of all saying, "They will respect my son." But the tenants said to one another, "This is the heir. Come, let's kill him and the inheritance will be ours." So they took him and killed him, and threw him out of the vineyard. What then will the owner of the vineyard do? He will come and kill those tenants and give the vineyard to others.

Mark 12:6–9

How would you have advised God? I would have shouted a warning to Him across the gulf of eternity, "Don't do it! Don't send Your Son, whom You love, to tenants who have killed Your servants!"

The best indicator of future behavior is past performance. Over the course of time, the vineyard tenants had demonstrated that they wouldn't give the owner what was due him and, instead, would kill whomever he sent.

But the owner wouldn't give up! Last of all he sent his son—and this was no ordinary son. The father didn't send him to get rid of him. The son wasn't just a chief operating officer of the company, or a business representative of the father. Oh no, he was the son "whom he loved."

Surely the father knew the risk because he was aware of how all his servants had been treated. But the son didn't balk when the father chose to send him.

The tenants had not changed. They had no regard at all for the one who made possible their livelihood. They wanted ownership and control of what was not theirs.

Isn't that the problem with all organized religion—the temptation to assume ownership of what is God's? Even God Himself is prevented from reclaiming His church. Religious leaders and hierarchy too easily can assume that the church is theirs. Not so!

Even in the New Testament era we have a picture of Jesus being locked outside His own church, knocking to gain entrance (Revelation 3:20). What is often true for organized Christianity is true also for the Israel to which Jesus came. The religious leaders loved their religion far more than they loved God. They loved their ceremonies, rituals, and income more than the One who gave them all that.

This story of the vineyard tenants must have filled Jesus with much emotion as He told it. After all, He was the Son who came after the tenants; through the long history of Israel, they had ignored, beaten, or killed the prophets who preceded Him. Jesus knew that in their heart of hearts they recognized Him as the Son. They were not killing a pretender. They hated the Son because they hated the Owner.

The crucifixion of Jesus on the part of the religious establishment wasn't a case of mistaken identity. Deep down they knew what they were doing. That is what Jesus was saying in this story.

But patience has its limits. Hoping that someone will change lasts for a season, until a point of no return.

Jesus knew that such a point had been reached with the religious leaders who opposed Him. They had had enough chances to say yes to God.

This story also has a personal application. We can resist the grace of God for so long that we reach a point of no return. Let that never happen to you!

A Prayer

Lord Jesus, help me always to understand that my life is not my own. May I never want to possess for myself what is Yours by right.

OUR CAPSTONE

Haven't you read this scripture: "The stone the builders rejected has become the capstone; the Lord has done this, and it is marvelous in our eyes"? Then they looked for a way to arrest him because they knew he had spoken the parable against them. But they were afraid of the crowd; so they left him and went away.

MARK 12:10-12

IT WAS TUESDAY IN what we call Passion Week. The events of the day began in the temple courts (11:27ff.) with a series of questions various interest groups asked Jesus. The first question from leadership asked the source of His authority. Jesus responded by (1) asking them if the baptism of John was from God or men and (2) telling them the story of the vineyard tenants who killed the owner's servants and finally the owner's son.

As a follow-up to the vineyard tenant parable, Jesus then gave the post script about the rejected stone.

Near the end of every Passover meal, Psalms 113 through 118 were sung—even until today. Most likely these were the Psalms Jesus and the disciples sang later in the Passion Week at the conclusion of what we know as the Lord's Supper (14:26), since these songs are integral to the liturgy of the occasion.

Given the fact that the verse Jesus quoted against the religious opposition was from this most familiar part of the Psalms—and next to the very last words sung at a Passover meal conclusion—it's no wonder Jesus asked incredulously, "Haven't you read this Scripture"—meaning Psalm 118:22-23.

Jesus knew He was both the killed son spoken of in the vineyard tenant parable and the rejected stone.

The question now is: Do I know that? Do you know that?

Our Lord knows He is not only the rejected stone, He is the capstone. What's that? It's the final piece placed at the top of a stone arch. It holds everything together. Jesus is God's first and last gift of God's revelation to us. He completes the Law and the prophets. He is the One who holds everything in place by the power of His word.

Jesus also knows the verse following verses 22 and 23 of Psalm 118—a verse we know very well: "This is the day the LORD has made; let us rejoice and be glad in it."

When Jesus, the capstone, is in place in our lives, then we, too, have reason for rejoicing. There can be no ultimate joy so long as He remains the stone not used in the construction of our lives. If we leave Him lying unattended, alone, neglected, then our lives have no completion, no destiny, and no fulfillment.

But, put Him in His proper place and our lives, like a stone arch, are works of beauty, function, purpose, and fulfillment.

The religious leaders of Jesus' day made the wrong choice—a choice that capped off the series of wrong choices they had made throughout the three-year ministry of Jesus.

They wanted to kill Him. What is it about those in religious authority that compels them to use force against others? Something is wrong with any faith that forces its way through violence or compulsion.

Jesus always gives us a choice. He appeals to us with love and not coercion. We make the decision whether to treat Him as a rejected stone or as our capstone!

A Prayer

Lord Jesus, I want You as the capstone of my day, every day, all my days. You bring completion to all I am and ever hope to be.

THE ATTACK DOGS

Later they sent some of the Pharisees and Herodians to Jesus to catch him in his words. They came to him and said, "Teacher, we know you are a man of integrity. You aren't swayed by men, because you pay no attention to who they are; but you teach the way of God in accordance with the truth. Is it right to pay taxes to Caesar or not? Should we pay or shouldn't we?"
MARK 12:13–15A

WE LIVE IN A TIME of "gotcha" attacks. Anyone in political or spiritual leadership faces this all the time. People with an agenda are out to get you, to smear the totality of your life by trapping you over one item they think will do you in.

That is what was happening to Jesus. First, the chief priests and others who were part of the temple ruling establishment—dominated by the Sadducees—attempted to trap Jesus on the question of authority. Failing at that, they sent the Pharisees and Herodians with a question over which they themselves were divided.

Their purpose was not to learn or to get the question settled. Their intention was to trap. What a shame! They had so much to learn from Jesus. He could tell them about the Father, about creation, about heaven, about eternity, about God's great love. He could unfold for them so much they did not know, could not know, and would not know.

They were only interested in stumping Him and tricking Him so they could bring an accusation against Him.

When you're determined to destroy someone you bring in unlikely allies. The Pharisees, unlike the Sadducees, believed in the resurrection, angels, and a life of separation from worldly culture. The Herodians, as their name indicates, were allied to the political interests of Herod. Earlier the Herodians and Pharisees had plotted to kill Jesus early on in His ministry (Mark 3:6).

It's amazing even today how many people of different perspectives all come together around one thing: opposing Jesus. Many can "swallow" Him as a teacher but not as Lord, not as King, not as Savior.

In this passage we see the blatant hypocrisy of those who opposed Jesus. They didn't believe at all in the three compliments they give Him. They only wanted to lure Him into a false sense of security by flattery. But what they said about Him is true.

First, Jesus is a person of integrity. That term comes from a word used in mathematics, *integer*, and is used to describe a whole number, an undivided number. Jesus is not one thing today and another thing on a different day. There is no difference between what He is in private and public. His person and persona are the same. Truly we can find no moral fault or fault of any kind in Him.

Second, Jesus is not swayed by public opinion. He doesn't take a poll in order to frame His position. He is not political or trying to score points. He treats the high and low, the rich and poor, the minority and majority exactly alike. He is no respecter of persons, yet He does respect each person.

Third, Jesus teaches the way of God in truth. If you want truth, then listen to Jesus. He said of Himself, "I am the truth!" He has the truth because He is the Truth!

A Prayer

Lord Jesus, I embrace You today as the One whom I trust. Help me to follow in Your steps by being a person of integrity, not a respecter of persons, and living truthfully as Your follower.

WHAT BELONGS TO GOD

But Jesus knew their hypocrisy. "Why are you trying to trap me?" he asked. "Bring me a denarius and let me look at it." They brought the coin, and he asked them, "Whose portrait is this? And whose inscription?" "Caesar's," they replied. Then Jesus said to them, "Give to Caesar what is Caesar's and to God what is God's." And they were amazed at him.
MARK 12:15B-17

THE FIRST "TEST" QUESTION, "What is the source of your authority?" had been put to Jesus by the chief priests and religious authorities (11:27–12:12). Jesus deftly parried their question and infuriated them.

Next, the Pharisees and Herodians asked the question of taxes. These two groups were on the opposite sides of the religious and political spectrum. The Pharisees resented the rule of Herod and the Romans, looking to the day when there would be no heathen occupation.

On the other hand the Herodians, a small, more secular group of Jewish people, were allied with the Herod family, whose interests were in lockstep with Roman occupation. The Herodians benefitted from the presence of Rome so they had no problem with everyone paying taxes.

Jesus didn't need a miracle of prescience to determine their motive in asking. They already had established opinions. They wanted to force Him to take sides.

Jesus asked for a denarius. He already had anticipated their question and was prepared with one of His own. Nothing takes Him by surprise. If you have worked out your theology of life, then you won't be rocked when a crisis comes. Jesus already had formulated the answers long before they asked Him the question. What will we do when tough questions are thrown at us?

Like Jesus, we should be careful to assess whether a compliment ("you are a man of integrity" in v. 14) is genuine or should be taken

WHAT BELONGS TO GOD

with a grain of salt. And like Him, we should live every day with settled convictions so that when we are tested we can respond out of the reservoir of His Word and Spirit living in us.

Jesus asked them to bring Him a common unit of currency, the denarius. Unlike the temple coinage called the shekel, the denarius was the occupier's currency, and Pharisees were loath to use it because of the image of Caesar. But Jesus had a point to make.

He asked them an obvious question. He could have skipped the question altogether, held the coin up for all to see, and then just made His point: "This bears Caesar's inscription and portrait." But Jesus is a Master at forcing the opposition into a corner. He made them acknowledge—especially the Pharisees—the nature of the currency in circulation.

They had come intending to trap Him. Instead He laid the trap for them. Never get into an argument with Jesus. He is much smarter than you!

The image on the coin was that of Caesar. Thus Jesus said, "Give that to Caesar." Then He added, "Give to God what is God's." Ask yourself, "What belongs to God?" The answer is "You!"

The coin bore Caesar's image, but we bear the image of God—created in His likeness.

We give to the government what is outside ourselves, the coin; but to God we give what is on our inside—our hearts.

We have a duty both to the government and to God. What we give to God is far more important than what we give to "Caesar."

A Prayer

Lord Jesus, may I always bear Your image and likeness. Stamp Your image deep on my heart.

SEVEN BROTHERS, ONE WIFE

Then the Sadducees, who say there is no resurrection, came to him with a question. "Teacher," they said, "Moses wrote for us that if a man's brother dies and leaves a wife but no children, the man must marry the widow and have children for his brother. Now there were seven brothers. The first one married and died without leaving any children. The second one married the widow, but he also died, leaving no child. It was the same with the third. In fact, none of the seven left any children. Last of all, the woman died too."

MARK 12:18-22

IT WAS "MEET THE PRESS" time for Jesus. His interrogators sought to trap Him on the Tuesday prior to His crucifixion.

The first questioners, the religious leaders, asked Him about the source of His authority (11:27–12:12). Next, the Pharisees and Herodians asked Him whether taxes should be paid to Caesar (12:13–17). Jesus avoided both their attempts to box Him in.

The Sadducees were the third group to try their hand at tripping up Jesus. This group held only to the authority of the five books of Moses, and asserted that belief in things like the resurrection and angels were later additions by man, not God.

The Law of Moses demanded that a man not have sexual relations with his brother's wife (Leviticus 18:16). However, there was an exception to this: if the brother died without his wife having had a child, then the surviving brother was to marry her, and the first son born to that union would carry on the name of the dead brother. The surviving brother, however, could opt out of that obligation (Deuteronomy 25:5–10).

This provision did protect the livelihood of the widow, for it permitted the property of the deceased to remain in her control through the son she bore who carried her dead husband's name. Even before Moses, this rite was practiced (Genesis 38:6–10).

We see it in full view in the book of Ruth, when Ruth's "kinsman redeemer" opted out of marrying her, ceding his place to Boaz.

The practice may also help explain why there is a difference in the genealogies of Luke and Matthew. In Luke, Joseph's father is Heli; and in Matthew, Jacob. Could either Heli or Jacob be the brother who generated a child for the deceased?

Given the practice spelled out in Deuteronomy and exhibited in Ruth, the Sadducees came with a wildly extended example: seven brothers in succession marrying the same woman. All the brothers die, and at last the woman also dies, childless!

Pity the poor woman! Only the first husband wanted to marry her. The other six took her by obligation. Their sexual relationship to her wasn't from love, but from duty. In the most intimate relationship of life, she was used rather than loved. Her value came only in her ability to bear a child.

Pity the poor woman! She had to follow seven brothers in succession to the cemetery, gaining the reputation in the community of being really "bad luck." Her only relief came when she died!

Obviously, the Sadducees fabricated this story, and I suspect they had stumped the Pharisees with it on more than one occasion.

So many people experience the same as this woman, heartbreak after heartbreak. As far as the Sadducees were concerned, death was the end for her. Not so with Jesus! Not so with you!

A Prayer

Lord Jesus, in every adversity in my life, You are there to help me and not to use me. You always care for me.

LIKE THE ANGELS

"At the resurrection whose wife will she be, since the seven were married to her?" Jesus replied, "Are you not in error because you do not know the Scriptures or the power of God? When the dead rise, they will neither marry nor be given in marriage; they will be like the angels in heaven."

MARK 12:23-25

THE SADDUCEES DID NOT BELIEVE in the resurrection. Thus, their question to Jesus about "whose wife will she be?" was an intellectual tease that they probably had lobbed many times at their opponents, the Pharisees, who did believe in the resurrection of the dead.

If I didn't know Jesus' answer, I ponder how I would have answered. Probably, I would have said, "The one she loved." Or, "None—after seven husbands, she's finally free to not have any of them imposed on her!"

I would have muddled through with an answer, but not Jesus. Since He came from "the other side," He was qualified to answer! He nailed the issue with a question: "Are you not in error?"

The Sadducees committed the same error liberal theologians do today. Both then and now people may know the Scriptures intellectually. There are experts in what we know as source criticism, form criticism, and textual criticism—the tools modern scholars use to dissect the Bible. But that doesn't mean one knows the Scriptures at the level of trust and obedience. We must never sit in judgment on the Bible or be critics of the Scripture. Rather, let it judge our lives.

In not truly knowing the Scripture, the Sadducees didn't know God's power. The two are intertwined. Those who know the Scriptures best know best the power of God. Why? Because He's the same yesterday, today, and forever!

If anyone should know what life in heaven is like, it is Jesus. He came from there. In His earthly ministry He didn't expand a great deal on what life in heaven is like. He did tell us there are many rooms (John 14) and that He wanted us to be with Him in the home He is preparing.

In this dialog with the Sadducees, He gives us a glimpse at the quality of life within that eternal home and He says there will be no marriage in heaven. Is that really good news?

At first blush, it may be disappointing. Isn't the greater part of life on earth taken up with marriage and family? On the other hand, there are many married persons who may be secretly relieved there is no marriage in heaven, since the one they had on earth was so full of trouble, sorrow, and discord.

If you go back to Genesis and the creation of Adam and Eve, one of the main functions of marriage was bearing children. In not having marriage in heaven, we know that there will be no children born there. When the human race is done on earth, it is finished with propagating itself. Earth marks the terminus for the reproduction of human life.

For those with happy and fulfilling marriages, it may be inconceivable that living as an angel could be an improvement on human life. We'll just have to leave that in the Lord's hands. He will never disappoint us; thus we can trust Him that always the next phase will be better—better than all we can ask or imagine!

A Prayer

Lord Jesus, I trust You in this life and in the life to come.
I do believe in Your Word and in Your power.

THE GREAT "I AM!"

Now about the dead rising—have you not read in the book of Moses, in the account of the bush, how God said to him, "I am the God of Abraham, the God of Isaac, and the God of Jacob"? He is not the God of the dead, but of the living. You are badly mistaken!

MARK 12:26-27

TWO OF THE MOST POPULAR current books relate the stories of after-death experiences. A five-year-old boy talks about his after-death experience in heaven, and a neurosurgeon relates his journey in the afterlife. It's important that we compare their testimonies with the Scripture, as there are elements in their stories that bear scrutiny.

However, we do have the testimony of Jesus and we can absolutely rely on Him. Why? Because He came from heaven and knows exactly what life there is like. Jesus affirmed, "No one has ever gone into heaven except *the one who came from heaven*—the Son of man" (John 3:13, emphasis mine).

On the Tuesday before His death and resurrection, the Sadducees asked Jesus a question about the woman who had married in succession seven brothers, each of whom had died. Pity the poor woman! The Sadducees, who didn't believe in the resurrection, asked Jesus whose wife she would be in the afterlife.

Key to Jesus' answer is the fact that He was very aware of their belief system. Their theology did not accept or believe in the resurrection or the existence of angels. They accepted only the validity of the first five books of the Bible, the Pentateuch, and held that belief in the resurrection or angels was a latter addition beyond the revelation of God to Moses.

Jesus flatly told them they were in error because they didn't know their own Scriptures.

He used their own Scriptures to illustrate the error of their thinking. Moses lived hundreds of years after Abraham, Isaac, and

Jacob; yet God said to Moses: "I AM the God of Abraham, Isaac, and Jacob." Jesus was saying that the present-tense "I AM" applies to both God and the patriarchs.

God would be God even if God said, "I *was* the God of Abraham, Isaac, and Jacob." How so? Because God would still be speaking after those men were gone. God's existence goes on while theirs does not. Had Jesus used that phrase, "I was," it would mean that these three were no more. They could be spoken of as in the past tense.

Let's reflect for a moment on how that applies to us. The "I AM" should be internalized by us. If He is the God of the "I WAS," we are left without His presence today. If He is the God of the "I SHALL BE," the result is the same. But He is the God of the "I AM." As His follower, you may even feel at times that He is not with you, but the reality is "I AM." God is present with you this and every moment.

Jesus flatly tells the Sadducees they were badly mistaken. The "I AM" means that when Abraham, Isaac, and Jacob passed from this life God did not switch to "I WAS." He remains eternal, and they remain eternal.

When your body lies in the ground, you don't cease to exist. He continues to not only be the God of Abraham, Isaac, and Jacob, but your God as well.

A Prayer

Lord Jesus, I place my confidence in You that, whether I live or die, You are always with me. You will never forsake me in time or eternity.

THE MOST IMPORTANT

One of the teachers of the law came and heard them debating. Noticing that Jesus had given them a good answer, he asked him, "Of all the commandments, which is the most important?" "The most important one, answered Jesus, "is this: 'Hear, O Israel, the Lord our God, the Lord is one.'"

MARK 12:28-29

I T WAS THE TUESDAY before Jesus' crucifixion on Friday. He was in the temple courts, and the others who questioned Him that day sought to trip Him up. They asked Him about His source of authority (11:28), whether taxes should be paid to Caesar (12:14) and even an absurd question regarding the wife who had seven husbands who died in succession, and whose wife would she be in the resurrection (12:23). None of these questioners really wanted answers, even though they received them.

Now came one who appeared to be an honest man. He was impressed with Jesus, as well he should be. He noted that Jesus had previously given a "good answer."

As an expert himself in the Law, he had listened to Jesus parry the trap questions. He became impressed that Jesus indeed might know the answer to the question all the others had missed. The essential question was not about taxes or whose wife a widow would be. The question was: "What's life all about? What are the basic principles by which we must live? What are the core values that guide us in the journey of life? Is there a road map to get us through?"

The answer to all these questions becomes settled if we know the primary question—the question that separates the main things from the subordinate things. The right question keeps us from chasing hobbyhorses or side trails. We must focus on the important things, not the lesser. So the teacher asked Jesus, "What is the main thing?"

Jesus' answer is not original to Him. It is given in Deuteronomy 6:4. Every Jewish child is taught this response from the earliest age of learning. The name of the recitation is called the *Shema*, which in Hebrew means "to hear" or "listen."

Let's consider the meaning of the first words of the *Shema*: "Hear [Shema], O Israel, the Lord our God, the Lord is one." This phrase is a preface before we get to the two main commandments: Love God and love one another.

Jesus' answer shows His alignment with the faith of Israel. He affirmed that there is only one God. God is not divided. Jesus did not send mixed messages. There aren't many varieties of avenues to God that contradict one another. He is One. As Christians, we understand that Oneness of God as Father, Son, and Holy Spirit—one God, not three.

And the One God is the God of Israel. That is to say, Jesus affirmed the revelation of God given to Israel through the Law and the Prophets—that they have the correct representation of God. Jesus did not say, "God of the Greek philosophers, God of Roman pagans, or God of anything else." While the existence of God may be seen through His creation, and the moral force of God may be seen through conscience, the revelation of His identity and character can be found only within the revelation given to Israel.

Jesus would complete that revelation by bringing to fulfillment everything that the Hebrew Scriptures pointed toward.

A Prayer

O God, I thank You that You have not hidden Yourself, but have revealed who You are through the Law and the Prophets, and at the last, through Jesus Christ, Your Son.

THE GREATEST COMMANDMENT

*"Love the Lord your God with all your heart and with all
your soul and with all your mind and
with all your strength."*

MARK 12:30

IN ANSWER TO the question from the religious expert as to what was the greatest commandment, Jesus responded by quoting Deuteronomy 6:4.

How easy it is to get distracted and become so busy in religious things and spiritual fads of the day. I knew a pastor who was always riding the wave of "what's next" in his personal life and spiritual leadership. He focused on what was the "new" thing God was doing, and often that "new" thing was either not described in the Bible or was peripheral to its message.

One day he asked me, "George, what new thing is God showing you?" I probably answered flippantly because I was young and judgmental. So I said to him, "Well, what the Lord is showing me lately is that I must love Him with all my heart, soul, mind, and strength." For me, as a Christian, the main things are the plain things; and the plain things are the main things.

The words "your" and "all" are each used four times in Jesus' reply.

Why the focus on "your"? Because love toward God is personal. You must make it your mission. The word is singular, not plural; therefore, Jesus' command is for you and not for a group en masse.

The word "all" is far more difficult. I don't know that I can do that. Would "love the Lord your God with some of your heart, or most of your heart" fit us better? Aren't our hearts, souls, minds, and strength often divided and spent on many things?

How do we respond to that word "all?" Are you loving Him completely with your affections (heart), with your intellect (mind), with your inmost being (soul), and with your efforts (strength)?

Surely the Lord has given each of us a daunting and perhaps impossible task when He said "all."

But "all" is a word that is limitless and therefore brings with it the prospect of continued growth and maturity. It provides us a goal to reach for, one that we may never completely fulfill in this life. "All" represents an aspiration, but it also speaks to us of how we fall short from living up to the relationship God seeks with us.

In the sacrifice of the cross, Jesus truly fulfilled God's love toward you—for God has loved you with all His heart, soul, mind, and strength. Love isn't love if it's only commanded. You can't order anyone to love you. The only way another will love you is if you give love. Love then becomes a response to love far more than a response to a commandment.

When Jesus quoted Deuteronomy 6:4 as the answer to the man's question, He satisfied the orthodoxy test since He quoted from the Scripture. However, He knew the only way to possibly fulfill that command was for Him to go to the cross and demonstrate first God's love toward us.

When you see how dearly God loves you, then you respond to His love—not because He has ordered it, but because His love for you has been demonstrated and thereby evokes from you the strongest passions. Then you can begin to move toward fulfilling what He asks: to truly love Him with your "all."

A Prayer

*Lord Jesus, forgive me for loving You partially
and incompletely. Help me to give You
the "all" You seek from me.*

THE SECOND GREATEST COMMANDMENT

*"The second is this: 'Love your neighbor as yourself.'
There is no commandment greater than these."*
MARK 12:31

A MAN ASKED JESUS, "What is the most important commandment?" Jesus answered that there were two: love God and love your neighbor.

In effect, Jesus gives us the cross. The vertical relationship is to love God; the horizontal crossbeam in life is to love others. When you see Jesus' arms outstretched on the cross, ask yourself how much He loves you. Look at his extended arms and hear Him say, "I love you this much."

In Luke 10, Jesus defines who our neighbor is. It is not necessarily the person who lives next door or a family member or even a friend. According to Jesus, the neighbor includes even a person from a different religion and racial group—the Samaritan. The word *neighbor* as used by Jesus is an elastic term stretching from the persons relationally nearest to us and outward to any other human being.

This second greatest commandment assumes we love ourselves: "Love your neighbor *as yourself.*" In other words, you can't love another better than you love yourself.

Many of us have a hard time loving ourselves. We still listen to the "tapes" drummed into us when we were kids, words spoken to us that had hard edges such as: "You're stupid," "You're clumsy," "You're lazy," "You're so ugly no one would every marry you."

Jesus is saying that we will never love others better than we love ourselves, that if we have poor self-love then that poverty of spirit will impact how we relate to others. This does not mean we have permission to become narcissistic or ego-centered.

Do you love yourself in a wholesome, Christ-centered way? What keeps you from loving yourself? Will you make that a matter of prayer and take the steps needed to bring you to spiritual, mental, and emotional health?

If, however, we think that loving others as we love ourselves is tough, then Jesus ratchets up the difficulty even more when He tells us, "As I have loved you, so you must love one another" (John 13:34). Self-love thus becomes the minimal and threshold standard for loving others as compared to the higher standard of loving others as Christ has loved us.

How does He love us?

He loves us with words. Look at how Jesus talked kindly, lovingly, and encouragingly to people. The only ones He had harsh words for were the religious hypocrites. The words Jesus speaks to us are spirit and life. That's also how we must love others. Do our words bring others encouragement, hope, and good cheer?

He loves us with actions. Jesus was always acting to help others. In His own words He said, "It is more blessed to give than to receive" (Acts 20:35). Do our actions help to heal the wounds in others, whether those wound are hidden or apparent? Do we serve the needy? Do others say of us, "You have a helping hand?"

Jesus goes far beyond loving with words and actions. He actually lays down His life for us. Are we willing to lay down our own lives for others? It may not be a physical death; it could involve subordinating or relinquishing our own desires to serve another.

These are hard questions that seek good answers: "Do I love others as I do myself? "Do I love others as Jesus loves me?"

A Prayer

Lord Jesus, I admit I fall short of loving others. Help me to properly love myself and learn how to love others even as You have loved.

NOT FAR

"Well said, teacher," the man replied. "You are right in saying that God is one and there is no other but him. To love him with all your heart, with all your understanding and with all your strength, and to love your neighbor as yourself is more important than all burnt offerings and sacrifices." When Jesus saw that he had answered wisely, he said to him, "You are not far from the kingdom of God." And from then on no one dared ask him any questions.

MARK 12:32-34

ON THE TUESDAY before His death, various people asked Jesus four questions, and He concluded the dialog by asking a question of His own.

His opponents desired to arrest Him when He answered the authority question (11:27-12:12). Then, His critics were amazed at His answer on the question of taxes (12:13-17). No response is recorded after His answer to the question of "whose wife will she be in the resurrection" (12:13-27)? The questioner responded positively when Jesus answered to the fourth question "What is the greatest commandment" (12:28-34)? It's the only question someone asked honestly with no intent to trap.

The man repeated what Jesus answered and then added to it this phrase: "is more important than all burnt offerings and sacrifices." Why did he add those words?

Remember that this dialog with Jesus occurred in the temple precincts not far from the altar of burnt offerings—an especially busy locale of animal sacrifice at Passover season. The opposition prized attention to religious ritual. Jesus had chastised His opponents for their rigid adherence to ritual and their neglect of the fundamental commandments to love God and others. Thus, this man sized up Jesus' response as one that was in agreement with the prophets (Isaiah 1:11; Jeremiah 6:20).

Love is more important than crossing off a performance list of religious observances. They may have their place, but they have no place without love for God and others.

Jesus commended the man for his answer. Jesus said, "You have answered wisely." He knew, from His own eternal association with the Father, that love for God and others are the two things God desires.

However, Jesus knows that love for God by itself doesn't get us into God's kingdom; it brings you close to the kingdom of God. Jesus didn't indicate to the man that his response brought him within that kingdom. Jesus simply said, "You are not far from the kingdom of God." In other words, the man was close but not there yet.

What was lacking? The answer is found in the requirement of the sacrifices. Hebrews 9:22, in reference to the Law, states that "without the shedding of blood there is no forgiveness." The sacrificial system had been established as a tutorial leading to the death of Christ on the cross as a substitute for us.

Thus, love for God and love for others isn't enough to bring us into the kingdom of God, commendable as that love is. We are powerless to bring ourselves into that kingdom despite our best and most honest efforts. We are stained indelibly by our sin. But, "at the right time, when we were still powerless, Christ died for the ungodly" (Romans 5:6).

Loving God and others does bring us, however, near the kingdom! If the man's response had been sufficient to enter that kingdom, then Jesus never would have had to go to the cross.

A Prayer

*Lord Jesus, thank You that You took no half measures
but set Your face to die on the cross.
Thank You for dying for me.*

AT THE RIGHT HAND

While Jesus was teaching in the temple courts, he asked, "How is it that the teachers of the law say that the Christ is the son of David? David himself, speaking by the Holy Spirit, declared: 'The Lord said to my Lord: "Sit at my right hand until I put your enemies under your feet."'"

MARK 12:35-36

VARIOUS PEOPLE HAD ASKED Jesus four test questions (11:27–12:34). Now it was His turn to ask one.

He began with the recognized premise that the Messiah would be a son of David and that his kingdom would last forever (2 Samuel 7:16). He prefaced the quotation from David in Psalm 110:1 by referring first to the origin of David's word. It didn't come from his imagination or thinking, but by the Holy Spirit. Clearly Jesus regarded the words of David as from divine origin.

Psalm 110:1 is quoted or referred to in the New Testament more than any other verse from the Old Testament (Matthew 22:44; Mark 12:36; Luke 20:43; Acts 2:34; 1 Corinthians 15:25; Hebrews 1:13; and 10:13).

The theme of Jesus being at the right hand of God occurs throughout the New Testament.

- The Father will make the decision as to who sits at Jesus' right hand (Mark 10:37–40).
- Jesus told the high priest at his arraignment before the Sanhedrin that in the future they would see the Son of Man sitting at the right hand of the Mighty One and coming on the clouds of glory (Mark 14:62).
- Jesus was taken up into heaven and sat down at the right hand of God (Mark 16:19).
- Peter declared that Jesus was exalted to the right hand of God, from whence He poured out the promised Holy Spirit (Acts 2:33–34).

- Peter and the apostles declared to the Sanhedrin that God exalted Jesus to His own right hand as Prince and Savior that He might give repentance and forgiveness of sins (Acts 5:31).
- In his dying declaration, Stephen saw heaven open and the Son of Man standing at the right hand of God (Acts 7:55-56).
- Jesus now intercedes for us at the right hand of God (Romans 8:34).
- The risen Christ is seated at the right hand in the heavenly realms, far above all rule and authority, power and dominion, and every title that can be given, not only in this present age but also in the one to come (Ephesians 2:20-21).
- We must set our hearts on things above, where Christ is seated at the right hand of God (Colossians 3:1).
- To persecuted believers the writer of Hebrews asserted five times that Jesus is seated at the right hand of God (Hebrews 1:3, 13; 8:1; 10:2; 12:2).
- Peter declared that Jesus has gone into heaven and is at God's right hand—with angels, authorities, and powers in submission to Him (1 Peter 3:22).

The suffering early church always knew where the final source of authority lay—in Jesus, exalted at the right hand of God! Thus, those believers could endure persecution, deprivation of rights, suffering, or martyrdom because they knew Jesus held eternal power over all human thrones.

Finally, by quoting Psalm 110:1, Jesus indicates to us that there will be a delay before "His enemies" are under His feet. He is to sit until that has been accomplished. Our deep desire is that His enemies be placed under His feet now—that sin, death, and sorrow be no more! However, we are to wait patiently as that Day will come!

A Prayer

Lord Jesus, because You are secure on Your throne,
I am secure in You on this earth!

SON AND LORD

"David himself calls him 'Lord.' How then can he be his son?" The large crowd listened to him with delight.

MARK 12:37

DO YOU ENJOY watching contests? Perhaps a football or basketball game, a NASCAR event or a tennis match?

People in Jesus' day in Jerusalem had none of those contests. But they loved to listen to the rabbis debate one another. The intellectual volleys back and forth were a professional verbal ping-pong match of words.

The crowd that gathered around Jesus in the temple courts on the Tuesday before His death on Friday saw and listened to it all. Jesus had come out the winner in five of the debates, and His opponents' scores were zero.

He bested them on the question as to the source of His authority (11:27–12:12). He deftly parried their question on whether to pay taxes to Caesar (12:13–17). He demolished the Sadducees in answering their ridiculous question about the widow who married seven brothers in succession, telling His opponents that they didn't know their own Bible or the power of God (12:18–27). Then Jesus superbly answered the question as to what was the greatest commandment (12:28–34).

Jesus finished off the theological jousting by asking a question arising from Psalm 110—How can David's Son also be his Lord?

When Jesus received no answer from His critics, the crowd loved it. Default—they couldn't return His volley.

It was indeed a delight to witness Jesus trounce the despised religious hypocrites, to see the comeuppance given them by the Galilean. At the same time, the crowd, like the religious experts, could not figure out the answer to Jesus' question: "How can David's Lord be his Son?"

We know the answer now. He is both. As David's Son, our Lord is fully human; as David's Lord, Jesus is fully divine.

If Jesus had come solely as God, then He wouldn't have known what it was like to be human. The writer of the letter to the Hebrews explains the importance of Jesus' humanity by saying, "For we do not have a high priest who is unable to sympathize with our weaknesses, but we have one who has been tempted in every way, just as we are—yet was without sin" (4:15). Jesus did what the first man, Adam, did not do. Adam sinned, and his disobedience brought downfall to all who followed; but Jesus' obedience brings uplift and restoration to all who follow Him (Romans 5:19).

Yes, Jesus was fully human: born to Mary in the poverty of a manger and secluded for thirty years in a small village where He learned and worked in the construction trade before launching His public ministry.

But we also know Him as Immanuel—God with us (Matthew 1:23). Jesus, in fact, declared: "Anyone who has seen me has seen the Father" (John 14:9). The apostle Paul wrote, "For in Christ all the fullness of the Deity lives in bodily form" (Colossians 2:9). Thus, God is not remote. He is not Aristotle's Unmoved Mover. He is not a capricious dictator, an absent or cruel father.

Through His divinity, Jesus shows us who God is and what He is really like—that He is the God of grace and mercy (1 Timothy 1:2). His essential and core character is love (1 John 4:8).

As David's Son, we embrace Him as Human; as David's Lord, we bow down and worship.

A Prayer

*Lord Jesus, thank You for being One with us, One of us—
but also One above us, One over us. We are so grateful
You are both our Friend and our God.*

RELIGIOUS FAKES

As he taught, Jesus said, "Watch out for the teachers of the law. They like to walk around in flowing robes and be greeted in the marketplaces, and have the most important seats in the synagogues and places of honor at banquets. They devour widows' houses and for a show make lengthy prayers. Such men will be punished most severely."

MARK 12:38-40

PHONY RELIGIOUS LEADERS may fool their followers, but they don't fool Jesus. He tells us how to spot them in any generation by giving six characteristics of their behavior and attitude.

First, attire to attract attention: In Jesus' day, it was "flowing robes." In our day it may be a shirt hanging outside of blue jeans to show the congregation how "hip" the pastor is. Nothing wrong with flowing robes, a shirt hanging out, or a three-piece suit and tie. The issue is the intent of the wearer. Is it to impress others with one's persona? Is there puff or substance? Is the purpose to convey a spiritual mystique about the speaker, or to develop a hunger for God in those who listen?

Second, a desire for recognition: The religious leaders of Jesus' day loved to be "greeted in the marketplaces." This admonition from Jesus to watch out for them is not meant to be a restraint on friendliness. Instead, it's an indictment against religious leaders who seek to grab attention, who delight in others fawning over them and according them an importance not merited. It warns the followers of Jesus who serve in leadership roles not to think of themselves more highly than they ought, not to indulge in self-congratulation and self-promotion. Friendliness should be genuine and not an artifice to gain favor from others.

Third, religion as a prop: The teachers of the Law loved "the best seats in the synagogue." In other words, they used religion to enhance their own personal recognition by others. The "church" was a place to show off. It was simply the set on which their own drama unfolded, rather than the stage from which true worship to God took place. Christian leaders today are not immune to this temptation to be seen by others rather than to point others toward the unseen God. Even worship leaders at their instruments and microphones who are called to lead the congregation in worship may instead only be a performing band that's enamored with its own talent and showmanship.

Fourth, focus of attention: Jesus noted that the teachers of the Law not only used religion as a prop, but carried their thirst for attention into the secular arena, loving the "places of honor at banquets." Jesus sees life differently. He desires His leaders to serve rather than be served, to put to death the desire for recognition and applause.

Fifth, unethical and crooked behavior: How many widows have emptied their wallets into some prominent preacher's personal bank account? Crooked religious leaders in any generation prey on the vulnerable and gullible. That's why Jesus says they "devour widows' houses."

Finally, spiritual pretense: Jesus says the fake religious leaders mask their hypocrisy by making a show of lengthy prayers. But they don't fool Jesus.

He cut right to the heart of the matter. His critics were frauds, and He was not afraid to call them that. Mark's account is the abridged version. Read Matthew 23 for Jesus' full denunciation of spiritual fakes, of persons who use religion to advance themselves.

A Prayer

Lord Jesus, may I be pure in heart so that what I present to others about myself is really who I am.

COUNTING THE OFFERING

Jesus sat down opposite the place where the offerings were put and watched the crowd putting their money into the temple treasury. Many rich people threw in large amounts. But a poor widow came and put in two very small copper coins, worth only a fraction of a penny.

MARK 12:41–42

JESUS WAS ONLY THREE DAYS away from being crucified, yet He took time to sit down in the temple precincts and watch a procession of people bring their offerings to support God's work.

He could have been doing so many others things: cramming last-minute lessons into the disciples, conducting mass healings and deliverances, teaching multitudes in the temple plaza or elsewhere, retreating to some lonely place in solitude to contemplate and pray as He approached His passion. But He did none of these.

He wanted to watch people give.

He is still doing that! He watches us as we bring our offerings.

First, He watched the rich people give. The temptation for any religious leader is to scan the donor list and see who the "heavy hitters" are so that they can be given special attention and preferential treatment. Jesus watched the big donors also but not to single them out to curry their favor and continued giving.

Unfortunately, the large donors Jesus watched made a parade of their gifts. They weren't paying in paper money, credit card, or check—for such didn't exist in Jesus' day. They gave in coins, often making a considerable clatter as they ostentatiously dropped their coins into the offering box.

Interestingly, Jesus wasn't concerned with the total amount given that day. His focus was not on the result but on the process. How sincerely was the money given?

The context for Jesus watching the offering is that it had been preceded in the temple courts by an extensive dialog with His opponents. That dialog ended with Jesus excoriating the teachers of the Law for their hypocrisy. Jesus verbally flailed them for showing outward religion without true faith, for demonstrating pride rather than true piety, for focusing on what gains the attention and applause of men rather than God.

The poor widow came at the end of a long line of donors. The ones with more magnificent gifts preceded her, giving in order to gain recognition. She had only a little. She knew it. She recognized she belonged at the end of the line, not the front.

She didn't, however, let the example of others discourage her. She could have said, "What difference does my little bit make?" Or, "Let the well-to-do take care of the Lord's work; the Lord will understand if I keep this for myself. I need it more." She didn't display envy or greed because of what others were giving, nor did she feel that the insignificant amount she had to give should be withheld from the Lord's work.

She came—not to be seen, but because she loved God, sought to honor Him, and was concerned to support the place where worship was given to God.

It's so easy to get our eyes on others and to let their bad example deter us from doing what we should. We must not think of how little we have to offer God, but whether we love Him enough to give what we have. Earth is the only place we can give offerings because everything has been provided for us in heaven.

A Prayer

Lord Jesus, may I love You and Your work so much that I always join those who support Your cause with my offerings.

MORE THAN A TITHE

Calling his disciples to him, Jesus said, "I tell you the truth, this poor widow has put more into the treasury than all the others. They all gave out of their wealth; but she, out of her poverty, put in everything—all she had to live on."

MARK 12:43-44

AT THE END OF A LONG DAY of difficult dialog in the temple courts on the Tuesday before His death, Jesus did one last thing before He left the premises. He watched as people placed their offerings in the temple coffers. What caught His eye was a poor widow who gave her all.

Today, an enormous amount of money is given by well-intentioned and deeply sincere people to ministries that are unproductive for the King and His kingdom. Instead of giving to reputable missionary, educational, and compassion organizations, they pour their limited funds into organizations in which the leaders lavish on themselves the offerings of the faithful.

To every poor widow, to every devout but gullible believer who contributes to such ministries, I want to shout, "*Stop*! This money could be better used!" (And, indeed, contributors do have a responsibility to assess the credibility of the ministries they give to.)

In this gospel account of the poor widow who dropped two small coins into the temple treasury, I would expect Jesus to draw the disciples aside and say to them, "You know how corrupt the temple establishment is. I am charging you to tell others not to do what this devout woman has done. Warn people of the dangers of supporting a religious racket."

But Jesus didn't do that. He didn't focus on the corruption in the system. Instead, He emphasized the piety of the poor widow. While others gave large amounts and used their financial contribution to draw attention to their piety, Jesus noted this woman who gave sincerely. He didn't indict her for giving to a corrupt ministry. He lauded her devotion. He would hold the ministry itself responsible for how it handled the gifts of devout people who made such great sacrifices.

Every once in a while I receive a letter or an essay arguing that tithing is Old Testament and doesn't apply to believers today. My standard answer is that if persons tithed under the Law (which was unable to save), how much more should we give under grace! Rather than seeing 10 percent as belonging to the Lord, and 90 percent to us, the Christian view is that everything is the Lord's and we seek to bless His name and His kingdom with as much as we possibly can, but with no less than the Old Testament minimum of 10 percent.

Without a doubt, if all Christians tithed there would be no lack in the ministries of the local and global church.

As I read Jesus' commendation of this woman, I ask myself, "What does the Lord think when He watches what I put in the offering? Is He able to commend me as He did this poor widow? Am I truly giving from the heart; not for show, but because I love Him?"

Can anyone say of you or me what the apostle Paul said of the Macedonians, that they gave not only as they were able, but beyond their ability—and that in their own impoverishment, generosity welled up with overflowing joy (2 Corinthians 8:1–4)?

A Prayer

Lord Jesus, help me to never be cautious when it comes to giving. Let me joyfully share what I have to honor You, to aid Your cause, and to help Your people.

DASHED EXPECTATIONS

As he was leaving the temple, one of his disciples said to him, "Look, Teacher! What massive stones! What magnificent buildings!" "Do you see all these great buildings?" replied Jesus. "Not one stone here will be left on another;
every one will be thrown down."

MARK 13:1–2

WHO KNOWS THE FUTURE? A lot of people get it wrong with their predictions. Not Jesus!

The disciples had it wrong. Matthew and Luke both report that the conversation among the disciples as they left the temple precincts that day had to do with the impressive temple structures. Mark notes that one of them personally exclaimed to Jesus his wonderment at the great and marvelous buildings.

You can see what they are up to. They still don't understand Jesus' mission. All that day they listened as Jesus verbally fenced with the opposition on the temple grounds, winning each engagement. No doubt now, as they began to leave the temple, they were thinking, *Soon all this will be ours. Jesus will show Himself as the true Ruler of Israel. He'll replace the hypocrites now running the temple, and we'll be with Him as He reigns. All this divine real estate will soon be ours.*

Granted, the buildings were impressive. Construction had taken, by this point, almost fifty years. The Temple Mount itself occupied almost thirty-seven acres—enlarged to that extent by Herod, who built massive retaining walls for the dirt in order to extend the temple area to its present size. If Herod used the dimensions of Solomon's Temple (1 Kings 6:2), then the size was similar to the present Sistine Chapel in Rome.

The comment on the magnificent buildings is also a tip-off that the disciple was not a Jerusalemite. All but Judas were from Galilee.

DASHED EXPECTATIONS

People who lived in Jerusalem, like those who live in most any famous place, became inured to the tourist sites that draw others from around the world. They no longer notice the specialness of what's in their neighborhood. But the Galileans were googly-eyed.

I have been to Jerusalem many times; even though Herod's Temple (the Second Temple) no longer stands, the Western Retaining Wall never fails to impress. Truly the stones are massive, and it's an architectural wonder that they got there without modern machines to lift them in place on top of one another.

Sometimes fellow pilgrims ask me when they see the Wall (also falsely called the Wailing Wall), how Jesus' prophecy could be true. Aren't the stones still standing on top of one another?

I explain that Jesus made no reference to the retaining walls, but to the temple on top—where the Dome of the Rock and Al Aqsa Mosque stand today. All the structures on the temple grounds were destroyed by the Romans in A. D. 70. In fact, you can stand at the bottom of the southwestern corner of the wall and see the massive boulders that were thrown down in that destruction.

Jesus knew the temple buildings were coming down. Within four decades, His prophecy came to pass.

Jesus came to save people, not buildings. One day all buildings will be destroyed. Even if the end of the world does not occur within this century, the world as we know it will end for us. We don't last on this earth as long as ancient buildings. The good news is that Jesus is building an eternal home for us that can never be destroyed!

A Prayer

Lord Jesus, my time is so short on this terrestrial ball.
Thank you for the assurance of an eternal home
You are preparing for me.

THE INSIDER QUESTION

As Jesus was sitting on the Mount of Olives opposite the temple, Peter, James, John and Andrew asked him privately, "Tell us, when will these things happen? And what will be the sign that they are all about to be fulfilled?"

MARK 13:3-4

JESUS' FOLLOWERS are at different levels of learning and curiosity. After Jesus declared that the magnificent temple would be thrown down, only four of the Twelve were curious enough to ask Him the follow-up question. They evidently pondered asking as they followed Jesus down from the temple, through the deep Kidron Valley ravine, and then up the slope of the Mount of Olives.

On three occasions in Mark's gospel, Jesus pulled aside the inner three of Peter, James, and John (5:37; 9:2; 14:33). This time the three are joined by Peter's brother, Andrew, completing the two sets of brothers. They got to ask their question when Jesus sat down on the Mount of Olives and looked west toward the temple mount.

The location provided a superb panorama, both then and now, of history past and future. Did it go through the Lord's mind that the location opposite Him was where Abraham prepared to offer Isaac? Where David purchased the threshing floor from Araunah the Jebusite? Where Solomon built his temple? Where the siege of Jerusalem occurred under Hezekiah, or the destruction of Jerusalem by Babylon? I'm sure He saw it all; not only that, but the future was well. The Temple Mount, which now is occupied by the Muslim faith and serves as their third holiest site, is the piece of land on which final battles will be waged and won.

Jesus knew it all.

When Jesus said that the temple buildings would be torn down and not one stone left on another, the disciples knew that when that happened it would be because of foreign invasion. It meant the end of Israel as they knew it. They could extrapolate further:

"If the temple is destroyed, then Israel is destroyed, and therefore the world is coming to an end."

Thus, in their minds, the destruction of the temple carried the harbinger for the immediate end of the world.

So the four of them asked two questions.

First, "When will these things happen?" That question refers to the prophecy Jesus made while on the Temple Mount that the buildings would be destroyed.

Second, "And what will be the sign that they are all about to be fulfilled?" Matthew's account of the question is: "What will be the sign of your coming and of the end of the age" (21:3)? The difference in wording of the questions may arise from the fact that four disciples were asking the questions. What we have, in comparing the Gospels, is the composite concern of the four disciples.

A summary of the questions reveals three components: the destruction of the temple, the sign of the Lord's coming, and the sign of the end of the age.

In the disciples' minds these three things would occur all together. From their point of view, the destruction of the temple meant the end of the age and the coming of Christ.

However, Jesus' answer would be different from what they expected.

For now, one thing is clear. The disciples had supreme confidence that Jesus knew what the future held. If they didn't believe this, they wouldn't have asked. We also know Jesus holds all our tomorrows.

A Prayer

Lord Jesus, You also know what the future holds for me.
I trust You every day, all the way.

WATCH!

Jesus said to them, "Watch out that no one deceives you. Many will come in my name, claiming, 'I am he,' and will deceive many."
MARK 13:5-6

FOUR OF JESUS' DISCIPLES came to Him and asked about the end times. Like them, we also want to know.

As I've grown older, I've become more understanding of the fact that we all live at the end of the age because this is the only age we have. Every generation is an end-time generation, in a practical sense, because this life is it for us.

I visited in the hospital with an elderly parishioner who was, as it turned out, within hours of her death. In a very weak voice she looked up to me from her bed and asked, "Pastor, do you think we are living at the end of time?" I almost said, "You are." But, of course, I did not. Instead, I prayed with her. Her question made me realize that I do live at the end of my time.

However, the disciples' question deals with the end of this age, the age that precedes the Messianic Kingdom. Their concern is, "When will all this sickness, grief, oppression, occupation, and death be over? When will the lion lay down with the lamb? When will we study war no more?"

How did Jesus begin to answer their question?

Surprisingly, He warned them first against deception, telling them to "watch out!" The term conveys the sense of active looking, as in a night watchman patrolling and on the lookout for intruders, or a soldier at his post of sentry duty.

Clearly, Jesus knew that deceivers would come. Not only that, they would come "in my name." Plus, there would be "many" who deceived "many."

History has clearly borne Jesus out on this. Look through the ages between the first century and now and you see the evidence in the schisms, cults, sects, and deviations that have occurred. Each group claims they have "Christ"—that is, that they have the true interpretation or the added revelation of who He is.

Read Revelation 2 and 3 and you discover that at the end of the apostolic age, the early church was already struggling with movements that were heretical. John's epistles dealt with persons denying that God came in the flesh.

But the phrase "in my name" can also be extended to mean any religion that claims to represent God. Certainly the revival going on today in Islam, Buddhism, and Hinduism testifies to the fact that these world religions vie for exclusive franchise in representing the Almighty.

The bottom line for Jesus' grave admonition for His disciples to watch, is that Jesus did not envision His teaching, atonement on the cross, resurrection from the dead, and ascension into heaven would result in unifying all the peoples of the world around Him. He saw continued plurality in religions, and split-away groups from within the church He established.

The mark of a true prophet is whether what that person says actually comes to pass. Jesus had no sugarcoated optimism that everyone was going to embrace Him. His prophecy has proven true.

He was deeply concerned about deception. We can slide into deceiving ourselves or permitting others to deceive us about who Jesus really is, what He wants us to believe, and how He wants us to behave. So, like His first disciples, we too must "watch!"

A Prayer

Lord Jesus, help me to be aware of deception in my own life whenever I start down a direction You do not approve.

WARS AND EARTHQUAKES

When you hear of wars and rumors of wars, do not be alarmed. Such things must happen, but the end is still to come. Nation will rise against nation, and kingdom against kingdom. There will be earthquakes in various places, and famines. These are the beginning of birth pains.

MARK 13:7-8

IT WAS TUESDAY AFTERNOON, just three days prior to Jesus' crucifixion. He was sitting on the slope of the Mount of Olives, facing west toward the Temple Mount and Jerusalem. The disciples had asked Him about the end of the age.

Jesus saw the course of human history in stark terms. He laid down four markers.

He first predicted there will be growing plurality of religions and deceptive leaders coming in His name (vs. 5-6).

The second and third markers are in verses 7 and 8: not only will there be "trouble" in religion, but also "trouble" in society (wars and rumors of wars) and in nature (earthquakes).

Let's look at each of these in turn.

Jesus said there would be no peace among peoples, just as there would be no unity in forming a one-world religion around Him. He knew that His life and ministry would not unite the human family. The promise of the angels at His birth was only that there would be "peace to those on whom his favor rests" (Luke 2:14)—in other words, the peace was not to all humans.

Jesus saw the conflict as between ethnic groups and kingdoms. The underlying word for "nation" is *ethnos*; thus we should hear Him saying, "ethnic group against ethnic group." But the conflict is also between kingdoms or political alliances. For example, in World War II, Japan and Germany were enemies of the U.S. but now they are allies. Political alliances shift over time, but there will always be power blocs vying for supremacy and territory.

At the beginning of the twentieth century, a liberal Protestant journal was launched titled *The Christian Century*. The idea behind it was that the 1900s would witness a world at peace through humanitarian and social effort. War would be a thing of the past; disease and poverty would greatly diminish.

The title of the journal demonstrates how far off the mark you can be in forecasting the future. The twentieth century was riddled with the most violent wars and bloodshed ever seen on earth, and the twenty-first century may ultimately be even worse with the sword of nuclear war now hanging over our heads.

Jesus also said there would be trouble in nature—earthquakes. Added to earthquakes were famines, pestilences and fearful events, and great signs from heaven (Luke 21:11).

Jesus compared these violent events in nature to pregnancy—they are the beginning of birth pangs. Jesus cautioned the disciples to not think that His return was immediately at hand just because some wars broke out or earthquakes and natural disasters began to happen.

In the words of Jesus, this age is pregnant with the age to come. In order for His eternal kingdom to come, first there will be trauma on earth. Things will not get better, only worse. As the birth pangs in pregnancy progress, the contractions become more frequent and painful.

The one certainty is that He is who He says He is, and that the present age will be followed by the age in which He rules and reigns.

A Prayer

Lord Jesus, my end is also coming. I don't know when. You do. Help me to ever trust You in whatever adversity I face between now and the time I see You face to face.

TROUBLE AND TRIUMPH FOR DISCIPLES

You must be on your guard. You will be handed over to the local councils and flogged in the synagogues. On account of me you will stand before governors and kings as witnesses to them. And the gospel must first be preached to all nations.
MARK 13:9-10

IN JESUS' DISCOURSE on the future, He gave four indicators or signs of what would happen between His first and second coming: division in religion (vv. 5, 6), societal and social conflict (vv. 7-8a), and environmental disasters (v.8b).

But He spent the most time talking about the fourth indicator: trouble for disciples (vv. 9-25). At the beginning of His ministry, He had invited them to "Come and see" (John 1:39). Earlier and here near the end (8:34-38), He invites them and us to "Come and die."

In North America and in other places, we may have a skewed understanding of following Jesus. Some tell us that if only we give our money to ministry or have faith, then nothing ill will happen to us. We are falsely promised health and wealth.

That's not the experience of millions of Christ-followers across the globe. We know, for example, that Christians are the single most persecuted group in the world. Not only are Christians denied civil rights, but they are hunted down, burned, pillaged, imprisoned, tortured, and executed.

Jesus stated in verses 7 and 8 that the persecution for first-century disciples would begin from religious people (synagogues) and political leaders (governors and kings).

In the book of Acts, we read about both types of persecution. However, it would be dishonest to not to note that so-called organized Christianity more than made up for any suffering of the early believers through the relentless and shameful persecution of the

Jews. Jesus never wanted the victimization of the Jews to occur. Better to be persecuted than to persecute.

These same two types of opposition—religious and political—happen today with increasing velocity. We only have to look to countries that have made it a crime to evangelize and to convert. The punishment could be imprisonment or death.

Even in America and the West, we see the opposition from these two sources. See what is happening in our culture to those who believe that Jesus is the exclusive means of salvation and in His teachings on morality. You need only look at the efforts to erase all references to Christ from the public market place as evidence. If that is not enough, then look at how the entertainment industry, the media, and even major sectors of the government seek to isolate Christ-followers by branding them as intolerant, not progressive, and even hateful.

There is a ramped up persecution coming to American Christians, and it is just over the horizon. Jesus knew that persecution would happen to His first followers and to us His latest followers. He regards such activity as normative rather than exceptional.

However, there is one positive indicator: "The gospel must first be preached to all nations." That's the one hopeful sign amidst all the negative indicators about the course of the age. Despite all the adversities and calamities, the good news of Jesus will be proclaimed to all ethnic groups. Jesus clearly saw that His story would reach beyond the narrow perimeters of Galilee and Judea—that it would touch the whole world!

So . . . for now, trouble . . . but at the end, triumph!

A Prayer

Lord Jesus, I am so privileged that Your good news has come to me. May I take this good news to others who have not yet heard.

WARNING AND PROMISE

Whenever you are arrested and brought to trial, do not worry beforehand about what to say. Just say whatever is given you at the time, for it is not you speaking, but the Holy Spirit.

MARK 13:11

JESUS NEVER PROMISED His disciples immunity from trouble or deliverance from trial. But He did give us two anchors that steady us in the turbulence.

First, we are not to be anxious. "Don't worry beforehand," Jesus said. How do you do that? How can you not be anxious when facing dreadful circumstances? Because you are there for a higher purpose—to represent the King of Kings and Lord of Lords. You're not there just for your own honor or safety. You are on assignment for Him. It's not what happens to you that is most paramount; it's whether what happens to you honors Him and advances His kingdom!

We need to take seriously Jesus' words about anxiety. I know for many of us this is not an easy thing to do. But, if we haven't discovered the means to have peace in our everyday lives (Matthew 6:25-34), then we will really have high distress in more horrific moments.

The prophet Jeremiah put it this way, "If you have raced with men on foot and they have worn you out, how can you compete with horses?" Jeremiah knew a greater trial was coming than a footrace (Jeremiah 12:5-6).

Second, we are to be confident that the Holy Spirit will give us the words to say. Look at what happened to Pastor Mehdi Dibaj, martyr for the gospel in Iran in 1994. See how the Holy Spirit helped him with the words to say.

Dibaj had spent over nine years in prison solely because he was a Christian. For two and a half of those years, he was in solitary: a space no larger than four feet by four feet.

Near the end of his time of imprisonment he was asked by his prison commander, "You are an old man. You are sixty years old. You have gray hair. You have been here ten and a half years. Only say no to Christ and we will release you. Once, only once with your words. You may keep your Christian faith in your heart."

Dibaj answered: "There is a long time until I become 120 years old. And if you keep me another sixty years, I'm not going to deny my Lord."

This same commander asked him on another occasion: "If you see Jesus in a dream and Jesus tells you that 'After me another prophet will come. Follow him.' What would you say to Jesus?"

Dibaj answered: "I'll fall on my knees. I'll cry and I'll say, 'Lord Jesus. If You want to send me to hell, please do so. If You want to execute me, please do so. Do whatever You will. But please don't send me away from You to another person.'"

How could Dibaj say things like that? Because Jesus' promise was true for him—the Holy Spirit gave him what to say in the moments he needed it.

It's the same for you. Are you going through trial right now? Would you take some moments to shut yourself in with Jesus and ask the Holy Spirit to give you a word to speak to your situation at this very moment? He will!

A Prayer

Lord Jesus, help me to rely on You today, trusting the Holy Spirit to give me the right words at the right time for every need I face.

FAMILY BETRAYAL

"Brother will betray brother to death, and a father his child. Children will rebel against their parents and have them put to death. All men will hate you because of me, but he who stands firm to the end will be saved."

MARK 13:12-13

ON THE TUESDAY before His crucifixion, Jesus prepared His disciples for what lay ahead.

We have a fairly good picture of what they expected when they first began to follow Him. Their question after the resurrection telegraphs what motivated them to follow Him in the first place because they asked, "Lord, are you at this time going to restore the kingdom to Israel" (Acts 1:6)?

Like them, we want to follow Jesus toward good times. We also want the kingdom—the external manifestation of His authority and control over governments, educational institutions, the entertainment industry, the media, and all adversity. In short, it would be nice to have heaven now: no pain, sorrow, crying, or death.

But Jesus saw a different picture for disciples in the first century, the twenty-first century, and all the centuries in between. He forecast division in religion, enmity among peoples, natural disasters, and persecution for disciples (Mark 13:5-23). The persecutions come from several sources, beginning with limited religious and civic authorities (synagogues and local councils) and progressing to higher strata of government (governors and kings). But the worst form of opposition will come from family.

Of all the warnings Jesus gave about what is to come, His statements on betrayal by family members are the most severe and haunting for they cut to the heart of the closest relationships we have in life.

Jesus doesn't spare His disciples the hard words. Their allegiance to Him will sometimes cost them not only death, but also the wrenching agony of the process that leads to death: betrayal by a sibling, a parent, or a child.

Dietrich Bonhoeffer, a German Christian pastor martyred by the Nazis, summarized it best: "When Jesus calls a man, he bids him 'Come and die.'" We would rather be healthy, wealthy, and undisturbed. "Shouldn't following Jesus better our lifestyle?" we may ask.

Of the original Twelve whom Jesus talked to about the future, ten would die a martyr's death. Jesus calls His disciples to pay a tremendous emotional and relational price to follow Him.

Would that all families could be united in coming to faith, as with Cornelius (Acts 10); but the fact remains that families divide over Jesus. Most times that division doesn't lead to outright betrayal and martyrdom. Sometimes it just results in distance, arguments, withdrawal of emotional or financial support, or disinheritance. Jesus knew that division within the family was a real potential consequence for following Him. We must choose Him even above our own family.

As the end times approach, Jesus sees that His disciples are in for a really tough time—not only from local authorities, big governments, and family. No, the despising of Christians would become universal, from "all men."

The good news, however, is twofold: (1) the gospel will be preached in all ethnicities (v. 10), and (2) the end will come (v. 13). In fact, the disciple who endures persecution all the way to the end will be saved. There is going to be a good end because Christ is Victor!

Your end and mine will come one way or another. Our task is to remain faithful and loyal to Jesus no matter what comes our way.

A Prayer

Lord Jesus, I pray today for believers who suffer and are persecuted for their faith. May they be true to you, and may I be true as well.

THE ABOMINATION OF DESOLATION

> *"When you see 'the abomination that causes desolation' standing where it does not belong—let the reader understand—then let those who are in Judea flee to the mountains. Let no one on the roof of his house go down or enter the house to take anything out. Let no one in the field go back to get his cloak.*
>
> MARK 13:14-16

THE DISCIPLES ASKED Jesus two questions that precipitated His outline of the future: (1) When will these things happen? (2) What will be the sign that they are all about to be fulfilled?

Instead of answering immediately, Jesus provided an overview of the course of human history following His time on earth (vv. 4-13). Then, He came to the crux of their question. Earlier that day He had said of the temple that not one stone would be left standing on another. They wanted to know when that would happen and how that would be linked to the end.

Jesus took them back to Daniel 9:26-27, which prophesied a future anti-God ruler coming to the temple and setting up "an abomination that causes desolation."

Clearly, the early Christians took Jesus' warning seriously. When the Roman army began to encircle Jerusalem less than forty years later, they fled. In A. D. 70, Rome sacked the city and destroyed the temple.

However, that wasn't the end to human history. It was a precursor to a later fulfillment that comes at the end of time. Thus, Jesus's words give direction to the first and last generations of Christians. The first generation witnessed a foreshadowing of what was to come. The last generation will witness the Antichrist desolating the Holy Place (that is, the temple).

After A. D. 70, the temple was never rebuilt. Today Muslims consider the temple mount their third most holy site, with the

Dome of the Rock and two mosques built on the former temple grounds.

At some point in the future, the Antichrist is going to set up an abomination where the temple stood; or if rebuilt, where the temple will stand. Jesus warned those alive at the time—get away from Jerusalem.

So urgent is the need to flee that Jesus gives two urgent instructions: if you are on the house roof, don't go back inside to take anything; and if you are out in the field, don't go back to get your cloak.

A friend of mine was in a commercial airliner that crashed. When it hit the ground, skidded, broke in two, and fire raced down the aisle, he nevertheless took a precious moment to grab his briefcase. The momentary delay almost cost him his life.

What a lesson for us! There is coming a time when we will not be able to take anything with us. Have we become so preoccupied with our possessions, our leisure time, and our work that we aren't ready when it is time to leave? The ongoing lesson for all disciples, in every era, is that we not treasure things above our own lives.

I well realize that in this passage Jesus is talking to end-time saints about a terrible time when the Antichrist will be revealed in Jerusalem. Jesus tells them not even to try and stand their ground, but to get out of town. Flee! There are occasions then and now when we don't have to try and be a hero.

A Prayer

Lord Jesus, help me to balance prudence with courage, to know when to take a risk or avoid it, to discern real danger from false alarm; and to be more concerned about saving my life than my things.

WOMEN AND WINTER

"How dreadful it will be in those days for pregnant women and nursing mothers! Pray that this will not take place in winter, because those will be days of distress unequaled from the beginning, when God created the world, until now— and never to be equaled again".

MARK 13:17-19

THREE DAYS BEFORE His crucifixion, Jesus looked through the telescope of time into the future and saw the prophecy of Daniel coming to pass in the "abomination of desolation"—the sacrilege of the temple at the end of time.

Based on Jesus' warning, the first-century Christians took flight from Jerusalem when they saw the Roman armies coming to destroy the city in AD 70. But the prophecy of Jesus has a double fulfillment. The first fulfillment was relatively minor compared to the terrible end-time fulfillment yet to come.

Having warned His disciples to flee Jerusalem (vv. 15-16), Jesus next provided a lament for the terrible toll this will exact from pregnant and nursing mothers.

But let us leap from the future to the present. There is already stark evil in the world, and the abomination spoken of by Jesus has not even yet occurred. Instead, there's an abomination of a different kind today. There are women pregnant with child who destroy their own babies, and mothers of newborns who abandon them for a variety of reasons: inconvenience, work, pursuit of self-fulfillment.

The abomination of desolation occurs today all over the world for countless millions of children who are abandoned, neglected, abused, trafficked; and babies are killed inside the womb in horrific numbers.

Add to that the mistreatment of pregnant and nursing mothers—abandoned by husbands or lovers, living as victims of rape and violence, refugees fleeing for safety from cruel armies, mothers beaten down by the culture in which they live. How dreadful it is for them, not just end-time mothers, but today's mothers.

Our attention must never be exclusively on end-time events but also on events right now. We must be focused on today and what we can do in this day to combat evil, especially for the defenseless in or outside of the womb.

Jesus additionally asked His disciples to pray that the horrible events in the future not occur in winter. Why? Because winter will make it more difficult for them to flee. They will want to go back home and get some blankets and proper footwear and retrieve their coats to keep warm. Young mothers will find winter flight especially difficult as they are routed out of their places of comfort. I have been in Jerusalem in winter and know how cold, damp, and windy the weather can get.

Jesus clearly looked beyond the destruction of Jerusalem in AD 70 to see the end-time when the worst suffering ever known on earth will take place.

Many take His warning to refer to post-rapture saints. My practical suggestion is that we hold these warnings close to our heart now. All over the world today believers are being hunted, imprisoned, marginalized, persecuted, discriminated against, and even martyred for their faith.

Their suffering right now is a precursor to the conditions that disciples at the end of the age will face. We need always to pray for our contemporary suffering Christians and do everything we can to help them.

A Prayer

Lord Jesus, You do not paint a pretty picture for the future. I pray today for those presently suffering for You, that they will remain faithful in their fierce hour of trial. Help me to remain true to You.

NO QUICK FIX

"If the Lord had not cut short those days, no one would survive. But for the sake of the elect, whom he has chosen, he has shortened them."

MARK 13:20

THE MICROWAVE AND FAST FOOD restaurants changed how we prepare and eat food. They epitomize the whole of life—we want everything in a hurry, along with instant solutions for complex problems.

Jesus sees the opposite for His disciples living at the end of the age. There is no short-term fix except for the fact that the number of terrible days will be shortened.

The question immediately arises, "If the Lord can shorten the days, why doesn't He just eliminate them altogether?" This is not only the mystery of the end time; it's the mystery also of the present time. Why doesn't the Lord move more quickly? Why do we have to suffer in anything?

When we are in the midst of adversity, danger, sorrow, illness, it seems as if time stands still. The emotional or physical pain doesn't end. I think of the brother who gave a woeful testimony in a church service and concluded with, "Pray for me that I will hold out till the end." A listener quietly said, "I think he's about to let go."

Indeed, there are seasons when we feel we are just holding on for dear life. If the Lord has power to heal, then why not just prevent the disease in the first place? If He has power to restore after an accident, then why not just prevent the accident? If He can help us endure the destruction of bad relationships, why doesn't He just clue us in at the beginning so we can avoid the subsequent nightmare? Why not stop hurricanes, tornados, and tsunamis before they hit and cause such devastation?

There are so many mysteries attached to the sovereignty of God, the problem of evil, the short leash that God seems to place at times on goodness. He seems to us on occasion to be as late in intervening as He was at Lazarus' tomb. We all prefer a shorter leash on the bad we endure, and we pray that the Lord will intervene sooner rather than later.

But the good news in every trial is that the Lord is truly Lord—that, in fact, He holds ultimate power. What happens to us is not random. We are not in this world without God, left to the fate of time and circumstance. The Lord remains on His throne above every tragedy, every hardship, and heartache. In His mercy, He often does shorten the days.

If the Lord just eliminated the difficult circumstance to begin with, then we would have no testimony on earth or in heaven. Without adversity there is no heroism, only blandness. The example of Jesus instructs us that where there is no cross there is no crown.

The end time heroes of the faith who go through the horrific season Jesus spoke of will have stories to tell that will keep us in rapt attention for endless days on the other side. We will hear the retelling of evil, but it will only be a story then, not a reality anymore in the land where there is no pain, sorrow, crying, night, curse, or death.

Evil will be banished there, no more to afflict us.

A Prayer

Lord Jesus, I cry out for shortcuts and instant answers. But I thank You for the assurance that great trials are no comparison to the weight of glory You have prepared for all who love You.

WHEN NOT TO BELIEVE

"At that time if anyone says to you, 'Look, here is the Christ!' or, 'Look, there he is!' do not believe it. For false Christs and false prophets will appear and perform signs and miracles to deceive the elect—if that were possible. So be on your guard; I have told you everything ahead of time."
MARK 13:21–23

AS JESUS CONTINUED His discourse on the future while sitting on the slope of the Mount of Olives facing Jerusalem, He knew the natural tendency. His followers would desire His deliverance from Him when they walked through the midst of all the trauma of wars, conflicts, natural disasters, and horrendous calamities.

He promised them that the "days will be shortened," but while the days are in full flower, pretenders will come and promise immediate relief.

We do want instant solutions. We want to trust someone who promises they can get us out of a mess. You see this all the time in daily life. A person comes along and offers a quick return on an investment. It is tempting to follow after them. Or a young person is promised a shortcut to education—only to discover later that the degree they obtained is worthless. At all ages in life, we can be so easily duped.

What Jesus said about the end times happens all the time. Every day there are voices (including religious voices) that cry out, "I am the answer" or "I have the solution."

Even in the Christian world we are quick to put our faith in leaders who promise quick cures, easy shortcuts to health and wealth, and life without pain. They all have their followers—and these are the "anyone" Jesus talked about—who try to win us over.

What does the Lord want from us when we are hard pressed and someone is offering us a quick way out? He wants us *not* to believe them. Jesus, who emphasized so much the need for faith, tells us there are times *not* to believe!

Faith must be deeper than our experience because experiences do not always tell us the truth about God. That is why Jesus warned against putting our trust in someone with miracle working powers. Why is it that a healing ministry always draws more attendees than a prayer meeting? It is because we want God to do something *for* us more than we want Him to do something *in* us!

The end-time and present-time deception involves persons of considerable spiritual power, but not all spiritual power is from God.

However, Jesus gave a word of hope to His followers, the "elect." The miracle workers would deceive them only "if possible." Left unsaid is whether or not it's possible. That's up to us—"by standing firm you will gain life" (Luke 21:19).

To be forewarned is to be forearmed. That's why Jesus concluded His panoramic sweep of human history with the warning, "Be on your guard." There is nothing more about the future we need to know because He has told us "everything."

The world will get progressively worse. Disciples will face increasing hostility. Religious voices and miracle workers will continue to arise and say, "I am the way. Follow me." We know all that will happen and, indeed, is happening now.

So, "Be on guard. Don't believe everything." Remain true to Him when faced with impulses, voices, and advice that would take you away from Him!

A Prayer

Lord Jesus, as I face strong and harsh winds—whether from persecution, temptation, discouragement, or doubt—help me to remain strong!

CATASTROPHE AND CLIMAX

> *"But in those days, following that distress, 'the sun will be darkened, and the moon will not give its light; the stars will fall from the sky, and the heavenly bodies will be shaken.' At that time men will see the Son of Man coming in clouds with great power and glory."*
>
> MARK 13:24–26

DOES HUMAN HISTORY have a culminating point? The prophet Isaiah, eight hundred years before Christ, made very clear that an ultimate day was coming. He declared: "See, the day of the LORD is coming. . . . The stars of the heaven and their constellations will not show their light. The rising sun will be darkened and the moon will not give its light. . . . Therefore I will make the heavens tremble; and the earth will shake from its place at the wrath of the LORD Almighty, in the day of his burning anger" (Isaiah 13:9–13).

As Jesus sat with His disciples on the slope of the Mount of Olives facing Jerusalem, He neared the end of His answer to the question posed by Peter, James, John, and Andrew: "When will these things happen? And what will be the sign that they are all about to be fulfilled?"

In summary, Jesus did not hold a hopeful view that life on earth would become more righteous. It will not. In fact, there will be continued division in religion, conflict and wars among ethnic groups and political alliances, natural catastrophes, and persecution from all quarters against disciples.

But the day will come when it is over. Jesus paraphrased the language of Isaiah to describe that day. The same catastrophe was also prophesied by Joel and quoted by Peter in his sermon on the day of Pentecost (Joel 2:28–32; Acts 2:19–21). The Holy Spirit revealed to both Joel and Peter the two mountain peaks: the pouring out of the Holy Spirit in the last days and the breaking up of the heavens. However, the Spirit did not enable them to see the valley of time between these two peaks.

Jesus also did not delineate the long era between the launch of the last days (the pouring forth of the Spirit) and their fulfillment. Why? I suspect it was because He wanted us to be ready for everything in each generation.

Jesus said that human history will be wrapped up with cataclysmic cosmic events (see also Revelation 6:12–14; 8:12). Others can guess about the fate of the earth, but our Lord knows! It will come to an end with dramatic pyrotechnics in the three lights now in the sky: sun, moon, and stars.

The good news is that the Son of Man is coming in clouds with great power and glory! That's the moment all believers wait for.

Matthew's parallel account of the Olivet Discourse tells us that "all the nations of the earth will mourn" (24:30). Those who follow the path of other religions or adhere to no religion at all will mourn like a defiant person headed for the gallows—unrepentant even to the last. We know that from the book of Revelation (9:20–21).

They mourn because He comes with great power and glory—all their weapons and arsenals are useless against Him. He comes as Conqueror and makes His entrance like no other. In history, generals, leaders, and dictators entered a conquered territory on a horse or armored car surrounded by battalions. He comes from the sky with all His holy angels!

A Prayer

Lord Jesus, on that day may I rejoice at Your coming and not be found among those who mourn.

GATHERED BY ANGELS

*"And he will send his angels and gather the elect from the
four winds, from the ends of the earth to
the ends of the heavens."*

MARK 13:27

DO YOU BELIEVE in the existence of angels? The Bible certainly does. It contains almost 300 references to angels and always takes their existence for granted. In fact, the book of Revelation tells us there are "ten thousand times ten thousand" angels (5:11) and the book of Hebrews speaks of "thousands upon thousands of angels in joyful assembly" (12:22).

Angels were especially active in the ministry of Jesus. Not only was his birth heralded by angels (Luke 2:9–15), but twelve legions of angels were at His disposal if He had desired to avoid the cross (Matthew 26:53). Angels ministered to Him following His temptation (Mark 1:3). An angel strengthened Him in Gethsemane (Luke 22:43), and two angels were present at the empty tomb following His resurrection (Matthew 28:2–7).

Jesus is going to return to earth in great glory and with *all* the angels (Matthew 25:31). What a re-entry! His return is described as being revealed in blazing fire with His powerful angels (2 Thessalonians 1:7).

The angels accompanying Jesus at His return are harvesters for all humankind. They are not only sent to gather the elect to join Jesus, they also take unbelievers to judgment (Matthew 13:41–42).

Could there be a connection with Luke 16:22 where angels carried the beggar Lazarus to Abraham's bosom and Matthew 13:39, "The harvest is the end of the age, and the harvesters are angels"?

The above passages give a prominent role to angels in transporting persons into eternity: the elect to meet Jesus, the wicked into hell, and Lazarus—representing those who die before the final judgment.

You don't have to look very hard to find numerous popular, current books about angels. You will also find many books on near-death or after-death experiences. A frequent phenomenon occurs in these stories—the presence of a light. Could the existence of a light actually be an angel who has arrived to escort the individual to their eternal destiny?

We do know that angels project powerful light. When the angels appeared announcing Jesus' birth, the glory of the Lord shone around the shepherds, and the angels at the empty tomb on the morning of the resurrection had an appearance like lightning and clothes as white as snow (Luke 2:9, 24:4; Matthew 28:3).

We may not know for sure that an angel will meet us at death, although we do know that angels will escort all humans at the end of the age. But their presence with Lazarus may give us a clue. It would also explain why unsaved people, in describing near- or after-death experiences, relate that they also saw a bright white light. What they may be seeing is not an angel of mercy taking them to heaven but an angel assigned to take them to hell.

We do know that angels are so powerful they cannot be resisted. The Bible often calls them "mighty." In fact, it takes just one angel coming down out of heaven at the close of this age to manhandle the devil with a chain and personally throw him into the bottomless pit (Revelation 20:1–3).

There are many mysteries we would like to know. One thing for sure—the end is coming for all of us. When Christ dispatches an angel to gather you, where will that angel take you?

A Prayer

Lord Jesus, on the Day of Your appearing, I'm ready for one of Your mighty angels to take me home to be with You.

THE FIG TREE

"Now learn this lesson from the fig tree: As soon as its twigs get tender and its leaves come out, you know that summer is near. Even so, when you see these things happening, you know that it is near, right at the door."

MARK 13:28-29

JESUS WAS THE MASTER storyteller, but He didn't tell stories to entertain or to fill time. He told them to make a point.

In Mark's gospel the fig tree story is the only story from the Olivet Discourse that Mark reported. He wrote what has been called the Reader's Digest gospel. It has fewer words and chapters than the other three gospels. Thus, it's not surprising that only one story is related from Jesus' discourse on the future.

Matthew's fuller account tells us that Jesus told four additional stories to illustrate the various aspects of the course of the age and His return to earth: The Wise and Faithful Servants (24:45-51); The Wise and Foolish Virgins (25:1-13); The Talents (25:14-30); and The Sheep and The Goats (25:31-46).

Altogether, in the Olivet Discourse, Jesus told us the five ways we are to live in the course of our age: (1) act responsibly (the wise servant); (2) be prepared for Him at any moment (the wise virgins); (3) be prepared to live a normal lifetime (the talents); (4) act compassionately (treating those in need as if they were Jesus Himself); and (5) be prepared to suffer (Mark 13:9-13).

Jesus' use of stories plants firmly in our memories the lesson He taught about the future. In particular, Mark's account of the fig tree as a metaphor for the close of the age tells us that human history is coming to a point of culmination.

The blooming fig tree represents the flowering of the four "things" Jesus referred to that mark the course of the age following His ascension into heaven until He returns: trouble in religion (deception and false Christs); trouble in society (ethnic and political conflicts); trouble in nature (earthquakes, famines, pestilences); and trouble for disciples (persecution from government, religion, family, and society).

In Mark 13:8, Jesus identified these four "things" or "markers" as "the beginning of birth pains." Drawing from His analogy of birth pains, we know that as a mother's labor continues the contractions come more rapidly and the pain becomes more intense. As Mark's account of the Olivet Discourse draws to a close, the analogy switches from birth pains to the fig tree blossoming—in other words, the discourse shifts from the beginning of the end time to the close of the end time.

How do we apply this to our own lives, here and now?

First, Jesus is essentially telling every generation—because every generation lives with these "markers" or "things"—that we are to consider ourselves as living at the end. We are always "right at the door." Eternity could come to us in a moment of time.

As Christians, we are to live with our bags always packed for the journey home!

Second, there is coming a last generation. We could be that generation. Certainly, in our time, the birth pangs of human history are becoming far more intense and more closely compacted together. The flowering fig tree story puts us on alert as we see the signs intensify that Jesus told us would herald the end of the age.

The good news is that Jesus is the Lord and has the times in His hand!

A Prayer

Lord Jesus, if today is the day, I know You will welcome me home. Thank You for the gift of life eternal!

THE LAST GENERATION?

"I tell you the truth, this generation will certainly not pass away until all these things have happened. Heaven and earth will pass away, but my words will never pass away."

MARK 13:30–31

ARE WE IN THE LAST generation before Christ returns? Various prophetic teachers over the years have tried to establish a timeline for Jesus' words about "this generation."

The most popular "teaching" went like this. A generation is forty years. Israel was established as a nation in 1948. Therefore, the rapture of the church must be no later than 1981, with the great tribulation ending in 1988, exactly forty years after Israel's independence. The problem is that 1981 and 1988 have now come and gone.

So, like other failed predictions, those who held this view moved the goalposts. They then took 1967—the reunification of Jerusalem—as the starting point for forty years. This meant the rapture would take place by 2000. (Of course, all computers would also fail in 2000, so this date became extremely popular with so-called prophetic experts!) Under this scenario, the great tribulation would end in 2007. What's the problem? Well, 2000 and 2007 have now come and gone.

The real problem is a failure to stick with Jesus' words. He linked the "this generation will not pass away" with "until all these things have happened." What things?

The "things" He talked about in the discourse on the Mount of Olives. Go back to the question that initiated His teaching. The disciples had asked Him, "When will these things happen?" By that they meant the destruction of the temple in conjunction with the signs fulfilled at the end of the age.

Jesus responded with four major "things" that would mark the course of human history, which we may summarize around the word "trouble." There will be trouble in religion (vv. 5–6), society (vv. 7–8a), nature (v. 8b), and for disciples (vv. 9–23). These, Jesus said, will be the major movements over the course of the age between His first and second coming.

Did this all happen to the first generation of believers? Yes, indeed! That first generation did not pass away until all those things had been fulfilled. Thus, the coming of Christ is always "at the door." We cannot set a timetable. He could have returned in the lifetime of the first generation; He could return even today.

"These things" continue to happen in all the generations between then and now. Just look at the events in today's world for evidence of their fulfillment.

Jesus then followed with two affirmative statements.

First, He clearly asserted that the heavens and earth are not going to last. He knew long before astronomers and futurists came to the conclusion that one day our planet would flame out.

Second, He clearly asserted that His words are eternal. When you look at the context, these words are amazing. He spoke them only seventy-two hours before His death on a cross. Who would have believed at that moment in time that the Galilean's life and words would be the most remembered of anyone ever to live on earth? His enemies simply thought He would disappear from history like all others who had made outsized claims.

But Jesus' words not only live for time, but for all eternity. His Word is so powerful it never goes away. The grass withers, the flower fades, but the Word of Jesus abides forever!

A Prayer

Lord Jesus, may Your words ever live in me!

THE UNKNOWN DAY OR HOUR

"No one knows about that day or hour, not even the angels in heaven, nor the Son, but only the Father. Be on guard! Be alert! You do not know when that time will come."

MARK 13:32–33

ON THE MOUNT OF OLIVES facing Jerusalem, Jesus neared the end of His teaching about the future. Less than seventy-two hours before His crucifixion, He outlined the course of human history.

We now look back and see the remarkable accuracy of Jesus' prophecy about events that would mark all ages leading up to the end time when He would return. Disciples in all centuries would need this information that the road wouldn't be easy nor their burdens light. They would witness the growth of false religions both inside and outside the church, ethnic and social conflict, disasters in nature, and persecution against them from all sides. In spite of all the travail, Jesus knew that His story would be told throughout the whole earth and that those who endured to the end would be saved.

The news about the course of the age may be gloomy, but the future for Jesus' followers is bright. He lets us know that He will return in great power and glory with all the angels and gather His elect from the ends of the earth.

In His statement, Jesus made a clear distinction between the Father and Himself as the Son. He did not explain the nature of that relationship (that is left to other parts of God's Word), but His statements tell us there is a distinction in the midst of their unity within the Triune God. One piece of knowledge is exclusively known by the Father—the day and hour when Christ returns.

Bible scholars may disagree as to whether Jesus, in His present exaltation at the right hand of the Father, now knows. But clearly, at the time Jesus made these remarks, He didn't know.

My question is this: If even the angels do not know, and Jesus did not know, why do we have so many "date-setters" even today? You can research and discover that there have been numerous false prophecies in the past centuries where authors and so-called prophets set a date for the return of Christ. Date-setters will always be wrong; you can count on it. What we know for sure is what Jesus told us—what the course of the age would be like.

The Lord encourages and warns us to be prepared at any moment. I think of the young woman in the news recently who was at church and in an adjacent room a man was showing off his gun. It discharged. The bullet pierced the wall and the woman. She did not know the hour or the day.

It is so with us. None of us know our own time—either by death or by Christ's return. You do not know the time when He will come for you.

Jesus' concern is that we stay awake. The temptation is to be hypnotized by the cadence of everyday routine so that we forget He is always at the door. You must therefore be on guard and alert in all moments—when you are tempted to sin, to despair, to think that you have all the time in the world to correct what you have done or left undone.

Today is indeed the day of salvation. Today, you might go home!

A Prayer

Lord Jesus, may I not fall asleep spiritually, but always be awake—living with no regrets!

WORK AND WATCH!

"It's like a man going away: He leaves his house in charge of his servant, each with his assigned task, and tells the one at the door to keep watch."

MARK 13:34

I AM CONFIDENT the disciples were having a difficult time understanding Jesus at this point. In this discourse on the future, Jesus was already talking about His return and He had not even left yet from His first coming to earth.

They had asked Him about the end of the age and when the destruction of the temple would occur, little realizing that His response would be lengthy and detailed. Jesus withheld His systematic teaching about the future until right at the end of His ministry. The disciples could not have understood it earlier, and even now were foggy in their understanding of His going away (as also reflected in John 14–17).

Jesus similarly does not disclose everything to us at the beginning of our walk with Him.

Clearly, some things we only see in retrospect. The original disciples and the entire church would see it later—Jesus was identifying Himself as the "man going away." The house is His church. We are the servants in charge and the watchpersons at the door.

I do not think we should segregate these two functions of being "in charge" and "at the door to keep watch." They comprise the two sides of our obligation as His followers.

The church is going to be, to a very large extent, what we make it. Although the Holy Spirit graciously infuses and fills us at our request, what happens in the Lord's church is largely left to us. Bad leadership, jealousy, strife, lack of vision, laziness, petty squabbles—all that and more mean the "house" falls into disrepair. On the other hand, where there is good leadership, vision, kindness, the fruit of the Spirit, decisions made from pure hearts—then the "house" prospers. We are more in charge than we think.

But our task is not just to settle down in the house and decorate its walls and keep it clean. It is His house. He is returning to His house. We must be ever expectant that the Owner will return, so we must never think that the house is ours. We are just keeping it ready, in tip-top shape, so that when He returns He will be delighted.

Watching is an important function in a Near Eastern home because robbers were always on the prowl. Watchmen served as the ancient version of an alarm system. The idea of a watchman is to keep watch for the owner's approach so that the home is fully ready, but also to guard it against all intruders so that when the Owner returns He will find everything intact.

Paul warned the Ephesian elders to be on guard because "savage wolves will come in among you and will not spare the flock. Even from your own number men will arise and distort the truth in order to draw away disciples after them. So be on your guard" (Acts 20:29–30)!

Paul added emphasis regarding the true nature of a watchman: not only to look down the street to ascertain the approach of the Owner but also to guard against anything that will harm the house.

A Prayer

Lord Jesus, help me to be on guard today, recognizing that You have put me in charge of myself and the responsibilities life has assigned to me. May I carefully watch over what You have entrusted to me so that no loss, theft, or spoilage occurs.

STAY AWAKE!

"Therefore keep watch because you do not know when the owner of the house will come back—whether in the evening, or at midnight, or when the rooster crows, or at dawn. If he comes suddenly, do not let him find you sleeping. What I say to you, I say to everyone: 'Watch!'"

MARK 13:35-37

WHEN YOU SEE THE WORD "therefore," you always need to ask, "What is it there for?"

In this instance it connects the whole of Jesus' discourse about the future, given on the Mount of Olives three days before His death, with the practical action His disciples must take. Jesus used the illustration of the owner going away and leaving his house in the care of his servants.

Jesus is the owner, and we are the servants. We have two responsibilities: to be "in charge"—that is, to take care of the Master's business—and to "Watch!" Five times in verses 33 to 37 Jesus admonished us to wakefulness: "Be on guard" and "be alert" each occurs once, with commands to keep watch occurring three times.

Notice that the instruction to watch doesn't occur in the daytime. The four periods of time are all at night when we are most likely to fall asleep: evening, midnight, rooster crow, and dawn. They are all the heavy sleep periods when it is most natural not to be awake.

Simply put, Jesus was saying to us that there are going to be times in life when it is dark. You can't see clearly. You are surrounded by trouble: heartbreak, loss, despair, discouragement, depression, illness, adversity, financial need or ruin, or persecution. All you can see is the darkness of your situation. The temptation for you will be to give up, to forget that the Owner is returning and we must, even in our most desperate moments, keep watch.

In watching for Christ's return, we are keeping the lights on in our own lives. We are making His house—our bodies, families, places of work and worship, "for in Him we live and move and have our being" (Acts 17:28)—an attractive place for Jesus. We want our lives to be ones where He makes Himself at home. The "dark" represents those moments when we have no sense of His presence, when we are most likely to sin or act in ways that don't bring honor to Him.

He wants to return to a "home" that is prepared for Him, a home that when He returns doesn't have to keep the door shut and the occupant saying, "Wait outside while I clean up some things and clear away the clutter."

We must be ready to meet Jesus at any moment, whether through His return or our going to meet Him.

So, given the five times in these short verses that Jesus instructed us to be alert—how do we watch? The expanded version of the Olivet Discourse in Matthew's gospel gives four ways:

- Don't mistreat others for whom we have responsibility. We don't have a license to abuse people (24:15–51).
- Be ready for Him to return at a moment's notice. We won't have time to make wrongs right; therefore we must live with a clear conscience (25:1–13).
- Watchfulness doesn't mean idleness. We are to plan and work as though we had a lifetime of service (25:14–30).
- Watchfulness means caring with compassion for fellow believers and for those who suffer (25:31–46).

Jesus' entire teaching on the future bids us to practical service rather than prophetic speculation.

A Prayer

Lord Jesus, my desire is to be ready if
You should come for me today.

THE ROOT OF RELIGIOUS PERSECUTION

Now the Passover and the Feast of Unleavened Bread were only two days away, and the chief priests and the teachers of the law were looking for some sly way to arrest Jesus and kill him. "But not during the Feast," they said, "or the people may riot."

MARK 14:1–2

THE ATTITUDE OF THE CHIEF PRIESTS and the teachers of the Law is repeated throughout history. When religious leaders are unable to win in the battle of ideas, they resort to force. Why is it that even today, in this twenty-first century, there are restrictive laws in multitudes of countries regarding conversion to Christ? In many places, conversion results in execution, imprisonment, discrimination, or marginalization.

It happens because the religious/political powers can't win in the arena of persuasion. Their belief system is so weak that they have to defend it with laws, with force, and with violence.

The Gospels spend more time chronicling the events of Jesus on the Tuesday before His crucifixion than any other comparable day in His life. A major portion of that day was taken up with questions thrown at Him by His opponents. They lost in that engagement.

So, instead of giving in to Jesus; instead of recognizing the force and truth of His teaching and His miraculous authority as given by God, they did a very ungodly thing. They plotted His death.

These were people who knew the sacred Scriptures, maintained the temple establishment with all its sacrifices and rituals, and ran the academies that taught young people the faith. But their hearts were hard. They represented all that is wrong with religion that has gone away from God. The God of love and kindness wasn't in their hearts.

They were losing control because of Jesus. Would that they had surrendered to Him! It's a lesson for us. Do we want our own way

THE ROOT OF RELIGIOUS PERSECUTION

instead of His? His resurrection from the dead validates everything He did and said. It validates the whole of Scripture as well. Will you surrender to Him or try to obliterate Him from your life?

Clearly, Jesus was popular with the masses. It was Passover time, and Jerusalem thronged with pilgrims from all over the world including, in all likelihood, a good number from Galilee. Jesus will always be popular with people unless the authority structures suppress the good news He brings and restrict or persecute those who bring that news.

In culture today, the "killing" of Jesus isn't being done by the masses. Instead, the masses are being turned against Jesus by the media, the entertainment industry, and even the political and religious establishments.

The authority structures are all opposed to Jesus' teaching that He is the one and only way to God, that the resurrection of Jesus is a reality and establishes Jesus' exclusive claim to truth. Thus, we witness the concerted and orchestrated attempt to push Jesus' followers out of the public square and into the four walls of their churches; or out of existence altogether.

However, the authority structures should have no fear. Jesus' true followers don't riot. Like Jesus, they will take a punch rather than give one, turn a cheek rather than strike one, lay down their life rather than take one.

As Jesus walks into the final hours of His life, we should remember that the common people heard Him gladly. The masses were on His side. It was the establishment that turned against Him.

A Prayer

Lord Jesus, I ever want to be included on the side of those who believe in You, who receive with joy Your words and deeds.

THE EXTRAVAGANCE OF LOVE

While he was in Bethany, reclining at the table in the home of a man known as Simon the Leper, a woman came with an alabaster jar of very expensive perfume, made of pure nard. She broke the jar and poured the perfume on his head.

MARK 14:3

THERE ARE TWO TIMES in the Gospels when Jesus had perfume poured on Him.

Luke records the first instance, when a sinful woman poured an alabaster jar of perfume on Jesus' feet while He reclined at table in the home of Simon the Pharisee and wiped His feet with her hair (Luke 7:36–50). This occurred fairly early in Jesus' ministry.

Mark, as well as Matthew and John, records this second occasion. A woman poured an alabaster jar of very expensive perfume on Jesus' head as He reclined at table in the home of Simon the Leper (see Matthew 26:6–13 and John 12:1–8). This anointing occurred just three days before His crucifixion.

John's gospel identified Mary as the woman who poured perfume on the Lord and wiped his feet with her hair (11:2). Most likely this Mary was the sister of Martha and Lazarus. She lived in the same village, Bethany, as Simon the Leper.

The anointing by the unnamed woman in the home of Simon the Pharisee was heavily criticized by the Pharisees present at that dinner, just as the disciples of Jesus also criticized the woman in the home of Simon the Leper. The difference between the two women resulted from their motives. The first one came because she had led a sinful life and had been forgiven much. The second woman appears to have no other motive than her love for Jesus.

As we look at the anointing recorded in Mark's gospel, we recognize that, although Jesus' opponents were looking for a way to kill Him (vv. 1, 2), He was very much relaxed as He reclined at table. What an example for us who face potential life-threatening or stressful circumstances! Just three days from His agonizing death, Jesus showed no sign of anxiety, worry, or dread. Amazing!

The home in which Jesus dined also raises eyebrows. The home of Simon the Leper? Was this someone whom Jesus had healed and was still being referred to as a leper, or did he currently have the disease? Certainly, the chief priests and teachers of the Law would not have stayed in such a house; but Jesus is equally at home with Simon the Pharisee or Simon the Leper.

Jesus made friends with unlikely people, and so must we! If we hang out only with the people we know or whom others approve, how can our light shine in a dark world?

In a home which was not on the "religiously approved" list of the day, another incident occurred that brought offense—this time, not to Jesus' opponents, but to His own friends. Without prior notice a woman dumped a jar of very expensive perfume on His head. Did Jesus see her approach and choose not to stop her, or did she sneak up on Him? Mark does not tell us.

But, we do know the gift was lavish! It is much harder to receive a gift than to give one. Yet Jesus makes no move to stop her. We need to be as gracious as Jesus when others bestow on us something totally unexpected and generous. There is a grace not only in giving, but in receiving. Jesus demonstrated both kinds of grace.

A Prayer

Lord Jesus, You gave lavishly for me.
May I give the very best to You.

QUICK TO CRITICIZE

Some of those present were saying indignantly to one another, "Why this waste of perfume? It could have been sold for more than a year's wages and the money given to the poor." And they rebuked her harshly.

MARK 4:4-5

HERE IS A KEY PROBLEM in the Christian community: We are often quick to criticize.

The disciples were upset. Rather than go to Jesus directly to complain about the extravagant gift from the woman who poured expensive perfume on Him, they grumbled among themselves. They didn't know the woman's motivation or even what Jesus thought of her act; they jumped to conclusions without knowing the facts. They asked, "Why this waste?"

Their indignation is a great lesson for us not to jump to conclusions without knowing what's really going on. Peace and fellowship among believers have often been disturbed or destroyed by those who have made conclusions not based on reality. Instead of following the principle laid down by Jesus in Matthew 18, that we are to go directly to the person against whom we have "aught," we choose the indirect route instead.

Gossip is simply called "sharing information." I see it all the time. Individuals who don't know the inside story jump to conclusions at the first sign that someone, in their opinion, has done something wrong or associated with someone of whom they disapprove. Rather than deal directly with the person involved, they use social media or private gossip to discredit and express their indignation. Had they been in the home of Simon the Leper, they would have been part of the clique criticizing the woman.

The question is whether we would have been part of that group. Or would we have waited to get more information before rushing to judgment?

The friends of Jesus who were in the house were upset and angry. They didn't know the woman's heart or what Jesus thought about what she had done. Had they just gone to Jesus, they would not have been bent out of shape. That is also a good lesson for us. We need to come first to Jesus in prayer and let our spirits become quiet so we can hear His voice, His perspective on how best we can deal with the matter that causes us concern.

They asked, "Why this waste?" Nothing done for Jesus is ever wasted! We are to love Him with all our hearts, minds, souls, and strength!

Jesus' friends didn't reckon on the fact that He had received no financial benefit from His words and works in His three years of ministry. He had given freely, lavishly of Himself. How much more ought we to respond similarly in our love for Him!

Are we willing to give all for Jesus? I have friends who, at this very moment, are laying down everything in their lives for Jesus. How could you and I do less? This woman who poured a lavish gift on Jesus is an example for us. Rather than thinking, *How little can I give?*—our question should always be, "How much can I give—of my time, talent, and treasure?"

I am simply amazed that the friends of Jesus spoke harshly to this woman. After all, they were closest to Him. Had they not learned to be gentle and kind from watching Him and how He dealt with sincere people? Let's not make the same mistake. Jesus would rather we practice extravagant love than indignant criticism.

A Prayer

Lord Jesus, may I never be quick to judge. Only You know the heart of another. Only You know my own heart.

SOMETHING BEAUTIFUL FOR JESUS

"Leave her alone," said Jesus. "Why are you bothering her? She has done a beautiful thing to me. The poor you will always have with you, and you can help them any time you want. But you will not always have me."

MARK 14:6–7

WHAT PROFOUND WORDS from the lips of Jesus: "Leave her alone."

The friends of Jesus had jumped quickly to criticize the woman who poured a vase of expensive perfume on Jesus. They not only grumbled among themselves, but they shamed the woman by rebuking her. Jesus turned and rebuked them instead.

We live in a day of attack journalism. You see it on cable news or in blogs. It is the era of "gotcha." Make one misstep, one wrong statement—and that defines your whole life. Unfortunately, this worldly style has invaded the church. Social media provides unlimited opportunity for believers to attack other believers.

In fact, there are some specific websites whose sole mission is to "watchdog" against anyone who does not toe their line. These sites are never marked by persons who are fruitful in evangelism or growth in discipleship. Their sole mission is to attack, and often their view is as distorted as the friends of Jesus in the house of Simon the Leper. Rather than see the motive and the heart of love for Jesus, the modern "friends of Jesus" leap to criticize, all the while believing they are doing a good thing.

We need to hear in our own hearts what Jesus says. We too need to do "a beautiful thing" for Him. The woman poured expensive perfume on Him—not just a few drops, but the whole bottle! She was lavish and extravagant in her gift. Do we do the same? Are we lavish with Jesus? How would He describe our love for Him? Do we just give Him a drop or two of our time, talent, and treasure, or are our hearts, souls, minds, and strength fully vested? *All* for Jesus!

What beautiful thing can you do today for Jesus?

This woman had a one-time chance to honor Jesus when He was physically present. Her example continues to inspire us to this day. Throughout the history of the church, multiplied millions have followed her example.

Too often Jesus' next statement, "the poor you will always have with you," has been misinterpreted and taken out of context to mean we need do nothing to help the poor. "After all," some think, "there's really not much we can do because poverty is a state of being that will always be with us."

That interpretation misses the rest of the sentence, "You can help them any time you want." We are called upon as believers to care for those in need. In the last day, we will be commended if we have clothed the naked, fed the hungry, and sheltered the poor. Jesus blesses the merciful with mercy.

When we minister to the poor, the sick, the captive, and the prisoner, we join the company of this woman. For in pouring out our love on them, we are pouring it out on Jesus. "Whatever you did for one of the least of these brothers of mine, you did for me" (Matthew 25:40).

Our acts of love for Jesus are seen not only in our extravagant devotion to Him, but also in our concern and compassion for the poor whom we have with us always.

A Prayer

Lord Jesus, may I never live for self alone. May I be ever more extravagant in my generosity of devotion to You and in my love for others.

WHAT YOU COULD

"She did what she could. She poured perfume on my body beforehand to prepare for my burial."
MARK 14:8

WHAT IF JESUS SAID to you and every one of His professed followers, "You did what you could"? What a difference that would make in this world!

It is far easier to lay back and let someone else "do it," to give Jesus our minimum rather than our maximum. Too often, we reserve our time, our talent, and our treasure exclusively for our use. But the story of this woman pouring a jar of expensive perfume out on Jesus serves as an example for our own devotion. Do we really love Him with our deeds, or just with our words? Of course, words are important—but what are we doing for Him? What love are you pouring out on Him today?

Of course, in the flesh He is not with us now. Thus, what we do for Him in devotion is what we do for others and what we do to advance His kingdom. This woman was not stingy in her devotion to Jesus. Don't you want to be just like her?

In all likelihood, the woman did not realize the deeper significance of her gift, that she was anointing Jesus for burial. She just wanted to say thanks to Jesus for what He had done for her. If the woman was Mary, then her anointing of Jesus came in gratitude for the raising of her brother, Lazarus. Jesus saw a deeper meaning in her act, and He does the same with us.

I wonder if we realize that our expressions of love for others—the gifts of our time, energy, and substance—touch others in far deeper ways than we may realize at the time. The recipients of our generosity may find a far more extensive meaning and impact to our gift than we perceive.

I think of simple gifts I gave my nieces when they were very young. I did not have much money as a high school student, but with what little I had I bought the three of them small red plastic stools that they could either roll or sit on. Fifty years have gone by, and they still have those gifts. For my nieces, the stools became an enduring symbol of my love. From a monetary point of view, they cost little—but, at the time, they cost all I had. I just wanted the girls to have something to play with as they had so few toys. But they cherished the stools and gave them a significance far beyond what I intended in the gifts themselves.

We must give our very best to Jesus, and we do that through our care for others and involvement in His kingdom. He then takes our gift to the next level. Perhaps we will wait until eternity to see the full consequences of what we do for Jesus.

There is another way of looking at this. Perhaps you may have given something very valuable and the recipient treated it as ordinary. Remember how disappointed you felt? Think, then, of what it cost Jesus to save us and provide for us eternal life.

He gave everything. He held nothing back! Do you value what He has done for you? Or do you take for granted what He has done for you? Do you respond to His extraordinary love with nonchalance or with heartfelt adoration and worship?

A Prayer

Lord Jesus, I join with the apostle Paul in saying thanks for a gift so great that it is indescribable (2 Corinthians 9:15)!

REMEMBERED

"I tell you the truth, wherever the gospel is preached throughout the world, what she has done will also be told, in memory of her"

MARK 14:9

EACH DECEMBER, Charles Dickens' *A Christmas Carol* remains a perennial favorite. Ebenezer Scrooge had been exactly that—a scrooge. But one night the ghost of his former business partner, Jacob Marley, appears to him seven years after Marley's death. The ghost was in chains, sentenced to roam endlessly.

Marley had been much like Scrooge: tightfisted and lacking any streak of generosity. In death, he had discovered his error. The ghost's most classic lines to Scrooge come when he says, "Mankind was my business. The common welfare was my business; charity, mercy, forbearance, benevolence were all my business. The dealings of my trade were but a drop of water in the comprehensive ocean of my business."

Marley's ghost effectively warns Scrooge to not suffer a similar fate as he. Scrooge awakens to a life of generosity.

You and I are all going to be remembered for something. Will it be for our generosity, or for what we held on to? (We cannot take any of it with us anyway!)

How much better it is that you and I are remembered for what we gave away than what we kept for ourselves! Our goal must never be a selfish one, asking "How can I be blessed?" Rather, our focus is, "How can I be a blessing? How can I help?" Jesus put it this way, "It is more blessed to give than to receive" (Acts 20:35).

Jesus immortalized the woman who poured an expensive jar of perfume on Him, stating that her gift would be remembered "wherever the gospel is preached throughout the world." We still remember her today!

When Jesus said these words, He was within sixty hours of His crucifixion. From a human point of view, it would be over for Him.

He would be just another Roman statistic of execution, a despised dead false prophet as regarded by the religious leadership. His life and impact were coming to a close. Every external indication would tell us that, for Him, it was the end. He would not be remembered except by those who knew Him in their lifetime. Within a generation or two, the memories of Him would cease.

But Jesus saw far beyond the generational and geographical borders of His own ministry. On the verge of His crucifixion, He saw His story going to the world. The gospel—the good news—would go beyond Jerusalem, Judea, and Galilee. It would go beyond the confines of the first and second centuries, all the way into the twenty-first century! This woman's act of devotion would be told because His story was not ending and will never end!

Jesus is not a false prophet who forecasts something that never happens. He knows, even at the verge of His death, that the resurrection will be around the corner. And the story of this woman serves as an everlasting example for all Jesus' followers that when our all is poured out for Him, our story will be told as well.

You can count on the words of Jesus. When He says something will happen, it will happen. Do you trust Him when He says that He has a home prepared for you (John 14:2), or when He declares: "I am the resurrection and the life . . . whoever lives and believes in me will never die" (John 11:25–26)?

You can always trust the words of Jesus. What He says will come true!

A Prayer

Lord Jesus, may I pour out my devotion for
You without any reserve.

KEEP ME TRUE!

*Then Judas Iscariot, one of the Twelve, went to
the chief priests to betray Jesus to them.*
MARK 14:10

WE ARE NEVER GIVEN the circumstances of Judas' calling as we are with Peter, Andrew, John, James, Levi, and Nathanael. When we see the listings of the Twelve in the gospels of Matthew, Mark, and Luke, Judas' name always appears last along with the this descriptor: "who betrayed him."

There are so many mysteries attached to Judas. We know so little about him. He was from Iscariot—the only one of the Twelve not from Galilee. We also know he kept the purse for the community of people who were with Jesus and he stole from it (John 12:5-6).

Why did Judas betray Jesus? Some say it was because He had a good motive: He wanted to precipitate the moment when Jesus would be forced to reveal Himself in power as King over Israel, vanquishing His enemies and restoring the physical throne of David.

But the Gospels strip away the speculation. Note the word "then" that begins verse 10. What does "then" refer to? It refers to the extravagant gift of perfume poured on Jesus by the woman in the home of Simon the Leper at Bethany, and Jesus' refusal to censure her or reject the gift. For Judas, this was the catalyzing moment that impelled him to action. Judas publicly rebuked Jesus for this waste of resource that could have been given to the poor (John 12:4-6).

John's gospel adds that the real reason Judas objected wasn't because of his concern for the poor, but because he wanted the money for himself. As the treasurer, he regularly stole from the purse.

The Bible tells us that we are never given more testing than we can endure. Surely, Jesus knew Judas would be tempted if he held the cash for the group. Even though Judas had that vulnerability in his life, he didn't have to yield to the temptation to enrich himself.

It's the same with you and me. The Lord allows certain situations to arise in our lives where we are most vulnerable. He lets that happen as a test for us. It's not a test He wants us to fail, nor is it one that we have no will power to resist. At any time, we can call upon the Lord's help.

But once we begin stepping over the line, as Judas did, and continue in a pattern of doing wrong in regard to where we are vulnerable, it becomes harder and harder to break the encircling cords of habit. Finally, that corrosion in our spirit can lead us to make catastrophic judgments that not only affect ourselves but others as well.

What we began as sinful acts to bring us pleasure ends up stripping us of everything, including life and reputation—as it did with Judas.

Judas' bad example serves as a warning to us as Jesus' disciples. Each one of the Twelve knew in his heart he had serious vulnerabilities, and that's why when Jesus said, "One of you will betray me," they all "were saddened, and one by one they said to him, 'Surely not I'" (Mark 14:19)?

If we're honest with ourselves, we know that deep in our hearts there are things that, if we let them, could blossom into betrayal of the Lord Himself. Our heart's cry must always be, "Keep me true, Lord Jesus."

A Prayer

Lord Jesus, from my heart I want to be close to You.
Reach Your arms around me and keep me safe, daily
cleansing me from sin and washing me with
Your forgiveness and righteousness.

DIVIDED LOYALTY

They were delighted to hear this and promised to give him money. So he watched for an opportunity to hand him over. On the first day of the Feast of Unleavened Bread, when it was customary to sacrifice the Passover lamb, Jesus' disciples asked him, "Where do you want us to go and make preparations for you to eat the Passover?"

MARK 14:11–12

ONE DISCIPLE, Judas, looked for an opportunity to turn against Jesus. The other disciples looked to Jesus for direction. What group do you belong to?

Let's start with the opportunity Judas looked for. It's clear that the religious leadership hadn't been able to figure out how to seize Jesus. They were delighted when Judas provided the opportunity. It would give them a chance to seize Jesus privately since they feared the crowd if they attempted to arrest Him publicly (11:18). Their antipathy against Jesus began near the beginning of His ministry when He forgave the sins of the paralytic man who was dropped through the roof for Jesus to heal (2:6–7). Now, their long three-year wait to seize Him was nearly over.

Judas' motive is also revealed. The perfume poured on Jesus' head upset him. He complained that the money could have been used for the poor; actually, he wanted it for himself. As the treasurer for the company of Jesus, Judas consistently stole from the funds entrusted to him (John 12:4–6). His motive in betraying Jesus wasn't noble; he simply wanted money for himself.

Judas' intention to betray Jesus wasn't a momentary whim. He actively looked for an opportunity to betray Jesus. In legal terms we define this as lying in wait—not a crime of passion, but of intention.

The rest of the disciples didn't look for opportunities to betray or desert. Instead, they wanted to eat the Passover meal with Jesus. At the time, they were staying in Bethany, a small village near the top of the eastern slope of the Mount of Olives (Mark 11:11; Matthew 21:17; John 12:1). Pilgrims to Jerusalem desired to eat the Passover meal within the city. Thus, the disciples' question to Jesus indicates they were uncertain as to whether He wanted to remain in Bethany or observe Passover elsewhere.

The disciples' question brings a practical observation. When you don't know what the Lord wants you to do, ask Him.

I realize that in all probability He won't answer you audibly as He did the disciples. But if you ask Him for direction, He will give it.

Sometimes that direction will come to you as you pray, other times as you open God's Word and let the Scripture speak to you. On other occasions, His counsel may come to you as you worship, or through the advice and counsel of people whose spiritual judgment you respect. I have found that He can even speak through our circumstances. Actually, there are no circumstances for the child of God—just God-instances.

There may also be times when you seek God's will and He is silent; you don't have a clear sense of direction. In those seasons, He may be saying to you, "I gave you a free will. I trust you. What do you want to do?"

Before making a decision, consider whether you have consulted the Lord. We do a lot of damage to our lives by rushing into situations without first seeking His will. Trust Him. Wait for His answer. He will not lead you astray.

A Prayer

Lord Jesus, may I never look for opportunities to turn away from You. Help me to always turn toward You.

ANONYMOUS FOR JESUS

So he sent two of his disciples, telling them, "Go into the city, and a man carrying a jar of water will meet you. Follow him. Say to the owner of the house he enters, 'The Teacher asks: Where is my guest room, where I may eat the Passover with my disciples?'"

MARK 14:13-14

HAVE YOU EVER TRIED to find a hotel in a busy holiday season in a major city without having made reservations? Then you know the potential dilemma Jesus faced. With Jerusalem packed with pilgrims, where could He find a room large enough for His company to celebrate the Passover?

It's obvious that Jesus had made reservations, because a man carrying a water jar and the owner of a house were waiting.

While Jesus knew where He would celebrate the Passover, His disciples did not. So He waited for them to ask Him. This is a great lesson in leadership. Too often we are eager to tell others what to do rather than waiting for them to come to a point where they want to know and need to know.

It's also evident that Jesus was being secretive about the location for what we now call the Last Supper. The reason for that is obvious from the Gospels. He had a last "download" of teaching to give the disciples centered on the person and work of the Holy Spirit, on heaven, and the institution of what we know now as Communion (John 13-17). Jesus didn't want that last time of privacy with the disciples to be interrupted by Judas' betraying Him. Thus, He sent only Peter and John (Luke 22:8).

A common myth in leadership is that everyone should be treated equally. Jesus didn't lead that way. He narrowed His disciples to seventy. Within the seventy, He had twelve; and within the twelve, He had three who were closest to Him—Peter, James, and John. Thus, on the day when the Passover Lamb was sacrificed, the first day of the Feast of Unleavened Bread, He sent the two most trusted disciples to make the arrangement: Peter and John.

Even they weren't told the location. They were given the mysterious instruction that a man carrying a water jar would meet them within Jerusalem. That man would then take them to the unnamed house owner.

We are never given the names of these two anonymous men, but they proved vital to Jesus' mission.

This raises a question: "Am I willing to be an unknown servant of Jesus?" If all He asks me to do is carry a water jar or prepare a room, am I willing to do that?"

Perhaps you feel that what you are doing is not all that important. Maybe the water jar man or the owner of the house felt that way. But if you removed them from the picture, the two disciples wouldn't be able to locate the room for the Passover. If the room wasn't located, then Jesus wouldn't have a place to have the Last Supper. If He didn't have that place, John 13 through 17 would be missing from our Bibles.

Every one of us is a link in the chain of activity that advances the Lord's mission. You may be a very small link. You may feel that what you do isn't all that consequential. Leave that with the Lord. What you do is important to Him!

A Prayer

Lord Jesus, may I always be willing to do the smallest things, even if I am not recognized. May I be satisfied with a menial task, so long as it is for You.

PREPARING A ROOM FOR JESUS

"He will show you a large upper room, furnished and ready. Make preparations for us there." The disciples left, went into the city and found things just as Jesus had told them. So they prepared the Passover.

MARK 14:15-16

DR. ROBERT MUNGER, my seminary professor, wrote a little booklet called *My Heart, Christ's Home*. It compared our lives to an ordinary house. Have we made room for Jesus in our living or family room, dining room, kitchen, bedroom? All of these are "rooms" within our hearts where Jesus must be present.

When you read that Jesus told the two disciples to go into Jerusalem and find the owner of a home that had an upper room, you need to make application from this simple statement to your own life.

Is your heart a large "upper" room for Jesus? If you have room for Him, is it small? Do you let Him into the living room, but not the bedroom? Or, is there no room for Him at all? Prepare your heart for Him and He will come (Revelation 3:20).

Think for a moment of another place that Jesus is preparing (John 14:2). It truly is an "upper" room, outside time and space. And it's large enough for everyone who believes in Him.

The owner made the upper room available and ready; but the two disciples had their responsibility: to prepare the meal, the Passover. Jesus always has something we must do.

What if the other disciples had arrived that evening at the larger upper room and discovered there was no food? What if the two Jesus had sent to prepare the Passover had grumbled and said, "It's not fair. We're doing all the work getting the meal prepared while the others are enjoying their time off with Jesus. We're not going to work if they aren't."

Have you ever felt that way about your work for Jesus? You are working hard and, when you look around, others aren't working for

Him. You feel you have the wrong end of the deal. Why should you be saddled with so much responsibility when others have time off?

It's not your place to compare yourself with others. Your task is simply to do what Jesus asks you. If you don't do what He requests, His work will suffer.

Can you imagine a large upper room where Jesus arrived and there was no food? Jesus wouldn't have been able to celebrate the Last Supper with His disciples.

If Peter and John, the two disciples who made preparations, hadn't arranged for the unleavened bread, Jesus couldn't have broken bread and said, "This is my body, which is broken for you." If they hadn't prepared the wine, He couldn't have said, "This is the blood of the new covenant which is poured out for many for the remission of sins. Drink this in remembrance of me."

No bread? No wine? The seemingly inconsequential assignment given the two disciples to prepare the Passover meal became monumentally consequential when Jesus took what they had prepared.

Never think that your task in serving Jesus is menial or unimportant. Just do what He asks, and you will be surprised at what He does as a result of you fulfilling your responsibility.

A Prayer

Lord Jesus, may no task be too small for me if it is for You. Help me not to compare my responsibilities to another who seemingly has less to do. May I be faithful in all You ask of me.

SURELY NOT I?

When evening came, Jesus arrived with the Twelve. While they were reclining at the table eating, he said, "I tell you the truth, one of you will betray me—one who is eating with me." They were saddened, and one by one they said to him, "Surely not I?"

MARK 14:17-19

BETRAYAL! What a strong word!

It's a far deeper term than *neglect* or *denial*. Betrayal is an intentional act to turn against someone. It always damages and inflicts pain.

We see this word playing out all the time in our culture. A business owner defrauds his partner. A wife commits adultery against her husband. The victim is always left wounded—emotionally, spiritually, and economically.

Jesus knew who would betray Him that night. He always knows which of His followers will betray Him, because He sees past all of our pretenses of spirituality and performance of religious duties. He sees our heart. He observes our spiritual coldness. He knows that even though we have "shared in this ministry" (Acts 1:17), we may be far from Him in our spirit.

On that fateful night of His betrayal, Jesus nevertheless invited Judas to the table. I would have kept Judas far away. So would you. But, then, we aren't Jesus. His love keeps reaching to Judas even though He knows that Judas has set his path unalterably away from Him.

There were two responses from the disciples to Jesus' announcement that one of them would betray Him: (1) sadness, and (2) concern on the part of each disciple that Jesus might be referring to him.

These two reactions are best explained when we open John's gospel and read of something that happened just prior to Jesus sharing the information that one of them would betray Him. As the Last Supper was being served, Jesus got up from the meal and washed the disciples' feet (John 13:1–17). This act must have stunned the disciples because it nonverbally pointed out their own lack of willingness to serve one another. No one had even offered to wash Jesus' feet!

We can only imagine their chagrin and shame about their own lack of hospitality when Jesus added to their discomfort the announcement that one of them would betray Him. No wonder they asked, "Is it I?" If they neglected to even wash His feet, would that be followed by an overt and intentional act to betray Him?

Every honest believer has had the same reaction, "Is it I?" We ask ourselves introspectively if we could betray Jesus. Only the proud and super-spiritual would never ask that question. It's the tender and honest heart that asks, "Is it I?" When faced with temptation or the severe pressure of discrimination or persecution, could our own hearts possibly fail Him?

The disciples were sad for not having washed Jesus' feet and one another's; that sadness was compounded when each realized what he was capable of—betrayal.

Other than Judas, we know that ultimately the answer for the other Eleven was "No." Not a one would betray Him throughout their entire lifetime. They would all remain faithful to the end.

Our hearts are sad when we realize that we might not be as loyal to Jesus as we profess, that we really haven't served our fellow believers, or even our family, as we ought. Honest self-examination forces us to ask the question of ourselves, "Is it I?"

A Prayer

Lord Jesus, when I ask "Is it I?" I'm so grateful that Your answer to me is "No. You will be faithful to me."

SO CLOSE, BUT SO FAR

"It is one of the Twelve," he replied, "one who dips bread into the bowl with me. The Son of Man will go just as it is written about him. But woe to that man who betrays the Son of Man! It would be better for him if he had not been born."

MARK 14:20-21

JESUS WAS IN THE UPPER ROOM with His disciples for the Passover meal. It would be the last night in His pre-resurrection body. The mood around the table had to be one of foreboding and tenseness.

The Twelve weren't seated at dinner as we would sit today or as Leonardo da Vinci pictured them in the most famous painting of the event. Rather, they were reclining—most likely all around the table rather than in da Vinci's single row all "facing the camera."

When Jesus said that one would betray Him, the betrayer was sitting close enough to Jesus so they could dip bread together into the bowl. We know from John, the beloved disciple who never named himself in his gospel, that he was sitting at Jesus' right hand because he was reclining against Jesus (John 13:23). How do we arrive at that placement?

The normal custom involved eating with the right hand. In order for John's right hand to be free, he would be reclining against his left side, on Jesus' right side. A fair conclusion, therefore, is that Judas was at Jesus' left with Jesus reclining toward Judas. They could dip the bread together.

Judas was physically close but so far away in his relationship to Jesus. He wasn't the last to keep up appearances. Could it be that even today a person can attend church, be deeply involved in its activities, even be a leader, but have a heart far away from Jesus? The seating arrangement at the Last Supper tells us that Jesus still may have held out hope for Judas. The place of nearness is given to draw us spiritually close. We choose the distance between ourselves and Him; His desire is only to be near.

Jesus referred to Himself as the Son of Man. No one in the gospels ever called Him that. It was His self-designation and is a concept much like those used in His parables—revealing truth or concealing it. The title seems to indicate His humanity; but, to the spiritually discerning, it is the term from Daniel describing the Son of Man who was "given authority, glory and sovereign power; all peoples nations and men of every language worshipped him. His dominion is an everlasting dominion that will not pass away, and his kingdom is one that will never be destroyed" (Daniel 7:14).

The One who has been given all dominion—who has all power—that One is betrayed by a mortal human being. It's one thing to betray another person; it's quite another matter to betray the One to whom the entire world will ultimately bow down and worship.

No wonder Jesus said, "It would have been better for him if he had not been born."

That is not only a word about Judas. It's a sentence describing every person who refuses Jesus entry into his or her heart and life. Measured from eternity, rejection of Jesus in this life is the single worst decision an individual can make. Hell is filled with great regret and the incessant repetition of the words, "If only..."

A Prayer

Lord Jesus, I pray You will never say of me that it would be better if I had not been born. Help me be true to You.

GRATITUDE

While they were eating, Jesus took bread, gave thanks and broke it, and gave it to his disciples, saying, "Take it; this is my body." Then he took the cup, gave thanks and offered it to them, and they all drank from it.

MARK 14:22–23

WE LEARN FROM JESUS that Communion is taken within community. It isn't meant to be a solo act in which an individual goes off by himself to take it alone. Jesus broke the bread to His disciples as a group. Communion involves presence and participation. We take it together rather than by ourselves.

Over the centuries there has been much discussion as to the meaning of Communion. For example, when we take the bread or the fruit of the vine, do they literally change substance so that we ingest the actual body and blood of Jesus?

Certainly, that view can't be derived from this text. When Jesus took the bread and said, "This is my body," His body and the bread were two separate substances. In that moment of time His body hadn't morphed into bread.

Jesus simply gave us an object lesson. Even as the bread was broken and distributed; so His body is broken and the nourishment from His life gives life to us. Through Jesus' choice of bread as a symbol of His body, we picture Jesus as the Bread of Life. Without bread—the common staple of food—we cannot live.

Next, Jesus took the cup. He didn't have to take it. Several hours after this moment, Jesus declared that He could call the Father and twelve legions of angels would be put at His disposal (Matthew 26:53). When you consider that it was only one legion of human soldiers—the Tenth Legion and some auxiliary troops—that destroyed Jerusalem and Masada forty years later, you get an idea of the "fire power" Jesus had at His command.

So many of us have circumstances from which we wish we could escape. It's easy to fantasize what life would be like if we just exited from the difficulty we are in. Are you willing also to drink a cup of trial, suffering, adversity, and endurance in order to follow His will for your life?

Jesus gave thanks as He faced the immediate hours before Him that involved betrayal, Gethsemane, disciples forsaking Him, trials and scourging and crucifixion. It's a lesson for us, that we may also give thanks in all things. We don't give thanks for the things themselves, but for what God is working through all things.

Jesus faced the cross with an attitude of gratitude. He was grateful that He had done—to this point—all that the Father had asked of Him. He gave thanks for the past. But He also gave a present thanks as He took the bread with the men into whom He had poured His life. He knew their weaknesses and failures; but He also anticipated what they would do in subsequent years. He had faith in them, and He was grateful for them.

There are so many things that happen to us that could make us bitter. But Jesus sets the example. Facing a horrible death that He did not deserve, He nevertheless gave thanks. How could we do less in our hour of trial? Giving thanks in all things isn't easy. It's hard; at times, seemingly impossible. But gratitude must grow in our hearts or bitterness will take root and destroy us.

A Prayer

Lord Jesus, may I never have a bitter or ungrateful heart.
I want to always live with an attitude of gratitude.

THE THIRD AND FOURTH CUP

> *"This is my blood of the covenant, which is poured out for many,"* he said to them. *"I tell you the truth, I will not drink again of the fruit of the vine until that day when I drink it anew in the kingdom of God."* When they had sung a hymn, they went out to the Mount of Olives.
>
> MARK 14:24–26

I HAVE HAD THE PRIVILEGE of taking the Passover meal with Jewish friends. Four times in the dinner they drink a cup containing the fruit of the vine: at the beginning of the meal, before eating the lamb, and the third time after the lamb. In between the third and fourth cups, the liturgy lengthily concentrates on the coming of Elijah and the Messiah. The meal ends by singing the Hallel (Psalms 113–118), and concludes by drinking the fourth cup.

Jesus finished the Hallel without taking the fourth cup, the cup of consummation. Deliberately Jesus appears to have prematurely ended the Passover meal. Why? Because the third cup that we drink in all our Communion services is yet the cup of redemption—setting forth the Lord's death until He comes. (See 1 Corinthians 11:26.)

When will we finish the meal and drink the fourth and final cup, the cup of consummation? Not until the church is all together in one room again.

The day of Pentecost was the last time the church was under one roof, but we will soon all be in one place again—at the Marriage Supper of the Lamb (Revelation 19:6–9).

Picture that banquet hall—so vast it stretches as far as the eye can see, yet so intimate each feels a part. Look at the tables set with linens, dishes, and utensils of heaven, ornamented with dazzling elegance and beauty. Banners stream from the vaulted ceilings, and visual delight presses on the senses from rainbows of color fashioned from the palette of the Master Artist. The room is breathtaking in its beauty.

Throughout the banquet room, orchestras are playing instruments known and unknown with such symphony in praise. Harps are singing, cymbals flashing, trumpets sounding, wind chimes ringing. There are bells and horns, lutes and violins, dulcimers and clarinets. From time to time, the instruments die down so the vast angel choirs positioned throughout the assembly room can break in with such melody of joy and praise to God as to banish every memory of the pain-filled night of earth.

A powerful angel steps to the rostrum and announces to the assembled crowd: "Please stand at your places. I present to you the King of Kings and Lord of Lords, Jesus of Nazareth!"

Trumpets begin their fanfare, and myriads of angels lift their harmony of hallelujahs.

Then He enters, majestic in His beauty. The Son of Man, the Son of God strides to His place of honor. Silence falls. His voice breaks the stillness: "Welcome to My Marriage Supper. Let us take the cup of consummation."

And together with Him, saints of all ages, nations, languages, cultures, from villages and cities, farms and desert places—all will take the chalice and lift our golden cup in toast to Him and His finished work. In that moment, as we drink the fourth cup of consummation, redemption's saga will be complete and the eternal age opened before us.

The invitation is still open. The guest list is yet incomplete. Will you be there?

A Prayer

Lord Jesus, we drink the cup of redemption in memory of You, anticipating the day when we will drink the cup of consummation in Your kingdom!

THREE PROPHECIES

"You will all fall away," Jesus told them, "for it is written: 'I will strike the shepherd, and the sheep will be scattered.' But after I have risen, I will go ahead of you into Galilee."

MARK 14:27-28

JESUS LEFT THE UPPER ROOM with His disciples, walked down through the Kidron Valley and up on the slope of the Mount of Olives. Here is what He told them.

First, they would all fall away. What dreadful words the Lord spoke to them and even to us. Have you ever felt the sting of those words in the midst of a failure or transgression? Have you experienced a time when, despite your desire to follow Jesus and be obedient, you nevertheless fell away?

Why does this phrase, "fall away," impact us so deeply? Because we know it's true. None of us is perfect. We have all sinned and come short of the glory of God. Not one of us can say, "I have never failed the Lord."

Second, Jesus said that the shepherd would be stricken. He quoted the prophecy given in Zechariah 13:7. We know why the Good Shepherd was stricken—for our sins, for the fact that we too have fallen away. He knows and loves us more deeply and intimately than any other; therefore, He doesn't give up on us. We're like a tire with many flats. He keeps patching and resealing us, not trading us in for a new tire so long as we throw open our arms to Him and cry anew, "Save me, Lord, for I am a sinful human being."

Our imperfections grieve us. But that's the reason Jesus came. He knew there was no other way than to be stricken for us. His name is Jesus because He saves us from our sins.

Third, Jesus told them He would go ahead of them into Galilee after He was risen. In His first appearance to the women early Easter morning, He also instructed them to tell the disciples that He was going ahead of them into Galilee (Matthew 28:7), but said nothing about meeting them first in Jerusalem. Why did He not tell them that He would first appear to them in Jerusalem?

Jesus is always one step or more ahead of us. Rather than telling us the next thing, He may reveal a direction for us that is the "next" beyond the "next." We get frustrated at times because we want to know everything in advance. But Jesus often chooses not to reveal to us the "in-between."

The Lord wanted His disciples to learn obedience when He was no longer physically present. If the disciples obeyed His instructions to go to Galilee, then that would be a building-block lesson for them to obey when He would later tell them to wait for the gift of the Holy Spirit (Acts 1:4).

Just before His ascension into heaven, Jesus told His followers that they must wait in Jerusalem until the Spirit was given, I wonder if some of them after a few days said, "Well, I'm going home. No use waiting any longer. Nothing is going to happen." But no, the 120 kept waiting and praying because they knew that Jesus would keep His word. On the tenth day in the upper room, their obedience was rewarded with the gift of the Spirit, just as their obedience was rewarded for going to Galilee.

We must always take Jesus at His word; and often there is a waiting period until that word comes to pass.

A Prayer

Lord Jesus, may I always be obedient to what You tell me.

GOOD INTENTIONS

Peter declared, "Even if all fall away, I will not."
MARK 14:29

HAVE YOU EVER HIT a bad spot in your Christian walk? You didn't see the black ice of adverse circumstances or temptation's power? Your feet slipped out from under you. You fell hard.

That's where we find Peter at this moment in his life. It had not been a good week for him, that last week before Jesus' crucifixion. In the short space of forty-eight hours, he failed eight times. Remarkable!

On the Tuesday night of Jesus' last week, the disciples protested indignantly about the woman who poured an alabaster jar of expensive perfume on Jesus (Matthew 16:8). Since the word "disciples" is used without qualification, we can infer that the protest involved all of them—including Peter.

His second misstep was on Thursday evening as Jesus prepared to eat the Last Supper with the disciples. Jesus began by washing their feet. Peter vehemently protested that the Lord would never wash his feet. Peter's protest came as he realized that neither he nor any of the disciples had done the courtesy of offering to wash the Lord's feet.

As the lead disciple who had heard Jesus teach on more than one occasion that the greatest must be servant of all, Peter had failed to actualize the Lord's teaching. (How many times do we know what the Lord wants us to do, but we also fail to do it?) The Lord provided a gentle retort that if He didn't wash Peter's feet, then Peter had no part with Him. Peter then went overboard with an opposite reaction and told the Lord to wash his hands and head as well (John 13:8–9).

Peter's third failure came the same evening. Peter demonstrated that he was unsure of his own commitment to Jesus; he asked, along with the other disciples, if he was the one who would betray Jesus (14:19). Peter instinctively knew that a dormant potential lay within him to turn against Jesus.

But Peter plucked up his resolve a few hours later. After leaving the upper room and walking through the Kidron Valley to the Mount of Olives, Peter switched 180 degrees. At the Last Supper he had asked, "Is it I?" Now he was adamant he would never fall away—his fourth bungle.

Peter was ricocheting emotionally like a pinball. Even more erratic acts were to follow.

Number five, he fell asleep three times when Jesus wanted company to pray with Him in Gethsemane (14:37).

Number six, he took out his sword in violation of Jesus' orders to be nonviolent. Instead, Peter cut off the ear of the high priest's servant (John 18:10). Jesus corrected Peter's failure by reattaching the ear—a nonverbal rebuke to Peter.

Number seven, Peter deserted, along with all the other disciples, when Jesus was arrested (14:46). Despite his earlier braggadocio, he fled when the heat was on. His earlier good intentions melted like snow on a hot summer day.

Finally, and most grievously, Peter disowned Jesus altogether—three times (John 14:66-72).

The Bible doesn't cover up Peter's failures, and that gives us hope; because despite Peter's failures, the Lord loved him.

Would that there would never be a failure in your life, that you would never be weak or vulnerable! That you would never give in to temptation or pressure! But sometimes, like Peter, we fall down hard. No failure need be permanent. The good news is that Jesus also extends grace to us, even as He did to Peter!

A Prayer

Lord Jesus, thank You for Your never-failing love.

KNOWS US BEST, LOVES US MOST

*"I tell you the truth," Jesus answered, "today—yes, tonight—
before the rooster crows twice you yourself will disown me
three times." But Peter insisted emphatically, "Even if I have
to die with you, I will never disown you." And all
the others said the same.*

MARK 14:30-31

DOES JESUS KNOW in advance when we are going to fail Him? From His words to Peter, we know the answer is, "Yes." He knows exactly how and when we are going to fail, just as He did with Peter.

Life brings to us hard circumstances and temptations. We don't always do the right thing. We need to be careful that we don't pretend we are better than Peter. We have the same arrogance as Peter if we say, "Well, had I been Peter I would not have failed the Lord."

When we posture ourselves as better than others—more spiritual, more committed, more gifted—the Lord will have a hard lesson for us even as He had for Peter. Better to not be cocky. We are clay vessels, and sometimes the Lord has to use a hammer and break us in pieces so He can remold us.

Jesus obviously loved Peter. He made him His lead disciple—always the first one listed in the enumeration of the Twelve; however, the greater the privilege, the greater the need for humility. If an arrogant angel got tossed out of heaven, as did Lucifer, then it's impermissible for a follower of Jesus to elevate their level of commitment to Jesus above that of others.

Jesus even emphasized Peter's coming failure by using the reflexive pronoun "you yourself will disown me." He could have simply said, "you." But the use of the reflexive pronoun made Jesus' pronouncement emphatic to Peter. It carried the meaning, "you, and no other."

Jesus' love particularizes—it focuses on us personally; but His discipline also particularizes. He singles us out from the group with an individual word; sometimes He speaks words of correction and sadness over our misbehavior or lack of love for Him. We don't want to grieve Jesus any more than Peter did, but the fact is that we, too, fail. We aren't better than Peter. The good news is that Jesus will use our failure to make us a more perfect follower.

Let's also recognize that every one of the disciples said the same thing, "We will never disown you." Earlier in the evening they had been more honest. At the Last Supper, Jesus announced that one of them would betray Him, and they all said, "Surely not I?" (Mark 14:19). Now, on the Mount of Olives, they had transitioned to certainty. They were no longer asking, "Surely not I?" Instead they were saying, "I will never disown you." They had moved from doubting themselves to falsely reassuring themselves.

The lesson for us is to recognize that only the Lord's grace and love saves us. He knew the disciples better than anyone else. He knows us better than anyone else. The miracle is that He moves toward us rather than away from us or against us. Like the disciples, we are held secure because He loves us and died for us.

Even though the disciples did indeed disown Jesus by fleeing away, He didn't disown them. That is the breathlessness of wonder we should feel at the marvelous grace of our loving Lord: grace that exceeds our sin and our guilt.

A Prayer

Lord Jesus, my failures do not catch You by surprise.
Thank You for loving me nevertheless.

THE PRAYER LIFE OF JESUS

They went to a place called Gethsemane, and Jesus said to his disciples, "Sit here while I pray."

MARK 14:32

IF YOUR LIFE IS MARKED by prayer, then prayer will be your constant companion in crucial moments. If you're grateful in ordinary times, you'll be grateful in times of loss and stress. If you grumble all the time, you won't react well when you face great adversity.

We find Jesus praying as He enters the most crucial hours of His life. But He didn't wait until Gethsemane to pray. All through His ministry He prayed. Look at the key moments in His ministry when He prayed.

At His baptism. Luke notes, "As we was praying, heaven was opened" (Luke 3:21). Jesus was praying as began His ministry with His baptism by John. Heaven is likewise open when we pray. The skies aren't made of brass. Our prayers don't bounce off the ceiling. When we pray, God listens.

Prior to the selection of the Twelve. Luke tells us that Jesus spent the night in the hills praying before He selected the disciples in the morning (Luke 6:12). We do well to imitate Jesus when we face key decisions. Do we make such choices with prayer? There has never been an effective servant of Jesus who led a prayerless life.

After rejection. Jesus did mighty works in Korazin, Bethsaida, and Capernaum, but was rejected by the people in those towns (Matthew 11:25–26). The rejection had to sting. What did Jesus do? He said, "I praise you, Father, Lord of heaven and earth" (v. 25). How do we respond when others turn against us, when a spouse walks out on us, a child rebels, or a friend betrays? We must do what Jesus did—repair through prayer. We get refocused when our heart turns toward Him.

THE PRAYER LIFE OF JESUS

Prior to a breakthrough. A turning point came when Jesus asked His disciples, "Who do you say that I am?" That question arose as Jesus finished a time spent in private prayer (Luke 9:18-20). If we want others to come to Jesus, then let us follow His example. People aren't birthed into the kingdom unless someone prays. Who are you praying for that they, too, will confess Jesus as the Christ?

At a high moment of revelation. The transfiguration of Jesus occurred as a result of Jesus going away with Peter, James, and John to a high mountain so they could pray privately (Matthew 17:2; Luke 9:28-29). We can also experience times of great joy and intense exhilaration in prayer, just as the disciples were filled with Spirit and with joy (Acts 2:4, 46).

In others' moments of need. Mary and Martha were overwhelmed at the death of their brother, Lazarus. Jesus ordered the stone removed from Lazarus' grave and then prayed (John 11:41-42). In moments of great sorrow, we can affirm our faith by praying as Jesus did, "Father, I [know] that you always hear me."

Now we find Jesus praying in Gethsemane. Escape was possible. It was just a quick walk up the slope of the Mount of Olives and He could have disappeared into the Judean desert. But He stayed and prayed—for us! There are moments when no miracle happens, when we must not run away but must stick to our post of duty. What stabilizes and gives us fortitude to remain is prayer.

A Prayer

Lord Jesus, may I follow Your example and pray in the key moments of my life, even as I do day by day.

JESUS: OUR MODEL FOR DEALING WITH DEPRESSION

He took Peter, James and John along with him, and he began to be deeply distressed and troubled. "My soul is overwhelmed with sorrow to the point of death," he said to them, "Stay here and keep watch."

MARK 14:33–34

GETHSEMANE IS WHERE no miracles happen. Sorrow sits like a leaden blanket on Jesus' heart. The Phillips translation states, Jesus "began to be horror-stricken and desperately depressed."

Jesus then told Peter, James, and John that His soul was overwhelmed with sorrow to the point of death. The Greek text has one word for "overwhelmed with sorrow": *perilupos*. This word can be used to describe a tight-fitting girdle. Jesus was encompassed or, literally, girded about or surrounded with sorrow.

Too often we think of depression as something akin to sin. And it may shock us to describe the Lord as depressed. But isn't that what depression is—a deep sadness, being overwhelmed with sorrow or grief? Luke tells us that Jesus' sorrow was so great He was in "anguish" and "his sweat was like drops of blood falling to the ground" (Luke 22:44).

Gethsemane is clearly the lowest moment in Jesus' earthly experience. His way of dealing with overwhelming sorrow provides a six-step pathway out of depression:

Jesus didn't isolate Himself. He let others into the inner circle of His apprehension, trouble, and grief. Too many believers have imprisoned themselves by treating their depression as a deep, dark secret that can't be talked about with others. Jesus openly revealed His sadness to His closest and most trusted friends. Do you?

Jesus didn't put on a mask. He avoided the trap of saying to Himself, "I am the Son of God, and therefore, I can't let anyone know the trial I'm going through." He didn't pretend to be happy when He wasn't. He verbalized what He was experiencing. Do you have anyone to talk to when you are feeling low?

Jesus prayed. He didn't try to handle His problems without the Father's presence, comfort, and help. In the privacy of Gethsemane's garden, He poured out His heart to His Father. He exemplified for us the power of accepting the things we cannot or should not change when He said, "Your will be done" (Matthew 26:42). Are you praying for God to help you accept what has been thrust on you?

Jesus didn't dissipate His strength with bitterness or blame. Even the failure of His closest friends to stay awake and pray with Him didn't deter Jesus from a right spirit and continued prayer. Are you keeping a sweet spirit in a difficult season?

Jesus rose to action. Events of life can momentarily paralyze or even cause people to flee in the wrong direction. Jesus could have abandoned the way to the cross by quickly leaving Gethsemane, ascending the Mount of Olives, and disappearing like David in a southeastern direction into the Judean wilderness. Instead, from His place of sorrow He rose to face what confronted Him.

Jesus is able to empathize with us in our sorrows because He has been sorrowful Himself.

What would you be doing today if you weren't depressed? The challenge is to go ahead and do it anyway. May the Lord give you strength to face your difficulties and not run from them. Remember, the same wind that uproots a tree can lift a bird because the opposing force becomes a lifting force if faced in the right direction.

A Prayer

Lord Jesus, thank You for showing me how to face sorrow in my own life.

YOUR WILL BE DONE

Going a little farther, he fell to the ground and prayed that if possible the hour might pass from him. "Abba, Father," he said, "everything is possible for you. Take this cup from me. Yet not what I will, but what you will."

MARK 14:35–36

IN THE MOMENTs before Jesus was arrested, He gave us an insight from His own experience on how to face the hardest circumstances of life.

First, He called God "Abba, Father." *Abba* is a term of endearment, much like we would use the word "Daddy."

For Jesus, God wasn't an abstract idea, a policeman in the sky, a remote ruler, or a king dispatching orders from his palace. No! God was personal. We learn that from Jesus. We, too, have a Father in heaven, a Father so endearing that we are as welcome to come into His arms of love and care, as a small child comes to his daddy.

We have a personal relationship with the God who made the heavens and the earth, God over all! Thus, in our "Gethsemanes," we come—not to a remote father who sits behind a desk, but to a "Daddy" who welcomes us into His presence with open arms.

Second, our confession of faith must always be, "God, You can do anything. Nothing is impossible with You." We recognize, as did Jesus, that we serve an all-powerful God. We must never let that reality slip from us when we are tempted to doubt and say, "But where is God?" or "Where was God?" He is always there; but also here. He has ultimate power and authority.

Third, our confession of faith must also include the words Jesus used, "Your will be done." God wasn't going to deliver Jesus from the evil decisions of others. In order for free will to work, people must have the freedom to do right or wrong.

Too often, people wrongly attribute an evil outcome to God's omnipotence, forgetting that we are responsible for our own actions.

For example, if my daughter were killed by a drunk driver, that wouldn't be God's decision. It would be the choice of a person who made a wrong and evil decision to get drunk and drive. God's will in that circumstance is that I would not become bitter or let the loss of my daughter destroy my life and those around me. "Your will be done" means that I ask the Lord, "How now do I respond to this? What good can come from this? Help me, Lord!"

We don't always get what we want. That's why it's so important for us to repeat the words of Jesus, "Not what I will, but what You will." To condition our prayers with "Your will be done" isn't a lack of faith; it's the evidence of a faith that trusts deeply in the character and goodness of God.

Finally, we should note that in the garden of Gethsemane Jesus went "a little farther." He went farther than the eight disciples left on the perimeter or the three disciples chosen to be closer to Him. He also went further—not only in prayer, but in agony, laying down His life for us. None of us will ever go further than Jesus. Only He could bear our sins in His body on the cross. That is what drove Him from Gethsemane to Calvary.

A Prayer

Lord Jesus, may my prayers be requests and not demands.
I know You can do anything, but I pray most for
Your will to be done in my life.

FALLING ASLEEP?

Then he returned to his disciples and found them sleeping. "Simon," he said to Peter, "are you asleep? Could you not keep watch for one hour? Watch and pray so that you will not fall into temptation. The spirit is willing, but the body is weak."

MARK 14:37–38

PETER ISN'T THE LAST disciple to fall asleep on Jesus. It's hard work to pray. Often it's much easier if the Lord simply asks us to spring into action. But He knows that actions can go terribly awry for the follower who hasn't preceded action with prayer. No wonder Peter later cut off an ear of the servant of the high priest. If he had done what the Lord asked him to do—pray—there would have been a different result.

It wasn't a comforting word that Jesus spoke to Peter. It was a sorrowful word. At the most critical juncture in the Lord's life, He found that He couldn't count on the disciples—the very closest disciples in whom He had invested the three years of His public ministry.

The prayerlessness of Peter and the others must have been an added weight on Jesus' heart as He agonized in Gethsemane. But how many times have we broken the heart of the Lord? Were we asleep when we should have been awake to what He wanted from us? Not necessarily physically, but asleep to opportunity, vision, need, or prayer. The Lord asks us to stay awake.

Jesus' words contain both warning and grace.

The warning is that if we don't watch and pray we will fall into temptation. Watching is an attribute of staying awake. It relates to more than just keeping our eyes open. It has to do with alertness.

You can be awake physically, with eyes wide open, yet stumble into sin. Morally, spiritually, emotionally—you fell asleep. It's like driving a car. When you take your eyes off the road, get distracted, reach for your cell phone or map, you can quickly drift off the road or into an approaching car. You took your eyes off what you should be doing.

That's one of the crucial aspects of sin. We fall asleep to danger—often not willingly, but carelessly. What Jesus says to Peter, he also says to us: "Watch!"

Immediately after the warning comes the word of grace. Our Lord knew how frail Peter was, and He knows how frail we are. He acknowledged what Paul later talked about in Romans 7—that what we want to do we fail to do. We want with all our hearts to please Jesus, but our human nature is also weak. Implicit in Jesus' warning for Peter to stay awake was His knowledge that Peter might not. That didn't lessen His love for Peter. He wanted Peter to succeed, but Jesus loved him even though he failed.

Ultimately, Peter's failure hurt him more than it did the Lord. He experienced subsequent shame and embarrassment. Twenty centuries later, we still see his failure. But Peter's failure also gives us hope, for it shows us that the Lord's love and grace toward us does not fail. He never gave up on Peter and He doesn't give up on us.

That grace isn't meant to give us an excuse to go ahead and fall into temptation. The Lord is serious when He says, "Watch!" Let's pay heed ahead of time more to His warning than to His grace lest we, too, fall as did Peter.

A Prayer

Lord Jesus, may I remain alert today, not fail
You nor bring shame to myself.

THE AGONY OF GETHSEMANE

Once more he went away and prayed the same thing. When he came back, he again found them sleeping, because their eyes were heavy. They did not know what to say to him.

MARK 14:39-40

MARK WRITES a condensed gospel. On occasion, we need to turn to Matthew and Luke to find fuller detail. Such is the case with our Lord's agony in Gethsemane. The disciples had fallen asleep twice when Mark notes their "eyes were heavy" and "they did not know what to say."

Matthew and Luke fill in two details regarding what happened while the disciples slept. First, Jesus prayed, "My Father, if it is not possible for this cup to be taken away unless I drink it, may your will be done" (Matthew 26:42; see also Luke 22:42). Second, Luke adds a detail found nowhere else: "An angel from heaven appeared to him and strengthened him. And being in anguish, he prayed more earnestly, and his sweat was like drops of blood falling to the ground" (Luke 23:43-44).

You and I have never prayed so intensely that our sweat was as drops of blood. It's vital that we remember Jesus did this for us. If He didn't drink the cup of taking our sins upon Him, we don't have eternal life. Our sins become a permanent barrier from God because there's simply no way to expunge them. Only the blood of Jesus can wash away our sin. His death means life for us.

We can never imitate the sacrifice of Jesus because His role is unique. But we can follow His example. Do we intercede with passion for others who don't know Jesus?

The agony of Jesus in Gethsemane was so great that the Father sent an angel to strengthen Him. Notice, the angel's mission was not to deliver Jesus, but to help Him endure.

Too often in our lives, we only want deliverance. We prefer to be released rather than strengthened. We may not have an angel to strengthen us, but we do have the Holy Spirit who comes for that very purpose. The apostle Paul put it this way, "I pray that out of his glorious riches he may strengthen you with power *through his Spirit* in your inner being, so that Christ may dwell in your hearts through faith" (Ephesians 3:16–17, emphasis added).

Paul wrote from a prison cell. God had not granted him release, but the Spirit strengthened him in his fierce hour of trial, even as an angel strengthened Jesus. In our own Gethsemanes (which pale in comparison to what Jesus went through), let us also pray, "Thy will be done," with expectation that the Spirit will strengthen us.

The disciples had no response to Jesus when He returned to them the second time. Even the normally talkative Peter was silent. They seem unaware of the danger just around the corner.

There are times in our lives when we are embarrassed and ashamed that we have not done what the Lord asked. We have no defense for doing the opposite of what He wanted. We have no response when our conduct is bad. But the Lord knows why—our eyes are also heavy. We fell spiritually asleep when we should have been wide awake and, like the disciples, we fell asleep more than once.

Even though the disciples failed, Jesus didn't write them off. Nor does He write us off. We may fall asleep, but He never does. He ever lives to make intercession for us.

A Prayer

Lord Jesus, help me to stay awake spiritually.
Strengthen me by Your Spirit.

TIME TO WAKE UP

Returning the third time, he said to them, "Are you still sleeping and resting? Enough! The hour has come. Look, the Son of Man is betrayed into the hands of sinners. Rise! Let us go! Here comes my betrayer."

MARK 14:41–42

SLEEP IS VERY NECESSARY. Unless we get proper rest, we don't function well. God has so designed our bodies that we must take about one-third of every twenty-four hours to rest and biologically recharge our batteries.

We even find Jesus sleeping. On one occasion He was so exhausted from ministry that when He got into the boat with the disciples, He promptly fell asleep with His head resting on a cushion (Mark 4:38). In fact, His sleep was so deep that the panicked disciples had to awaken Him.

Now, in Gethsemane, it was the opposite situation. The disciples were sleeping, and Jesus awakened them—not once, but three times. They, too, were exhausted. They didn't know the violence of the storm that was immediately around the corner.

In His parable of the Wheat and Weeds, Jesus taught about the inherent dangers with sleep. "The kingdom of heaven is like a man who sowed good seed in his field. But while everyone was sleeping, his enemy came and sowed weeds" (Matthew 13:24–25). Jesus explained that the good seed was sown by Him, but the Devil sowed the weeds.

How does the Devil do his work in our lives? It happens while we are spiritually, morally, or emotionally sleeping. We aren't awake to the dangers of temptation or the dangers that come with trial.

This is what the Lord warned us about in His discourse on the future, given just two days prior to Gethsemane: "If he comes suddenly, do not let him find you sleeping" (Mark 13:36). While this warning is attached to the end of days, clearly it has immediate application.

The disciples were asleep in Gethsemane. If they fell asleep in this crisis, will they be awake when the Son of Man returns suddenly? If we can't watch when Jesus tells us to discern the signs of the end times, will we be watchful of our own conduct in the everyday of now?

The story, perhaps apocryphal, is told that when Muslim armies surrounded the historic city of Constantinople (now Istanbul), the capital of the Christian eastern empire, inside the city theologians were debating whether Mary had blue or brown eyes and whether a fly falling into the Communion chalice would be sanctified or the wine be contaminated. The city was asleep to the danger all around it.

Too often the church has also been asleep to the internal and external threats all around. The Enemy does come and sow seeds of false doctrine, division, and spiritual lethargy. Jesus wants His church to be wide-awake.

Remember the first murderer, Cain? Before he killed his brother, Abel, the Lord warned Cain that "sin is crouching at the door; it desires to have you, but you must master it" (Genesis 4:7). Cain didn't heed the Lord's warning, even as the disciples didn't heed Jesus' warning to stay awake and pray. Thus, they weren't prepared for the events that would immediately unfold.

Something or someone evil is always "crouching at our door." Fervent and regular prayer in our lives keeps us awake so that we're well prepared for whatever spiritual danger is just around the corner.

A Prayer

Lord Jesus, with all my heart, I want to watch and pray that I may do Your will in my life.

FALL FROM GRACE

Just as he was speaking, Judas, one of the Twelve, appeared. With him was a crowd armed with swords and clubs, sent from the chief priests, the teachers of the law, and the elders.

MARK 14:43

HOW CAN ANYONE EXPLAIN the behavior of Judas? The early 1970s rock opera, *Jesus Christ Superstar,* tried to rehabilitate Judas. It chronicles the last seven days in the life of Jesus as seen through the eyes Judas, who had become disillusioned. After leading the soldiers to Gethsemane and watching events unfold, Judas realizes he has been tricked by God into being an instrument of Jesus' martyrdom. Furious that the man from Nazareth will be remembered as a "Superstar," Judas hangs himself.

Opposite to this modern attempt to rehabilitate Judas is the writing of fourteenth-century author, Dante. In his work *The Inferno,* Dante placed Judas is the lowest pit of hell, frozen in a lake of ice—a lake formed by the tears of humanity. With Judas in the lake is the Devil, depicted as a huge craggy monster with three faces and great batlike wings. In each mouth he crushes a traitor—Brutus and Cassius on each side and in the center mouth, Judas.

For Dante, Judas' sin was against love. His head is now mangled by the teeth of the Devil in memory of the crown of thorns his treachery brought Christ, and his back is lacerated by the Devil's claws in repayment for Jesus' scourging.

In contrast to *Jesus Christ Superstar* and *The Inferno,* the Scriptures give us the real story.

Judas started out as a regular disciple. He followed Jesus from John's baptism (Acts 1:22); was selected after Jesus spent a night in prayer (Luke 6:12–13); was sent out to preach, heal, and cast out demons (Mark 6:6–13); witnessed the miracles of Jesus; and listened to His teachings. Judas didn't accept Jesus' invitation to be a member of the Twelve in order that he would later betray Him.

So, what happened? Judas didn't deal with his disappointments in Jesus. Why was Jesus not advocating the overthrow of the Roman government? If He could do miracles, why wasn't He using His powers militarily?

Judas' disappointment with Jesus grew gradually as evidenced by the fact that he stole from the money bag (John 12:6). Finally, the Devil himself entered Judas (Luke 22:3; John 13:27), and Judas sold Jesus for thirty pieces of silver (Matthew 26:15), the price set for a slave (Exodus 21:32).

Notice the descent in Judas from disappointment in Jesus, to moral failure as a thief, ending in being possessed of the Devil. His life is a lesson for us lest we fall into greater and greater sin.

Nineteen-century hymn writer and theologian F. W. Faber said: "He who dallies with temptation . . . is never safe. People say that such and such a man had a sudden fall, but no fall is sudden. In every instance, the crisis of the moment is decided only by the tenor of the life; nor, since the world began, has any man been dragged over into the domain of evil, who had not strayed carelessly, or gazed curiously, or lingered guiltily, beside it edge."

Jesus said that if we are faithful in small things, He will make us rulers over much. The reverse is also true. If, like Judas, we are unfaithful in small things, then we open ourselves to greater and greater unfaithfulness until the Devil himself enters us.

A Prayer

Lord Jesus, guard my heart. Guard my life. May I choose not to sin small, lest I become capable of sinning greatly.

BETRAYED WITH A KISS

Now the betrayer had arranged a signal with them: "The one I kiss is the man; arrest him and lead him away under guard." Going at once to Jesus, Judas said, "Rabbi!" and kissed him.

MARK 14:44-45

WE LEARN THE COMPLETE detail of Judas' arrival in Gethsemane from reading the first three Gospels.

Matthew and Mark tell us the crowd was armed with swords and clubs. Matthew records that they were sent from the chief priests and elders of the people.

Mark, the condensed gospel, records Judas as speaking only one word to Jesus, "Rabbi." That one word tells us Judas' frame of mind. He had repudiated the confession of faith in Jesus as the Messiah; to Judas, Jesus was only another rabbi, a teacher.

Luke's gospel notes that Jesus asked him, "Judas, are you betraying the Son of Man with a kiss" (Luke 22:48)? In Matthew's Gospel, Jesus called him "Friend," and said, "Do what you came for" (Matthew 26:50).

From these brief accounts, we mine some sobering truths.

Judas followed Jesus for three years, but at the end, his opinion of Jesus had diminished. How many, like Judas, began to follow Jesus, witnessed Him do wonderful things, and marveled at His teaching; but, in the end, devotion failed? The earlier faith was repudiated. Jesus was no longer the One, He was just another one.

It's sobering to recognize that multitudes throughout Christian history have done the same as Judas. Visit any church today and you will find the same thing. Those who once sang the songs of Zion and testified of faith in Jesus have, like Judas, fallen away.

How about you? Is that the best title you can give Jesus, "Rabbi?"

Judas' devaluation of Jesus did not change Jesus' love for Judas. He called the traitor, "Friend." We should be amazed at that. Even when we are at our worst, Jesus gives grace to us and, like Judas, calls us friend.

Mark gives us very few words that we can't find in the other Gospels. When these words occur, we recognize they must come from someone positioned very close to Jesus. For example, Mark is the only gospel writer to record that Jesus was asleep on a cushion in the storm (4:38). We know from early second-century tradition that Peter influenced the writing of Mark. Likely, Peter is the one who awakened Jesus, and that is why we have the detail of the cushion.

In the Gethsemane betrayal of Jesus, Mark gives us a detail not found elsewhere. Peter must have been standing very close to catch the nuance. Mark notes that the betrayer had given them a sign saying, "The one I kiss is the man." In Greek, the word for kiss is *philein*.

However, when Judas came and actually kissed Jesus, the word for kiss in the Greek is *kata-philein*. The prefix, *kata*, in front of *philein* changes the nature of the transaction. *Kata-philein* is a kiss of intensity—as when the woman kissed Jesus' feet (Luke 7:38), or the father kissed the prodigal (Luke 15:20), or the elders at Ephesus kissed Paul goodbye (Acts 20:37). Judas didn't give Jesus an ordinary courtesy kiss.

The intense kiss makes the act of betrayal even more dastardly. Yet, according to Matthew's gospel, Jesus responded by calling him, "Friend." Judas' betrayal couldn't shake the love of Jesus for him.

No one who goes to hell can ever say, "Jesus didn't love me."

A Prayer
Lord Jesus, I pray to always be true to You.

RETURNING GOOD FOR EVIL

The men seized Jesus and arrested him. Then one of those standing near drew his sword and struck the servant of the high priest, cutting off his ear.
MARK 14:46-47

JESUS NEVER LAID hands in anger on anyone. Whenever He touched someone, it was from love and compassion.

I recently had an experience where I thought I had done my very best. Long days and hours, difficult negotiation, and roller coaster moments combined to bring a good result. Inwardly I felt I deserved appreciation and thanks for the leadership I provided. None was forthcoming. I felt like the poor wise man in Ecclesiastes 9 who saved a city by his wisdom, but no one remembered or thanked him.

Well into my self-pity, I come to this moment in Jesus' life. Look at all He had done for others: healing persons of incurable diseases, casting out demons and returning the possessed individual to sanity and normality, even raising dead people to life. What did He receive in return?

Instead of a pat on the back, or a hug of endearment, violent hands were laid on Him. He was "seized." Our Lord, who never caused harm, was now harmed.

It's a lesson for us in several ways. First, we must serve Jesus and do our best whether anyone thanks us or not. Our task is to do His will. Second, our hands must be used to help and never to hurt. Not only must our hands never hurt, our words must never hurt either. Better to give thanks than curse. Better to help than harm.

It wasn't Roman guards who came to arrest Jesus in Gethsemane, but a "crowd" from the chief priests, teachers of the Law, and elders. In other words, the religious establishment felt threatened by Jesus; and thus, the decision to detain Him. Their example is mimicked all over the world.

Whenever religion has to use force to defend itself, it has no spiritual power from God; and thus, it must resort to defending itself with force. We see that all over the world today where dominant religions in a country persecute, seek forced conversion, discriminate against, tax more heavily, or marginalize those who don't practice the dominant religion. A religion that must use coercive power to uphold itself is a religion that isn't from God.

All the gospel writers record the arrest of Jesus and the fact that one of His companions took his sword and cut off the ear of the high priest. From the gospel of John, we know who that disciple was—Peter! We also know the name of the servant, Malchus (John 18:10–11).

The mention of Malchus by name intrigues us. We don't know the names of almost all the people whom Jesus healed except for Jairus, because of his daughter, and Bartimaeus and Lazarus. Now, we have the name of Malchus. Why?

Could it be that these individuals subsequently served Jesus and became a vital part of the first Christian community? I suspect so.

Malchus got more than the reattachment of his ear. His hard heart was healed. He would never be the same. When we do as Jesus did, when we return good for evil, the heart of the perpetrator is also touched. And, even if their heart continues to harden after we have done the good, we must never let our own hearts harden. We must do the good no matter what.

A Prayer

Lord Jesus, may I learn anew from You the power of love—even for those who wrong me.

RELIGION GONE BAD

"Am I leading a rebellion," said Jesus, "that you have come out with swords and clubs to capture me? Every day I was with you, teaching in the temple courts, and you did not arrest me. But the Scriptures must be fulfilled."

MARK 14:48-49

FROM TIME TO TIME I talk with people who have been wounded by the bad conduct of persons in spiritual leadership. Sometimes, the wound was inflicted by a pastor or minister, other times by a deacon or persons in positions of authority in the church.

Some of the wounded never again darken the door of a church.

What happened? The same spirit that motivated the religious leadership in Jerusalem to arrest Jesus is alive in those who lead with unkindness and authoritarian "my way or the highway" attitudes within the church.

I will never forget conducting a business meeting in a church where there was a confidence vote on the pastor. Under his leadership many new people had come to Christ. He had reached out to young people and they had found a welcome home in the church.

But the "old guard" was threatened. They perceived that their power to control the church was slipping from their grasp. So they petitioned to have a business meeting and conduct a vote of confidence on the pastor. The pastor was several votes short of the two-thirds he needed to remain as pastor.

After the meeting adjourned, I noticed two groups. The older group members, who engineered the vote, were in the back of the church congratulating one another. The young people were at the altar weeping and embracing the pastor. That "old guard" in the church was actually like the religious leadership who arrested Jesus. They used power to protect their position.

I have often wondered how many of the youth weeping at the altar that night became so disenchanted with the church that they became lost to the family of God in their adult lives.

I wonder the same about the Christian family where a husband or wife asserts authority in such a domineering way that the spouse and kids walk on eggshells lest they incur displeasure. That spouse is attempting to lead his or her family from the vantage point of power rather than from love.

The "old guard"—the chief priests, elders, and scribes—got their way with Jesus. They knew they could not openly arrest Him. That's why they did it at night, sending a group led by Judas with swords and clubs. They knew Jesus was not leading a rebellion. They recognized that their position was being undermined by His attack on their religiosity and godlessness.

We know from secular accounts that the temple authorities were extremely wealthy. Religion, for them, was a matter of profit. Thirty pieces of silver for the betrayer was a mere pittance for them to pay.

It's easy to condemn those religious authorities for what they did to Jesus. But we must always put ourselves in the text of Scripture. How important is power to you or me? When you are criticized, do you easily take offense and attempt to get even? When your leadership is questioned, do you respond with the graciousness of Jesus or the belligerence of the temple establishment?

Followers of Jesus are willing to suffer rather than to impose suffering, to be reviled rather than to revile, to live with an open hand rather than a clenched fist.

A Prayer

Lord Jesus, may I serve others with love, rather than attempting to manipulate or coerce them into doing what I want.

THE COME-BACK DISCIPLE

*Then everyone deserted him and fled. A young man,
wearing nothing but a linen garment, was following Jesus.
When they seized him, he fled naked,
leaving his garment behind.*

MARK 14:50–52

AT THE LAST SUPPER, just hours earlier, Jesus told His disciples they would all fall away, that the prophecy of Zechariah 13:7 would be fulfilled: "I will strike the shepherd, and the sheep will be scattered" (Mark 14:27).

The passion of Jesus finds us at the intersection of God's sovereignty and human freedom. Greater minds than ours have attempted to resolve the interplay between these two choices— God's and man's. The Bible doesn't attempt to resolve it, however. Both realities are laid side by side (Acts 2:23–24).

We experience moments when we cannot interpret the significance of an event at the time it happens. We can only look back later and gain perspective. Thus, at the time of Jesus' arrest in Gethsemane, the disciples all deserted Him and fled.

Much later in their lives, all would be willing to suffer and die for Him, but not at this moment. That would only come when they knew "the rest of the story." Don't make the mistake of the disciples in assuming the worst during a powerless moment in your life, a moment when you even feel God is powerless. God is working out purposes you don't presently see.

The disciples deserted Him and fled. So did a young man.

Have you noticed that the gospel writers never name themselves within the text of their gospels? The superscription giving authorship was placed there by others later on.

However, verses 51 and 52 probably give us an autobiographical reference by the author. These two verses are found in no other gospel, and it's most likely that the young man who fled naked into the night was none other than John Mark.

THE COME-BACK DISCIPLE

John Mark wasn't one of the Twelve. He may have been a teenager at the time, curious about unfolding events as the group left the upper room following the Last Supper. Since he was only dressed in a linen garment, the assumption can be made that he was prepared for bed, but surreptitiously decided to follow Jesus. In Gethsemane, none of the disciples had hands laid on them, so we can also assume John Mark hung around just a little too long and was grabbed. But he was agile and got away, minus his garment.

We know John Mark was the cousin of Barnabas (Colossians 4:10); that his mother was Mary who had a house in Jerusalem (Acts 12:12); that he accompanied Barnabas and Paul on the first missionary journey but deserted them (Acts 13:3, 13); that Paul refused to take him on the second missionary journey, thereby producing a split from Barnabas (Acts 13:37–39); but that years later from prison Paul asked for Mark to come because he was helpful to him (2 Timothy 4:11).

Think of it! John Mark twice ran away from danger. Once, when Jesus was arrested and secondly, when the going got difficult on the first missionary journey! But in the end he was no longer a runaway. He headed straight to Rome where Paul was held in Nero's prison and where great danger awaited.

Is there hope for you if you have failed the Lord in the past? Absolutely! The man who failed twice was chosen by the Holy Spirit to write the second gospel! God didn't give up on him, and He doesn't give up on you!

A Prayer

Lord Jesus, I am grateful You give me another chance when I flee from You or fail You.

TOO NEAR THE FLAME

They took Jesus to the high priest, and all the chief priests, elders and teachers of the law came together. Peter followed him at a distance, right into the courtyard of the high priest. There he sat with the guards and warmed himself at the fire.

MARK 14:53–54

WHEN JESUS MET PETER for the first time, He changed his name from Simon to Peter (John 1:41–42).

We often think of Jesus' authority in reference to the miracles He did, His insightful teaching, and His power over death. There's an additional way to look at Jesus' authority—the authority to give us a new identity.

He did that with Simon. Just imagine telling a person the first time you meet them, "I don't want to call you by the name your mother gave you, or the name others have called you all your life. I'm giving you a new name."

We would look askance at such a person, either turning away from them or saying indignantly, "Who are you to change my name?"

But Jesus acted with a clear intention toward Peter, as He does with us. The underlying common word for Peter in the language spoken then is "Rock." Jesus called Simon by the term *rock*. Why did Jesus do that?

Jesus was out to build His church. Not a structure of wood, stone, brick, and glass, but a structure of people. He Himself is the cornerstone.

Peter, along with the other apostles and prophets, became the foundation stones upon which the whole building rests. We now are the living stones, built into that edifice (Ephesians 2:20–22; 1 Peter 2:5). The purpose of a foundation stone is to bear the weight that will be placed on it.

Jesus gave Peter a new identity because He saw the fisherman's potential. No one else had seen it. Jesus had faith in Peter before

Peter had faith in Him. And that's the way it is with us. We often talk about having faith in Jesus, and can easily forget that He has far greater faith in us. He believed that Peter would become a great fisher of men (Mark 1:17)!

Think of that as we come to this moment in Peter's walk with Jesus. Immediately preceding Peter's presence in the courtyard of the high priest was his experience in Gethsemane. He fell asleep three times. He couldn't rouse himself to stay awake and pray with Jesus no matter how much Jesus wanted him to do that.

Jesus specifically told Peter to pray lest he fail (14:38). Peter only roused himself when the arresting contingent came from the religious leadership, resorting to violence in an attempted defense of Jesus (John 18:10).

We find Peter now, like a moth being drawn toward the flame. He wants nearness to Jesus, but He is also going to be badly singed. Better if he had heeded Jesus' counsel in Gethsemane, "Watch and pray so that you will not fall into temptation."

Have you found yourself in a situation similar to Peter? You know the Lord loves you; you know He believes in you. But you have had some failures. Like Peter, you have adamantly expressed your loyalty to Jesus (Matthew 26:33), perhaps even setting yourself up as more committed than all the others.

We capture Peter warming himself by the fire at the precipice of his failure. He didn't know that in the coming moments he would fail terribly. We can be grateful that Jesus didn't fail him; nor will He fail you.

A Prayer

Lord Jesus, I always want to stay close to you. When I fail, as did Peter, I am so grateful You do not cast me aside.

THE RIGGED TRIAL

The chief priests and the whole Sanhedrin were looking for evidence against Jesus so that they could put him to death, but they did not find any. Many testified falsely against him, but their statements did not agree. Then some stood up and gave this false testimony against him: "We heard him say, 'I will destroy this man-made temple and in three days will build another, not made by man.'" Yet even then their testimony did not agree.

MARK 14:55–59

TWO EVENTS RECENTLY happened in our city of Springfield, Missouri, that outraged us.

A ten-year-old girl was grabbed by a passing motorist. Onlookers got the license plate number and immediately reported it to the police. Within hours the man was captured, but the girl had been assaulted and shot to death. How could anyone be so cruel as to seize a little girl, walking home from visiting with a friend, and then subject her to violence and death by a bullet?

A few weeks later in a very visible area, two Canadian geese had made their home. The male goose was deliberately run over by a car, leaving the mother goose alone with her unhatched eggs. Not only did the motorist run over the goose, as captured by a surveillance camera, he turned around and ran over the goose for a second time. What causes such madness?

A report came across the Internet today that an eight-month pregnant mother had been condemned to death by an Islamic court. She is scheduled to be flogged before she is executed. Her crime? Converting to Christianity and marrying a Christian man.

I could write the rest of this article about injustices that proliferate exponentially on a daily basis. There is madness in the world.

We open the Gospels and find Jesus—the purest, kindest, wisest person who ever lived—as the object of deep acts of injustice.

Can religious people, even religious leaders, do horrible things? Absolutely!

Even the history of institutional Christianity is rife with acts of injustice: Martin Luther making awful statements about Jews and peasants; John Calvin presiding over Servetus burning at the stake as a heretic; the popes of the past violently acting to take the lives of those who disagreed with them. Yes, religious people sin—no matter what faith they claim.

Nonreligious people sin as well—just witness the horrible acts of a Hitler, Stalin, or Mao. Or, how about the present injustice that discriminates against persons who value life and advocate sexual behavior that is taught in the Bible?

We live in an unjust world. No doubt about it! You see it in the religious trial of Jesus.

Every trial is supposed to have an indictment, with clear evidence presented of wrongdoing. This is totally absent in the trial of Jesus before the Sanhedrin. First, they couldn't find a witness. Then they found witnesses whose stories didn't agree. Finally, they simply gave false testimony. No one presiding at the trial stepped in to stop it. It was rigged from beginning to end.

God lets people make choices. That's the nature of free will. If we can select to do what is good, it must mean we can also select to do what is wrong. We live in a world that's often violent. It's the world Jesus came into, the world for which He died. His example teaches us that it's better to be wronged than to inflict wrong; better to suffer than to impose suffering.

A Prayer

Lord Jesus, when hate was breaking out around You,
You didn't let it enter You. Help me to do the same.

JESUS' OWN TESTIMONY

Then the high priest stood up before them and asked Jesus, "Are you not going to answer? What is this testimony that these men are bringing against you?" But Jesus remained silent and gave no answer. Again the high priest asked him, "Are you the Christ, the Son of the Blessed One?" "I am," said Jesus. "And you will see the Son of Man sitting at the right hand of the Mighty One and coming on the clouds of heaven." The high priest tore his clothes. "Why do we need more witnesses?" he asked. "You have heard the blasphemy. What do you think?" They all condemned him as worthy of death. Then some began to spit at him; they blindfolded him, struck him with their fists, and said, "Prophesy!" And the guards took him and beat him.

MARK 14:60–65

AS YOU READ THROUGH the first three Gospels, you find a gradual unveiling of Jesus' identity. Bible scholars call this the Messianic secret.

Jesus took great care in calibrating the revelation of Himself. You see this in the details that unfold in Mark's gospel.

The first to recognize the Lord's true identity was the demon-possessed man in the Capernaum synagogue. Jesus didn't want the testimony of this evil spirit and commanded him to be silent (Mark 1:24–25). The same evening he commanded other demons not to speak "because they knew who he was" (1:34).

Shortly afterward, Jesus healed a leper and ordered him not to tell anyone. The man disobeyed and, as a result, Jesus stayed in "lonely places" (1:44–45). Even there, out in the countryside, crowds found Him and again He gave demons "strict orders not to tell who he was" (3:12).

How do we explain Jesus' seeming reluctance to self-identify throughout the first couple years of His ministry? The answer is that He wanted the disciples to understand He was not the Messiah of their expectations. He wasn't going to be political, overthrow Roman occupation, or toss out the corrupt religious leaders in Jerusalem.

The kingdom of God was going to be split into two eras. In the present age, the kingdom is internal. It is "within you" (Luke 17:21), and is "of righteousness, peace and joy in the Holy Spirit" (Romans 14:17). In the age to come, the kingdom is external—visible to all. Jesus will reign until all enemies are under His feet (1 Corinthians 15:25).

Spiritually, the disciples were like the Bethsaida blind man whose eyes at first saw only opaquely. At the second touch of Jesus, he saw clearly (8:22–26). Immediately following the healing of that man, the eyes of the disciples were opened to identify Jesus for who He presented Himself to be. Thus, Peter declared: "You are the Christ," and Jesus immediately commanded His disciples not to tell anyone else (8:29–30). Why? The secret must be kept lest the crowds attempt to make Him their political king.

In His trial before the Sanhedrin, the high priests pressed Jesus, "Who are you?" At first, Jesus demurred. That was his right, to avoid self-incrimination. But Jesus knew His silence would only raise the attention level of the religious court. Thus He waited for the dramatic moment because He knew the high priest would ask again.

Jesus' answer reveals the second part of the kingdom of God, its external dimension. He will reign visibly! He will be seated at the right hand of the Majesty on High. He will come on the clouds of glory!

A Prayer

Lord Jesus, may Your kingdom reign in my life today even as I long for the day when You reign over all.

CRACKED UNDER PRESSURE

> *While Peter was below in the courtyard, one of the servant girls of the high priest came by. When she saw Peter warming himself, she looked closely at him. "You also were with that Nazarene, Jesus," she said. But he denied it. "I don't know or understand what you're talking about," he said, and went out into the entryway. When the servant girl saw him there, she said again to those standing around, "This fellow is one of them." Again he denied it. After a little while, those standing near said to Peter, "Surely you are one of them, for you are a Galilean." He began to call down curses on himself, and he swore to them, "I don't know this man you're talking about." Immediately the rooster crowed the second time. Then Peter remembered the word Jesus had spoken to him: "Before the rooter crows twice you will disown me three times." And he broke down and wept.*
>
> MARK 14:66–72

PETER HAD A DEEP fault line in his personality, and it shows here. He didn't do well under pressure.

I think every follower of Jesus identifies with Peter. We don't want to exhibit braggadocio like Peter did in the upper room at the Last Supper, and say: "Lord, that would never be me" (14:29). Jesus knows the stuff we are made of, even when we do not.

Peter's problem with pressure continued well into his Christian journey. Look at what happened in Antioch. Gentile believers were coming to Christ in great numbers. Peter broke kosher dietary rules to eat with them. For the first time in his life he was eating meat and dairy products at the same time.

However, certain members of the very observant Jewish believers came to Antioch and were not happy with Peter's conduct. What did Peter do? The same thing He did in the high priest's courtyard. He wilted! Paul rebuked him (Galatians 2:11).

Peter withdrew from table fellowship with the Gentile believers because he couldn't take the pressure of adverse opinion. This cracking under pressure comes long after the resurrection! It represents a fault line in Peter's personality that the Enemy exploited.

Perhaps you identify with Peter. There is an area in your life where the Evil One knows you are susceptible. He will keep coming back to your weakness time and time again.

Did Peter ever get over his vulnerability to pressure? Yes, most definitely! At the end of his life he has made his "calling and election sure" and was prepared to soon put aside "the tent of this body" (2 Peter 1:10–14). Early church tradition says that Peter chose to be crucified upside down because he wasn't worthy of being crucified as was his Lord.

Luke's gospel tells us that after his third denial, "The Lord turned and looked straight at Peter" (22:61). No wonder Peter "broke down and wept."

Do you also weep when you have failed the Lord? Is there remorse? Granted, the Lord sees that we crack under pressure, but does that nevertheless grieve us when we fail? Or do we go on sinning or failing in a cavalier manner?

Don't you love the Lord's great grace? Jesus never gave up on Peter. In fact, after the resurrection, Peter was the first of the eleven disciples to whom Jesus appeared (Luke 24:34; 1 Corinthians 15:5). The Lord looks at us when we fail, but He holds out His arms afterward to enfold us in His amazing love.

A Prayer

Lord Jesus, I am so grateful that You continue to love me even when I fail. I love you.

THE ARRAIGNMENTS

Very early in the morning, the chief priests, with the elders, the teachers of the law and the whole Sanhedrin, reached a decision. They bound Jesus, led him away and handed him over to Pilate. "Are you the king of the Jews?" asked Pilate. "Yes, it is as you say," Jesus replied. The chief priests accused him of many things. So again Pilate asked him, "Aren't you going to answer? See how many things they are accusing you of." But Jesus still made no reply, and Pilate was amazed.

MARK 15:1-5

JESUS FACED FOUR judicial events the morning before He was crucified.

The first came from the religious leadership. The effort to push Jesus to the cross didn't come from the Jewish people themselves. The masses supported Jesus, and that's why the religious authorities weren't willing to risk arresting Him openly. Those responsible for pushing Jesus toward the cross were from the corrupt religious establishment.

Luke's gospel provides additional detail about the preliminary hearing before the chief priests, elders, scribes, and the Sanhedrin. Their concern was a religious one: "If you are the Christ, tell us." Jesus initially didn't answer their question directly except to say they wouldn't believe Him if He told them, and that "from now on, the Son of Man will be seated at the right hand of the mighty God." So, they asked a second time, "Are you then the Son of God?" Jesus answered, "I am" (Luke 22:66-71).

The first arraignment before religious authorities confirmed in their minds that Jesus had committed the sin of blasphemy. Their problem was that blasphemy wasn't an indictable offense under Roman law, and only Rome had the power to put to death an individual who committed a capital offense.

Thus, Jesus was next handed over to Pilate, the Roman governor of Judea. The charge they brought against Jesus before Pilate was not, "He claims to be the Son of God." Rather, they accused Jesus of political sedition in opposing payment of taxes to Caesar and claiming to be king (Luke 23:2).

Pilate focused on the issue of Jesus claiming to be the king of the Jews. Jesus gave a short response to the indictment, "Yes, it is as you say." In legal terms, this was an admission against self-interest. Jesus' statement was enough to convict Him. Pilate, however, did nothing. Apprehensive lest Jesus be released, the religious leadership pressed their case accusing Jesus of "many things."

Jesus was silent when asked to respond further, and Pilate was amazed. He had sat in judgment on many others whom he had put to death, but never one like Jesus who remained calm and declined to defend Himself.

Luke's gospel tells us that upon learning Jesus was a Galilean, Pilate sent Him over to Herod Antipas, the ruler of Galilee who had executed John the Baptist. Herod was in Jerusalem for the Passover. Jesus refused to speak with Herod in the third arraignment of the day. Herod mocked Jesus by dressing Him in an elegant robe and sent Him back to Pilate (Luke 23:5–12). The fourth arraignment of the morning—again before Pilate—resulted in the death sentence.

What is the lesson for us? People who claim to be religious can do terrible things. Perhaps there are those you thought were spiritual, but subsequently they negatively impacted you by their evil example. Don't let their bad behavior influence you away from God. Focus instead on the goodness of Jesus.

A Prayer

Lord Jesus, help me to keep my eyes on You rather on those who claim to be spiritual but are not.

THE CROWD, THE GOVERNOR, AND THE RELIGIOUS LEADERS

> *Now it was the custom at the Feast to release a prisoner whom the people requested. A man called Barabbas was in prison with the insurrectionists who had committed murder in the uprising. The crowd came up and asked Pilate to do for them what he usually did. "Do you want me to release to you the king of the Jews?" asked Pilate, knowing that it was out of envy that the chief priests had handed Jesus over to him. But the chief priests stirred up the crowd to have Pilate release Barabbas instead.*
> MARK 15:6–11

EACH OF THE FOUR Gospels provides details that give us a composite understanding of Jesus before Pilate. Mark gives the condensed account.

First, there was the crowd. At first glance, the crowd was neutral. They simply asked Pilate to do what he customarily did at the Passover time—release to them a prisoner. However, crowds are easily swayed by authorities and propaganda. How else can one explain entire populations falling sway under a persuasive leader as happened in Germany in the events leading to World War II? Propaganda and coercion work.

It is alarming to see this same phenomenon happening today in American culture. Just look at how the populace has been swayed on issues of sexual morality by the influence of politicians, entertainment personalities, and the media. These sources are the "chief priests" of our day, influencing the masses to make the wrong choices.

Second, there was a group known as the chief priests. In Jesus' day, they were the ones leading the religious establishment, with control over the temple and its functions. Jesus' popularity was a threat to them. Out of envy, they pressed the crowd to ask for the release of Barabbas so that Pilate would deliver Jesus to the cross.

THE CROWD, THE GOVERNOR, AND THE RELIGIOUS LEADERS

Whenever religious leaders resort to or urge force to impose their will, you know they are corrupt at the heart. Jesus never used violence, intimidation, threat, or coercion. His disciples are to follow His example. Persons must be free to say yes or no to God's love. It must be against our religion to impose our religion.

Third, there was Pilate.

Luke's gospel gives the added detail that the case of Jesus was sent by Pilate over to Herod, and then back again to Pilate for a second hearing (23:6-12). Pilate attempted to avoid making a decision even after Jesus had been returned to him (23:13-23).

Matthew's gospel relates that Pilate's wife sent him a message telling him that she had suffered many things in a dream and that Jesus was an innocent man (27:19). Pilate would have done well to heed his wife's counsel. But, like many a husband, he ignored the good advice she gave.

John's gospel tells us that Pilate took Jesus inside the palace and privately questioned Him. Jesus told Pilate that His kingdom was not of this world but that Pilate was right in saying He was a king. When Jesus said that He came "to testify to the truth," Pilate dismissively answered with, "What is truth?" Clearly, Pilate didn't believe there is ultimate truth (John 18:28-40).

As we meditate on Jesus before Pilate, the practical question for us is this: do we identify with the main actors: the crowd, the religious leaders, or Pilate? I hope not! All of them made the wrong choices. What will you do with Jesus?

A Prayer

Lord Jesus, You are Lord, King, Savior, Messiah—
the only One who can save us from our sins
and give us eternal life.

THE VERDICT

"What shall I do, then, with the one you call the king of the Jesus?" Pilate asked them. "Crucify him!" they shouted. "Why?" What crime has he committed?" asked Pilate. But they shouted all the louder, "Crucify him!" Wanting to satisfy the crowd, Pilate released Barabbas to them. He had Jesus flogged, and handed him over to be crucified.

MARK 15:12–15

JESUS' ARREST IN GETHSEMANE the night before came not from the Romans, but from a crowd armed with swords and clubs sent by the religious leaders. They had no authority to condemn Jesus to death, so they brought Him to Pilate.

Pilate didn't want to make a decision. He hemmed and hawed. Upon hearing that Jesus was from Galilee, Pilate sent Jesus over to Herod Antipas, the murderer of John the Baptist (Luke 23:6–12). Next, Pilate's wife warned him not to have anything to do with Jesus (Matthew 27:19). Finally, Pilate tried to get out of sentencing Jesus by proposing that the crowd in front of him choose a prisoner to be released, evidently hoping they would select Jesus over the terrorist Barabbas.

When the crowd asked instead for Barabbas, Pilate then insulted them. He asked, "What shall I do, then, with the one you call the king of the Jews?" In fact, the crowd before him and the religious leadership egging them on had never called Jesus "king of the Jews." In using the term, Pilate mocked them. Essentially he was saying, "If you have a king, this is what he looks like—powerless."

The crowd ignored the insult and shouted, "Crucify him." Pilate still vacillated and asked, "What crime has he committed?" Clearly, Pilate—as the administrator of Roman justice—had no business sentencing a man to crucifixion without even knowing the crime he had committed.

Pilate, however, had a troubled history with the Jews. He was thinking, *They could get me in trouble with Caesar by alleging that*

I refused to deal with a threat to the security of Rome. So, when they shouted all the more, "Crucify him," Pilate gave in.

Matthew's gospel gives this additional detail: "All the people answered, 'Let his blood be on us and on our children'" (27:25). That statement has led to much misinterpretation and tragically has led some so-called Christians to assume that henceforth and forever all Jewish persons were under a curse and were collectively responsible for the crucifixion of Jesus.

Such is not the case. This crowd had no authority, under God, to speak for anyone but themselves. The masses clearly adored Jesus as is seen in His triumphal entry into Jerusalem and the fact that the religious leaders were so afraid of Jesus' popularity they arranged for a stealthy arrest at night and a quick and illegal trial. The crowd who shouted that day had no authority to bind their children or subsequent generations of Jewish people.

No, the Jews did not kill Christ. A cabal of conspiring religious authorities pushed a spineless Roman procurator into putting Jesus on the cross. The sin of Jew and Gentile alike is not believing in the One God sent to save us from our sins.

Pilate caved in. In an act of sheer cruelty, he ordered Jesus flogged. The leather ends of Roman whips were affixed with small pieces of metal that flayed the skin. Jesus sweat drops of blood in Gethsemane. Now, His wounds began for our transgressions.

A Prayer

Lord Jesus, may I never do what is wrong to save my own skin. Thank You for going to the cross to atone for my sins.

THE ABUSE

> *The soldiers led Jesus away into the palace (that is, the Praetorium) and called together the whole company of soldiers. They put a purple robe on him, then wove a crown of thorns and set it on him. And they began to call out to him, "Hail, king of the Jews!" Again and again they struck him on the head with a staff and spit on him. Falling on their knees, they worshiped him. And when they had mocked him, they took off the purple robe and put his own clothes on him. Then they led him out to crucify him.*
>
> MARK 15:16–20

PILATE HAD JESUS FLOGGED before handing him over to the soldiers. This flogging (v. 15) was far different from that experienced by Jesus in the hearing before the high priest. There Jesus was spit on, blindfolded and struck with fists (14:65). As grievous as that treatment, it was child's play compared to what our Lord now experienced.

After Pilate's flogging, the soldiers could have led Jesus away to crucify Him. Instead, they took the moment as an occasion for sport.

I remember as a child in northwest China watching a puppy that some boys had thrown into the river. As it valiantly tried to swim to shore, the boys pelted it with rocks just as it was about to get to safety. I watched, horrified.

That scene has never left my memory. I was powerless to prevent it, and that moment engraved itself on my mind as an example of the extraordinary inhumanity that we see every day somewhere in the world.

But when you witness the mistreatment of Jesus by grown men, the boys' cruelty pales in comparison to what the Roman soldiers did to Jesus. They assailed Him through taunts and violence.

The taunts were three. First, they put a robe on Him that was of the color worn by nobility, purple. Second, they mocked Him with what they believed to be a slur on the Jewish people whom they had subjugated: "Hail, king of the Jews." They not only mocked Christ by doing this, they mocked the Jewish nation; in effect, they were telegraphing their feelings that if the Jews produced a king he would be helpless and hopeless like this condemned prisoner. Third, they ultimately knelt on their knees, feigning obeisance to Him.

The violent acts against Jesus were also three in number. First, they put a crown of thorns on His head. The needle-like spines of the crown dug into Jesus and made His head bleed and throb with excruciating pain. Second, they kept striking him on the head with a stick—again and again. The stick or staff drove the thorns further into his scalp and brow; not only did they strike Him there but on His face as well. Third, they continually spit on Him.

From the beating before Pilate and the violent acts in the palace, Jesus' back had been flayed and massive hurt had been inflicted upon His head.

Little did the soldiers realize that the One whom they mocked was indeed the King—not only of the Jewish people, but of all humanity and for all time. Despite this dishonoring, Jesus spoke amnesty to them from the cross: "Father, forgive them, for they do not know what they are doing" (Luke 23:34).

What amazing grace from Jesus, and a reminder to us that we also should practice grace to those who mistreat us.

A Prayer

Lord Jesus, thank You for also extending Your forgiveness to me even when I have deliberately failed You. You are full of grace and mercy.

GOLGOTHA

A certain man from Cyrene, Simon, the father of Alexander and Rufus, was passing by on his way in from the country, and they forced him to carry the cross. They brought Jesus to the place called Golgotha (which means The Place of the Skull). Then they offered him wine mixed with myrrh, but he did not take it. And they crucified him. Dividing up his clothes, they cast lots to see what each would get.

MARK 15:21–24

MULTIPLIED THOUSANDS of pilgrims each year visit Jerusalem to trace the steps of Jesus along the Via Dolorosa (the way of grief). The twenty-first century route differs considerably from that of the first century; Catholic tradition has added a number of "stations of the cross" that cannot be found in Scripture. The essential components of this journey come from the Gospels themselves.

Matthew, Mark, and Luke give us the name of Simon as the person compelled to carry the cross. He was from Cyrene, which we know to be in North Africa. Some have suggested he was African; others, that he was a Jew of the Diaspora.

Mark gives us a detail found nowhere else. It is a rather surprising piece of information because there is so little in Mark's account that cannot be found in the other Gospels. Mark notes that Simon was the father of Alexander and Rufus. Why does Mark give the names of Simon's sons?

We do know from early church tradition that Mark's gospel was directed to the Roman believers. Years later, Paul wrote to the Romans. Near the end of his letter he expresses greetings to a number of folks, including "Rufus, chosen in the Lord, and his mother, who has been a mother to me, too" (16:13). Could it be that the reference to Rufus in Paul's letter relates back to Mark's inclusion of Rufus' name, that Rufus ultimately relocated to Rome;

and that the greeting to his mother was in recognition of her being the widow of Simon, the man who carried the cross of Christ?

If so, then the original onerous task of carrying the cross ultimately became a badge of honor belonging to Simon's family—even as our willingness to bear the cross of Christ in our own time brings honor to those who come behind us.

Luke's gospel tells us that a large crowd followed Jesus and the cross-bearing Simon, including women who mourned and wailed for Him. Jesus spoke words of sorrow and warning to the women (Luke 23:27–32).

The first three Gospels note that Jesus refused the wine mixed with myrrh, a concoction designed to lessen the pain and cognition of the sufferer. But, Jesus refused. He chose to die clear-headed, able to express Himself with words from the cross—words He could not have spoken if He had allowed Himself to be drugged. He wanted us to hear those words. The first sentence from the cross, recorded by Luke, stamps on us our response to injustice, "Father, forgive them for they do not know what they are doing" (23:34).

Finally, we note the callousness of the soldiers who began to cast lots for Jesus' clothes as He began His suffering on the cross. John notes that the garments were divided four ways except for Jesus' seamless inner garment over which they cast lots (19:23–25).

No words can ever adequately describe what Jesus suffered for us. Are we callous as the soldiers were, or ready to carry His cross as did Simon?

A Prayer

Out of love, Lord Jesus, You suffered for me.
May I always be grateful.

THE CROSS AT 9 A.M.

It was the third hour when they crucified him. The written notice of the charge against him read: THE KING OF THE JEWS. They crucified two robbers with him, one on his right and one on his left. Those who passed by hurled insults at him, shaking their heads and saying, "So! You who are going to destroy the temple and build it in three days, come down from the cross and save yourself!"

MARK 15:25–30

MARK'S GOSPEL ALONE tells us the start time of Jesus' crucifixion—the third hour or 9 a.m. Mark opens his literary gaze by noting the written charge affixed to the cross, the robbers crucified with Jesus, and the taunting from Jesus' opponents. Let's take each of these in turn.

Pilate is known from secular history for his troubled relationship with the Jews. John's gospel tells us it was Pilate who ordered the notice prepared and fastened to the cross that read in three languages—Aramaic, Latin, and Greek—"The King of the Jews." Clearly, this was no confession of faith on the part of Pilate. Rather, he mocked the chief priests who had forced him into his decision. Pilate let the insult stand, not realizing that the title actually spoke truth. Jesus is King—not only of the Jews but of all humankind!

Mark's gospel also notes, as do the other Gospels, that two others were crucified with Jesus. In the beginning moments of the Jesus' crucifixion, these two said nothing. They spoke sometime later in the morning (v. 32), and one of them would subsequently have a change of heart (Luke 23:39–43).

Mark next points his word camera at the observers. They were heartless with rage, hurling insults and taunting Jesus to save Himself and come down from the cross. After all, Jesus had said three years earlier, "Destroy this temple, and I will raise it again in three days" (John 2:19). They didn't know that Jesus wasn't speaking of the physical temple but of His own body.

In the midst of all this rancor and shouting, Jesus spoke. Luke alone records His first word from the cross, "Father, forgive them, for they do not know what they are doing" (Luke 23:34).

Jesus' invocation from the cross is personal. Others may say, "God" because God lacks definition to them. But Jesus knew God as Father.

Commentator James Stalker reminds us that Jesus' use of the word "Father" tells us "His faith is unshaken by all through which He had passed and was now enduring. When righteousness is trampled underfoot and wrong is triumphant, faith is tempted to ask if there really is a God, loving and wise, seated on the throne of the universe. . . . But, when the fortunes of Jesus were at the blackest, when He was baited by a raging pack of wolf-like enemies, and when He was sinking into unplumbed abysses of pain and desertion, He still said, 'Father.'"[4]

Jesus looked down on those mocking Him—cruel and callous soldiers, crooked politicians, corrupt religious leaders. What did He do about them?

What He didn't do is as important as what He did. He didn't ball his fists and say, "I'll get even with you for this. I'll send you to hell for this." Rather, He opened His hand to receive the nail, demonstrating for us that it is more important to be oppressed than to oppress, to be wounded than to wound, to be hated rather than to hate.

His first word from the cross was one of forgiveness. Amazing!

A Prayer

Lord Jesus, I too need forgiveness.
I am grateful You forgive me also.

---

[4] James Stalker, *The Trial and Death of Jesus* (London: Valde Books, 2010).

FAITH AND FAMILY

In the same way the chief priests and the teachers of the law mocked him among themselves, "He saved others," they said, "but he can't save himself! Let this Christ, this King of Israel, come down now from the cross, that we may see and believe." Those crucified with him also heaped insults on him.

MARK 15:31-32

IN JESUS' FIRST THREE HOURS on the cross, He suffered more than excruciating physical agony. He was assaulted by the taunting words of passersby and the religious leadership who had engineered His death.

Even the robbers being crucified on His right and left mocked Him. Luke's gospel, however, gives us a more expanded version. As the morning wore on, one of the thieves had a change of heart. He had listened as Jesus began His hours on the cross with a word of forgiveness towards those crucifying Him (Luke 23:34). No crucified person would respond to suffering by pardoning those who had nailed him to the cross.

After several hours, the truth sunk in. One of the robbers came to faith. He said, "Jesus, remember me when you come into your kingdom" (Luke 23:42). In those words, the robber revealed the depth of his faith—he didn't believe the spirit died with the body, he did believe Christ had a kingdom, and he believed that Jesus could bestow the favor asked.

Jesus didn't ignore him. He didn't say to him, "I'm dying for the sins of the whole world; I don't have time for you." Nor did Jesus deny that He had a kingdom to offer. Instead, Jesus promised the thief instant access to paradise—no waiting period, no purgatory—just, "Today you will be with me!" Salvation is instant upon our request to be saved!

This is the only request made of Jesus while He hung on the cross. It's the request Jesus desires to grant for every human being who asks. It is why He came into this world—to save us from our sins! While Jesus was dying for the sins of the whole world, He took time to save one individual.

Martin Luther wrote: "This [man's request] was for Christ a comfort like that supplied to Him by the angel in the garden. God would not allow His Son to be destitute of subjects and now His church survived in this one man. Where the faith of St. Peter broke off, the faith of the penitent thief commenced."

Near the end of His first three hours on the cross, Jesus also addressed his mother and the beloved disciple (John 19:25–27). We know Jesus had four brothers and at least two sisters (Mark 6:3). Only His mother was at the cross. The rest of His family wasn't there. It is a testimony to the rejection experienced by Jesus that "his own did not receive him" (John 1:11).

There's something infinitely moving in the fact that Jesus, in the agony of the cross and in the moment when the salvation of the world hung in the balance, thought of the loneliness of His mother in the days when He would no longer be on the earth.

Thus, He honored the faith of the robber and honored the love of His mother.

From 9 a.m. until noon, Jesus spoke in short sentences three times from the cross. His dying themes were forgiveness (Luke 23:34), faith, and family. These are words also for us to live by!

A Prayer

Lord Jesus, receive me also—when my day is done—
into Your eternal kingdom. I cannot do this
for myself; only You can save me.

FINAL WORDS FROM THE CROSS

At the sixth hour darkness came over the whole land until the ninth hour. And at the ninth hour Jesus cried out in a loud voice, "Eloi, Eloi, lama sabachthani?" which means, "My God, my God, why have you forsaken me?" When some of those standing near heard this, they said, "Listen, he's calling Elijah." One man ran, filled a sponge with wine and vinegar, put it on a stick, and offered it to Jesus to drink. "Now leave him alone. Let's see if Elijah comes to take him down," he said. With a loud cry, Jesus breathed his last.

MARK 15:33–37

IN HIS FIRST THREE HOURS on the cross, Jesus spoke three times: to those crucifying Him (Luke 23:34); to the thief dying beside Him (Luke 23:43); to His mother and to John (19:25–27). At noon, as darkness descended, He gave what is called the cry of dereliction—of being forsaken of God.

But Jesus' cry from the cross is more than one of being abandoned. It shows that Jesus was praying through Psalm 22, written by King David a thousand years before Him. Read the Psalm, and you will see that while it begins with being forsaken, it ends with triumph: "They will proclaim his righteousness to a people yet unborn—for he has done it."

On the cross, Jesus knew that He would win the victory for us. In His most difficult hours He told us of His relationship with the Father by using the personal pronoun twice: "My God, My God." In our own moments when we feel abandoned by God or others, let us follow the example of Jesus. Even when the heavens are dark, we aren't alone. God is still our God!

The other Gospels tell us of three other short utterances Jesus made in His final dying minutes.

His fifth word from the cross was "I am thirsty" (John 19:28). Jesus had refused a pain-alleviating drink at the beginning (Mark 15:23) in order to experience the full measure of the cross and to remain alert to speak from the cross. Mother Teresa took these words of Jesus' thirst as a theme for her own life, saying, "Our acts of love are meant to satisfy the thirst of Jesus."

Jesus' sixth word from the cross was, "It is finished" (John 19:30). He didn't say, "I am finished." Rather, the work He came to do was forever done!

A young man approached an evangelist after the last night of a gospel meeting. The crowd had already been dismissed, but the young man implored, "What must I do to be saved?" The old evangelist replied, "You're too late."

"Too late?" the young man asked. "Surely not just because the meeting is over!" The wise evangelist replied, "What must you *do* to be saved? You are hundreds of years too late. It is finished. Believe in the Lord Jesus Christ, and you will be saved!"

Jesus died a victor with a word of triumph on His lips. All hell heard it and trembled. All heaven heard it and rejoiced!

Finally, Jesus recited a phrase from Psalm 31:5, "Into your hands I commit my spirit"—the first bedtime prayer every Jewish child learned to say. Jesus made one change. He added to the prayer, "Father" (Luke 23:46). That one word makes all the difference. God is personal. Even in death, our life is in the hands of our loving heavenly Father.

A Prayer

Lord Jesus, Your dying words bring me life and hope.
I thank You for dying on the cross for me.

THREE POST-CRUCIFIXION MOMENTS

> *The curtain of the temple was torn in two from top to bottom. And when the centurion, who stood there in front of Jesus, heard his cry and saw how he died, he said, "Surely this man was the Son of God!" Some women were watching from a distance. Among them were Mary Magdalene, Mary the mother of James the younger and of Joses, and Salome. In Galilee these women had followed him and cared for his needs. Many other women who had come up with him to Jerusalem were also there.*
>
> MARK 15:38–41

IMMEDIATELY AFTER JESUS DIED on the cross, God let His opinion be known.

Rabbinic literature and the first-century Jewish historian Josephus tell us that the curtain or veil that hung in front of the Holy of Holies in the temple was eighty-two and a half feet high and twenty-four feet wide, measuring a handbreadth in thickness. It was impossible for two human hands to tear; and, even if it were, the human would have had to start at the bottom and tear upward.

God reacted to the crucifixion of His Son by tearing the curtain from top to bottom, opening the Holy of Holies to all. The writer of Hebrews picks up on this when we says that we have a firm and secure anchor for the soul because Jesus entered the inner sanctuary behind the curtain on our behalf, not a man-made sanctuary but heaven itself to once and for all put away sin by the sacrifice of Himself (Hebrews 6:19–20; 9:23–28; 10:19–22). God ripped open the earthly curtain to let us know that heaven was now open for all who would come through Jesus.

The centurion, on the other hand, knew how Jesus died even though He did not know what happened in the temple. He saw the whole event unfold. As a military man, he was used to watching criminals die. He had never seen a death like that of Jesus.

THREE POST-CRUCIFIXION MOMENTS

Jesus had one convert as He died, the thief next to Him. The Roman soldier, a pagan, believed when Jesus expired. The title affixed to the cross in three languages, "King of the Jews," was not sufficient to describe the One who died. For the centurion, Jesus was more than a king of one ethnic group; He was the Son of God.

The third post-crucifixion moment comes in the observation that women at a distance watched Jesus die. Some are named, many are not.

When you compare the gospel of John to the other three Gospels, you know that there were two groups of women at the cross. John tells us about the women close in during the morning hours—Mary, the mother of Jesus, His mother's sister Mary, and Mary Magdalene (John 19:25).

Mary Magdalene is mentioned again as being among those at a distance, leaving us to assume that sometime during the afternoon she moved further away from the cross to join the other women. Perhaps the crucifixion became so overwhelming for Jesus' mother and aunt that they left sometime in the afternoon.

What the Gospels do tell us is that women were loyal to Jesus and served Him throughout His ministry. They did not run away from Him when He was nailed to the cross. Women were the last to leave the cross and the first to see Him again on Easter morning.

Jesus ennobled women by drawing them into His inner circle both then and now.

A Prayer

Lord Jesus, may I remain as loyal to You as the women who served You and stayed with You even through Your darkest hours.

THE BURIAL OF JESUS

It was Preparation Day (that is, the day before the Sabbath). So as evening approached, Joseph of Arimathea, a prominent member of the Council, who was himself waiting for the kingdom of God, went boldly to Pilate and asked for Jesus' body. Pilate was surprised to hear that he was already dead. Summoning the centurion, he asked him if Jesus had already died. When he learned from the centurion that it was so, he gave the body to Joseph. So Joseph bought some linen cloth, took down the body, wrapped it in the linen, and placed it in a tomb cut out of rock. Then he rolled a stone against the entrance of the tomb. Mary Magdalene and Mary the mother of Joses saw where he was laid.

MARK 15:42-47

THINK OF THE GOSPEL writers as literary photographers. They place their word cameras in different positions, and it requires us to examine all their photographs to gain a composite understanding of the burial of Jesus.

Their main perspective is to establish clearly that Jesus was dead. He didn't swoon or fall into a coma on the cross. The centurion who oversaw the crucifixion affirmed to Pilate that Jesus was indeed dead. Then they took Jesus' body down from the cross and buried it in a tomb.

You don't bury someone who is alive. Had there been any sign of life, pulse, or breath in Jesus, Joseph of Arimathea and Nicodemus wouldn't have swathed Him in burial cloths and placed Him in a dark tomb.

A subtheme to the burial is the story of the ones who took Jesus down from the cross and buried Him. All the Gospels identify Joseph of Arimathea as the one who took initiative to secure the body of Jesus; however, John's gospel notes that Nicodemus assisted in removing the body from the cross, wrapping it with spices, in strips of linen, and burying Jesus in a new tomb near the place where He was crucified.

If you visit Jerusalem today you know that there are two different sites that are held as possibilities for the crucifixion and burial: The Church of the Holy Sepulcher and the Garden Tomb. It matters not which one is the "real" site—the important thing is that Jesus is *not* in either place! He is alive and is seated at the right hand of the Majesty on high!

Both Joseph and Nicodemus were prominent members of the Sanhedrin, the ruling body of Jewish elders. At the beginning of His ministry, Jesus talked with Nicodemus about the importance of being born again. That conversation must have borne fruit in Nicodemus' heart because we see his love for Jesus in his defense of the Lord at the Feast of Tabernacles and in his participation in the burial (John 3:1–21; 7:45–42; 19:38–42). Certainly, such an act would not have had the approval of his colleagues, who disdained Jesus.

Luke's gospel notes that Joseph had not consented to the action and decision of the Sanhedrin (Luke 23:50–51).

These two prominent religious leaders showed a loyalty to Jesus that not even His own disciples demonstrated. They risked their lives by going to Pilate and asking for the body of Jesus, and risked their reputations with their religious colleagues as well.

Why did they do this? Because even though Jesus was dead, they were still looking for the kingdom of God. Jesus wouldn't disappoint them! And He will never disappoint you!

A Prayer

Lord Jesus, I too have hope because I know
You are the King of the kingdom of God.

WOMEN AT THE TOMB

When the Sabbath was over, Mary Magdalene, Mary the mother of James, and Salome bought spices so that they might go to anoint Jesus' body. Very early on the first day of the week, just after sunrise, they were on their way to the tomb and they asked each other, "Who will roll the stone away from the entrance of the tomb?" But when they looked up, they saw that the stone, which was very large, had been rolled away.

MARK 16:1-4

SABBATH ENDED AT sundown; thus, the women bought spices on Saturday evening and headed for the tomb the next morning. No one gospel writer lists all the women who came to the tomb but we know from reading all four Gospels that there were at least six. Mary Magdalene is listed first in each gospel.

The remaining women were the "other" Mary (Matthew 28:1), who was the mother of Joseph and James (15:47; 16:1; Luke 24:10); Joanna (Luke 24:10); Salome (16:1); and at least two other unnamed women (Luke 24:10). The mother of Jesus didn't come to the tomb, no doubt too grief-stricken to make the effort.

Some of these women could have come from different directions, at even slightly different times, which would explain the varieties in details of that morning among the gospel writers.

But let us focus on Mary Magdalene. Here is what we know about her.

She was a leader. Even as Peter's name is always listed first when the Twelve are mentioned, so also Mary Magdalene's name is always first when listed with other women except for the one time she is listed at the cross with Mary (the mother of Jesus) and her sister (Mary, the wife of Clopas, John 19:25).

She had suffered greatly until Jesus delivered her from seven demons; thereafter, she became a loyal follower of Jesus who with other women helped support Jesus and His disciples from their own means (Luke 8:3). The fact that Mary Magdalene could financially support Jesus tells us that she was a woman with some degree of wealth and independence. Like millions of other women through the centuries, she made her time and resources available to Jesus.

She evidently was a go-between for two groups of women at the cross—being listed near Jesus (John 19:15) and those women who were watching from a distance (Matthew 27:55–56). We are left to assume, from a comparison of the Gospels, that she stood with each group at different times.

Finally, Mary Magdalene's love and loyalty is shown not only by her presence at the cross, but as a witness to the placement of the body in the tomb (Matthew 27:61) and her presence at the tomb on resurrection morning. A poet said of her:

> *Not she with traitorous kiss her Master stung,*
> *Not she denied Him with unfaithful tongue;*
> *She, when Apostles fled, could dangers brave,*
> *Last at the cross, and earliest at the grave.*

What does her example teach us?

She had lost hope, but had not lost love. Love brought her and the women to the tomb. Love had kept her loyal when hope had died. On resurrection morning, Jesus restored Mary's hope, but He didn't need to restore her love. She never lost that!

Is your love holding even when adversity impacts your life, when faith and hope have taken a monster hit? Hold on to that love. Jesus will make His presence known to you as He did to Mary Magdalene.

A Prayer

Lord Jesus, all of our shattered dreams
You are mending. I love you, Lord!

UNLIKELY RECIPIENTS OF GOOD NEWS

> As they entered the tomb, they saw a young man dressed in a white robe sitting on the right side, and they were alarmed. "Don't be alarmed," he said. "You are looking for Jesus the Nazarene, who was crucified. He has risen! He is not here. See the place where they laid him. But go, tell his disciples and Peter, 'He is going ahead of you into Galilee. There you will see him, just as he told you.'" Trembling and bewildered, the women went out and fled from the tomb. They said nothing to anyone, because they were afraid.
>
> MARK 16:5–8

WE HAVE NOTED numerous times that Mark is the "condensed" gospel. Thus, when we come to the resurrection, we see again that his is a shorter account.

We know at least six women were at the tomb that Easter morning (Mark 16:1; Luke 24:10). Mark focuses on only three. We know from Matthew's gospel that there was a violent earthquake and an angel rolled back the stone, leaving the grave guards shaking and becoming as dead men (28:2–4). Luke's gospel tells us that two angels were at the tomb (24:4), while Matthew and Mark's literary cameras focus only on the one who spoke to the women.

John's gospel focuses exclusively on Mary Magdalene (John 20). In comparing the first three Gospels' accounts with John, we can see the sequence. Mary evidently immediately left the scene of the tomb when she saw the stone had been rolled away. The other women, who remained, went inside and heard the angel's word, "He is risen." But Mary had run back to Simon Peter and John to tell them the body of Jesus was missing from the tomb. The two men raced to the tomb. Mary Magdalene trailed them. By the time she got there, they were gone as were the women. Mary Magdalene was then met by the risen Lord.

What do we make of this?

UNLIKELY RECIPIENTS OF GOOD NEWS

People are fascinated today with the possibility of extraterrestrial life. Well, it exists! Angels were present at the birth of Jesus (Luke 2:8–15) and at the tomb—bringing the greatest good news ever: "The Savior is born" and "The Lord is risen!"

The Lord reveals Himself in unlikely ways. At His birth, shepherds got the good news first. Why them? Why not some people with connections, power, and political influence? God just likes to surprise ordinary people with extraordinary good news! And He repeated the strategy of giving good news to unlikely people by having the first announcement of His resurrection made to a group of loyal and grieving women. They were told to go share the news with His disciples and Peter.

Peter! Peter is the one who denied Jesus three times and then wept (Mark 14:66–72). Peter's failure didn't keep Him from the love of Jesus. In fact, the first man Jesus appeared to after His resurrection was none other than Peter (Luke 24:34). Jesus came to Peter even before He revealed Himself to the Twelve as a group (1 Corinthians 15:5).

Except for Judas, Peter failed Jesus more deeply than any other disciple. But Jesus reached out to him first, and I suspect He would have done the same for Judas. The problem with Judas was that he gave up too soon.

What great hope there is for us! After our worst failures, Jesus doesn't turn His back on us. He still wants us! Don't give up on Jesus; He hasn't given up on you!

A Prayer

Lord Jesus, Your promise is true. You will never leave me nor forsake me.

SHATTERED DREAMS MENDING

When Jesus rose early on the first day of the week, he appeared first to Mary Magdalene, out of whom he had driven seven demons. She went and told those who had been with him and who were mourning and weeping. When they heard that Jesus was alive and that she had seen him, they did not believe it.
MARK 16:9-11

THE EARLIER MANUSCRIPTS of Mark's gospel end at verse 8. Why? Perhaps the last part of the original manuscript, which would have been at the outside of the scroll, broke off. Perhaps Mark was interrupted by some danger just as he was completing his gospel. What we do know is that the longer ending, verses 9 to 20, contains no new information not found in the other gospels. Thus, we can rely completely on the veracity of these verses without knowing who or when they were appended to the abrupt break in Mark's gospel at verse 8.

The account of the appearance to Mary Magdalene is told in detail in John's Gospel (20:10-18), of which Mark provides only a brief summary.

By reading and comparing the accounts of all four gospel writers, we can conclude that Mary set out ahead of the other women since she headed to the tomb while it was still dark (John 20:1), while the others went "just after sunrise" (Mark 16:2). When she saw the stone rolled away from the tomb, she ran to tell Simon Peter and John. They both ran and came to the tomb, but didn't see Jesus. However, the evidence of the grave cloths was enough to convince John that Jesus had risen from the dead (John 20:1-9).

Mary must have trailed Simon Peter and John, because after the two men left she remained outside the tomb, disconsolate. Two angels asked her why she was weeping. Unlike John who had already believed on the basis of what he saw, Mary didn't arrive at the same conclusion. So, she said to the angels, "They have taken my Lord away and I don't know where they have put him." She suggested the same idea to the One she mistook as the "gardener."

Can you imagine our shock if we were to discover that a recently buried loved one's body had disappeared? We would do exactly as Mary—seek to recover the body. Thinking the "gardener had taken away Jesus' body, she implored him, "Tell me where you have put him, and I will get him" (John 20:15).

How do we apply Mary's experience to our own lives?

First, Mary was looking in the wrong direction. She was facing the tomb. We know that because she "turned" to see Jesus (John 20:16). Sometimes we look at the wrong things, and they discourage us. Turn your gaze away from your loss toward Jesus, the resurrected Lord.

Decades later the apostle John would do that very same thing. Imprisoned on the Isle of Patmos, he looked away from his circumstances to see the all-powerful and risen Lord (Revelation 1:17).

Second, sometimes our tears prevent us from seeing Jesus enter our situation. Human sorrow is real. But the resurrection of Jesus tells us that sorrow is only for a season. There will be a day in which there are no more tears (Revelation 21:4).

In the 1970s, Byron Jeffrey Leech wrote these haunting lines in a hymn: "All of our shattered dreams you're mending." Indeed! Mary's experience is not unique to her alone. We, too, shall see Him face to face!

A Prayer

Lord Jesus, Your promise is true—after tears, joy comes at the breaking of the day!

REFUSING TO BELIEVE

Afterward Jesus appeared in a different form to two of them while they were walking in the country. These returned and reported it to the rest; but they did not believe them either. Later Jesus appeared to the Eleven as they were eating; he rebuked them for their lack of faith and their stubborn refusal to believe those who had seen him after he had risen.

MARK 16:12-14

THE DANISH THEOLOGIAN Søren Kierkegaard defined faith as a leap in the dark. But that's not what true Christian faith is all about. Faith is resting in the sufficiency of the evidences.

Jesus' disciples had a hard time accepting the evidence of His resurrection. They disbelieved the report of Mary Magdalene (16:11) and the two to whom Jesus appeared as they were walking in the country. When Jesus met with the Eleven, He upbraided them for their stubborn refusal to believe.

Every other major or minor religion derives its existence from the teachings or purported revelations of its founders. There is only one faith that claims validity because of an act of its Founder. Only Christianity has a risen Lord. All the other religious leaders are dead. Jesus' resurrection validates all His teachings and the claims He made of Himself.

The French philosopher-atheist, Voltaire, was reputed to have said sarcastically: "Gentlemen, it would be easy to start a new religion to compete with Christianity. All the founder would have to do is die and then be raised from the dead."

Mark's gospel gives the condensed account of Jesus' appearance to the two disciples on the Emmaus Road, shared in more detail by Luke (Luke 24:13-35). Mark also briefly reports on Jesus' appearances, one week apart, to His disciples (Luke 24:36-40; John 20:19-29).

The refusal of the disciples to believe shows them as persons not easily duped. Chuck Colson (of Watergate scandal fame), a top aide to President Nixon, later became a Christian. He said,

"When I am challenged on the resurrection, my answer is always that the disciples and 500 others gave eyewitness accounts of seeing Jesus risen from the tomb. . . . [The Watergate] cover-up could only be held together for two weeks and then everybody else jumped ship in order to save themselves. . . . The disciples, . . . powerless men, peasants really, were facing not just embarrassment or political disgrace, but beatings, stonings, execution. . . . The apostles could not deny Jesus because they had seen Him face to face. . . . You can take it from an expert in cover-ups, nothing less than a resurrected Christ could have caused those men to maintain to their dying whispers that Jesus is alive and Lord." [5]

The story of Jesus comes down to this: Did He rise again from the dead? The disciples were certainly in no frame of mind to steal the body from a guarded tomb and then suffer and die for a concocted lie. The opposition did not steal the body or they would have produced the corpse when the disciples started preaching the resurrection.

There is only one answer that makes sense. Jesus rose again on the third day, as He had promised! He thereby demonstrated that everything He taught, everything He said about Himself was true. The great news is that His resurrection is not limited to Himself. When we die, we have the assurance that we, too, will be raised from the dead at His coming. His good news is our good news!

A Prayer

Lord Jesus, I confess with my mouth and believe in my heart that You are risen from the dead!

---

[5] *Leadership Journal*, Spring, 2003.

COMMAND AND PROMISE

He said to them, "Go into all the world and preach the good news to all creation. Whoever believes and is baptized will be saved, but whoever does not believe will be condemned. And these signs will accompany those who believe: In my name they will drive out demons; they will speak in new tongues; they will pick up snakes with their hands; and when they drink deadly poison, it will not hurt them at all; they will place their hands on sick people, and they will get well."

MARK 16:15–18

WE KNOW THAT, following His resurrection, Jesus appeared to His followers at various times and places over the course of forty days (Acts 1:3).

As Mark's gospel draws to an end, it doesn't attempt to provide a compendium of those appearances and conversations. Rather, the gospel summarizes the essential command and promises Jesus made.

The command can be summarized in one word: "Go." We know that the disciples at the end of His post-resurrections appearances were still thinking that Jesus might restore the kingdom to Israel (Acts 1:6). Their attitude toward the nations might best be summarized as: "come." They would have preferred to remain where they were and for the peoples of the earth to come and visit them to hear the good news. It's difficult to relocate—especially when that relocation calls you into another culture, language, and place.

After Jesus' ascension into heaven, the disciples didn't willingly go. They never held a missions convention, never strategized about how to reach their world. What drove them out of Jerusalem was persecution (Acts 11:19).

But let's not be too hard on those first disciples. We, too, would rather be comfortable in our own circumstances. But Jesus keeps insisting "Go!" Thus, He calls us to our neighbor, to our community, and beyond that to the far reaches of this world. Why is this so? Jesus answered that question: "Whoever believes is saved . . . whoever does not is condemned." The eternal destiny of others hangs upon our willingness to go and spread the good news.

When we do so, He promises that miraculous events will happen, and so they have. Demons fled (Acts 5:16; 8:7; 16:16-18), believers spoke in languages they had not learned (Acts 2:4-11; 11:46; 19:6), protection was given from snake bites (Acts 28:1-6), and sick people were healed (Acts 3:1-10; 5:15; 8:7; 9:35-43; 14:8-10; 19:11-12; 28:7-10). Nothing is recorded in Acts regarding protection from poison; however, my missionary father was once poisoned by nomadic Tibetans with whom he had shared the gospel. When they later saw him alive they said: "You must have a very strong God. We gave you enough poison to kill ten men."

Jesus is the same yesterday, today, and forever (Hebrews 13:8). The command and the promises are not only for the first Christians, they are for us today. However, the promises are conditioned on getting out of our comfort zones and telling others about Jesus. No signs accompany believers who sit around and do nothing.

We learn also from the experience of the early believers that Jesus does not turn us into supermen and superwomen. A man lame from birth was healed when Paul prayed for him, but the next moment Paul had no immunity when he was nearly stoned to death (Acts 14:8-20). In both signs and sorrows, miracles and persecutions, the underlying promise is always this: "I am with you always" (Matthew 28:20)!

A Prayer

Lord Jesus, may I never decide to stay when You tell me to go.

TO BE CONTINUED . . .

After the Lord Jesus had spoken to them, he was taken up into heaven and he sat at the right hand of God. Then the disciples went out and preached everywhere, and the Lord worked with them and confirmed his word by the signs that accompanied it.

MARK 16:19–20

MARK'S GOSPEL BEGAN with an incomplete sentence, "The beginning of the gospel about Jesus Christ, the Son of God."

It was his way of saying, "All that I'm going to tell you about Jesus is only the start. His earthly ministry was but the launch. The story of Jesus will actually go on forever."

The close of Mark's gospel is almost as abrupt as its beginning. He briefly recounts Jesus' resurrection appearances to Mary Magdalene, two disciples walking in the country, and to the Eleven. Then, Mark is "over and out" with a brief conclusion.

The last two verses tell us that Jesus' story continues in two ways.

First, the story of Jesus continues in the heavens. He is now seated at the right hand of God. This is what Jesus had promised. In His dialogue with the opposing teachers of the Law, He quoted Psalm 110:1, "The LORD said to my lord, 'Sit at my right hand until I put your enemies under your feet.'" Jesus then asked how David could call his son his Lord? They didn't know the answer; but Jesus did. As David's son, He is human; as David's Lord, He is divine (Mark 12:35–37).

Jesus flatly declared to the high priest at His trial, "You will see the Son of Man sitting at the right hand of the Mighty One and coming on the clouds of heaven" (Mark 14:62).

From the first disciples until now, Christians know that Jesus isn't finished. His story continues. We know where He is now—seated at the right hand of the Majesty on High (Acts 2:25, 33, 34;

5:31; 7:56; Ephesians 1:20; Hebrews 1:3, 13; 8:1; 10:12; 12:2; 1 Peter 3:22).

The one exception to Him being seated was when Stephen, as he was dying from being stoned, saw Jesus standing at the right hand of God (Acts 7:56). How gracious of Jesus to stand when the first believer to die after His own resurrection entered heaven!

From the apostle Paul we learn what Jesus is doing while seated at the right hand of God. He is interceding for us. Rather than bringing a charge against us or condemning us, He is our advocate in the most important position in heaven or on earth. We have a Friend in heaven who believes in us (Romans 8:33–34)!

Second, the story of Jesus continues on earth through us. When the disciples first began following Jesus, they really didn't know who He was—except that He attracted them to Himself. He walked and talked with them. They heard His words and witnessed His deeds. They saw the strength of His character, His insight into life, His humor, His courage in the face of death, His certainty of the ultimate triumph of good. They couldn't keep the good news to themselves so they went everywhere, backed by His power working with them.

In our time, we must do the same. Jesus' story is too important to keep to ourselves. If we will go everywhere we can to everyone we can, then Jesus will continue working with us.

Jesus is alive! That is the enduring good news of the gospel!

A Prayer

Lord Jesus, thank You for all You did so that I could have forgiveness of sins and eternal life. Amen.

ABOUT THE AUTHOR

DR. GEORGE O. WOOD is the chief executive officer of the Assemblies of God. As general superintendent of the Assemblies of God, USA, part of the largest Pentecostal denomination in the world, he is a member of the denomination's Executive Leadership Team and Executive Presbytery. The church has over 12,800 congregations in the United States with over three million members and adherents.

The U.S. Assemblies of God is part of a larger World Assemblies of God fellowship with a membership of over 67 million. Dr. Wood also serves as chairman of the World Assemblies of God fellowship as well as the global co-chair for Empowered21.

Prior to his present position, Wood served the church as its general secretary for fourteen years. He was assistant superintendent of the Southern California District from 1988–93. Wood pastored Newport-Mesa Christian Center in Costa Mesa, California, for seventeen years.

The son of missionary parents to China and Tibet, Wood holds a doctoral degree in pastoral theology from Fuller Theological Seminary in Pasadena, California, and a juris doctorate from Western State University College of Law in Fullerton, California. He did his undergraduate work at Evangel University (College) in Springfield, Missouri, and served the college in several capacities, including being director of spiritual life and student life from 1965–71. He was ordained by the Southern Missouri District in 1967.

Dr. Wood is author of a number of books including *Road Trip Leadership, Living in the Spirit, A Psalm in Your Heart, Living Fully, The Successful Life*, and a college text on the book of Acts. Sermons by Dr. Wood may be heard at www.georgeowood.com.

Wood and his wife, Jewel, currently reside in Springfield, Missouri. They have a daughter and a son.

For More Information

*about this book and other valuable resources
please visit www.vital-resources.com*